Challenging the
Prison-Industrial Complex

Challenging the
Prison-Industrial Complex

Activism, Arts, and Educational Alternatives

Edited by
Stephen John Hartnett

University of Illinois Press
Urbana, Chicago, and Springfield

Library of Congress Cataloging-in-Publication Data
Challenging the prison-industrial complex : activism, arts,
and educational alternatives / edited by Stephen John Hartnett.
p.   cm.
Includes index.
ISBN 978–0–252–03582–1 (cloth : alk. paper)
ISBN 978–0–252–07770–8 (pbk. : alk. paper)
1. Prison-industrial complex—United States.
2. Imprisonment—United States.
3. Prisons—United States.
I. Hartnett, Stephen J.
HV9471.C46   2011
365'.973—dc22   2010024101

Contents

Illustrations follow page 148

Acknowledgments

This book began in the autumn of 2002 as a conversation in the political poster-filled office of Dr. David Roediger, the Kendrick C. Babcock Professor of History, tireless activist, all-around good guy, and first director of the University of Illinois Center on Democracy in a Multiracial Society (CDMS). David's groundbreaking work on our nation's history of race-making and racism intersected with my commitments to studying and dismantling the prison-industrial complex, and so we hatched the idea of hosting a conference, which unfolded in January 2004 as "Education or Incarceration? Schools and Prisons in a Punishing Democracy." A rousing success, the conference drew scholars, activists, and artists from around the nation; the presentations were expert and the dialogue was spirited. I will never forget our closing party, at which the creaky old prairie-colonial that houses the CDMS was filled to bursting with students, faculty, staff, local activists, and our guests, all eating piles of pizza while enjoying the performances of Michael Keck (who sang and danced) and Tori Samartino (who read poems). Michael and Tori were two of the many talented artists and activists who came to the conference to help shape our critique of the prison-industrial complex into searing aesthetic forms that can both speak to our heads and inspire our hearts. The conference also produced a wave of organizing in Champaign-Urbana, meaning the academic gathering melted slowly but surely into political work carried out on the local level. I therefore want to acknowledge David Roediger, everyone in the University of Illinois's Office of the Chancellor, the CDMS's remarkable staff (Aprel Thomas was a magician with the details), our conference participants, and the local activists who helped make both the conference and its follow-up activities such a success.

I will also confess, however, that by the time we had cleaned up from the long weekend's events, even while being spiritually fulfilled and politically motivated, I was also exhausted—*there will be no book from this conference*, I swore. And for a while I kept that promise, but then, in the spring of 2006, the CDMS hired a new director, Dr. Jorge Chapa, professor of sociology and Latina/Latino studies, voting-rights scholar, and leading advocate for diversity in higher education. Jorge believed that the CDMS was producing world-class work and that we should do a better job of spreading the evidence of our efforts, and so he partnered with the University of Illinois Press to launch a new book series tackling the dilemmas of how to move our nation away from its long addiction to racism and toward justice and liberty for all. Working at Jorge's urging, I invited some of the participants from our 2004 conference to submit essays and also commissioned new works for this occasion. Throughout the early stages of assembling this book, Jorge and the CDMS generously supported my efforts by enabling me to receive a semester release from teaching in order to focus on the project. And so I owe a giant thank-you to Jorge for his vision, to my CDMS colleagues for their ongoing efforts to end racism, and to Ruth Mathew, who has kept the CDMS and this book organized. At the University of Illinois Press, I would like to thank Laurie Matheson for her deft handling of this manuscript, Cope Cumpston for her aesthetic vision, Jennifer S. Clark for her help shepherding the book toward publication, Geof Garvey for his expert copyediting, and the anonymous reviewers, whose insightful commentary on an early draft of the manuscript helped me to help the authors shape their essays into more powerful statements. As ever, cultural production entails collaboration across fields and specialties, races and classes, and ages and genders—we fly together or sink alone.

Because I worry about the ways even the best-intentioned scholarship can sometimes address social justice issues while marginalizing the voices of the people we work with and for, I wanted to make sure that prisoners are represented in this volume. Each chapter of the book is accordingly followed by a poem written by an incarcerated artist, thus making sure that as we read about the crisis of the prison-industrial complex, and as we consider pragmatic ways to move forward, we also encounter the heartbreaks and hopes of the men and women trapped within America's gulags. Special thanks, then, to our poets: Dennis Mansker, Marvin Mays, Erika Baro, William T. Smith, George Hall, Robert "Chicago" McCollum, Nicole Monahan, and K. Sean Kelly. Because we know of these writers only through the efforts of writing workshop facilitators who have brought their imprisoned students' and collaborators' work to our attention, I want to thank Buzz Alexander for convening the Poet's Corner in Jackson, Michigan; Kal Wagenheim for hosting his workshop in

Trenton, New Jersey; University of Colorado–Denver students Linda Guthrie, Vlad Bogomolov, and Gordana Lăzīc for their support of the writing workshop in Denver, Colorado; and all the University of Illinois students who joined the writing workshop in Urbana, Illinois, including Sarah Franseen, Katie Healey, Justin Lensing, Jennifer Mussman, Sejal Patel, and Ashley Reibel. As these workshop facilitators and tutors will tell you, and as the poems printed here attest, our imprisoned neighbors are capable of producing poems full of unspeakable pain yet also inspiring beauty.

To accompany these poetic contributions, I also thought readers would benefit from having the opportunity *to see* what the men and women snared within the prison-industrial complex experience each day. And so I contacted Janie Paul, one of the founders and curators of the annual Exhibition of Art by Michigan Prisoners, and asked her to select what she thought were ten representative images made my imprisoned artists. I am therefore proud to include here artwork made by Frankie Davis, Gary English, Dara Ket, Nancy Jean King, Fred Mumford, Bryan Picken, Wynn Satterlee, Kinnari Jivani, Martin Vargas, and Virgil Williams III. We know of these imprisoned artists because Janie and her colleagues at the Prison Creative Arts Projects, in Ann Arbor, Michigan, spend each winter and spring driving thousands of miles, crisscrossing Michigan, visiting dozens of prisons, so that they can collect and then display hundreds of pieces of art on the lovely University of Michigan campus each April. Many thanks, then, to Janie, her PCAP associates, and to all the imprisoned artists, teachers, and friends who make it possible to produce art under even the most dire circumstances. The images show us that the men and women in our prisons are fellow human beings with dreams, visions, and remarkable talent. Printing the images as full-page color-plates was an expensive endeavor, and is made possible by the generous support of the University of Colorado–Denver's Office of the Associate Vice Chancellor for Research and the UCD College of Liberal Arts and Science's Dissemination Grant Program.

On a more personal note, I want to thank my darling existential soul-mate, Dr. Lisa Keränen, who has stood by me as this project has winded its way toward completion. When I depart for prison events in faraway places, she sends me off with unconditional love; when I come home late from another night teaching at the prison, she meets me at the door with whiskey; when prose needs pruning, she cheerfully gets down to it—she is my everything, a source of support and encouragement, a reason to continue.

Finally, I want to thank the authors, both for their remarkable contributions to this book and for their ongoing efforts to model decency and dignity while trying to transform our punishing democracy. During the course of the book's long march toward publication, I had the opportunity to marvel at the organizing efforts of Rose Braz, Myesha Williams, and their Critical Resistance colleagues while participating in their efforts in Oakland, California; to share in Buzz Alexander's and Janie Paul's community-building and consciousness-changing PCARE events in Ann Arbor, Michigan; to watch proudly as Daniel Larson and Julilly Kohler-Hausmann finished their dissertations and pushed on with their promising careers; to share stages and efforts with Erica Meiners in Illinois, where she continues to amaze me with her energy and vision; to join Robin Sohnen on prison visits and beach walks in California, where her Each One Reach One program continues to save lives; to invite Garrett Albert Duncan to Denver, Colorado, where he rocked the minds of my students and colleagues while discussing his educational work in St. Louis, Missouri; to visit with Lori Pompa in Boston, Massachusetts, where she spoke to a room of rapt colleagues and students about her Inside-Out Program; and to break bread with Travis Dixon, who, even while raising his new twins, continues to do strong work demonstrating how television makes you fearful. Special thanks go to Jonathan Shailor, who, when someone backed out of the project at the last minute, stepped up to write a gorgeous chapter about teaching and performing Shakespeare in prison. When I finally met Jonathan, at a conference in San Diego, California, he impressed me even more, as he embodied the Buddhist calm described in his lovely essay. The authors included herein thus amount to a list of leading intellectuals, teachers, artists, and activists; they span the nation geographically and implement a stunning array of critical methods, pedagogical strategies, artistic programs, and political goals, thus offering us a tribute to the persistence of democratic hope and good will in hard times. They would tell you that what they do each day is not so much heroic as simply necessary, but they are nonetheless my heroes—to count them as my friends is a blessing, to publish their work an honor.

Challenging the
Prison-Industrial Complex

Empowerment or Incarceration: Reclaiming Hope and Justice from a Punishing Democracy

Stephen John Hartnett

Stacked atop one another on the same page on the same day, juxtaposed clues to a catastrophe, two *New York Times* articles illustrate some of America's obsessions, fears, and blind spots regarding crime, violence, and punishment. The top story tells the tale of Gilberta Estrada, a twenty-five-year-old Mexican immigrant who hanged herself and her four children. Recently separated from her long-time partner, working the morning shift at a Wendy's, living in a trailer park outside Dallas, raising four children by herself, and "struggling with depression," Estrada's days were difficult. Then something snapped one night, as Estrada took her eight-month-old baby and her two-, three-, and five-year-old daughters and strung them and herself up by their necks in a closet. The infant survived, but Estrada and her three older daughters died, leaving Sheriff Larry Fowler stunned: "It's horrendous" he said, thus casting the event in the gothic genre wherein human actions are inexplicable, monstrous, bizarre, and macabre. From one perspective, Fowler is correct, for this group murder and suicide is "horrendous" and defies explanation: Estrada's actions are the stuff of dark and mysterious forces, they gesture toward the worst capacities of humans to inflict violence upon themselves and others. From another perspective, however, Fowler is wrong, for the circumstances leading to Estrada's violence are painfully typical. Consider the array of Estrada's all-too-familiar tribulations: She was struggling to hold together a broken family, escape a life of poverty, survive a dead-end job, raise four children in a state with infamously bad family support services, prosper in a state rife with racism, and live with a debilitating health condition that was not being treated. *No partner, no money, no prospects, no support, no justice, no health care.* We cannot reduce these circumstances to some crude formula that produces violence, for most poor and even desperate people do not commit crimes, let alone hang themselves and their children. But we cannot settle for Sheriff Fowler's characterization of Estrada's actions as "horrendous," for they are more than that: They are indicative of the near-total breakdown of what Americans once called community, they illustrate the consequences of decades of mean-spirited public policy, they demonstrate how the intersection of neoliberal economics, racism, gender inequity, failing schools, and just plain bad luck leaves millions of our neighbors in grueling positions, struggling on the fringes of a society that notices them only when they get busted for dealing drugs, hang their children, or fight for the kinds of political rights and human services that the middle class takes for granted.[1]

Indeed, the second *New York Times* article, sitting just below the news about Estrada, chronicles the aftermath of the 2007 May Day riot in Los Angeles, at which between 500 and 600 police officers attacked a crowd of 6,000 Angelinos, mostly people of color, who had assembled peaceably in MacArthur Park to rally in support of immigrants' rights. When folks like Estrada participate in the public sphere, doing what democracy asks them to do, they are physically beaten by police trained to see gatherings of poor people of color not as a movement but as a gang, not as a celebration of democracy but as a threat to law and order. In response to this mêlée, Los Angeles Police Chief William J. Bratton fired some of his top officers and instituted new training programs for others. Nevertheless, if you consider the history of the Los Angeles police, including their performance in the so-called Zoot Suit riots in 1943, their response to the Watts uprising in 1965, their implication in the Tijuana/L.A. cocaine cartels of the 1980s, their violations of human rights in the Ramparts scandals of the late 1980s and early 1990s, their handling of the Rodney King affair in 1991, and their most recent attacks on Angelino activists, then it is hard not to conclude that Bratton is not engaging in systematic institutional transformation so much as another round of crisis management. For the past seventy-five years, rogue elements within the L.A. police have been among the most brutal and lawbreaking gangs in the land— does anyone really think that Bratton's public relations band-aid is going to change that fact?[2]

These two stories prompt a series of questions: Can it be any surprise that many hardworking Americans, like Estrada in Texas and the riot victims in California, awake each morning to a sense of hopelessness? Because neoliberal economics have left millions of Americans without any reasonable chance of social ascent, and the courts frequently appear to function as little more than private clubs for the wealthy, and millions of our neighbors are arrested each year by police forces that many see as bureaucratized versions of street gangs, can there be any wonder that the norms of U.S. democracy have fallen into ill repute? To begin answering these questions, many of the essays in this collection argue that the institutionalized law-and-order violence unleashed when the L.A. police attacked peaceful protesters is interlaced with the personal violence committed by Estrada and others in her dire condition, and that both kinds of violence—the political and the personal—undermine our collective faith in the democratic process. As Mumia Abu-Jamal argues in *Live from Death Row*, a government that supports the brutality of the prison-industrial complex teaches its citizens to be "more cynical, colder, and more calculating," and hence to be less likely to participate in the daily mechanisms of governance and cultural renewal that keep democracy afloat.[3]

At the same time, the dilemmas of the democratic process—including our collective refusal to think compassionately about schools, health care, and immigration; our national failure to pay for human services instead of imperial wars; and our longstanding inability to end racism, just to skim the surface of our national paralysis—also fuel the desperation, cynicism, and dropout mentality that lead to crime and violence. This cycle of violence and failing democracy has reached such dismal proportions that many Americans have begun to wonder if it is not too late—whether perhaps we have passed the tipping point beyond which any talk of democracy and justice is delusional. Cornell West warned back in 1993 that many young people, especially in hard-hit black communities, were drowning in "the murky waters of despair and dread." He was pointing to how the "monumental eclipse of hope, the unprecedented collapse of meaning, [and] the incredible disregard for human (especially black) life" had combined to produce a "nihilistic threat" to the "very existence" of black America. In the time since West offered this diagnosis, the number of African Americans locked up in America's prisons has ballooned by 22 percent, reaching to well over half a million. This book responds to West's call for a transformative "politics of conversion" while also expanding his demands, for nihilism knows no race: The eclipse of hope creeps into the hearts of everyone attuned to the times, the rising tide of despair and dread leaves us all damaged, our lives less beautiful, our communities less welcoming, our futures less enticing.[4]

. . . .

If we hope to turn back this nihilistic threat, America will need a national mobilization based on the understanding that abolishing the prison-industrial complex should be at the head of a new human rights agenda for the twenty-first century—this collection of essays hopes to inspire nothing less. Some readers may charge that this ambition is based on a naïve forgetfulness wherein we pretend that America's millions of prisoners are not hardened men and women who have broken the social contract, sometimes violently. To short-circuit that criticism, let me state from the beginning that the authors in this collection do indeed recognize that many of the men and women warehoused in our prisons and jails have committed crimes. Patriots of all political persuasions want their children to be safe, their neighborhoods to be prosperous and caring, their lives to be fulfilling and hopeful—and crime destroys those wishes. In fact, the U.S. Bureau of Justice Statistics reports that in 2005 Americans suffered "an estimated 23 million violent and property crimes"—that is 23 million lives irreparably damaged, 23 million families forever scarred, 23 million times that someone chose to rob or assault another human being, thus violating his or her body, property, and sense of safety. These heartbreaking numbers provide evidence of a culture desperately out of balance. We therefore offer this book not because we are "soft on crime" but because we want to stop it: The violence must end, the wasted lives must be reclaimed, the abandoned communities must be rebuilt, the nihilism must be transformed into passionate participation in the messy mysteries of civic life. The crucial questions, then, are "How can we reverse the avalanche of crime and violence?" "How can we address the underlying social dilemmas that lead to nihilism?" and "How can we reclaim hope and justice from our punishing democracy?"[5]

Because the prison-industrial complex has proven to be a failure at providing answers to these questions, perhaps it is time to consider its abolition, perhaps it is time to move toward empowerment instead of incarceration. Angela Davis accordingly suggests that abolition will "involve the shifting of priorities from the prison-industrial complex to education, housing, [and] health care." Davis and the most ardent prison abolitionists understand that even while pursuing abolition in the long run, the state will need to provide facilities for housing repeat violent offenders. Abolition therefore does not mean the immediate and complete closing of prisons but their long-term transformation and dramatic downsizing. To achieve that goal, Davis calls on activists, scholars, and artists to "generate a conversation about the prospects for abolition," hence beginning "a project that involves reimagining institutions, ideals, and strategies" for moving U.S. democracy away from its love of imperialism and imprisonment and toward something more like equality and justice for all. The difficulty in arguing for abolition, then, is that shutting down the prison-industrial complex will require nothing less than a revolution—the question is not only how to abolish prisons but *how to reimagine a democracy* that does not need such institutions. As Erica Meiners argues:

Working toward abolition means creating structures that reduce the demand and need for prisons. It is ensuring that communities have viable, at least living-wage jobs that are not dehumanizing. It means establishing mechanisms for alternative dispute resolution and other processes that address conflict or harm with mediation. It means ensuring that our most vulnerable populations, for example, those who are mentally ill or undereducated, do not get warehoused in our prisons and jails because of the failure of other institutions such as healthcare and education. It means practicing how to communicate and live across differences and to rely more on each other instead of the police.[6]

That is a tall order. For Davis's and Meiners's abbreviated lists point toward economic and urban reforms, judicial and policing reforms, health and education reforms, and communicative and communal reforms. They are talking about a wholesale reconceiving of democracy as we know it. With the persistence, even under an Obama presidency, of widespread public support for chest-thumping imperial arrogance and gung-ho mass incarceration, that does not seem likely in the immediate future. Tiyo Attallah Salah-El, who founded the Coalition for the Abolition of Prisons while serving a life sentence in Pennsylvania, thus notes that when we say abolition, we are talking about considering the conditions under which it might be feasible. For Salah-El, "we must construct the groundwork for future generations to build a world that is safe and just. Let us begin working at the edges of what is possible. Let us strive toward a new possibility." When we say abolition, then, we do not mean the immediate closing of all prisons; rather, we point toward the creative work of reinventing the nation, of beginning to explore "the edges of what is possible," and thus of beginning the project of reclaiming hope from nihilism.[7]

· · · · · · · · ·

Working from the assumption that abolishing the prison-industrial complex will be driven by a combination of critical analysis and daily practice, both hard-edged criticism and practical imaginings of what is possible, this book is divided into two parts. The first half of the book, consisting of five essays, offers analyses of the prison-industrial complex and focuses on its economic infrastructure (Meiners, chapter 1), its policing mechanisms (Kohler-Hausmann, chapter 2), its relationship to the so-called Drug War (Larson, chapter 3), its mediated constructions of race and racism (Dixon, chapter 4), and its debilitating impact on our public schools (Braz and Williams, chapter 5). Taken as a whole, these five chapters demonstrate how the prison-industrial complex is undermining America by turning the nation into what this Introduction calls a "punishing democracy." That phrase indicates how the daily mechanisms of governance, the everyday habits of citizenship, our embodied modes of consumption and sense-making, the very fabric of our national life, have become enmeshed in technologies and rituals of punishment. We appear to have reached the point where putting our neighbors in cages is taken for granted, where it is understood that our popular culture is based largely on the endless repetition of narratives of cops-and-robbers, where our tax dollars are poured into facilities that have shown no ability to lower crime rates, where crumbling schools are other people's problems—we appear to have become a nation addicted to the notion that harsher punishments doled out to more of our neighbors will somehow make us safer or happier or healthier. Our national character would appear, then, to be increasingly rooted in a collective thirst for punishment. Whether addressing corporations and politicians for whom mass incarceration means massive profit (Meiners), or police who engage in torture to coerce false confessions from beaten suspects (Kohler-Hausmann), or law enforcement agencies who use fear of drugs to militarize their organizations while locking up urban youth (Larson), or media conglomerates that numb viewers with systematically racist news coverage (Dixon), or legislators and educators who seem more concerned with trimming difficult students from the class rolls than empowering them to succeed (Braz and Williams), these chapters illuminate how punishment has become a driving force in contemporary American life. Indeed, as these essays demonstrate in heartbreaking detail, we have become *a punishing democracy*.[8]

The range of critical perspectives offered in these five chapters is by no means comprehensive, and it could be extended in a number of directions. For example, as those of us committed to abolishing the prison-industrial complex move forward in our work, we will need to know more about the relationship between incarcerated parents and the life chances of their children; about the impact of gerrymandering on how districts are represented in state assemblies, and how this affects laws about crime and punishment; about the many ways that gender affects crime, how it leads to different responses and sentences for men and women, different postimprisonment opportunities, and different types of stigma and trauma; about the relationships among disappearing work opportunities and discouraging work experiences and those young men and women who turn to crime as a means of sustenance; about the possible links between depression, learning disorders, and other psychological conditions that seem to correlate with antisocial behavior; and on and on it goes, a veritable shopping list of future topics for research and activism. I mention these other areas of concern by way of indicating that the five chapters offered here are meant to open the conversation, not to end it.[9]

Still, the five chapters that comprise the first half of this book establish a devastating critique of the economic policies, policing strategies, rhetorical habits, mediated fantasies, and educational failures that fuel the prison-industrial complex. The second half of the book then begins the hard work of moving toward abolition by celebrating what is possible. Consisting of another set of five essays, this part of the book chronicles the practical lessons learned from using the arts and education, both in prisons and the public, as tools of self-empowerment, community building, and social change. Because many of us have lost faith in our elected officials, activists fighting against the prison-industrial complex increasingly rely upon grassroots strategies of resistance. This turn to the local means working directly with prisoners and the communities hit hardest by the prison-industrial complex; as West describes what he calls "the politics of conversion," "it stays on the ground among the toiling everyday people." Indeed, the activists, teachers, and artists included here work with prisoners and in their communities to forge new means of self-expression, to explore new means of community organizing, and ultimately to reclaim hope from the peddlers of fear and cynicism. The second half of the book thus offers personal observations, how-to suggestions, and fiery calls to action from longtime activists who use writing and acting workshops to empower prisoners and change communities' attitudes (Alexander, chapter 6), write and stage plays and host follow-up tutorials to enable incarcerated youths to begin reclaiming their lives (Sohnen, chapter 7), work in inner-city schools to shut down the schools-to-prisons pipeline by encouraging a new culture of achievement among so-called at-risk youth (Duncan, chapter 8), produce updated versions of the plays of William Shakespeare, in prison, as occasions for exploring agency and accountability (Shailor, chapter 9), and break down the barriers of separation by taking college students into prisons where they learn side-by-side with incarcerated classmates (Pompa, chapter 10). Chronicling successful programs deployed in Michigan (Alexander), California (Sohnen), Missouri (Duncan), Wisconsin (Shailor), and Pennsylvania (Pompa), these chapters offer a sustained examination of the aesthetic, pedagogical, and political strategies that are helping us move toward abolition. Indeed, whereas the first half of the book diagnoses the crisis, the second half of the book offers tributes to the heroism of those who work each day—in classes, on stages, in prison cells, on the streets, and in workshops—to end America's debilitating addiction to mass incarceration.[10]

Some observers of the projects chronicled in this second half of the book will note with dismay that they involve working not only against but also *in* prisons. The charge will be raised, then, that such work is not so much about abolishing the prison-industrial complex as sustaining it, even putting a human face on its daily operations. From this perspective, the works included herein are not so much radical as complicit; they are not models of change but of cooptation. This accusation may be true, and indeed it seems to me that this is the risk we take when working not only inside prisons but within any organization that we hope to transform: because such transformative work forces us into close proximity with entrenched power, we risk becoming pawns to its needs rather than agents of change. It seems to me, however, that the chapters offered here illustrate in unwavering terms how the authors have dared to take that risk precisely because they are so committed to the educational, artistic, and cultural needs and aspirations of the people with whom they work. In fact, the authors address this challenge directly, chronicling how they have had to shift their priorities, or change their programs, or alter their strategies to be able to continue doing daring work in the shadow of hostile prison administrations. Still, the authors have faced that challenge precisely because they so desperately believe in sharing the gift of speech, the thrill of creativity, and the spark of recognition that comes from learning and making art together. There is no doubt that all of us involved in movements against the prison-industrial complex could be more active on legislative fronts, but the assumption underwriting these chapters is that legislative work cannot be successful until the nation begins to experience an even more fundamental change in consciousness. And so the chapters included herein offer us roadmaps of how to begin moving from being a punishing democracy to one rooted in mutual respect, community-building, and redesigned arts and educational opportunities. Moreover, I argue that the pedagogical, artistic, and political lessons contained in these five chapters offer not only hopeful models for how to begin working toward the abolition of the prison-industrial complex but also toward a much-needed reframing of some of the core educational and artistic beliefs that drive our public schools and universities. Indeed, the longtime activists who have offered us these five roadmaps toward abolition are also some of our very best teachers—let us open their chapters then, not by noting what they do not do but by celebrating what they do: share stories of using the arts and education to open the minds and life opportunities of students whose choices have been constrained. Here is a pedagogy of hope and empowerment, and, moving from there, perhaps of social change.

To make sure that the arguments offered herein do not distract readers from the daily horrors, humiliations, and hopes of those suffering incarceration, I have interspersed throughout the book, layered between each chapter, poetic observations offered by our imprisoned neighbors. To add a visual dimension to the book, I have asked Janie Paul, one of the curators of the annual exhibition of art hosted by the Prison Creative Arts Project, to assemble ten color plates of art made by men and women imprisoned in Michigan; those images and an introduction to the art are in the Appendix. I have included these poetic and artistic components to remind readers that the prison-industrial complex does not house monsters but humans—this simple reminder may well point to the most daunting communicative challenge of the twenty-first century: trying to build a new democratic idiom that flourishes without obsessive othering and compulsive punishment, choosing instead to construct community by celebrating the pursuit of solidarity, equality, and liberty. As Bob Ivie argues in *Dissent from War*, we can continue down the bloody road of mass-produced barbarism, or we can begin the hard task of "weaving a web of reconciliation that would supplant the ruling paradigm of victimization and redemptive violence." Hoping to embody this transformative spirit, and offered as both critiques of the prison-industrial complex and inspiring roadmaps for how to abolish it, the essays collected here aspire to help us take another significant step toward social justice.[11]

I will close this introduction, then, by offering a vision of hope written by Mario Rocha, a once wrongfully incarcerated but now free young man who, since leaving prison, has entered George Washington University:

> I breathe the briskness of the wintry morning breeze
> soaking in nature's tranquil glory
> feeling the empowerment of solitude and prayer
> absorbing the blessings the day brings
> and evoke the Spirit of the Mountain
> offering me peace in mind and body
>
> I call upon the Mountain God to sustain me
> to give me the wisdom and strength
> to withstand these attacks of fear oppression hatred
> fading now mercifully as the morning sunlight
> warms my face within these prison walls
> alone now on the yard filled with spirit
> compassion wonder hope

Rocha used the educational and artistic opportunities provided to him in prison (by some of the authors included herein) to help him move from the prison yard to the campus quadrangle, where he has begun to blossom into a community leader and passionate voice for change. He is just one example of how, working together, we may reclaim hope and justice from our punishing democracy.[12]

Notes

1. Gretel C. Kovach, "A Mother, Depressed, Hangs Herself and Her Children," *New York Times* (30 May 2007), A14; on the relationship between the gothic genre and crime, see Karen Halttunen, *Murder Most Foul: The Killer and the American Gothic Imagination* (Cambridge, MA: Harvard University Press, 1998); on the relationship between mental illness and imprisonment, see the Sentencing Project, *Mentally Ill Offenders in the Criminal Justice System* (Washington, DC: Sentencing Project, 2002), where we learn that "16% of all inmates self-reported current mental illness or an overnight stay in a mental hospital, and an additional 14% had received other mental health services in the past. Almost one quarter of incarcerated women were identified as mentally ill" (p. 2); also see Human Rights Watch, *Ill-Equipped: U.S. Prisons and Offenders with Mental Illness* (New York: Human Rights Watch, 2003).

2. Randal C. Archibold, "Los Angeles Police Chief Notes Failures of Command at Rally," *New York Times* (30 May 2007), A14; on the historical narrative offered here, see Eduardo Obregón Pagán, *Murder at the Sleepy Lagoon: Zoot Suits, Race, and Riot in Wartime L.A.* (Chapel Hill: University of North Carolina Press, 2006); Jervey Tervalon and Cristián Sierra, eds., *Geography of Rage: Remembering the Los Angeles Riots of 1992* (Los Angeles: Really Great Books, 2002); *Board of Inquiry into the Ramparts Area Corruption Incident*, overseen by Bernard Parks, Chief of Police (Los Angeles: Police Department, 2000); and Mike Davis, *City of Quartz: Excavating the Future in Los Angeles* (New York: Random House, 1990), 223–317; sources on the drug war may be found in Daniel Larson's contribution to this volume (chapter 3).

3. Mumia Abu-Jamal, *Live from Death Row* (New York: Perennial, 1996), 64; on the declining state of opportunity in the U.S. economy, see the essays collected as "Inside the Income Gap," the *New York Times Sunday Magazine* (10 June 2007), 51–85; the fate of Americans under this economic arrangement is captured in the title of Louis Uchitelle, *The Disposable American: Layoffs and Their Consequences* (New York: Vintage, 2007); for a case study of the entwining of neoliberal economics and the prison industry, see Ruth Wilson Gilmore, *Golden Gulag: Prisons, Surplus, Crisis, and Opposition in Globalizing California* (Berkeley: University of California Press, 2007), 1–86; on those who profit from this crisis, see Daniel Burton-Rose, Dan Pens, and Paul Wright, eds., *The Celling of America: An Inside Look at the U.S. Prison Industry* (Monroe, ME: Common Courage Press, 1998), and Tara Herivel and Paul Wright, eds., *Prison Profiteers: Who Makes Money from Mass Incarceration* (New York: New Press, 2007).

4. Cornell West, *Race Matters* (Boston: Beacon Press, 1993), 12, 20; for more on the relationship between the prison-industrial complex and the production of dread amidst black Americans, see the essays by Manning Marable, Angela Davis, Marc Mauer, Salim Muwakkil, and Adrien Wing in *States of Confinement: Policing, Detention, and Prisons*, ed. Joy James (New York: St. Martin's Press, 2000), 53–105, and Travis Dixon's and Garrett Albert Duncan's contributions to this volume (chapters 4 and 8); whereas African Americans accounted for 473,300 of all U.S. prisoners in

1994 (Bureau of Justice Statistics, *Prisoners in 1994* [Washington, DC: Department of Justice, 1995], table 10, p. 8), by 2005 they totaled 577,100, an increase of 22% (Bureau of Justice Statistics, *Prisoners in 2005* [Washington, DC: Department of Justice, 2006], table 10, p. 8).

5. See Bureau of Justice Statistics, *Criminal Victimization, 2005* (Washington, DC: U.S. Department of Justice, 2006), 1—within the number of 23 million, the Bureau of Justice Statistics found 18 million property crimes and 5.2 million violent crimes (including "rape or sexual assault, robbery, aggravated assault, and simple assault"); for help making sense of the data on crime in America, see Steven Donziger, ed., *The Real War on Crime: The Report of the National Criminal Justice Commission* (New York: HarperPerennial, 1996).

6. Angela Davis, *Abolition Democracy: Beyond Empire, Prisons, and Torture* (interviews with Eduardo Mendieta) (New York: Seven Stories, 2005), 74–75, 89; Erica Meiners, *Right to Be Hostile: Schools, Prisons, and the Making of Public Enemies* (New York: Routledge, 2007), 168–69; and see the classic Mark Morris, ed., *Instead of Prisons: A Handbook for Abolitionists* (Syracuse, NY: Prison Research Education Action Project, 1976), available online at www.prisonpolicy.org/scans/-instead_of_prisons, and the materials available from the Prison Moratorium Project at www.nomoreprisons.org.

7. Tiyo Attallah Salah-El, "A Call for the Abolition of Prisons" (2001), as reprinted in *The New Abolitionists: (Neo)Slave Narratives and Contemporary Prison Writings*, ed. Joy James (Albany: State University of New York Press, 2005), 69–74, quotation from 74; to join projects working toward this goal, contact Critical Resistance at www.criticalresistance.org, or the Sentencing Project at www.sentencingproject .org; for additional information, contact the Prison Activist Resource Center at www .prisonactivist.org.

8. For studies addressing these and other prison-industrial complex-related issues, see Tara Herivel and Paul Wright, eds., *Prison Nation: The Warehousing of America's Poor* (New York: Routledge, 2003); Marc Mauer, *Race to Incarcerate* (New York: New Press, 1999); and Christian Parenti, *Lockdown America: Police and Prisons in the Age of Crisis* (London: Verso, 1999); although the notion of a "punishing democracy" is my term, I am drawing here upon a long line of scholarship that places violence at the heart of the American experience—in this regard, see Richard Maxwell Brown, *Strain of Violence: Historical Studies of American Violence and Vigilantism* (New York: Oxford University Press, 1975); Richard Slotkin, *Regeneration through Violence: The Mythology of the American Frontier, 1600–1860* (Middletown, CT: Wesleyan University Press, 1973); my *Executing Democracy, Volume One: Capital Punishment and the Making of America, 1683–1800* (East Lansing, MI: Michigan State University Press, 2010); and Jeremy Engels and Greg Goodale, "'Our Battle Cry Will Be: Remember Jenny McCre!' A Précis on the Rhetoric of Revenge," *American Quarterly* 61, no. 1 (2009): 93–112.

9. On the question of how prison affects families, see Erik Eckholm, "In Prisoners' Wake, a Tide of Troubled Kids," *New York Times* (4 July 2009), accessed online at www.nytimes.com; regarding the prison-industrial complex and gender, see the materials available from Women and Prisons at www.womenandprison.org; on gerrymandering and the impact prisons have on the electoral process, see Gary Hunter

and Peter Wagner, "Prisons, Politics, and the Census," in Herivel and Wright, *Prison Profiteers*, 80–89.

10. West, *Race Matters*, 20; this book is therefore situated amid the recent turn toward engaged scholarship and pedagogy committed to advancing the cause of social justice; for examples of this work across a wide range of concerns, see *Communication Activism*, 2 vols., ed. Lawrence R. Frey and Kevin M. Carragee (Cresskill, NJ: Hampton, 2007); for works on prison-related issues, see PCARE, "Fighting the Prison-Industrial Complex: A Call to Communication and Cultural Studies Scholars to Change the World," *Communication and Critical Cultural Studies* 4, no. 4 (2007): 402–20, and Patricia Yaeger, "Editor's Column: Prisons, Activism, and the Academy—a Roundtable with Buzz Alexander, Bell Gale Chevigny, Stephen John Hartnett, Janie Paul, and Judith Tannenbaum," *PMLA* 123, no. 3 (2008): 545–67 (this same issue contains another ten articles on prisons, education, and activism); for teachers' perspectives, see Judith Tannenbaum, *Disguised as a Poem: My Years Teaching Poetry at San Quentin* (Boston: Northeastern University Press, 2000); my "Lincoln and Douglas Engage the Abolitionist David Walker in Prison Debate: Empowering Education, Applied Communication, and Social Justice," *Journal of Applied Communication Research* 26, no. 2 (1998): 232–53; Eleanor Novek, "'The Devil's Bargain': Censorship, Identity, and the Promise of Empowerment in a Prison Newspaper," *Journalism* 6, no. 1 (2005): 5–23; and Jonathan Shailor, "When Muddy Flowers Bloom: The Shakespeare Project at Racine Correctional Institution," *PMLA* 123, no. 3 (2008): 632–41.

11. Bob Ivie, *Dissent from War* (Bloomfield, CT: Kumarian, 2007), 8; for a programmatic statement of these principles, see my "Communication, Activism, and Joyful Commitment," *Western Journal of Communication* 74, no. 1 (2005): 68–93.

12. Mario Rocha, "Four Years Down Today," *Broken Chains* (Summer 2001), 11; *Broken Chains* was the newsletter of the Coalition for the Abolition of Prisons, for which Kate Klehr and I edited this issue; regarding Rocha's now infamous case, see Susan Koch's award-winning documentary, *Mario's Story* (Cabin John, MD: Cabin Films, 2006), and "Visiting Mario," in *Incarceration Nation: Investigative Prison Poems of Hope and Terror,* ed. Stephen John Hartnett (Walnut Creek, CA: AltaMira, 2003), 135–54; for exemplary collections of writings by our imprisoned neighbors, see Bell Gale Chevigny, ed., *Twenty-Five Years of Prison Writing* (New York: Arcade, 1999); H. Bruce Franklin, ed., *Prison Writing in 20th-Century America* (New York: Penguin, 1998); Judith Scheffler, ed., *Wall Tappings: An International Anthology of Women's Prison Writings* (New York: Feminist Press, 2002); the resources listed by the PEN American Center, under "prison writing," at www.pen.org; and the offerings in Krista Brune, ed., *Creating behind the Razor Wire: Perspectives from Arts in Corrections in the United States* (privately printed, 2007).

PART I

Diagnosing the Crisis

Building an Abolition Democracy; or, The Fight against Public Fears, Private Benefits, and Prison Expansion

Erica R. Meiners

Several years ago, at St. Leonard's Adult High School, where we offer adults a second chance at earning a high school diploma, we started a college and career night to provide students with information about accessing postsecondary education. Students—men and women with still raw, or in some cases old, histories of incarceration—usually want to hear from representatives of local community colleges, drug and alcohol-abuse counselor training programs, truck-driving schools, or other trade apprenticeships and job-training initiatives. Our students make no requests for information about medical, law, dental, teaching, or business schools; if we had south-facing windows in our classroom, then the University of Illinois at Chicago (UIC) would be visible from our learning space, but we have no such windows, we receive no requests, and so do not schedule representatives from UIC, Northwestern University, the University of Chicago, Loyola University, or any of the other elite public and private institutions in Chicago. Even though these universities sometimes provide their students as tutors for our students, the unspoken and tacit consensus among St. Leonard's students (and many of us who organize the school) is that institutions like UIC are impenetrable fortresses. Even my public and relatively open-access university, Northeastern Illinois University, seems out of reach; institutions outside of Chicago might as well not exist. For example, "going downstate" in Illinois, an expression that generally refers to upper-middle-class families venturing south from the greater Chicago area to visit the University of Illinois at Urbana–Champaign or Illinois State University in Normal, means something completely different to our students and their families and friends, for whom the phrase signifies being shipped down to prisons located in the state's southern rural communities. And so, even on the occasion of trying to support the hardworking students of St. Leonard's Adult High School to exercise their right to access an education, we collide again with the fact that education in America often functions as what can only be called a caste or apartheid system.[1]

Despite these structural impediments, the representatives from the admissions or recruitment departments of colleges that attend our college night, and the many job developers who come as well, display patience and generosity. Year after year, I watch our participants anxiously press them with questions about programs for part-time students, access to financial aid and childcare, restrictions on services or programs for those with felony and other convictions, and their records on successful job placements. Even when supported by the contacts formed at these events, it will be extremely difficult for most of our students to consider even these affordable and open-access job training and academic programs. Some of these students, without stable and low-cost housing, will not be able to maintain or regain custody of, let alone provide daycare for, their children, thus making night school a virtual impossibility. Their nonliving-wage jobs, often physically exhausting, leave little time for school and provide barely enough cash to make rent, let alone plan for a better future. Others, because of the need to work, can attend classes only part-time and so are shut out of most financial aid. And, most infuriating to me, despite analytic brilliance, powerful poetry and art-making abilities, and sophisticated financial skills (incomprehensible to those of us who have never had to sleep for a week in a car while living on a twenty), many lack what Jesse Jackson has called the "cash language," and so will fail to score well on the admissions tests that would place them into required English or mathematics classes, meaning that they must take, and pay for, two or three remedial classes. Ostensibly offered to help undertrained students make the leap to college-level work, these classes also cost money our students often do not have and often reinforce students' anxieties that they are *not college material, not competent.*[2]

I will confess that on our college nights (and, increasingly, other evenings as well), I do a bad job of tethering my rage that the stratospherically wealthy local universities—institutions that hoard resources and are seemingly unaccountable for the ways they concentrate power and privilege along class and race lines—do not have to be present and respond to this audience. I also realize, however, that at the end of the day, my rage is self-indulgent and our students are better pragmatists than I: They do what they must to survive, even if that means long-term educational planning takes a back seat to short-term employment needs. During bleaker moments, I know that Malcolm X Community College, less than a half-mile from our high school, might as well be on another planet. Still, on my optimistic days, I think about the successes: Out of every graduating class of fifteen to twenty students, perhaps three women make the transition to community college immediately, and usually a couple of students make that leap a year or two later.[3]

While colleges and universities are thus virtually forbidden zones for my formerly incarcerated students, other public institutions are more receptive to this crowd and are much more generously endowed by the state. As of June 2007 (the most recent data available from the Illinois Department of Corrections), Illinois housed more than 46,000 prisoners in thirty-six prisons, work camps, and other centers of detention. These state facilities, the majority built and opened in the 1980s and 1990s, are paid for by tax dollars and warehouse a growing number of our neighbors, lovers, sisters, brothers, and parents. Consider, for example, the "supermax" Tamms prison, one of the priciest facilities in Illinois, with a construction cost of $120,000 per bed. Opened in 1998, Tamms was built, as the Illinois Department of Corrections states, to contain the "worst of the worst behavioral problems of the department." This language is echoed, albeit ironically, by those incarcerated in the supermax, in this testimony from Martell Gomez, who writes that "at the age of 23, I became one of the worst-of-the-worst in the Department of Corrections in the state of Illinois and was consigned to the six-year-old supermax security prison located in the southern town of Tamms, in Alexander County." Supermax prisons, also called control units, were first initiated at the United States Penitentiary in Marion, Illinois, in 1972; they are prisons, or sometimes separate parts of a prison, that operate under a supermaximum, or high-security, regime wherein imprisoned men and women are locked in solitary confinement between twenty-two and twenty-three hours a day. As the supermax model has spread, so critics have increasingly attacked them as human-rights violations and as factories of mental illness. Nonetheless, despite these concerns, as of 2008 the state of Illinois was paying roughly $59,000 per year for each prisoner condemned to Tamms. Our state educational facilities, ostensibly institutions for producing new leaders and good citizens, are thus virtually shut to my students at St. Leonard's Adult High School, yet the same state that will not invest in my students' educational opportunities will not hesitate to lavish $59,000 a year on sending them, allegedly the worst of the worst, to Tamms and other expensive penal facilities.[4]

In contrast to our neighbors who are shipped off to Tamms, consider those who matriculate to the University of Illinois at Urbana-Champaign (UIUC), where the fall 2010 full-time base-rate undergraduate tuition is estimated to be $10,386 a year. Listed as one of the nation's "top ten public national universities" by the marketers at the *2008 U.S. News and World Report College Guide*, UIUC and similar institutions refer to their incoming and graduating students and faculty as the "best and brightest" of our nation, or as "the cream of the crop." Politicians and postsecondary leaders emphasize the development and reproduction of human capital as a rationale for postsecondary funding, which is meant to keep our talent in the state, thus fueling its economy, its culture, and the health of its democratic practices. Juxtaposing the Fighting Illini and Tamms opens up a chilling comparison of how the state chooses to allocate its funds and resources, for these parallel public institutions—prison for the worst of the worst and university for the best of the best—are intertwined, planned pathways created by the state. That is, these institutions do not merely reflect existing structures of power but reproduce and even exacerbate them: Studying the relationship between prisons and schools thus enables us to dive into the structural question of how the state invests in punishment, how it disinvests in communities hit hard by crime, and how its economic and educational policies therefore fuel the prison-industrial complex.[5]

The Savage Ironies of the Prison-Industrial Complex

Considering that calls for fiscal restraint and tightened accountability are the frequent responses to demands for increases in public educational expenditures, our extraordinary public investment in the prison-industrial complex is striking. These "savage ironies," as Paul Street documents, of experiencing simultaneous social-welfare disinvestment and carceral augmentation, are in full display in Illinois, where, in the last twenty-five years, the state has built more than twenty new prisons, work camps, or other detention facilities. According to the Illinois Consortium on Drug Policies (ICDP), between 1985 and 2000, state appropriations for higher education in Illinois increased 30 percent, while corrections appropriations increased more than 100 percent. Trends in Illinois are indicative of national patterns; in fact, between 1984 and 2000, across all states and the District of Columbia, the increases in state spending on prisons were six times as high as the increases in spending on higher education. Such discrepancies are also evident at the K–12 level: In Illinois, the annual cost of incarcerating one adult is about "four and a half times the cost of one child's annual [K–12] education." The state is therefore increasingly shifting its financial support away from its educational institutions and toward its penal institutions. Thus, "between 1970 and 2001, the Illinois prison population increased more than 500 percent, from 7,326 to 44,348 people," placing Illinois among the top ten states in prison population. And so, even while affirmative action is increasingly contested in the public arenas of education and employment, it is aggressively promoted in another public venue: corrections. Consider the startling fact that in 1999, only 992 African American males were awarded undergraduate degrees in Illinois while approximately 7,000 were released from its prisons and jails; in 2001, Illinois had approximately 20,000 more African American men in prison than in a college or a university. These figures indicate how the state's systematic investment in prisons is exacerbating longstanding inequalities by shifting resources from education to imprisonment, from empowerment to incarceration—hence building a punishing democracy.[6]

This savage irony, of investing state monies in punishment while refusing to invest in the educational programs and institutions that could lower crime, runs counter to common sense, for research clearly documents that supporting students who choose to progress in their educational levels reduces the need for prisons and jails, hence costing taxpayers less in the long run than mass incarceration. But since when has financial common sense shaped public policy? For example, while 1998 capped five years of marginal but steady increases in budgetary advances for higher education in Illinois, the 1990s were also marked by heightened concerns about accountability and fiscal responsibly. According to the Illinois Board of Higher Education, the statewide "Priorities, Quality, [and] Productivity" (PQP) program forced the "elimination or consolidation of more than 600 outdated or duplicative programs in the state's 12 public universities and, to a lesser extent, in the 49 community colleges over the last six years. An average $36 million a year has been saved." Yet, in the rush to streamline academic offerings in the name of being cost-effective, there was no thought to offer college courses in prison, or to work to reinstate Pell Grants for people incarcerated, even when research documents that postsecondary education has the highest rate of reducing recidivism (Pell Grants for prisoners were cut in 1994). Indeed, the ICDP has calculated that in 2002, if postsecondary programs were offered to incarcerated men and women, then Illinois could have saved "between $11.8 and $47.3 million" from the reduced recidivism rates. "Get tough on crime" rhetoric thus pushes counter-productive legislation and budget choices that, when combined, lead to disinvestment in the one life choice that we know actually reduces crime and recidivism: education.[7]

The patterns of institution building and resource allocation noted here are intertwined yet uneven: For the best of the best, the state supports institutions that offer possibilities of enhancing human capital, but for the worst of the worst it builds warehouses that depreciate human capital. Acknowledging this relationship between prisons and schools in turn obliges us to think about questions of our personal and institutional accountability, about how those of us with positions and stakes in higher education (as students, staff, teachers, and leaders) participate in institutions that dehumanize others—and I mean not just in the prisons, but in our own colleges and universities. In order to have a UIUC, must we have a Tamms? Thus, even as I try below to explain how the neoliberal economics of antidevelopment have crippled some communities while enriching others, and privatized public spaces in the guise of promoting safety, I also want to encourage readers to recognize their own place within these questions. As Paul Street argues, those of us committed to social justice and the abolition of prisons must seek "a general redistribution of resources from privileged and often fantastically wealthy persons to those most penalized from birth by America's long and intertwined history of inherited class and race privilege." Following Street, and thinking again of my students at St. Leonard's Adult High School, it is important to ask: If we take decarceration movements seriously, how must our allegiances and relationships to our universities and colleges change? How can we redistribute the resources and life choices allocated to the supposed best of the best and worst of the worst? To begin answering those questions, I address below how neoliberal economics interweave with the legacies of white supremacy and the prison-industrial complex.[8]

The Assault on Big Government and the Persistence of White Supremacy

Ever since the presidency of Ronald Reagan, bipartisan public sentiment has clamored to reduce the financial burden of government on the people, to have "smarter" government, to try, to paraphrase Reagan, to "get big government off the backs of the working people." While this drive to shrink big government may, for some advocates, be motivated by an honest desire to lower taxes or to reduce the role and the cost of government in everyday life, hence supposedly opening the way for more efficient entrepreneurial development, for others these same claims amount to a useful lie, a persuasive bait and switch. For when some politicians and their supporters describe shrinking big government, they frequently mean cutting specific components of government services, typically those social services utilized by the poor and people of color, even while drastically inflating government spending in other areas. For example, in the last thirty years, the budgets of the Drug Enforcement Agency, the Bureau of Prisons, and the (since disbanded) Immigration and Naturalization Services (INS) swelled *at least 10 percent each year*, while funding for social welfare programs—such as housing programs for the poor, unemployment compensation, and food and nutrition assistance—decreased significantly.[9]

This shift toward becoming a punishing democracy not only has transformed the budgets of many government agencies but also has changed the goals and functions of these agencies. For example, the enforcement arm of the INS has grown—it is now called Immigration and Customs Enforcement (ICE) and has been subsumed by the Department of Homeland Security—yet that agency's service and assistance components have shrunk. In their discussion of the reframing of the welfare state into a neoliberal state, Rebecca Bohrman and Naomi Murakawa argue that "welfare retrenchment and punishment expansion represent opposite trends in state spending, but they rely on the same ideology. This ideology holds that the liberal welfare state corrodes personal responsibility, divorces work from reward, and lets crime go without punishment; consequently the lenient welfare regime attracts opportunistic immigrants and cultivates criminal values." To be anti–big government in this climate is to oppose offering welfare benefits to those with drug felony convictions but not to oppose the establishment of the Department of Homeland Security; it means opposing spending tax dollars on inner-city schools but not on the prisons that will house the children failed by our educational system (I exclude here anti–big government organizations such as Americans for Tax Reform, or certain civil libertarians, who tend to be consistent in wanting to defund the police and the welfare state). These twin shifts are not coincidental or arbitrary; rather, they are the hallmarks of neoliberalism, which pursues the remaking of nation-states and economies through the intertwined practices of deregulation and privatization, thus supposedly fueling the rise of a now unencumbered free market—which of course leads to the decimation of the public sphere. Neoliberalism in the United States has been forged, then, as David Harvey states, through the "long march" of corporations, media, think-tanks, and other powerful forces that have sought not only to change economic and political policies but the cultural understandings that ground our relationship to democracy and everyday life itself. Indeed, from pursuing deregulation and privatization to waging imperial wars to supporting mass incarceration, these shifts in the economic and political spheres have prompted transformations in the private sphere as well, including how we understand our identities, families, emotions, and relations to the state.[10]

Demands to reduce big government have always been popular in the United States—for example, John L. O'Sullivan, that antebellum gadfly and champion of Jacksonian democracy, preached in 1837 that "the best government is that which governs least"—but such demands possessed little traction after World War II, as white males took full advantage of public federal initiatives, especially the GI Bill and the federal subsidy of suburban housing. Because they benefitted directly from such New Deal–influenced programs, millions of white men favored government programs that enabled educational opportunities and economic mobility. But the global economic changes of the 1970s, fueling what some observers have called a phase of deindustrialization in the United States, or what Elizabeth Blackmar has called "lagging capitalism," provided an opening for those who favored neoliberal rather than New Deal policies. Entrenched in the middle class, the same white men who had once reaped the benefits of New Deal programs now turned against them, seeing the same assistance that helped them as constituting unnecessary handouts to others. Coupled with these economic shifts, the debacles of Vietnam and Watergate fueled increasing distrust of the government, hence fueling assaults on the welfare state. Trade-union membership, environmental regulations, and welfare and social services, far from providing a common or a civil society, were constructed as limits on both individual rights and the "free" market. According to this logic, the U.S. government had morphed into a monster that was antithetical to individual progress, yet the free market, framed as superior to ineffective and artificial public bureaucracies, could not be asked to bear responsibility for rising social or economic inequities. Private was now superior to public; as Blackmar observes, neoliberals argued that "common property offered no incentives to labor, and without incentives to labor, society faced the problem of 'free riders' and 'shirkers,' two groups who turned the *public* domain itself into a wasteful commons by taking something for nothing." From this neoliberal perspective, government was taking freedom from individuals; personal responsibility thus became the watchword of those who sought to destroy social welfare policies.[11]

To understand how these neoliberal transformations in the U.S. economy and culture affected the prison-industrial complex, we should approach this desire to shrink big government through the larger context of the history of white supremacy. For most people of color and women were specifically excluded from participation in the original structuring of the New Deal welfare state. Union membership, social security, and housing assistance either explicitly excluded most communities of color and women or did not apply to those categories of work that were available only to communities of color and women, thus affecting their ability to advance their careers, accumulate wealth, and participate in the public sphere. The Civil Rights movements of the 1950s and 1960s involved widespread challenges to white supremacy, in part by demanding that these programs (and other basic forms of civic life) be extended to all citizens. For example, African Americans and their allies fought for access to the Federal Housing Authority's resources, to equal public education, to the voting booth, and more. But as these groups worked to remove formal barriers to equality, resistance emerged from many quarters; deindustrialization thus coincided with a political backlash against the rights-based movements of minority groups. As Julilly Kohler-Hausmann demonstrates in this volume (see chapter 2), this combination of a backlash against the victories of the civil-rights movement, the rise of deindustrialization, and the production of a culture of fear led to a dangerous configuration in which African Americans were increasingly targeted as opponents of the state and as criminal monsters. The rise of neoliberalism therefore coincided with the production of a new racism based less on political disenfranchisement than on using an ascendant prison-industrial complex to enforce the norms of white supremacy.[12]

The dismantling of social welfare programs and the expansion of the prison-industrial complex therefore depended upon the maintenance and reinvention of longstanding tropes about race and gender. Downsizing of the welfare state was required because of all the freeloaders and shirkers who take advantage of the state's lax generosity; concurrently, the subsequent expansion of the punitive functions of the state was required to contain the supposed violence launched by those individually irresponsible losers who are unable to climb the social ladder. As Wahneema Lubiano observes, the stereotypical characters driving such thinking represent old stories in the United States:

> Categories like "black women," or particular subsets of those categories, like "welfare mother/queen," are not simply social taxonomies, they are recognized by the national public as stories that describe the world in particular and politically loaded ways—and that is exactly why they are constructed, reconstructed, manipulated, and contested. They are, like so many other social narratives and taxonomic social categories, part of the building blocks of "reality" for many people; they suggest something about the world; they provide simple, uncomplicated, and often wildly (and politically damaging) inaccurate information about what is "wrong" with some people, with the political economy of the United States.[13]

Although data consistently illustrate the same rates of welfare use across multiple races, the rhetorical force of these racializing categories means that welfare freeloaders manifest in the mass media as "lazy black mothers" or "illegal alien families." Bohrman and Murakawa note that "less than 1 percent of surveyed immigrants move to the United States primarily for social services"; moreover, "fear of deportation" and confusion about eligibility mean that immigrants are less likely to use state resources, meaning that the longstanding racial narratives that teach white Americans to fear certain Others are at odds with the facts. Such stereotypes resonate not because of their accuracy but because they echo deep-grained racist narratives, what Lubiano calls "the building blocks of 'reality.'"[14]

These "building blocks" point to a strategy of scapegoating, where the elite architects of social inequality and violence are masked while the victims of such policies are blamed. Rather than focusing on the causes of long-term economic shifts, or looking at employers' or corporations' culpability and greed, or addressing the consequences of the government's focus on expanding punitive and enforcement practices, blame is placed on communities and individuals that represent old anxieties about race, gender, and power. As Michelle Fine concludes from her study of deindustrialized white working-class men, these Americans came to understand themselves largely by constructing public enemies: "African-American men . . . are discursively imported to buffer the pain, protest the loss, and still secure the artificial privilege of whiteness. Occluded are the macro-structures that have forced white working class men out of the labor market and into an obsession with Black men, affirmative action, and welfare." Opposition to welfare and affirmative action therefore cloaks deeper unease over the norms of race, gender, class, and power. Members of the white "silent majority," as Howard Winant calls them, believe they are oppressed through governmental largesse that unduly benefits the least worthy. This persistence of working-class communities electing not to align themselves with communities of color, and instead supporting actions, policies, and larger cultural fictions that actually harm or decrease their social or economic options in order to preserve white supremacy is another familiar story in the United States. As Charles Mills argues, "white workers prefer incorporation into white domination, even as junior partners, to joining a trans-racial struggle that might endanger their privileged status." Seen from this perspective, the rise of the prison-industrial complex amounts to a massive reshifting of cultural anxieties: In the face of deindustrialization, declining wages (relative to the cost of living), rising unemployment, a string of legal successes advancing the civil-rights agenda, and the embarrassments of Vietnam and Watergate, many white Americans found solace in locating their troubles at the feet of poor blacks who would need to be imprisoned.[15]

The historical transformations noted here do not indicate that the state is withering, or that a now-liberated market dominates, but that the state's responsiveness to capital is strengthening. The so-called downsizing of big government has in fact resulted in various government agencies playing a greater role in the surveillance of the poor and marginalized. Far from reducing big government, these shifts in the role of the state, produced in tandem with global economic changes, have translated into dramatic increases in the government's roles in the lives of the poor. As James Ferguson argues, "the state, in this conception, is not the name of an actor, it is the name of a way of tying together, multiplying, and coordinating power relations, a kind of knotting or congealing of power." For example, the Pew Center on the State's Public Safety Performance Project documents that at the start of 2008, American prisons or jails held 2,319,258 adults, accounting for one prisoner for every 99.1 men and women. This unprecedented ratio of incarceration indicates that the government is not downsizing; rather, it is increasingly regulating the lives of poor men and women, especially those of color, hence reinforcing those building blocks of reality that support longstanding racist stereotypes. Thus neoliberalism intertwines with white supremacy, supports the rise of the prison-industrial complex, and so produces a punishing democracy.[16]

False Promises and the Political Economy of the Prison Boom

While neoliberalism and white supremacy mutually support the rise of a punishing democracy, another strong source of support for mass incarceration is the canard that building prisons creates jobs and economic opportunity for host communities. While prisons-as-economic-salvation is a ruse, it is true, historically, that prisons and criminalization participate in the regulation of the labor force. As Angela Davis documents, laws written after the Civil War, the so called Black Codes of the southern states, reworded the Slave Codes to target recently freed African Americans who would now be castigated not as slaves but as criminals. Once incarcerated in conditions that many observers called worse than slavery, these men constituted a ready supply of laborers after the Civil War. Ex-slaves were not the only targets of such Codes, however, as numerous mid-nineteenth century laws also addressed indigenous peoples, criminalized their behavior, and subsequently framed them as exploitable labor. As Stormy Ogden writes: "In 1850 the California legislature passed the Government and Protection of the Indians Act, which can only be described as legalized slavery. The act provided for the indenture of 'loitering, intoxicated, and orphaned Indians' and forced regulation of their employment. It also defined a special class of crimes and punishment for these Indians. Under the act, California Indians of all ages could be 'indentured or apprenticed to any white citizen.'" Such laws resulted in the economic exploitation of indigenous peoples in prisons, their treatment as second-class citizens outside prisons, and continued discrimination in many aspects of everyday life. Thinking historically, then, we need to realize that the prison-industrial complex amounts to the most recent manifestation of these other longstanding practices wherein imprisonment has been used both as a form of labor control and, more broadly, as a means of disciplining marginalized populations.[17]

There is of course profit to be made in such practices. While marginal, approximately 3 percent of U.S. prisons participate in private for-profit industries. For example, labor within prisons is contracted out to for-profit companies such as Victoria's Secret, often for as low as twenty-six cents a day. In U.S. prisons, minimum wage laws do not apply, and overtime and healthcare benefits are not an issue because companies simply do not offer them, meaning prisons offer some companies opportunities to lower their cost of production and hence raise their profits. For example, with 100 factories employing more than 21,000 inmates, the Federal Prison Industries (FPI) listed $546.3 million in net sales in 2003. More centrally than the possibility of exploiting the labor of the incarcerated, however, the construction of multibillion-dollar prisons and the subsequent staffing and maintenance of these institutions is touted by their supporters as an economic engine for rescuing depressed rural communities. For just as the new neoliberal mobility of capital translated into manufacturing jobs moving to nation-states where labor is cheaper, so agribusiness swept across the nation, capturing government subsidies and further reducing the economic viability of the small family farm. With this landscape of "surplus" land and deindustrialization, and with its corresponding under- and unemployment, those incarcerated, from one vantage point, are commodities. And so, starting in the mid-eighties, rural communities across the United States that were hard hit by the closing of manufacturing plants, the consolidation of farms, and the other historical shifts this article narrates, began lobbying for prisons as a way to support local economies. For example, Gilmore charts the establishment of the Corcoran supermax prison in Kings County, California, a former cotton town. Residents of Kings County were looking for a steady employer, and, as Gilmore documents, the California Department of Corrections's community relations expert, Theresa Rocha, argued that "'prison doors would 'unlock' the town from its persistent economic depression by putting labor and real property back to work." Yet local residents initially received only 10 percent of new prison jobs. This number was bumped up to 20 percent after the community organized to better prepare residents to fill out the necessary paperwork; still, the promise of town and county revitalization was not achieved. Gilmore suggests that when measured by specific indexes, prisons are not an economic success story: "When measured by jobs for current residents, residential development, locally sited related industries and services, or consumer retail, prisons have not delivered even on the modest employment and growth projections derived from the CDC's categorical assurances. Indeed, the biggest beneficiaries are those major shapers of the valley's economic development: utility companies." Seduced by promises of steady employment and economic revitalization, towns are betrayed by the mobility of prison workers, hurt by the inability of locals to qualify for the new employment, and suffer the rising domestic violence rates attached to families who work inside prisons. Indeed, Joëlle Fraser depicts how, when the High Desert Prison came to Susanville, her hometown in California, domestic violence skyrocketed, because, as a Susanville social worker asked, "What kind of husband and father do you think they [the guards] can be after what they have been around for 14 hours?"[18]

Like Fraser's disappointed California neighbors, many Illinoisans are learning that the promise of achieving economic development via the prison-industrial complex is often broken. In 2001 the maximum security Thomson Correctional Center—including 1,600 cells, eight cell houses, and a separate 200-bed minimum-security unit—was finished near the city of Lanark, in Carroll County. Thomson remained partially closed and waited for the state to appropriate the money necessary for it to open fully. Frustrated residents concerned about the county's development have lobbied for the state to open the facility and hence to fulfill what they thought was a program of economic uplift. Resident Lynn Kocal of Lanark, in a 2003 letter to the editor in the *Chicago Sun-Times*, connected local employment and economic growth to prison development. She asks the state why, when other prisons are overcrowded, the new Thomson Correctional Center has only 600 inmates "instead of the 3,000 promised by the state?" Kocal continues: "We have never asked for much, and this time, when we have asked the state for help with our 11 percent unemployment, we have, once again, been forgotten." The letter is accompanied by a photo of a demonstration protesting the "empty prison," complete with marchers carrying signs that read "We Want Your Felons" and "Jobs Not Empty Jails." Local residents finally got their wish when discussions started in 2009 to sell the Thomson Correction Center to the federal government to house those imprisoned in Guantánamo Bay, and White House officials were quoted as claiming that this move would create "3,000 new jobs." As Stephen John Hartnett summarizes this bizarre scenario: "rural white Illini thus rallied in favor of busting more urban black and Chicano youths whose bodies would serve as the raw material driving an anticipated economic boom. At a time when 'welfare' is a bad word, whites rallying for the mass-incarceration of poor people of color makes sense under the rubric of getting-tough-on-crime and lobbying for jobs in hard times. Spend money on urban schools and the jackals howl about 'hand-outs' and affirmative action; spend money on prisons, and the masses crow with pride."[19]

The angry citizens of Lanark are not alone, however, for Tracey Huling has documented that across the United States, as of 2001, "about 350 rural communities have acquired new prisons since the start of the prison boom began in 1980." Communities lobby for these prisons because they believe that they will provide a boost to local employment, yet as the citizens of Lanark and Susanville learned, they do not deliver on that promise. Indeed, most new jobs that prisons provide do not go to local workers, as the initial big construction contracts go to outside firms; moreover, the establishment of a prison may discourage other industries from opening in a "prison town." While the vast majority of prisons in the United States are public institutions, prison management and services such as healthcare and the commissary are also generally privatized, further facilitating private profit paid for with public money. Although often opposed by powerful corrections officers unions because of the fear that privatization will lead to non-union labor, corrections is thus a lucrative for-profit industry. Public or private, prisons are perceived as development. Marc Mauer cites an industry call to potential investors: "while arrests and convictions are steadily on the rise, profits are to be made—*profits from crime*. Get in on the ground floor of this booming industry now." Such advertisements talk about a booming industry, yet my assessment of the impact of the prison boom of the 1980s and 1990s suggests that we can more accurately characterize the prison construction era as *antidevelopmental*. For while these prisons are the result of intricate economic planning, the consequences of this planning do not develop the region's capacity for long-term economic growth; rather, they offer maximum profit to certain stakeholders, including construction corporations, utilities, prison guard unions, the makers of surveillance technologies, and so on. The prison-industrial complex thus redistributes wealth from the public to select private sources, in essence functioning as corporate welfare under the guise of getting tough on crime.[20]

There is, however, one clear advantage for a community that builds a prison, as inmates are counted for the U.S. census in these towns and not in their home locations. By building prisons, then, and because of these bizarre census practices, these once small, rural, and predominately white communities benefit from the reallocation of resources from urban centers (even while those in prisons cannot vote). For example, in Illinois most of the approximately 30,000 or so folks who are released from the state's prisons and jails each year return to six of Chicago's neighborhoods: Austin, Humboldt Park, North Lawndale, Englewood, West Englewood, and East Garfield Park. These neighborhoods are among the most economically disadvantaged in the state. Nonetheless, when their citizens are arrested and sent downstate, these communities lose the resources (and representation) that follow from the census. Despite an inquiry in 2006 that prisons inflate the numbers for small communities and direct resources away from needy urban centers, the 2010 census will continue to count those Illinoisans held in prisons as residents of the communities where the prisons are located (even while they cannot vote), thus increasing population counts by the thousands and affecting the corresponding resource allocations. This census-rigging is practiced across the nation, as seen in the startling example of Franklin County, New York, where the 2000 census documented a rapidly growing African American population—91 percent of the African American population was housed in the five prisons in the county.[21]

While these census-counting strategies reallocate resources from poor urban neighborhoods to rural prison towns, the same people who bulk up the census are denied their voting rights. According to a 2007 report from the Sentencing Project, "5.3 million Americans, or one in forty-one adults, have currently or permanently lost their voting rights as a result of a felony conviction." The Sentencing Project documents a national landscape of disenfranchisement coupled with cumbersome voting-rights restoration processes: "Two states deny the right to vote to all ex-offenders who have completed their sentences. Nine others disenfranchise certain categories of ex-offenders and/or permit application for restoration of rights for specified offenses after a waiting period (e.g., five years in Delaware and Wyoming, two years in Nebraska)." The incoherent laws surrounding disenfranchisement and restoration create confusions that often lead to election officials wrongfully disqualifying voters, hence lowering voter turnout. In fact, a 2005 report produced by the Sentencing Project included a thirty-three-state survey of disenfranchisement laws and concluded that "more than one-third (37%) of local officials interviewed in ten states either described their state's fundamental eligibility law incorrectly, or stated that they did not know a central aspect of that law." I see these confusions in Chicago, where the students enrolled in the St. Leonard's Adult High School can often find casual work on election day, yet confront persistent confusion about their own eligibility as voters. Thus, as our punishing democracy comes to rely more and more heavily on the prison-industrial complex as a form of corporate welfare and resource redistribution, so the nation's voting base is directly affected, in essence producing a new age of Jim Crow–style restrictions on who enjoys the right to vote.[22]

Remaking Public Space via Surveillance and Fear

I have thus far chronicled the savage ironies of the prison-industrial complex, traced its rise to a merging of neoliberalism and white supremacy, and debunked the promise that prison construction aids small-town economies; I want now to track how these historical transformations have produced new meanings attached to public and private spaces, including the *feelings* that accompany these shifts. This remaking of public emotions is a crucial consequence of the prison-industrial complex, for while Americans have been taught to fear crime and criminals, they have also been systematically denied information about the people and processes in question. Indeed, correctional facilities are frequently isolated from the public by their physical location far from urban centers. More than just their physical distance from most population centers, however, prisons, jails, and other detention centers are extremely difficult to enter, meaning communication to and from these carceral institutions is heavily controlled. As the activist/scholars of PCARE (Prison Communication, Activism, Research, and Education) argue, we are witness to a strange bait and switch: "while the prison-industrial complex churns out an infinite number of offerings for the society of the spectacle, so prisoners' lives, the conditions of prisons, the fate of prisoners' families, and the actual workings of the prison-industrial complex remain largely invisible." In short, we have become a nation obsessed with crime, violence, prisons, and prisoners, yet we know very little about these subjects.[23]

As public institutions protected from public scrutiny, prisons are thus an "absent site," a social institution that anthropologist Lorna Rhodes argues is represented through fetishized details and stereotypical fragments used to invoke racialized fears. The saturation of representations of violence in mainstream media, coupled with this absence of representations of the realities of life for those in prison, turns prisons into mythical places of terror:

> Looming cellblocks, stone-faced guards, dangerous and deranged felons: these tropes tell us in advance what to expect of prison. Allen Feldman writes of what he calls "cultural anesthesia": the fact that we are bombarded with images representing all kinds of violence but are also able, by means of these same images, to evade the disturbing physicality and immediacy of violence

itself. Many aspects of the contemporary representation of crime and punishment carry the danger of this kind of anesthesia. One consequence is that prison becomes an "abstract site" in the public imagination precisely through the fetishization of its concrete details.[24]

The combination of this absence and abstraction means that the public depends on mainstream media to supply information about prisons and those within prisons, yet the corporate media offer audiences very particular images and tools to interpret these individuals and institutions, which, as Travis Dixon demonstrates herein (chapter 4) systematically reproduce racism and fear more broadly. Such images tells us that public space is unsafe, that a sex offender is potentially lurking in every playground and school, that drug dealers stalk every corner, that crime is everywhere. In short, these images traffic in fear and enemies, and thus shape the public feelings needed to justify the maintenance and even augmentation of our punishing democracy.

As addressed in more detail in this volume by Rose Braz and Myesha Williams (chapter 5) and Garrett Albert Duncan (chapter 8), this culture of mass-produced fear has led to children becoming highly policed bodies and schools becoming highly policed public spaces. For example, almost every state has adopted drug-free zones around schools, but as a 2006 Justice Policy Institute Report identified, these zones blanket neighborhoods in urban areas where predominantly people of color reside, including "76 percent of Newark, and over half of Camden and Jersey City." These zones—ostensibly created in the name of safety—result in the targeting of communities of color by police, yet they fail to keep drugs away from schools. Along these same lines, the mobility and public space restrictions attached to sex offender registries, the most potent and current component of our expanding prison-industrial complex, center on public places where children congregate: schools and parks. But with the Bureau of Justice Statistics acknowledging that more than 70 percent of all reported sexual assaults against children are committed in a residence, usually the victim's, this emphasis on policing public spaces is odd. Indeed, it would appear that such policies have less to do with actually addressing the causes of crime and violence than with criminalizing certain spaces and classes of people, in essence functioning as public guides to whom we should fear and where we should fear to tread. This is not criminology but fear production.[25]

Because of this mass-produced fear, private spaces have proliferated, for they are perceived as less dangerous and more controllable than public spaces. For example, Setha Low offers some conservative figures on the growth of the gated community in the United States: In 1998, 4,013,655 households (or 3.4 percent) of the U.S. population lived in communities that require entry codes, key cards, or security guard approvals. By 2001, 16 million people lived in gated communities where privileges are based on property rights, not on citizenship, and where public services, roads, sanitation, and other communal goods may be paid for in part by the state even while access to these goods is restricted. Low also documents that "one-third of all new communities in Southern California are gated, and the percentage is similar around Phoenix, Arizona, the suburbs of Washington, D.C., and parts of Florida." These private associations frequently do the work that the state once did, including picking up the trash, organizing security, and maintaining the association's "common" property. These once public functions are not only being absorbed and regulated by private associations, but they are offered only to property owners. In short, the spaces, functions, and rights once associated with citizenship are being shifted—largely because of fear of crime—to the realm of consumerism.[26]

While neoliberalism thus shifts our understanding of what is public and what is private, in essence limiting the norms of citizenship along class lines, so the prison-industrial complex feeds a culture of resentment. In particular, feelings of disgust, anger, and fear have been harnessed expertly by those politicians committed to building a punishing democracy. The fear of terrorist violence infiltrating your neighborhood, of illegal aliens taking your job, of welfare freeloaders and prisoners using your hard-earned dollars, of confronting the worst of the worst, of a deviant sex offender teaching your children—these feelings of disgust, fear, and anger help to justify expanding the punitive arm of the state while cutting its social services. More directly, these fears fuel support for the surveillance of those public spaces and institutions that are perceived as inhabited by the working poor. For example, a 2005 Department of Justice study found that "blacks and Hispanics are roughly three times as likely as whites to be searched, arrested, or threatened or subdued with force when stopped by police." Fear fuels surveillance, which drives arrest patterns, which then feeds the fear again; it is a vicious cycle that distorts the reality of danger. Indeed, Patricia Allard, in her research analyzing the impact of drug laws on women, offers a snapshot of one aspect of these discriminatory policies and practices: "Although African-Americans only represent 13% of all monthly drug users (consistent with their proportion of the population), they account for 35% of those arrested for drug possession, 55% of drug possession convictions, and 74% of those sentenced to prison for drug possession." These disproportionate arrest rates refigure how people use public spaces, change how they think about their neighbors, and mean that communities of color are tracked into further state control and management. The rise of the prison-industrial complex therefore coincides with and further fuels dramatic transformations in how we think about what is public, what is private, who pays for and reaps the benefits of what services, and how such communal goods provide the building blocks of citizenship.[27]

Conclusion: Building an Abolition Democracy

I grew up on the edge of resource communities—land and lumber—in British Columbia, Canada. In the 1970s and 1980s, I moved through Mission, Whonnock, and Albion, a series of small towns that dot the Fraser River, where Douglas firs and western red cedars are still stripped and floated downstream to be milled into two-by-fours. My high school classmates were neither the best nor the worst, except for the smattering of First Nations kids (mainly Stó:lō), who were often stigmatized as education failures before they arrived at school. Risking nostalgia, I recall us as average kids of the lower-middle/working class, from an average B.C. town, with an average-quality high school that had average expectations for the white kids at the school: The kids from "good" families were expected to graduate from high school, and college or university was held out as a hope for the lucky few. While my sister dropped out of school at sixteen, I persevered, certain that I did not want the gendered path of marriage and a job at the local (at least, then, unionized) grocery store. I applied to a four-year research university by filling out a short form. Unless my memory is faulty, there were no essays, no SATs, no reference letters, no interviews, no family financial disclosure statements—if there had been any of these requirements, odds are that I never would have applied. I relate my own history in part because comparative analysis is always useful; how and why, for example, has deindustrialization affected Canada and the United States so differently? How and why did late capitalism facilitate the establishment of prisons throughout upstate New York while it shaped tourism, a wine industry, and expanded higher education across the border in the Canadian Niagara peninsula? Why does the surplus of land, in conjunction with global economic shifts, create such different trajectories in the agricultural valleys of British Columbia and California? Asking these questions points to the conclusion that neoliberalism, despite its economic power, is not a determining factor in a culture; we still have political agency and can shape our communities according to different political visions.

Moreover, I offer this truncated personal history and raise these brief comparative questions because they demonstrate how development and antidevelopment, these exigencies of place, labor, capital, and reproduction, *are written on and in all of our bodies*—best, worst, and average are not simply descriptions of different economic futures, or of different relations to the state and its resources, but of how we live our lives. Identities are internalized and the institutions, built around and for these identities, are naturalized. For example, by any standard measure, the students who have learned and worked through St. Leonard's are, if not the mainstream's perceptions of the so-called worst, then fairly close to it: They are high school dropouts, convicted criminals, parents who have abandoned their kids or had them seized, addicts, dealers who have sold to children, sex workers, and so on. But they are also competent, sometimes brilliant, driven, hardworking folks who deserve a chance to succeed. Indeed, my experiences at St. Leonard's consistently remind me that the ways we are taught to view my students are not useful, because the corresponding best and worst pathways of our culture often speak less to the individual than to their situation within deep histories of structural inequities. As the chapters in this book document, these pathways are visible *as early as preschool,* where youth of color are expelled and suspended at higher rates than white children. These best and worst identities are not just internalized, they form the foundations of many of our public institutions: Tamms and the Fighting Illini, supermaxes and universities.[28]

If we are invested in moving away from our punishing democracy, our schools-to-prisons pipeline, our incarceration nation, then we must challenge the prison-industrial complex by interrupting antidevelopmental policies and refusing those manufactured fears that lead us to privatize our public spaces. We must also challenge political institutions and personal practices across the spectrum. Decarceration and dismantling the prison-industrial complex will not come from a one-dimensional movement; it is not enough to take down prisons, we must name how our democratic institutions continue to shut out millions from the "best of" pathways, and then remake these institutions. This has never been more vital. Horrified at the downstate trips to adult prison offered to Chicago's fifteen-year-old youth of color? Then reshape institutions to ensure that other sorts of downstate trips are not just imaginable but materially feasible and socially expected—we must replace narratives of expected incarceration and educational disenfranchisement with a culture of across-the-board achievement and excellence. Indeed, an abolition-democracy, to use the term of Angela Davis and W.E.B. DuBois, requires reconstructing the structures and traditions that safeguard power and privilege. Prisons, Davis states, have "thrived over the last century precisely because of the absence of those resources and the persistence of some of the deep structures of slavery. They cannot be eliminated unless new institutions and resources are made available to those communities that provide, in large part, the human beings that make up the prison population." While challenging the prison-industrial complex means fighting to bring down Tamms, it also means doing the perhaps more difficult work of opening up and reconfiguring other institutions—especially schools—that have shut their doors to the men and women who have been abandoned by our punishing democracy.[29]

For those safely inside the categories of the better and the best, even the average, the solutions are visible and bold: be a radically transformative apprentice. Why not build a campaign for free postsecondary education, thus creating in the United States what is taken for granted in other nations? Why not challenge the restricted access to the institutions with the most resources, and why not debunk the thin discourses of quality and academic integrity that shield this access to power? Why not demand other measures for entrance into our educational institutions? Why not work to hold universities and colleges accountable to a more encompassing vision of their stated mission to serve the common good? Why not eschew charity and demand systemic and structural changes to those institutions and cultural practices that reproduce inequality and injustice? If the old structures are not able to change, then we shall build new ones; abolition therefore means *remaking our democracy*—nothing less is acceptable.

Notes

1. On "going downstate" in Illinois, see Paul Street, "Color Bind," in *Prison Nation: The Warehousing of America's Poor*, ed. Tara Herivel and Paul Wright (New York: Routledge, 2003), 30–40, "downstate" on 31–32; on apartheidlike schooling, see Jonathan Kozol, *Shame of the Nation: The Restoration of Apartheid Schooling* (New York: Crown, 2005); for more on the schools–prisons relationship, see the essays in this volume by Rose Braz and Myesha Williams (chapter 5) and Garrett Albert Duncan (chapter 8).

2. Jesse Jackson as quoted in Linda M. Christensen, "Teaching Standard English: Whose Standard?" *The English Journal* 79, no. 2 (1990): 36–40, quotation from 37.

3. I do acknowledge the Odyssey Project, in particular the staffs at the University of Chicago and the University of Illinois, who sustain small, part-time, and free college programs; credits for the classes are provided by Bard College, and resources come from the Illinois Humanities Council and their partner campuses; for more on these programs, see www.prairie.org/index.cfm/fuseaction/dir_programs.prog_detail/object_id/0ce31632-4076-4ce1-b839-bc9a63e67e5a/TheOdysseyProject.cfm.

4. Prisoner population is reported in Illinois Department of Corrections Summary, available by following the links at www.idoc.state.il.us; Martell Gomez, "Humanity Is Never Lost," in *Lockdown Prison Heart*, ed. K. Ryan and R. Hudson (Bloomington, IN:

iUniverse, 2004), 31–32, quotation from 31; information on Tamms is culled from the Illinois Department of Corrections, "Facilities: Tamms Correctional Center," available at www.idoc.state.il.us/subsections/facilities/information.asp?instchoice=tam; on the history of Tamms, see Rick Pearson, "Guard Union Seeking New Prison Cites Overcrowding," *Chicago Tribune* (5 February 1997), A6, and "Illinois Supermax Prison Comes with a Super Price Tag" *Chicago Tribune* (2 February 1996), A2; for mental health conditions in supermaxes, see Christi Parsons, "New State Prison Puts All Inmates in Solitary," *Chicago Tribune* (25 March 1998), A1, and Christi Parsons, "Inmates Sue State, Calling New Top-Security Prison Cruel," *Chicago Tribune* (8 January 1999), A4; and Human Rights Watch, *Ill-Equipped: U.S. Prisons and Offenders with Mental Illness* (New York: HRW, 2003); for an overview of supermax prisons, see Daniel Mears, "Evaluating the Effectiveness of Supermax Prisons," a March 2006 report from the *Urban Institute,* available at www.urban.org/uploadedPDF/411326_supermax_prisons.pdf.

5. 2010 UIUC tuition from the University of Illinois Urbana-Champaign, available at http://www.osfa.uiuc.edu/cost/undergrad/res_1011.html; see the annual "Best Colleges" report published by *U.S. News and World Report,* available at http://colleges.usnews.rankingsandreviews.com/college/national-top-public.

6. "Savage ironies" is a term borrowed from Street, "Color Bind," 34; ICDP data from Kathleen Kane-Willis, Jennifer Janichek, and Daniel Clark, *Intersecting Voices: Impacts of Illinois' Drug Policies* (Chicago: Illinois Consortium on Drug Policies, 2006), increase in corrections spending on p. 13, incarceration cost versus K–12 education on p. 13, available at www.roosevelt.edu/ima/pdfs/intersectingVoices .pdf; for analysis of the relationship between postsecondary and correction spending, see Justice Policy Institute, *Cellblocks or Classrooms? The Funding of Higher Education and Corrections and Its Impact on African American Men* (San Francisco: Vincent Schiraldi and Jason Ziedenberg, 2002), available at www.justicepolicy.org/ images/upload/02–09_REP_CellblocksClassrooms_BB-AC.pdf; Illinois prison populations statistics are from Nancy G. La Vigne, Cynthia A. Mamalian, Jeremy Travis, and Christy Visher, "A Portrait of Prisoner Reentry in Illinois," a 2003 report from the *Urban Institute,* available at www.urban.org/url.cfm?ID=410662, quotation on p. 1; for a discussion of affirmative action hiring in prison, see Dana M. Britton, *At Work in the Iron Cage: The Prison as Gendered Organization* (New York: New York University Press, 2003), 204–8; on the number of African American men in prison rather than a college or university, see Kane-Willis, Janichek, and Clark, *Intersecting Voices*, 13.

7. For discussions of the economic inefficiency of public policies that support incarceration and not education, see Lance Lochner and Enrico Moretti, "The Effect of Education on Crime: Evidence from Prison Inmates, Arrests, and Self-Reports," *American Economic Review* 94, no. 1 (2004): 155–89; Becky Petit and Bruce Western, "Mass Imprisonment and the Life Course: Race and Class Inequality in U.S. Incarceration," *American Sociological Review* 69, no. 2 (2004): 151–69; Jon M. Taylor, "Post-Secondary Correctional Education: An Evaluation of Effectiveness and Efficiency," *Journal of Correctional Education* 43, no. 3 (1992): 132–41; U.S. Department of Education, "Pell Grants for Prisoners: Facts/Commentary" (Washington, DC: Office of Correctional Education, 1995); Stephen J. Steurer, Alice Tracy, and Linda

Smith, *Three State Recidivism Study* (Lanham, MD: Correctional Education Association, 2001); and Michelle Fine, Maria Elena Torre, Kathy Boudin, Iris Bowen, Judith Clark, Donna Hylton, Migdalia Martinez, "Missy," Rosemarie A. Roberts, Pamela Smart, and Debora Upegui, *Changing Minds: The Impact of College in a Maximum Security Prison*, a 2001 report available at http://web.gc.cuny.edu/che/changingminds.html; information about the PQP program is from William Trombley, "Illinois at a Crossroads; National Cross Talk," *National Center for Public Policy and Higher Education* (1998), available at www.highereducation.org/crosstalk/ct1098/news1098-illinois.shtml; on savings from potential postsecondary programs, see Kane-Willis, Janichek, and Clark, *Intersecting Voices*, 4.

8. On the prison-industrial complex as a machine of resource allocation and planned disinvestment in certain communities, see Ruth Wilson Gilmore, *Golden Gulag: Prisons, Surplus, Crisis, and Opposition in Globalizing California* (Berkeley: University of California Press, 2007); Street, "Color Bind," 38.

9. On the neoliberal transformations noted here, see Lisa Duggan, *The Twilight of Equality: Neoliberalism, Cultural Politics, and the Attack on Democracy* (Boston: Beacon Press, 2003), and Stephen John Harnett and Laura Ann Stengrim, *Globalization and Empire: The U.S. Invasion of Iraq, Free Markets, and the Twilight of Democracy* (Tuscaloosa, AL: Alabama University Press, 2006), 139–211; on shifting federal budgetary priorities, see Rebecca Bohrman and Naomi Murakawa, "Remaking Big Government: Immigration and Crime Control in the United States," in *Global Lockdown: Gender, Race, and the Rise of the Prison Industrial Complex*, ed. Julia Sudbury (New York: Routledge, 2005), 109–26.

10. Bohrman and Murakawa, "Remaking Big Government," 110; David Harvey, *A Brief History of Neoliberalism* (New York: Oxford University Press, 2005), 40.

11. John O'Sullivan, "Introduction," *United States Magazine and Democratic Review* 1 (October 1837), 1–15, quotation from 6; Elizabeth Blackmar, "Appropriating the 'Commons': The Tragedy of Property Rights Discourse," in *The Politics of Public Space*, eds. Setha Low and Neil Smith (New York: Routledge, 2005), 49–80, quotations from 66, 70 (emphasis original); on the relationship of a shifting welfare state to white supremacy, see George Lipsitz, *The Possessive Investment in Whiteness: How White People Profit from Identity Politics* (Philadelphia: Temple University Press, 1998).

12. For discussions of the white supremacist backlash linked to shifting economic contexts, see Howard Winant, *The New Politics of Race: Globalism, Difference, Justice* (Minneapolis: University of Minnesota Press, 2004), and Michelle Fine, "Witnessing Whiteness," in *Off White: Readings on Race, Power, and Society*, ed. Michelle Fine, Linda Powell, Lois Weis, and L. Mun Wong (New York: Routledge, 1997), 57–65; for an overview of the rise of the right during this period, see Mike Davis, *Prisoners of the American Dream* (London: Verso, 1986), 157–300.

13. Wahneema Lubiano, "Black Ladies, Welfare Queens, and State Minstrels: Ideological War by Narrative Means," in *Race-ing Justice, En-Gendering Power: Essays on Anita Hill, Clarence Thomas, and the Construction of Social Reality*, ed. Toni Morrison (New York: Pantheon, 1992), 323–63, quotation from 330–31.

14. Bohrman and Murakawa, "Remaking Big Government," 119; on welfare and race, gender, and social assistance programs, see Jill Quadagno, *The Color of Wel-*

fare: How Racism Undermined the War on Poverty (New York: Oxford University Press, 1994), and Ange-Marie Hancock, *The Politics of Disgust and the Public Identity of the "Welfare Queen"* (New York: New York University Press, 2004).

15. Fine, "Witnessing Whiteness," 62–63; Winant, *New Politics of Race*, 181; Charles Mills, *From Class to Race: Essays in White Marxism and Black Radicalism* (Lanham, MD: Rowman and Littlefield, 2003), 169; for an overview of these processes, see Stephen John Hartnett, "The Annihilating Public Policies of the Prison-Industrial Complex; or, Crime, Violence, and Punishment in an Age of Neo-Liberalism," *Rhetoric and Public Affairs* 11, no. 3 (2008): 491–533.

16. James Ferguson, *The Anti-Politics Machine: "Development," Depoliticization, and Bureaucratic Power in Lesotho* (Minneapolis: University of Minnesota Press, 1994), 273; Pew Center on the States Public Safety Performance Project, "One in 100: Behind Bars in America 2008," available at www.pewcenteronthestates .org/uploadedFiles/One%20in%20100.pdf; for shifting state roles, see Ruth Wilson Gilmore, "Globalization and U.S. Prison Growth: From Military Keynesianism to Post-Keynesian Militarism," *Race and Class* 40, nos. 2–3 (1998–1999): 171–88, and Loïc Wacquant, "From Slavery to Mass Incarceration: Rethinking the 'Race Question' in the US," *New Left Review* 13 (2002): 41–60.

17. Angela Davis, "From the Convict Lease System to the Super Max Prison," in *States of Confinement: Policing, Detention, and Prisons*, ed. Joy James (New York: St. Martin's Press, 2000), 60–74, for her discussion of post–Civil War convict leasing; Stormy Ogden, "The Prison Industrial Complex in Indigenous California," in *Global Lockdown*, ed. Sudbury, 57–66, quotation from 63; the claim that the Reconstruction era was worse than slavery became ubiquitous after an 1874 Thomas Nast cartoon using the phrase to depict the rise of the Ku Klux Klan (the Nast image may be seen in Robert James Branham and Stephen John Hartnett, *Sweet Freedom's Song: "My Country 'Tis of Thee" and Democracy in America* [New York: Oxford University Press, 2002], 162).

18. On prison privatization, see Linda Evans, "Playing Global Cop: U.S. Militarism and the Prison Industrial Complex," in *Global Lockdown*, ed. Sudbury, 215–30; Judith Greene, "Bailing Out Private Jails," in *Prison Nation*, 138–47; and *Prison Profiteers: Who Makes Money from Mass Incarceration*, ed. Tara Herivel and Paul Wright (New York: New Press, 2007); FPI data from Major Philip C. Mitchell, "Federal Prison Industries: Ending Their Mandatory Source Status," *Michigan Bar Journal* 83, no. 9 (2004): 18–21, available at www.michbar.org/journal/pdf/pdf4article739.pdf; Rocha quoted in Gilmore, *Golden Gulag*, 149; on Corcoran employment figures, ibid., 159; on the economic failure of Corcoran, ibid., 175–76; Joëlle Fraser, "An American Seduction: Portrait of a Prison Town," in *Prison Nation*, 73–84, quotation from 79; more broadly, see Stephen John Hartnett, "About the Same as Commercial Fishing," in *Incarceration Nation: Investigative Prison Poems of Hope and Terror* (Walnut Creek, CA: AltaMira, 2004), 97–115.

19. Lynn Kocal, "Why Build a Prison and Not Use It?" *Chicago Sun-Times* (30 May 2006), A42; Helene Cooper and David Johnston, "Obama Tells Prison to Take Detainees," *New York Times* (15 December 2009), A27; Hartnett, "Annihilating Public Policies," 500.

20. Tracey Huling, "Building a Prison Economy in Rural America," in *Invisible Punishment: The Collateral Consequences Of Mass Imprisonment*, ed. Marc Mauer and Media Chesney Lind (New York: New Press, 2002), 197–213, quotation from 199; Marc Mauer, *Race to Incarcerate* (New York: New Press, 1999), 10; along these same lines, see Fraser, "American Seduction," and Evans, "Playing Global Cop."

21. La Vigne et al., "Portrait of Prisoner Reentry in Illinois," available at www .urban.org/url.cfm?ID=410662; Zachary A. Goldfarb, "Census Bureau, Activists Debate How and Where to Count People Who Are Incarcerated," *Washington Post* (29 January 2006), A15: Rose Heyer and Peter Wagner, "Too Big to Ignore: How Counting People in Prisons Distorted Census 2000," *Prisoners of the Census* (2004), 1, available at www.prisonersofthecensus.org/toobig/toobig.shtml.

22. The Sentencing Project, *Felony Disenfranchisement Laws in the United States* (Washington, D.C.: 2007), quotations from 1, available at www.sentencingproject.org/ Admin/Documents/publications/fd_bs_fdlawsinus.pdf ; on voter eligibility confusion, see Alec Ewald, "Civil Death: The Ideological Paradox of Criminal Disenfranchisement Law in the United States," *Wisconsin Law Review* (2002): 1045–1137; Alec C. Ewald, "A 'Crazy-Quilt' of Tiny Pieces: State and Local Administration of American Criminal Disenfranchisement Laws" (Washington, DC: Sentencing Project, 2005), i.

23. PCARE, "Fighting the Prison-Industrial Complex: A Call to Communication and Cultural Studies Scholars to Change the World," *Communication and Critical Cultural Studies* 4, no. 4 (2007): 402–20, quotation from 407; for more along these lines, see Jimmie L. Reeves and Richard Campbell, *Cracked Coverage: Television News, the Anti-Cocaine Crusade, and the Reagan Legacy* (Durham, NC: Duke University Press, 1994).

24. Lorna Rhodes, *Total Confinement: Madness and Reason in the Maximum Security Prison* (Berkeley: University of California Press, 2004), 8; for more on media representations of crime, see Elaine Rapping, *Law and Justice as Seen on TV* (New York: New York University Press, 2003); Stabile, *White Victims, Black Villains*; and Travis Dixon's essay in this volume (chapter 4).

25. Judy Greene, Kevin Pranis, and Jason Ziedenberg, "Disparity by Design: How Drug-Free Zone Laws Impact Racial Disparity—and Fail to Protect Youth" (Washington, DC: Justice Policy Institute, 2006), 26, available at www.justicepolicy.org/ reports/SchoolZonesReport306.pdf; Bureau of Justice Statistics, *Sexual Assault of Young Children as Reported to Law Enforcement: Victim, Incident, and Offender Characteristics* (Washington, D.C.: U.S. Department of Justice, 2000), 6, available at www.ojp.usdoj.gov/bjs/pub/pdf/saycrle.pdf.

26. Setha Low, "How Private Interests Take Over Public Space: Zoning, Taxes, and Incorporation of Gated Communities," in *Politics of Public Space*, ed. Low and Smith, 81–104, statistics on gated community growth and quotation from 86; according to Low, proponents of such living arrangements are lobbying to deduct the fees they pay for their private services from their taxes, hence further shifting the balance between public funds and private goods, but as of yet this scheme has not met with widespread success.

27. On sentiment and feeling as used by the right, see Lauren Berlant, "Compassion (and Withholding)," in *Compassion: The Culture and Politics of an Emotion*, ed. Lauren Berlant (New York: Routledge, 2004), 1–14; Department of Justice data as

reported in an ACLU press release, "ACLU Applauds Senate Reintroduction of Racial Profiling Bill, Urges Congress to Finally Pass Comprehensive Legislation Next Year" (Washington, DC: American Civil Liberties Union, 2005), available at www.aclu.org/racialjustice/racialprofiling/23090prs20051219.html; Patricia Allard, "Life Sentences: Denying Welfare Benefits to Women Convicted of Drug Offenses" (Washington, DC: Sentencing Project, 2002), 26, available at www.sentencingproject.org/tmp/File/Women%20in%20CJ/women_lifesentences.pdf; for more on the consequences of drug-related convictions for women, see Patricia Johnson, *Inner Lives: Voices of African American Women in Prison* (New York: New York University Press, 2004), and Juanita Diaz-Cotto, "Latinas and the War on Drugs in the United States, Latin America, and Europe," in *Global Lockdown*, ed. Sudbury, 137–54; more broadly, see Daniel Larson's essay in this volume (chapter 3).

28. On pre-K expulsion, see Walter S. Gilliam, "Pre-Kindergarteners Left Behind: Expulsion Rates in State Pre-Kindergarten Programs" (New York: Family Child Development Foundation, 2005), available at www.fcd-us.org/usr_doc/ExpulsionPolicyBrief.pdf; more broadly, see the essays in this volume by Rose Braz and Myesha Williams (chapter 5) and Garrett Albert Duncan (chapter 8).

29. Angela Davis, *Abolition Democracy: Prisons, Democracy, and Empire* (New York: Seven Stories Press, 2005), 95–96 on DuBois, quotation from 96–97; for more on abolition, see my *Right to Be Hostile: Schools, Prisons, and the Making of Public Enemies* (New York: Routledge, 2007), 165–86, and Tiyo Attallah Salah-El, "A Call for the Abolition of Prisons" (2001), as reprinted in *The New Abolitionists: (Neo)Slave Narratives and Contemporary Prison Writings*, ed. Joy James (Albany: State University of New York Press, 2005), 69–74.

Another Day in the Champaign County Jail

Dennis Mansker

An original member of the Writing Workshop at the Champaign County Jail, in Champaign, Illinois, Dennis Mansker responded to the challenge to write detailed and realistic poetry with this poem chronicling the monotony of a day in jail; this piece was published in *Captured Words/Free Thoughts* 1 (Summer 2006).

Another day another tray
That's how my world begins
6:30 every morning
The speaker bellows *Trays! Trays!*
And you can rest assured
It will be like all the other days
A carton of milk
A cup of instant coffee
The usual oats grits or farina
Maybe a hard-boiled egg

Then it's back to my cell for quiet time
Read a book maybe write a poem or letter

At 11:30 it all starts over again
Trays! Trays! Here they come full of
Turkey bologna turkey ham turkey burger
Two slices of bread
Dehydrated potatoes
Some soggy salad
And for dessert, lime Jell-O

Now it's back to my cement cage again
A few more hours of clanging and banging

Until at 4:30 it begins again
Trays! Trays! I hope you like beans
'cause it's been beans all week
Baked beans brown beans black-eyed beans
Have you ever spent time with 25 men
Who have lived on beans for a week?

It's evening now
Everybody's back in the pod

Playing cards, watching TV
Everyone is talking so loudly you can't hear the TV
The TV is so loud you can't hear what anyone is saying
And so it goes, loud and louder
And now somebody's mad over a game of spades
The words and cards are flying

Lockdown at 10:30
The doors are shut and the locks secured
The guards rattle the doors just to make sure
Time for that final five minute chat with your celly
You lie down on that two inch mat on top of a slab of steel
Knowing in the morning your back will hurt so bad
You can barely walk

And now all the heartache and sadness
Can no longer be ignored
The wife you cannot kiss goodnight
The children you cannot tell you love them
The friends you probably won't see again
All seem a million miles away

You want to cry but it won't do any good
So you hold back the tears
Trying to keep what little pride you have left
Say a little prayer
And hope to drift off to sleep

And so end
Another day
in the Champaign County Jail

Militarizing the Police: Officer Jon Burge, Torture, and War in the "Urban Jungle"

Julilly Kohler-Hausmann

"Our community is under occupation," Jesse Jackson told reporters at a press conference on February 18, 1982. "Our community is very tense. It is a war zone." Days earlier, in an effort to apprehend the murderers of police officers William Fahey and Richard O'Brien, the Chicago Police Department had initiated one of the largest manhunts in the city's history. Police saturated the African American community where the crimes took place, broke down doors, and rounded up scores of witnesses and suspects, many of whom were beaten, some of whom were tortured. Lieutenant Jon Burge led the search and apprehension of the alleged murderers, Andrew and Jackie Wilson, scoring one of the highest-profile convictions of his career and winning public accolades from the state's attorney and future mayor, Richard M. Daley. But the manhunt was conducted in harsh fashion: Jackson's organization received forty complaints of police brutality during the first week of the search alone; during that same time, the police department recorded eighteen calls reporting excessive force. In fact, the brutal police treatment of the suspects eventually derailed the state's efforts to sentence the Wilson brothers to death and initiated public scrutiny of a long history of tortures committed by detectives at Burge's Area 2 police headquarters.[1]

According to Andrew Wilson, police started beating him shortly after he was brought to the station. They suffocated him by putting a plastic bag over his head and handcuffed him to a radiator, causing second-degree burns on his chest and thigh. Because he was still unwilling to confess after this first round of abuse, officers then attached wires from a black box to Wilson's ears and turned a crank, sending excruciating electric shocks through his body. Later, Wilson would learn that this box was a modified army field phone that Burge had probably learned how to transform into a torture device during his service in the Vietnam War. After Wilson relented and issued a forced confession, police took him to the lockup facility where the intake officers refused to admit him out of fear that they would be held responsible for his multiple injuries. As seen in the torture of Wilson, the practices of Jon Burge and some of his fellow officers were particularly brutal, but their extreme nature should not distract us from how Burge's tactics were symptomatic of and predicated upon larger historical processes, particularly the militarization of domestic police forces and the treatment of urban youth as if they were a hostile and foreign enemy.[2]

In this chapter, I frame Burge's violent acts as a case study for examining the larger rhetorical patterns, police practices, and popular cultural productions that enabled decades of police torture to go unchecked. While the idiosyncrasies and sadistic tendencies of Jon Burge and his staff lie at the heart of this story, I am also interested in the larger historical question of how Vietnam War–era Americans came to imagine cities as urban jungles wherein public safety must be guarded not merely by traditional police forces but by militarized and increasingly vigilante-inspired urban assault forces. Indeed, I contend that examining the concentric circles of social, political, and cultural phenomena that cradled the actions at Chicago's Area 2 police headquarters offers both deeper understanding of Burge's actions and insight into the struggles over power that escalated in America's inner cities during the 1960s and 1970s. I argue, then, that Burge's specific acts of police torture were enabled by heightened racialized fear of "the ghetto," wide social acceptance of vigilante justice, and the militarization of police tactics in an age of foreign war and domestic revolt. In short, our contemporary punishing democracy flows from a cultural imaginary and a set of police practices profoundly shaped by the Vietnam War.

I therefore argue that the secret happenings of dark police interrogation rooms tell us as much about key social dynamics as the most public acts. Elaine Scarry's study of war and torture, *The Body in Pain,* explains that torture is a public practice meant to enact and display the power of the torturer. She argues that although the need to extract critical information always rationalizes torture, its core purpose lies elsewhere:

> "The question" [during interrogation] is mistakenly understood to be the "motive"; "the answer" is mistakenly understood to be the "betrayal." The first mistake credits the torturer, providing him with a justification, his cruelty with an explanation. The second discredits the prisoner, making him rather than the torturer, his voice rather than his pain, the cause of his loss of self and world. These two misinterpretations are obviously neither acci-

dental nor unrelated. The one is an absolution of responsibility; the other is a conferring of responsibility; the two together turn the moral reality of torture upside down.[3]

For Scarry, the scripted interrogation, the narrative ritual of asking "questions" and seeking "answers"—as if torture were concerned with producing information—obscures torture's more fundamental purpose of enacting power relations. Building on this notion of torture as public, other scholars recognize that ongoing torture is not possible without large sections of society accepting the supposition of the danger posed by the victims of extreme treatment. As criminologist Ronald Crelinsten writes, "to enable torture to be practiced *systematically* and *routinely,* not only do perpetrators have to be trained and prepared, but wider elements of society must also be prepared and, in a sense, trained to accept that such things go on. . . . A central feature of this reality construction is the creation of a powerful and dangerous enemy that threatens the social fabric." Following Scarry and Crelinsten, I propose that Burge's long-term, systematic torture would not have been possible without widespread social acceptance of the idea that urban police were engaged in warlike sieges in poor communities across the nation and that the state was the sole legitimate user of force in these struggles.[4]

To pursue these claims about how imagining inner-city space as enemy territory played a significant role in enabling decades of police torture in Chicago, the first section of this chapter examines how constructions of inner cities as the jungle, or hostile foreign terrain, enabled authorities' increasing reliance on military metaphors and strategies in their efforts to regulate urban spaces. I do not claim that the specific metaphor of a racialized urban jungle played the determining role in events; rather, I insist that the incessant use of war and jungle metaphors (by both white and African American activists, citizens, police, politicians, and journalists) reveals key dynamics of police–community relations and race relations in America. In addition to reflecting important assumptions about the relationship between the state and "the ghetto," these and other similar tropes were also *productive*: they helped construct inner-city residents (usually young, poor, African American males) as internal enemies and, therefore, helped condition society to accept their torture as an unpleasant but necessary part of defending the nation. Having established this historical context, I then examine the specific events at Chicago's Area 2 and 3 police headquarters, where detective Burge and his colleagues engaged in a decades-long program of systematic torture. I then broaden the scope from individual acts of torture to explore how rhetorical patterns and popular culture buttressed the violent practices of Area 2 detectives. I argue here that tolerance of Burge's actions extended beyond a culture of silence within police departments and reflected the assumption that law enforcement amounted to a war between racialized communities that demanded vigilante justice and extralegal techniques. The popularity of politicians' calls for "law and order," when coupled with the mass appeal of vigilante movies and television shows, suggests that large chunks of the American populace celebrated a tough, militarized response to crime. Indeed, because the vigilante violence of Burge was directed against African American men portrayed as internal enemies, it was implicitly tolerated by many Chicagoans, particularly among those tasked with law enforcement and criminal prosecution, and those voters mobilized by the crime issue. Once entire areas and populations were constructed as foreign, tactics of war, both sanctioned and unsanctioned, became reluctantly (and occasionally, enthusiastically) accepted by large sections of mainstream society.[5]

Many readers will be familiar with the now common notion of blowback, which suggests that covert military operations tend to produce deadly unintended consequences, such as training anticommunist paramilitary groups whose interests become inimical to U.S. foreign policy, or supplying arms to right-wing drug traffickers who then turn their weapons against U.S. agents. But few scholars have studied the ways blowback has also crippled police practices in the United States. In this chapter, I explore one site where specific punishing technologies migrated between foreign wars and domestic police stations, thus transforming how communities were monitored and how racialized class positions were policed at home. Burge is an ideal vehicle to illustrate these transfers because he brought home a technique ("the Vietnam treatment") and a torture device (the army field phone) used during the Vietnam War and turned them against U.S. citizens in Chicago. It is particularly important to recognize these transnational transfers today, when U.S. society wrestles with revelations of torture by U.S. soldiers in foreign wars, most notably at the Abu Ghraib prison in Iraq. While in Burge's case, knowledge traveled home from foreign wars, the torture at Abu Ghraib was perpetrated largely by soldiers and contractors who had first worked in U.S. prisons. Thus, as a theoretical contribution to our understanding of the infrastructure of our punishing democracy, I demonstrate how torture practices migrate between the military and prison-industrial complexes, and how, after the Vietnam War, militarism and the military played crucial roles in transforming police practices in urban affairs.[6]

I also emphasize how tough "law and order" rhetoric and practices at home were deeply enmeshed in public concern about the war in Vietnam. Many scholars see the demand for law and order as part of a backlash against the social movements, rising crime rates, and urban riots of the late 1960s. But important recent work has countered these backlash interpretations by re-centering the roles of racism, examining the longer historical roots of local struggles over residential segregation, and arguing that interpreting the rise of the right as a reaction against movements on the left obscures years of systematic and independent organizing by conservatives. Few scholars, however, have investigated the specific ways that the Vietnam War influenced police reactions to domestic conditions. Thus, to further our understanding of these phenomena, I argue that international events intervened directly in national affairs, that the war played a critical role in militarizing key social movements and law-enforcement agencies, and that international war provided a powerful set of metaphors to explain domestic conflicts in U.S. society. In sum, the domestic social upheaval of the "long 1960s" and the war in Vietnam were not experienced separately, as many Americans found the world to be unstable at home and abroad simultaneously: crime, rioting, and political resistance within inner cities seemed that much more threatening because of America's failure to subdue the resistance in Vietnam. As both domestic and international conflicts intensified, Americans increasingly used metaphors from or references to the war in Vietnam to organize their understandings of domestic conditions.[7]

Imagining the Jungle; or, Turning Neighbors into Enemies

The image of the jungle has long been used to describe marginalized spaces within the nation; the term evokes ideas of an untamed and foreign space that is simultaneously exotic, alluring, and dangerous. Long before the Vietnam War, the jungle was used to describe those spaces created by the ravages of industrialization, such as America's hobo camps and decimated manufacturing areas. For example, Upton Sinclair's 1906 novel, *The Jungle*, portrayed the horrors of Chicago's meatpacking industry and the surrounding impoverished community. Even before Sinclair's devastating depiction, the metaphor of the jungle became popular as a result of colonial and imperial encounters. In *Writing the Urban Jungle*, Joseph McLaughlin argues that British "writers in the late nineteenth century appropriated ways of thinking and talking about the colonies and discursively transformed the metropolis into a new borderland space: the urban jungle." The metaphor attached the racial and cultural assumptions that rationalized colonialism to the urban poor within western countries while simultaneously isolating social problems from their larger contexts by framing them as indigenous to a wholly separate, isolated ecosystem. This rhetorical logic obscured the fact that conditions in inner cities or developing countries were often the result of larger economic and political structures, such as imperialism, industrial capitalism, or institutional racism. Thus, as an elastic metaphor with origins in imperialism, the jungle designated a state of extreme otherness and degradation, all the while obfuscating the causes of these conditions.[8]

Much as the British came to use the jungle as an explanatory metaphor during the highpoint of their imperial age, so Americans, as domestic political unrest and the war in the jungles of Vietnam intensified during the late 1960s, increasingly referred to "urban jungles" to organize their comments about the home front. For example, Inspector Daryl Gates, field commander of the Los Angeles Police Department during the 1965 Watts rebellions, explained that "the streets of America had become a foreign territory." Making the link between urban crime and foreign war explicit, the Los Angeles police chief during the conflict, William Parker, told reporters that "this situation is very much like fighting the Viet Cong." Urban areas had long been constructed as foreign, racialized spaces; once they were in open revolt, their struggles with state authority were easily interpreted with the same rhetorical devices used for insurgent populations abroad. Thus, it is not surprising that over time, more and more voices called for the state to use the same tools and techniques employed overseas to subdue allegedly dangerous domestic spaces. And so, by the mid-to-late 1960s, domestic law enforcement agencies had begun to interpret the conditions in inner cities as wars and had begun to turn for answers to military training, technology, and terminology. This transference of knowledge and hardware was most blatant in the use of the National Guard in riot control and the subsequent involvement of military counterinsurgency experts in helping local police remap domestic spaces as possible battle zones. Indeed, domestic police engaged in extensive joint exercises with National Guard units. In another example, the LAPD borrowed a strategy used in Vietnamese villages when they painted huge numbers on the tops of public housing units to enable helicopter surveillance.[9]

These arrangements were further institutionalized in 1968, when the U.S. Congress passed the Omnibus Crime Control and Safe Streets Act, which, among other things, initiated a massive transfer of expertise and technology from the military to local law-enforcement agencies. Aiming to rationalize and strengthen the crime-fighting powers of the state, the bill weakened the federal legal protections of criminal defendants (which had recently been articulated by the Supreme Court) and allowed new limited wiretapping without warrants. The Safe Streets Act also created the Law Enforcement Assistance Administration (LEAA), which was intended to strengthen ties between local police and the federal government, thus enabling an influx of federal dollars into local police departments, funding primarily training and new technological gadgetry for surveillance and crime control. These federal subsidies to states helped police departments to retool their arsenals by gaining access to military hardware—including helicopters, movement sensors, and armored troop carriers—that were not previously deemed appropriate for domestic uses. LEAA's budget ballooned from $63 million in 1968 to almost $700 million in 1972. Although the program funded drug treatment and other "crime prevention" strategies, the majority of these funds were funneled toward police hardware and riot-control efforts. These grants also funded the new paramilitary organizations, or SWAT teams, that were soon employed by many urban police departments. Thus, by 1968, spurred by the Vietnam War, domestic rebellions at home, and funded by the LEAA, urban policing was increasingly militarized—and the new firepower was aimed directly at inner-city communities.[10]

These developments were driven in part by military contractors intent on expanding into domestic markets. Recognizing the opportunities presented by the new stream of LEAA funding, manufacturers such as Dupont, Motorola, and Kodak rushed to develop new commodities for police departments. One journalist explained in 1974 that "over the past several years, manufacturers have rushed out all manner of gadgets, including riot tanks, ballistics shields, machines that spew forth foam, bubbles and slippery substances, and disabling crowd control sprays including one spectacularly messy variety that causes loss of control of bowels and bladder." Some in the business called the practice of repackaging technologies originally developed for NASA or the Pentagon for domestic police forces the "paint it blue" phenomenon. Many of the new products were not particularly successful, such as the "slippery banana" machine that spewed a slick substance designed to make areas impenetrable to rioters. To the chagrin of Chicago police, the product made streets equally impassable for law officers and was evidently almost impossible for police to peel off the concrete.[11]

Paint-it-blue transfers from the military to the domestic police were rationalized by sensationalized language that equated the threats faced on foreign and on home fronts. For example, in a 1968 article in *U.S. News & World Report*, Colonel Robert Rigg, an army officer and author of the handbook *How to Stay Alive in Vietnam*, warned that the imperatives of urban warfare demanded new strategies of military intervention. In order to justify military-style campaigns in American cities, Colonel Rigg used the metaphor of the jungle to draw parallels between American cities and the battlefields of Vietnam. "Man has created out of steel and concrete a much better 'jungle' than nature has created in Vietnam," he explained, and "such cement-and-brick 'jungles' can offer better security to snipers and city guerillas than [the] Viet Cong enjoy in their jungles, elephant grass, and marshes." Rigg warned that incipient political organizations in the cities could pose an even greater threat to national security than previously unscripted urban revolts. He ventured the opinion that "we may find that the danger to a free America is greater from within than from without," and went on to emphasize the threats posed by the unique contours of the urban terrain: "Vietnam's jungles have no elevators and stair wells in their treetops, but city buildings do—and a multitude of vacant rooms to which to flee. No jungle tree branch is as secure. . . . Police, National Guard, and active army units could hardly carry out successful search-and-hold operations in the steel-and-concrete jungle of high-rise buildings without resorting to a campaign that would almost reach the destruction experienced by Stalingrad. . . . Plainly, the finest 'jungle' for insurrection was not created by nature; it has been built by man." Despite his focus on the physical environment, Rigg portrayed some U.S. citizens living in inner cities as wartime enemies and an insurgent force; he even envisioned combat against such forces leading to devastation comparable to the leveling of Stalingrad. To counter these dire threats, Rigg called for preparing troops for the challenges of this new battlefield: "Army units must be oriented and trained to know the cement-and-asphalt jungle of every American city. . . . This is the only way to solve the intelligence, social, economic and political problems associated with serious 'third front warfare,' which could bear the unfortunate label of 'Made in the USA.'" And so Rigg explained that military tactics and operations, conditioned by the experiences of Vietnam, were "the only way to solve" urban rebellions—what he called "third front warfare"—and the country's other social, economic, and political problems.[12]

While Colonel Rigg was portraying America's cities as imminent war zones, public discussion about these issues often reflected a frustration with the perceived limits of the state's response to rising crime and unrest in urban areas. During the 1960s, the Supreme Court dramatically revised criminal procedure by granting defendants a series of new protections: people charged with crimes won the right to a public defender if unable to pay for counsel, the right to have a lawyer present during interrogations, and the right to be informed of their rights upon arrest. Many journalists and politicians argued that these new legal protections had tied the authorities' hands just as poor communities reached the height of rebellion. Ronald Reagan used this issue to his political advantage in his successful gubernatorial campaign in 1966. In televised comments in which he held the new legal safeguards responsible for rising crime, he explained to a white, middle-class audience that every day when the sun goes down, "the jungle gets a little bit closer." The dawn of the age of Reagan was therefore marked by this historical irony: As the legacy of the Civil-Rights movement advanced in the courts, opponents argued for a compensatory return to vigilante justice. Legal and political gains in one realm of the republic would be accompanied by vigilantes and state military mobilization in the central cities of the United States.[13]

Indeed, some conservatives called for vigilante justice to restore order where formal state structures failed. For example, in 1979, right-wing political commentator Pat Buchanan wrote a column connecting the cry for vigilantism to debates over spending on social programs:

> Poverty is not the cause [of crime]: it is the convenient excuse in an affluent society where crime is five times as common as it was in the Depression, when a third of the nation was poor and a fourth of its labor force out of work . . . [now,] the criminal element runs little risk of being forced to pay an acceptable price. . . . On the old frontier, the answer would have been simple, direct, and instructive: a rope and a tree . . . an occasional reversion to vigilante justice which, though uncivil and crude, is preferable to no justice at all. . . . Only a fool would voluntarily disarm himself and his family in this urbanized jungle.[14]

Weighing into the raging public debate over how best to manage urban space, Buchanan invokes an idealized past where social hierarchies were honored and order maintained. As evidenced by Buchanan's calls for hanging, these sentiments were not merely linked with contemporary images of war but also drew on the most historically potent practice in the struggle for white supremacy: lynching. During the 1960s, many insisted that new social and financial support, such as War on Poverty programs, would address the root causes of urban malaise and therefore decrease crime, but others, like Buchanan, denied any relationship between poverty and crime and insisted that the only way to deal with disorder in the jungle was through the swift retribution of vigilante violence.

But military veterans, law enforcement professionals, and political elites were not the only people drawing parallels between domestic urban areas and foreign war zones. In fact, the rhetoric of activists and inner-city residents overlapped in key ways with the rhetoric of advocates for harsher discipline in poor communities. For example, African American activists often described inner cities as "internal colonies." Black Panther David Hilliard expressed this common sentiment in his autobiography: "we're a colony, a people with a distinct culture who are used for cheap labor. The only difference between us, and, say, Algeria, is that we are inside the mother country. And the police have the same relation to us that the American Army does to Vietnam: they are a force of occupation which will stop at nothing to keep us under control." This critique borrowed from anticolonial movements around the globe, but it also resonated with American elites' representations of inner cities as foreign spaces that were in mutiny against the state. Echoing both Hilliard and Colonel Rigg, the imprisoned activist and Black Panther George Jackson argued that "the cities of fascist U.S.A.—built straight up and with very little real planning or pattern, the twisting side streets, gangways connecting roofs, manholes, storm drains, concrete and steel trees—will hide a guerrilla army just as effectively as any forest." The internal colonialism thesis shaped activists' claims that African American soldiers had more in common with anti-imperialist insurgents, such as the Viet Cong, than with the U.S. government; it also contributed to the tendency to talk about police as "occupiers" in inner-city communities. For example, when talking about a raid on Black Panthers in Detroit, Huey Newton recalled how "the local police laid siege on that community and that house, and they used the same weapons they used in Vietnam (as a matter of fact, two tanks rolled up). The same thing happens in Vietnam because the 'police' are there also. The 'police' are everywhere and they all wear the same uniform and use the same tools, and they have the same purpose: the protection of the ruling circle here in North America." Metaphors of colonialism and the jungle conflated domestic and foreign spaces, but whereas the notion of the jungle explained urban conditions as the result of natural processes that were indigenous to that space, the metaphor of colonialism implied a system of exploitation in which white oppressors were directly implicated in the deliberate underdevelopment of inner cities in America and entire nations abroad.[15]

Moreover, it is not surprising that radical activists, such as the Black Panthers, employed war metaphors, since they were subjected to all varieties of military attacks and sabotage. In fact, so many different military and government agencies were involved in the surveillance and disruption of the Black Panther party that they often tripped over each other, by, for example, trailing each other's informants. Authorities also conducted military raids on activists; by the early 1970s, more than twenty Panthers had been killed in various confrontations. Perhaps the most infamous attack transpired in 1969, when Chicago police raided a Panther apartment and murdered Mark Clark and Fred Hampton, who was asleep next to his pregnant girlfriend when he was killed (after probably having been drugged by an FBI informant who had posed as the head of Panther security). Black Panther rhetoric depicting inner cities as colonized zones was therefore rooted in both their revolutionary ideology and daily experience.[16]

It is equally important to acknowledge the role of people's lived experience in Vietnam and how fighting abroad provided critical skills and technology that migrated home. In fact, in many of the cities with organizing by the Black Panthers, Vietnam veterans trained and drilled the membership in military exercises. Indeed, the experience of war probably intensified many African Americans' frustrations about the racial dynamics in American society while also familiarizing them with military tactics. Fear of this dynamic figured prominently in the mainstream press. For example, a national media frenzy erupted over the "De Mau Mau," a "secret terrorist group" composed of disgruntled African American veterans who allegedly murdered white victims. In one *Time* magazine article, "Black Power in Vietnam," the journalist found that 45 percent of the African American servicemen interviewed said they would "use arms to gain rights when they returned to the 'world' [United States]." A few others mentioned their plans to smuggle automatic weapons back to the United States. One African American marine pointed to the irony that the U.S. government trained him in the military skills he would use to challenge the state's authority at home: "What the beast [white man] has done for me, which is going to screw him, is teach me how to use a weapon. The Marines taught me how to improve." The article and its sensationalized tone reflected a general social awareness, and for some parties, acute fear, of the volatile relationship between the experience of fighting in a foreign war and struggles for domestic economic and racial equality at home. Thus, however dramatically the different groups noted here may have disagreed about the root causes of disorder and inequality, they often agreed about the nature of the conflict: whether Black Panthers, former

African American soldiers, white police or veterans, or conservative politicians, their rhetoric depicted a society cleaved apart and enmeshed in a confrontation that demanded military tactics to resolve.[17]

This rhetorical escalation was accompanied by law enforcement's increasing militarization, which had significant and often lethal consequences for urban communities. Indeed, as police gained new weaponry, surveillance technology, and torture strategies, the metaphors of war, jungles, and colonial occupation probably seemed less hyperbolic and more like graphic descriptions of everyday life. For example, when word spread of the new weaponry police acquired in anticipation of rioting in the summer of 1968, one Chicago community leader expressed the widespread feeling that police seemed to be "declaring war on the entire Negro community." An official in Chicago's Urban League complained that the military buildup risked validating "the line of extreme [Negro] militants that white society is intent on genocide." After hearing rumors about the possible use of tanks and other military gear on Chicago's streets, people's fears of an impending urban war were simply descriptive. For the media as well, military logic continued to saturate discussions of the daily relations between communities of color and state agents. For example, in October 1971, a *Chicago Tribune* journalist spent six nights with a police task force patrolling Chicago's West Side. His article explains how the officers moved between their homes in white communities and "the dirty streets and glass-littered alleys of the human jungle." The story focuses on Officer Simandl, who "buckles 9½ pounds of equipment around his waist, kisses his wife and three small sons, gets into his car on Chicago's Northwest Side and drives six miles to war. . . . The young man probably would object to that word 'war,' and so certainly would their superiors. But stripped of semantic camouflage, that's what it is. War. . . . Strange, occasionally boring, often savage, always unpredictable war, waged with the usual paradoxical objective—keeping the peace." The article thus explicitly constructs policing as a military exercise in hostile, foreign territory; the people living in these spaces are presented not as citizens but as adversaries of the state. And so, as the Vietnam War dragged on, Americans from all walks of life came increasingly to imagine inner cities as junglelike war zones and police work as a form of urban warfare.[18]

Representing the Jungle: Vigilantism in Popular Culture

Popular culture both reflected and heightened the notion that strategies from the Vietnam War could be used to quell domestic chaos, as the 1970s and 1980s featured a number of television series about veterans returning home and using their military skills to fight enemies in domestic spaces. For example, Vietnam veteran crime fighters appeared in the popular television shows "Miami Vice," "The A-Team," and "Magnum P.I." Some of the era's more popular films reflected these themes as well. In fact, vigilante movies could be considered one of the defining film genres of the 1970s. For example, in 1971, Clint Eastwood played the title role in *Dirty Harry*, a popular law-and-order film about a maverick San Francisco cop, Harry Callahan, chasing a serial killer called Scorpio. Callahan's embrace of violent, extralegal tactics clashes with the ineffectual state hierarchy committed to following legal procedures. In a key confrontation, Callahan tortures the killer until he reveals the location of his latest victim. As if to emphasize Callahan's deviation from sanctioned police policy, Scorpio repeatedly asserts his rights to a lawyer during the scene. Callahan soon finds the body and the murder weapon, yet the killer is released because police failed to follow proper procedure, meaning the key evidence is inadmissible in court. Infuriated by these legal hindrances, Callahan takes matters into his own hands, confronts the killer again, and, in a bravado performance that would cement Eastwood's public persona for the next twenty years, executes him. For a populace obsessed with crime and the supposed ineptitude of liberal crime-control strategies, the film dramatically illustrated the appeal of vigilante justice. Although leading reviewers criticized the film as a right-wing fantasy and as "the most disturbing manifestation of police paranoia I have seen on the screen," the film was popular and was followed by four other commercially successful *Dirty Harry* movies. Indeed, Eastwood's films from this period came both to embody and to fuel the conservative belief that vigilante violence was required to quell the "urban jungle."[19]

Following the model popularized by *Dirty Harry*, *Death Wish*, a popular 1974 vigilante film, also spawned four sequels exemplifying the public frustration with perceived rising crime and police inefficiency. In the film, Paul Kersey, played by Charles Bronson, is an architect who served in the Korean War and whose family is raped and murdered when he is away from home. Furious, he takes to the streets and kills a string of muggers. Instead of arresting him for the murders, police let him escape, fearing the wrath of the press and public who support Kersey's actions and consider him a hero. The vigilante violence depicted in the film is celebrated as an effective and appropriate reaction to a society rife with chaos and crime; the film helped make Bronson one of the most popular movie stars of the 1970s. In a more conflicted handling of these themes, the award-winning 1976 film *Taxi Driver* follows an unstable Vietnam veteran who violently rescues a young prostitute from her pimp. *Exterminator* (I and II) and *Rolling Thunder* also featured Vietnam veterans who draw on their military experience to fight crime. And so, in a society that had previously championed liberalism's therapeutic strategies as the key to social control, vigilante justice became a pop culture staple, depicting ruthless force as the antidote to disorder.[20]

One of the more complicated of these filmic narratives was *Rambo: First Blood*. In the blockbuster 1982 movie, Sylvester Stallone plays a decorated Vietnam veteran whose military instincts are triggered after being abused by police in a small American town. John J. Rambo, unable to handle the persecution, snaps and beats several guards during his escape from the police station. By the end of the prolonged confrontation with police and the National Guard, Rambo has morphed from a civilian back into a guerrilla fighter. Naked from the waist up and armed with a huge M60 machine gun, he transforms the sleepy American town into a war zone by blowing up most of the main buildings. As the first major film that depicted a soldier using high-tech weaponry against his own country, *First Blood* testified to the complicated and ambivalent legacy of the Vietnam War. Perhaps in an effort to sidestep politically charged issues of race and class, producers set Rambo's domestic war in a rural white town. The internal war that most Americans imagined and feared during the 1960s and 1970s, however, was the one waged in an urban landscape against a lower-class and racialized enemy. David Morrell, the author of *First Blood,* the book upon which the film was based, acknowledged that these cultural currents inspired his narrative. The plot idea came to him after seeing two juxtaposed news stories: one about the inner-city riots in the late 1960s and the other about returning Vietnam veterans.[21]

Through film and television, cultural producers struggled to make sense of domestic social unrest and the Vietnam War while negotiating a place in society for returning veterans. In some ways, the movies discussed above helped reassert the virtue of American soldiers and military might by transferring them to a new battlefront where they faced a new enemy: the shadowy, racialized American criminal. In these cultural imaginings, military skill and vigilante violence was far more successful at controlling domestic chaos than it had been in the jungles of Vietnam. Unfortunately, these ideas were never merely cultural fantasies or isolated to the silver screen, as millions of Americans sympathized with calls for a return to "law and order," and many embraced the notion that this could be achieved only through tough, militarized policing and, when that failed, extralegal violence. Jon Burge is a particularly poignant example of these processes, because through him we can trace the migration of military knowledge as it returned home from a foreign war to be directed against the marginalized people who lived in America's "urban jungles."[22]

Jon Burge and Police Torture in Chicago

Jon Burge was born in 1947 and raised in Merrionette Manor, a racially homogeneous housing development on Chicago's Southeast Side. After high school, Burge joined the Army in 1966 and two years later volunteered to serve in Vietnam. Assigned to the Ninth Infantry Division's military police, Burge's unit was responsible for, among other things, guarding, transporting, and processing prisoners of war. Although military intelligence officers conducted the interrogations, several veterans who served on the base acknowledge that military police moved prisoners between cells and often observed interrogations or stood guard nearby. Many also admitted that it was common for military intelligence officers to rig wires from hand-cranked field telephones to shock prisoners, ostensibly to extract confessions and information. But the use of field phones in torture was not limited to Vietnam, as the first reports of the device actually surfaced stateside, where it was allegedly assembled in the early 1960s by a doctor at the Tucker Prison Farm in Arkansas. Knowledge of this device, often called the "Tucker telephone," migrated to Vietnam and references to its use have subsequently been reported all over the world. Although Jon Burge denies any involvement with Vietnamese prisoners of war during his service, other veterans suggest that it would have been difficult to avoid interactions with detainees or knowledge of such practices.[23]

Burge joined the Chicago police force in March 1970, shortly after returning home from Vietnam. Two years later, he was promoted to detective and assigned to Area 2, which includes sections of the far South Side of Chicago between Cicero Avenue and Lake Michigan. The first reports of abuse surfaced shortly after Burge joined the force; the Tucker telephone reappeared in 1973 when Burge used it to torture Anthony Holmes during an interrogation. According to scores of testimonies, between 1972 and 1991, Burge tortured or supervised the torture of more than 100 people. He and the detectives under him used a variety of techniques, including beatings, Russian roulette, shocking, and mock executions to coerce confessions from crime suspects; these techniques were intended to inflict high levels of pain or fear without leaving any physical evidence of violence; most of these forms of torture would be familiar to people knowledgeable about the unsanctioned but pervasive interrogation procedures employed by U.S. forces in Vietnam. On other occasions, victims were handcuffed to hot radiators, forced to strip, and repeatedly beaten on the genitals. Officers suffocated some detainees by placing a plastic bag or typewriter cover over their heads; Burge and his colleagues also shocked victims on the scrotum, penis, anus, fingers, or ears with a cattle prod or the field phone.[24] These techniques were applied systematically; the longer those in custody resisted police demands, the more extreme the violence became. Officers advertised the methodical nature of their actions, often announcing to the suspect that they had a "scientific method" of making people talk.[25]

These physical acts were accompanied by verbal abuse that reveals how these patterns of torture were driven by issues of race, both in the community and the police department. Indeed, in the privacy of the interrogation rooms, the racial elements of the violence were explicitly and incessantly referenced. Every torture victim, except one, was African American, and most victims report being subjected to unrelenting racial slurs by police abusers. In one case, a man testified that after his arrest, police explained how they intended to beat him because he was "a smart ass nigger." When asked during his trial whether the police repeated this epithet more than one time, the man responded, "Yes, ma'am. In fact, every time he had something or anything to say." Another defendant reported that police "threatened to hang him as they had hung other niggers. They threatened to kill him if they ever saw him in a white neighborhood." Relying upon the historically potent language of lynching, these threats explicitly linked police violence to efforts to enforce a racial hierarchy and maintain all-white neighborhoods.[26]

While some torture victims were guilty of the crimes with which they were charged, the interrogation techniques described here were generally not employed to find the actual perpetrators of specific crimes. For, as the earlier quotations from Scarry and Crelinsten suggested, the torture was employed not so much as an intelligence-gathering technique as a weapon in the struggle for power over public spaces and the fate of communities. For example, testimony given by the sister of a police officer who worked with Burge provides privileged insight into frank discussions about the nature of police work at Area 2. According to the woman, Burge and her brother explained that "the purpose of the police is to punish." According to this witness, when her brother and Burge talked about their work, they "began to boast about power and what really happens in a police station"; one of them even bragged that "I can make someone confess to anything." The officers went on to explain that African Americans ruin neighborhoods and make life hard on the police. And so, when the police bring African Americans to the station, the officers revealed, "we give them hell." In fact, the witness recounted how her brother and Burge boasted about beating, burning, and smothering people in custody. These testimonies, from both victims of torture and the relatives of torturers, indicate that the violence used by Burge and his colleagues was not merely penological but also political: the information-gathering functions of the interrogations were secondary to asserting the power of these police officers to torture with impunity.[27]

In fact, on many occasions, police were aware that the person in custody had no direct knowledge of the events; in such cases, police rehearsed the specifics of the crime with the suspect before forcing him to make a confession. While the police hid their practices from the press and mainstream society, they encouraged their victims to share their experience with their neighbors; on one occasion, they drove an obviously beaten man around the streets, as if to broadcast their violence and their immunity from reprisals. These highly public acts were not directed against specific criminals; rather, they were intended to transmit a message to entire communities about state authority—private torture was therefore made public, with the bodies of beaten suspects functioning as warnings of the violence these Chicago police would use in their struggle to control neighborhoods. In some cases, officers fabricated evidence and hid information that would have exonerated the prisoner. In the case of Madison Hobley, police planted evidence and faked polygraph tests to frame him for a fire that killed seven people, including his wife and infant son. Hobley spent sixteen years in prison before being exonerated in 2003. It appears, therefore, that Burge and his colleagues were less concerned with unearthing the facts of any given case than with producing the spectacle of arresting, convicting, and punishing *someone* from the suspect territory.[28]

In terms of the perpetrators of these actions, the systematic police torture was executed by a group of white detectives, many of whom worked "midnights," the late-night shift. This group of men, headed by Burge, called themselves the A-Team, referencing the popular 1980s television show about a group of Vietnam veterans who used their military skills to dispense vigilante justice. The fact that Burge and his accomplices appropriated the moniker the A-Team is revealing on multiple levels. First, it acknowledged a shared commitment to using extralegal techniques to bypass the allegedly intrusive bureaucracy and formal safeguards of the criminal justice system. Second, like their television namesake—and like the Bronson and Eastwood characters discussed above—Burge's team probably imagined that its work was hamstrung by liberal government agencies that bungled the task of protecting American society from criminals and foreign threats. Third, by linking themselves to popular culture icons, the police officers positioned their actions not only as legitimate but as heroic, the stuff of television drama. Fourth, by seeing themselves as a Chicago version of the A-Team, Burge and his co-workers openly embraced the cultural and political trends discussed above of harnessing military knowledge and technology to handle domestic problems. In fact, Burge explicitly referenced such trends by naming the boat that he moored on Lake Michigan the *Vigilante.* Aboard the *Vigilante,* Burge hosted police gatherings where he would brag about his ability to break prisoners. His vicious practices were therefore deeply connected to the larger political and cultural trends of embracing militarism and vigilantism to manage a nation many feared was spinning out of control.[29]

Unlike television's A-Team, Burge's A-Team was an all-white operation. In Area 2, African American detectives were consistently assigned to "blind cases," crimes with little or no chance of resolution because of the lack of evidence or witnesses. Since job reviews were based in part on any given officer's number of arrests, this race-based allocation of case assignments both jeopardized the careers of African American officers and ensured that they would not rise to positions of authority from which Burge and his team might receive scrutiny. Moreover, African American detectives testified that it was an open secret at the station that the A-Team produced so many confessions precisely because they used violent, extralegal interrogation methods. Detective Walter Young remembers overhearing reference to a technique called "the Vietnamese treatment" or "the Vietnam special"; he gathered that such phrases meant using a field phone to shock detainees. Referring to the rumors about officers' use of the field phone, he explained: "There was the implication that . . . the suspect would be made to talk if, uh, the same techniques were basically used that were used in Vietnam." Law-abiding officers like Young, trapped between Burge and standard police protocol, endured professional sabotage while suspecting ongoing torture in their midst. Burge thus wielded immense influence, both on the streets and in the police station, and he liked to remind his victims of this fact. Indeed, during most of the interrogations, Burge and his associates would inform the man in custody of his social and cultural position, especially in reference to racial politics and police power. In a 1982 case, Burge explained to an African American prisoner that no one would believe his reports of torture, especially when contradicted by a police lieutenant. To highlight the point, Burge proceeded to detail torturing acquaintances of the prisoner, explaining how he shocked them and forced them to crawl all over the ground. By renarrating the previous abuse, Burge put on a performance inside a performance, an attempt to actualize his fantasy of absolute power and authority.[30]

Despite these violent performances of power, Burge's systematic strategy of torturing suspects and intimidating his fellow officers eventually faced concerted resistance. Although it would take years for their charges to be addressed, many of his victims found ways both within and without the criminal justice system to publicize their treatment. Starting in the 1980s, the People's Law Office, the high-profile activist law firm that first represented Andrew Wilson, took up additional cases of police torture after an anonymous letter from a police informer alerted them to additional victims. As word of lawsuits spread through jailhouses and prisons, more people came forward to testify against Burge and his subordinates. These lawsuits, coupled with community activism and Conroy's hard-nosed investigative reporting, relentlessly pushed the torture cases into public consciousness over the next decades.[31]

But even as victims forced the floodgates open, the racialized stamp of criminality was a powerful weapon for delegitimizing their claims. To combat this bias, lawyers for the victims brought in specialists to testify that their clients would not have the specific military knowledge or physical capacity to fabricate the details of their torture. For example, in one case, two prominent doctors with extensive international experience investigating torture described the physiological symptoms of torture. But during the cross-examination, lawyers representing the police officers continually glossed over the experts' medical evidence, instead redirecting the court's attention to the inherent untrustworthiness of criminal suspects. A typical exchange began with a question from the attorney representing the police:

> **Attorney Kelly:** Doctor, Is it fair to say based on your comment that you strongly believe that torture occurs at Area Two?
> **Dr. Kirshner:** That is correct.
> **Kelly:** All right. You base that on talking to convicted murderers and what you have read of other individuals convicted of murder testify about what happened to them, correct?

To discredit victims' claims about torture and the powerful testimony of medical experts, lawyers for the police sought to overwhelm the material evidence by making incessant racialized references to the criminality of the victims. Lawyers for the police thus hoped to override the claims of victims by persuading jurists that they should not believe criminals, even those criminals whose guilt was often established only by the very posttorture confessions under scrutiny at the trial.[32]

In the testimony of a second specialist, lawyers representing torture victims sought to prove the truth of their clients' claims by focusing on how they reported symptoms that would have been impossible to fake. According to Dr. Antonio Martinez, when torture victims are forced to recount their experiences, they display a series of reactions emanating from the sympathetic nervous system, including trembling, sweating, disassociating, crying, and startling easily. According to Dr. Martinez, these physical reactions cannot be faked: "Darrell Cannon [a torture victim] is not making up these reactions. The limbic system is responding to this. . . . You don't fake them. The only way to fake them is if you have years of training in yoga, years of training in deep meditation, years of training in hypnosis. Mr. Cannon doesn't seem to be the type of person who possesses that type of training." Thus, in order to legitimate the charges against the police, Cannon's lawyers, working with Dr. Martinez, sought to separate their client's physical body from his socially constructed status as a criminal. Bias was so strong against arrested African American men that the lawyers could not rest their cases on evidence that could be considered as originating from the criminal suspect; instead, specialists were forced to interpret the bodies of victims as proof of torture. And judging by the comments of the lawyer for the police, even physiological and material evidence from the body of a man charged with murder should not be taken at face value, for even that could be redeployed as proof of the "criminal's" infinite capacity for deception.[33]

Although the Chicago Police Department's Office of Professional Standards conducted scores of investigations, starting as early as 1973, into the allegations of torture in Area 2, Burge was not disciplined until he and two other officers were suspended in November 1991 for the abuse a decade earlier of Andrew Wilson. During the lengthy review before the Police Board, much of the police force, media, and political establishment sympathized with the accused officers, with many of these supporters arguing that Burge and his colleagues had already been exonerated in various other proceedings. And so, in February 1992, Chicago police organized a benefit to raise funds for the accused officers' legal fees; approximately 4,000 supporters overflowed the Teamster Auditorium while proclaiming Burge's innocence. A year later, the Police Board voted to dismiss Burge; they reinstated the other two officers after their fifteen months of suspension. Even after Burge's dismissal, many in the police force still viewed him as a martyr or believed him to be innocent. The following month, the police union planned to dedicate their float in the South Side Irish Parade to the accused officers; they withdrew the plan only after the African-American Police League voiced outrage to parade organizers. Even then, Patricia Hill, president of the league, expressed frustration with the union's support for Burge and his colleagues: "I knew that it was consistent with the Fraternal Order of Police, trying to further polarize the department and the community. I don't think changing the theme [of the float] really changes anything. All it means is that the banner won't be there physically, but it carries the same message." Soon thereafter, Burge moved to a modest house on the Tampa Bay in Florida, where he owns a new motorboat and continues to draws a full police pension.[34]

Despite the massive evidence compiled by lawyers, investigators, and journalists, and despite the millions of dollars in civil settlements that the City of Chicago paid to compensate victims, Burge and the other police officers were never criminally charged for their abuse and torture. A report by special prosecutors released in July 2006 finally and officially validated victims' torture claims; it was so long in coming, however, that the statute of limitations prevented prosecuting the officers involved. Victims and their families were dismayed but not shocked at the outcome. Mary Johnson, the seventy-three-year-old mother of one victim, explained simply that "people just don't care. . . . Guess what? My son is black. Guess what? His mother is poor." Unable to indict for the crimes themselves, federal authorities arrested Burge in 2008 for lying during proceedings for a civil lawsuit. A federal jury convicted Burge on three counts of obstruction of justice and perjury on July 28, 2010, decades after the first complaints of torture.[35]

Conclusions: Race, Justice, and Policing in a Punishing Democracy

The minimal public outcry in response to the torture at Area 2 and the ensuing controversy suggests that Burge's actions were more embedded in the U.S. social fabric than one might first assume. Even those swaths of the public who may have disagreed with his extreme tactics appear to have accepted the legitimacy of his targets, for many people shared his basic vision of a nation at war with itself. Indeed, by the early 1980s, structural critiques of U.S. society were increasingly inaudible; rehabilitation, reform, and social-welfare programs were largely discredited by the prolonged assault, from both the right and the left, on a problematic, conflicted liberalism and the U.S. semblance

of a welfare state. Many citizens increasingly came to believe that social order in marginalized communities was best achieved through surveillance and
punishment. Elites, who had long imagined inner cities as jungles, transferred
the tools, personnel, and machinery used in the Vietnam War to control domestic spaces. By treating poor, racialized communities both metaphorically
and literally as a foreign war zone, the state negated residents' claims to full
citizenship and silenced structural critiques of U.S. society. Eventually, once
large groups of people accepted that mainstream society was locked in a mor-
tal struggle with crime and disorder emanating from "urban jungles," they
saw torture as just another unfortunate consequence of war.[36]

Ultimately, however, these practices are no more successful at establishing
authority or legitimacy in inner cities than they are in foreign wars, for they
obviously discredit state agents in heavily policed communities and eventually cast a shadow over the government's punitive power among other groups
as well. Indeed, Burge's actions have implicated significant segments of Chicago's political elite, as exemplified by the persistent allegations that Mayor
Richard Daley failed to respond to torture charges during his tenure as state's
attorney. In fact, the state's propensity to convict and sentence innocent men
to death shook faith in the criminal justice system at the highest levels. After
activists and journalism students proved four of Burge's victims to be innocent
of the crimes for which they were convicted, Illinois governor George Ryan, a
Republican and long-time supporter of capital punishment, issued full pardons
and released the men from death row in 2003. The next day, Governor Ryan
sparked a national conversation about the inherent injustice of the death
penalty by commuting the sentence of every person on death row in Illinois
to a term of life in prison. Therefore, although brute violence and militarized
force certainly produce spectacles of power, they ultimately fail at establishing
order or overcoming the diverse strategies of resistance these tactics inevitably
inspire. These lessons, seared into American consciousness after hard failures
in Vietnam—and reprised in the tragic occupation of Iraq—have unfortunately
done little to diminish their appeal, either at home or abroad.[37]

Notes

For invaluable assistance and feedback, the author wishes to thank Mark Leff, Jim
Barrett, Stephen Hartnett, Kwame Holmes, Issa Kohler-Hausmann, Clarence Lang,
Victor Pickard, Leslie Reagan, David Roediger, the People's Law Office, and the Work-
ing-Class History Group at the University of Illinois, Urbana-Champaign.

1. Jackson quoted in "Cops Accused of Brutality," *Chicago Tribune* (18 February
1982): A3; Burge is praised in "Daley Hails 11 in Crime War," *Chicago Tribune* (20

May 1983): LF8; complaints filed to Jackson and the Chicago police are noted in "Cops Accused of Brutality" and in "Chicago's Slain Policemen," *Chicago Tribune* (28 September 1982): 13; testimonial evidence on the harsh search methods and the torture of suspects is available through the People's Law Office, "Petition and Memorandum in Support of Petition for Appointment of Special Prosecutor and Response to Motion for Clarifications" (23 July 2002)—this document was accessed under disc 1: "Pleadings, Findings, Decisions of Interest" and "DISQUAL for SAO and Judges, 7.23.02.SAOBrief," two of the thousands of legal documents that were provided to me on compact disc by the People's Law Office, the attorneys representing the torture victims in their suit against Chicago and Commander Burge; hereafter, all documents retrieved from these discs will list the document title and date, followed by disc number, folder titles, and the document page numbers containing the cited evidence.

2. The torture of Wilson is chronicled by Investigator Francine Sanders in "Special Project Investigative Summary Report" (26 October 1990), accessed on disc 1: "Goldston.Sanders.Reports," 45–49; for introductions to this argument about the militarization of police forces, see *Militarizing the American Criminal Justice System: The Changing Roles of the Armed Forces and the Police*, ed. Peter Kraska (Boston: Northeastern University Press, 2001), and Christian Parenti, *Lockdown America: Police and Prisons in the Age of Crisis* (New York: Verso, 1999).

3. Elaine Scarry, *The Body in Pain: The Making and Unmaking of the World* (New York: Oxford University Press, 1985), 35.

4. Ronald Crelinsten, "The World of Torture: A Constructed Reality," *Theoretical Criminology* 7, no. 3 (2003): 293–318, quotation on 295–96; on what Crelinsten calls "the creation of a powerful and dangerous enemy," see Erica Meiners, *Right to Be Hostile: Schools, Prisons, and the Making of Public Enemies* (New York: Routledge, 2007), and Carol Stabile, *White Victims, Black Villains: Gender, Race, and Crime News in U.S. Culture* (New York: Routledge, 2006).

5. On the indifference to Burge's actions, see John Conroy, "Town without Pity," *Chicago Reader* (12 January 1996), www.chicagoreader.com/policetorture/960112/; regarding the creation of a public fear so great that extreme measures are accepted as necessary responses to crime, see Travis Dixon's article in this volume (chapter 4); Jimmie Reeves and Richard Campbell, *Cracked Coverage: Television News, the Anti-Cocaine Crusade, and the Reagan Legacy* (Durham, NC: Duke University Press, 1994); and Clarence Lusane, *Pipe Dream Blues: Racism and the War on Drugs* (Boston: South End Press, 1991).

6. On blowback, see Chalmers Johnson, *Blowback: The Costs and Consequences of American Empire* (New York: Henry Holt, 2004), and Alfred W. McCoy, *The Politics of Heroin: CIA Complicity in the Global Drug Trade* (Brooklyn, NY: Lawrence Hill, 1991); on the migration of punishment practices from the United States to Abu Ghraib, see Stephen John Hartnett and Laura Ann Stengrim, *Globalization and Empire: The U.S. Invasion of Iraq, Free Markets, and the Twilight of Democracy* (Tuscaloosa, AL: University of Alabama Press, 2006), 22–23; on the links between international and domestic policing, see Dylan Rodriguez, "(Non)Scenes of Captivity: The Common Sense of Punishment and Death," *Radical History Review* 96 (2006): 9–32.

7. For an example of the backlash theory, see Thomas Byrne Edsall and Mary Edsall, *Chain Reaction* (New York: W. W. Norton, 1991); for the importance of rising crime rates in the appeal of law and order (with some attention to the role of the Vietnam War), see Michael Flamm, *Law and Order: Street Crime, Civil Unrest, and the Crisis of Liberalism in the 1960s* (New York: Columbia University Press, 2005); for works focusing on the role of white racism, see Parenti, *Lockdown America*, and Linda Williams, *The Constraint of Race* (University Park: Pennsylvania State University Press, 2003); for studies addressing local confrontations over neighborhoods, see Arnold Hirsch, *Making the Second Ghetto: Race and Housing in Chicago, 1940–1960* (Cambridge, England: Cambridge University Press, 1983), and Thomas Sugrue, *The Origins of the Urban Crisis: Race and Inequality in Postwar Detroit* (Princeton, NJ: Princeton University Press, 1996); for studies chronicling conservative organizing efforts, see Lisa McGirr, *Suburban Warriors* (Princeton, NJ: Princeton University Press, 2001), Rick Perlstein, *Before the Storm: Barry Goldwater and the Unmaking of the American Consensus* (New York: Hill and Wang, 2001), and Donald Critchlow, *Phyllis Schlafly and Grassroots Conservatism* (Princeton, NJ: Princeton University Press, 2005).

8. For information about hobo jungles, see Frank Tobias Higbie, *Indispensable Outcasts: Hobo Workers and Community in the American Midwest, 1880–1930* (Urbana: University of Illinois Press, 2003); Upton Sinclair, *The Jungle* (1906; New York: W. W. Norton, 2003); Joseph McLaughlin, *Writing the Urban Jungle: Reading Empire in London from Doyle to Eliot* (Charlottesville: University of Virginia Press, 2000), 2; for a recent version of this argument, see the editorial "'The Jungle,' Again," *New York Times* (1 August 2008), A22.

9. Gates and Parker are quoted in Tracy Tullis, "A Vietnam at Home" (Ph.D. diss., New York University, 1999), 105 and 102; for analysis of coordination between the military and police, see Frank Morales, "U.S. Military Civil Disturbance Planning," *Covert Action Quarterly* 69 (2000), available at www.covertaction.org//content/view/61/75/, and the 1983 oral history of Major General Anthony Palumbo, listed as "Law Enforcement, Emergency Planning, and the California National Guard, 1965–1974," in the collection Law Enforcement and Criminal Justice in California, 1966–1976 (OH R-23), as held by the California State Archives, Sacramento, California; for the numbers painted on roofs, see Gerald Horne, *Fire This Time: The Watts Uprising and the 1960s* (Charlottesville: University of Virginia Press, 1995), 165.

10. For information on LEAA, see Parenti, *Lockdown America*, 6–23, and Jonathan Simon, *Governing through Crime: How the War on Crime Transformed American Democracy and Created a Culture of Fear* (Oxford, England: Oxford University Press, 2007), 89–102, and Flamm, *Law and Order*, 119. On the growth of the LEAA's budget, see Peter Carroll, *It Seemed Like Nothing Happened: America in the 1970s* (New Brunswick, NJ: Rutgers University Press, 1990), 49; for examples of how this new military technology has been employed, see Stephen John Hartnett, "A Rhetorical Critique of the Drug War and 'the Nauseous Pendulum' of Reason and Violence," *Journal of Contemporary Criminal Justice* 16, no. 3 (2000): 247–71.

11. For the quoted passage and discussion of the paint-it-blue phenomenon, see G. Christian Hill, "Police Weapons Range from Electronic Cops to Growing Bacteria,"

Wall Street Journal (18 March 1974), 1; for further discussions of new military/police gear, see Tullis, "Vietnam at Home," 132–64, and Parenti, *Lockdown America*, 21–23.

12. Robert B. Rigg, *How to Stay Alive in Vietnam; Combat Survival in the War of Many Fronts* (Harrisburg, PA: Stackpole, 1966); Robert B. Rigg, "A Military Appraisal of the Threat to U.S. Cities," *U.S. News & World Report* (15 January 1968), 68–71; for another of the many articles linking domestic urban unrest to international military conflicts and uprisings, see "The City as a Battlefield: A Global Concern," *Time* (2 November 1970), 22.

13. The reaction against new protections for criminal defendants is discussed in Parenti, *Lockdown America*, 5; Reagan is quoted in Flamm, *Law and Order*, 74; on how the fears discussed here are marshaled during electoral cycles, see Kathleen Hall Jamieson, *Dirty Politics: Deception, Distraction, and Democracy* (Oxford, England: Oxford University Press, 1992), 15–101; for historical background on this process, see Lusane, *Pipe Dream Blues*, and Stabile, *White Victims, Black Villains*.

14. Pat Buchanan, "The Urban Jungle Where Crime Pays," *Chicago Tribune* (20 March 1979), B3. Editor's note: Historically, lynch mobs justified their actions—as Buchanan does here—as a corrective to lax law enforcement; lynchings were therefore understood by their perpetrators and supporters not as extralegal outbursts of racial hatred but as grassroots support for violated community norms (see James Elbert Cutler, *Lynch-Law: An Investigation into the History of Lynchings in the United States* [New York: Longmans, Green, 1905], and Orlando Patterson, *Rituals of Blood: Consequences of Slavery in Two American Centuries* [New York: Basic Civitas, 1998], 171–232).

15. For examples of the large body of works advancing the internal colonialism thesis, see Kenneth Clark, *Dark Ghetto: Dilemmas of Social Power* (New York: Harper and Row, 1965); Robert Allen, *Black Awakening in Capitalist America* (London: Gollancz, 1970); and David Hilliard and Lewis Cole, *This Side of Glory: The Autobiography of David Hilliard and the Story of the Black Panther Party* (Boston: Little, Brown, 1993); George Jackson is quoted in Eric Cummins, *The Rise and Fall of California's Radical Prison Movement* (Stanford, CA: Stanford University Press, 1994), 207; Huey Newton is quoted in *To Die for the People: The Writings of Huey P. Newton*, ed. Franz Schurmann (New York: Random House, 1972), 36. For examples of scholarly discussions of these themes, see Nikhil Pal Singh, *Black Is a Country: Race and the Unfinished Struggle for Democracy* (Cambridge, MA: Harvard University Press, 2005), and Robert Self, *American Babylon: Race and the Struggle for Postwar Oakland* (Princeton, NJ: Princeton University Press, 2003); for further discussion of the notion of "deliberate underdevelopment," see Meiners's essay in this volume (chapter 1), and Ruth Wilson Gilmore, *Golden Gulag: Prisons, Surplus, Crisis, and Opposition in Globalizing California* (Berkeley: University of California Press, 2007).

16. For the number of murdered Black Panthers, see Jeffrey Ogbar, *Black Power: Radical Politics and African American Identity* (Baltimore, MD: Johns Hopkins University Press, 2005), 199; on the role of the military in suppressing the Black Freedom Movement and in responding to the urban riots of the 1960s, see Horne, *Fire This Time*, and Gerald McKnight, *The Last Crusade: Martin Luther King, Jr., the FBI, and the Poor People's Campaign* (Boulder, CO: Westview Press, 1998); more broadly,

see Ward Churchill and Jim Vander Wall, *Agents of Repression: The FBI's Secret Wars against the Black Panther Party and the American Indian Movement* (Boston: South End Press, 2002).

17. For examples of veterans training Black Panthers, see Elaine Brown, *A Taste of Power: A Black Woman's Story* (New York: Anchor Books, 1994), 12, and Geronimo Il Jaga, "Every Nation Struggling to Be Free Has a Right to Struggle, a Duty to Struggle" in *Liberation, Imagination and the Black Panther Party,* ed. Kathleen Cleaver and George Katsiaficas (New York: Routledge, 2001): 71–77; for fear of the De Mau Mau, see "De Mau Mau," *Time* (30 October 1972), www.time.com/time/magazine/article/0,9171,906633,00.html; the quotations are from "Black Power in Vietnam," *Time* (19 September 1969), 22–23.

18. Fears of new police weapons are discussed in "Arms and the Ghetto: Police Weapons Buildup in Cities Intensifies Fear of Big City Clashes," *Wall Street Journal* (11 March, 1968), 1; the quotation is from "Six Nights with a Police Task Force," *Chicago Tribune* (10 October 1971), I25.

19. For the prevalence of Vietnam veteran crime fighters on television, see Robert McMahon, "SHAFR Presidential Address: Contested Memory: The Vietnam War and American Society," *Diplomatic History* 26, no. 2 (2002): 159–84; for the centrality of vigilante movies in the 1970s, see Peter Lev, *American Films of the 70s: Conflicting Visions* (Austin: University of Texas Press, 2000), 22–40; for the movie itself, see *Dirty Harry*, dir. Don Siegel (Los Angeles: Warner Bros. Pictures, 1971); the quoted reviews are cited in Lev, *American Films of the 70s: Conflicting Visions*, 35.

20. *Death Wish*, dir. Michael Winner (Los Angeles: Paramount Pictures, 1974); *Taxi Driver*, dir. Martin Scorsese (Los Angeles: Columbia Pictures, 1976); *Exterminator*, dir. James Glickenhaus (Los Angeles: VCO Embassy Pictures and Interstar, 1980); *Rolling Thunder*, dir. John Flynn (Los Angeles: American International Pictures, 1977); Bronson's popularity is discussed in Lev, *American Films of the 70s*, 39; for a contemporary filmic spin on this theme, see Jodi Foster—who had played the child prostitute rescued in *Taxi Driver*—return as a revenge-driven vigilante in *The Brave One*, dir. Neil Jordan (Los Angeles: Redemption Pictures, Silver Pictures, Village Roadshow Pictures, and WV Films III, 2007).

21. *Rambo: First Blood*, dir. Ted Kotcheff (Los Angeles: Anabasis N.V. and Carolco Pictures, 1982); the special edition DVD contains interviews with the producers and writers, and production notes about the film and the genesis of the book idea.

22. Not every film from the period celebrated the use of military strategies within the nation; for example, although Rambo's skills may have made him unstoppable, he ultimately had to surrender and acknowledge the inappropriateness of targeting (white) American civilians with war machinery; in the subsequent *Rambo* films, however, the U.S. state was portrayed as willing to harness Rambo's extralegal military prowess and direct it against foreign enemies; viewers can now see a post-9/11 version of Rambo, who returned with a new release in 2008.

23. Burge's biographical information is culled from John Conroy, "Tools of Torture," *Chicago Reader* (4 February 2005), 24–27, and David Heinzmann, "Scandal Muddied Bright Future," *Chicago Tribune* (20 July 2006), 17; for the history of the Tucker telephone, see Bruce Jackson, "Our Prisons Are Criminal" *New York Times* (22

September 1968), 49, and Michael Streissguth, *Johnny Cash at Folsom Prison: The Making of a Masterpiece* (Cambridge, MA: Da Capo Press, 2004), 49; the Tucker telephone's subsequent migration all over the world was discussed in the testimony of Dr. Kirshner in disc 4: "Cannon Witness, Dr. Kirshner," 59, and in interviews with veterans who served in settings similar to Burge's, who were featured in Conroy, "Tools of Torture"; I should note that John Conroy has covered this story closely since 1991, when his articles in the *Chicago Reader* began to provide comprehensive accounts of the events. His work subsequently became instrumental in bringing police misconduct to light (see David Carr, "Muckraking Pays, Just Not in Profit," *New York Times* [11 December 2007], C1), and eventually was published as *Unspeakable Acts, Ordinary People: The Dynamics of Torture* (New York: Alfred A. Knopf, 2000); the *Chicago Reader* was recently acquired and the new owners laid off four of the paper's senior writers, including Conroy, in December 2007.

24. Although it is tempting to present the actions by Burge and his colleagues in more detail, hence highlighting their brutality, I have tried to present these atrocities in a way that neither fetishizes the violence nor reinscribes the attempt to denigrate the victims; although the names of people tortured by Burge have been released in various articles and other public records, I have removed the last names in cases where the person's involvement was not widely documented in the media.

25. The dates of the torture and the number of victims is reviewed in Conroy, "Tools of Torture"; my synopsis of the kinds of torture employed was compiled after reviewing depositions, court testimonies, and numerous general reports by police boards from the case files; the "scientific method" of torture was mentioned in the testimony of Dr. Kirshner, as accessed from disc 4: "Cannon Witness, Dr. Kirshner," 87–89.

26. The first man is quoted from the testimony of Phillip _____ (26 April 2000), accessed from disc 2: "Victims Testimony, Phillip. __.4.26.00," 12; the second defendant is quoted from the "Motion to Suppress Statement of Rodney _____" (23 December 1982), accessed from disc 2: "Victims Testimony, _____.Rodney.12.23.82."

27. All quotations here are from a videotaped sworn statement by Eileen _____ (11 March 2004), accessible from disc 1: "_____.video.stmt.3.26.04," 6–9.

28. For an example of the police coaching a torture victim in how to make his "confession," see the "Deposition of Eric ___" (21 March 2005), accessed from disc 2: "Victim's Testimony, ___.Eric.3.21.05," 45–46; the story of driving a beaten man around the neighborhood is from the "Statement of Robert _____" (28 March 2005), accessed from disc 2: "Victim's Testimony, _____.Robert.3.28.05," 25; on the case of Madison Hobley, see "Memorandum Opinion and Order in Madison Hobley v. Burge (et al.)" (22 June 2004), accessed from disc 1: "Pleadings, Findings, and Admissions and Decisions of Interest, 6.22.04."

29. Burge's boat and dockside parties are discussed in Sasha Abramsky, "Trial by Torture," *Mother Jones* (3 March 2000), available at www.motherjones.com/news/feature/2000/03/chicops.html.

30. For the discussion about suspicions about torture within the police station, see the "Deposition of Walter ___" (2 November 2004), accessed from disc 1: "Walter ___ Statement," 8–9; for Burge's recounting of other tortures, see "Lawyers for

Superintendent of Police, Leroy Martin, Memorandum in Opposition to Motion to Bar Testimony Concerning Other Alleged Victims of Police Misconduct" (22 January 1992), accessed from disc 1: "Pleadings, Findings, Admissions, and Decisions of Interest, 1.22.92, City Memo Admitting Pattern of Torture," 8.

31. For how word spread about the People's Law Offices' efforts, see Conroy, *Unspeakable Acts, Ordinary People*, 237; the People's Law Office, founded in 1968, has played a historic role in a number of high-profile cases on state misconduct and abuse, such as the Attica massacre in 1971 and the 1969 police killings of Black Panthers Fred Hampton and Mark Clark; for their description of the work on police abuse and specifically the role of the anonymous police informer, see the People's Law Office website: www.peopleslawoffice.com/archives/last-10-years/.

32. This exchange is from the "Testimony of Dr. Kirshner in [the] Trial of Darrell Cannon" (1 November 1999), accessed from disc 4: "Cannon Witness, Dr. Kirshner," 136. Editor's note: in this regard, the burdens of testimony faced by torture victims echoes the old Slave Codes, which forbade any African American, whether free or enslaved, from testifying against any white defendant.

33. "Testimony of Dr. Antonio Martinez in [the] Trial of Darrell Cannon" (19 July 1999), accessed from disc 4: "Cannon Witness, Dr. Martinez.part 2.7.19.99," 107.

34. For a synopsis of these events, see Conroy, *Unspeakable Acts, Ordinary People*, 229–31; for example of the support for Burge, see Mike Royko, "Facts Don't Add Up to Police Brutality," *Chicago Tribune* (27 February 1992), 3; on the fundraiser, see Janita Poe and Sharman Stein, "Burge Supporters Come Out in Force" *Chicago Tribune* (26 February 1992), 1; for Burge's dismissal, see Sharman Stein, "Police Board Fires Burge for Brutality," *Chicago Tribune* (11 February 1993), 1; for the police union's support of Burge, see Andrew Gottesman, "Police Union Will Alter Float for South Side Irish Parade," *Chicago Tribune* (10 March 1993), 2; on Burge's move to Florida and his new boat, see David Heinzmann, "Scandal Muddied Bright Future," 17.

35. For the civil settlement of nearly $20 million for four victims, see Gary Washburn and Jeff Coen, "'Disgrace' Costs Millions; Aldermen Approve Payouts Totaling Almost $20 Million," *Chicago Tribune* (10 January 2008), 1; for the fallout from the special investigation, see "Suspects Tortured, Report Says; But Fired Cop Can't Be Charged Because Cases Are Too Old," *Chicago Tribune* (19 July 2006), 6; for the reaction of family members, see Stephano Esposito, "Lack of Charges No Surprise to Alleged Torture Victims," *Chicago Sun-Times* (20 July 2006), 7; for Burge's arrest, see Steve Mills and Jeff Coen, "Feds Catch Up with Burge—Notorious ex-Chicago Commander Charged with Lying about Torture," *Chicago Tribune* (22 October 2008), 1; for Burge's conviction, see Rummana Hussain, et al., "'A Long Time Coming'; Burge found Guilty of Lying about Torture," *Chicago Sun-Times* (July 29, 2010), 14.

36. For fuller treatment of how and why the United States increasingly abandoned therapeutic solutions and embraced punishment as the dominant strategy to handle crime, poverty, and drug addiction, see my "Forging a Punishing Consensus: The Punitive Turn in American Criminal and Social Welfare Policy, 1968–1980" (Ph.D. dissertation, University of Illinois at Urbana-Champaign, 2010).

37. For Mayor Daley's involvement, see Gretchen Ruethling, "Chicago Mayor Says He Shares Responsibility in Torture Cases," *New York Times* (22 July 2006), A11,

and Natasha Korecki, "Burge Foes Target Daley: They Seek to Add Mayor to Police Brutality Suit," *Chicago Sun-Times* (15 February 2007), 10; on Governor Ryan's pardons, see Jodi Wilgoren, "4 Death Row Inmates Are Pardoned," *New York Times* (11 January 2003), A13; on the context of the pardons, see Stephen John Hartnett and Daniel Mark Larson, "'Tonight Another Man Will Die': Crime, Violence, and the Master Tropes of Contemporary Arguments about the Death Penalty," *Communication and Critical Cultural Studies* 3, no. 4 (2006): 263–87.

Gotta Be Careful Where Ya Plant Ya Feet

Marvin Mays

A member of a writing workshop founded by Hispanic Americans for Progress (HAP) in the New Jersey State Prison, in Trenton, New Jersey, Marvin Mays writes poems portraying the harsh realities that lead to crime and punishment; this poem (and five other pieces by Mays) was published in *Inside/ Out: Voices from New Jersey State Prison,* ed. Kal Wagenheim (Livermore, CA: Wingspan Press, 2009).

All tears ain't weeps, all closed eyes ain't sleep,
So ya gotta be careful where ya plant ya feet.

Ya homeboy was gleamin', riding low and leaning,
Gettin' crazy money and his hustle was screaming.

Jump in gee, I'm a'gonna teach you how to be
A real smooth operator, just like me.

Hit you off with a package, showed ya how to move,
Ya started clocking crack, not taking ya butt to school.

He was ya tutor, mentor, ya first homeboy,
the one ya thought was all that and more.

Then the bust came down and he wasn't around,
ya screamed for his help, but he couldn't be found.

Now ya feel like hell, cause he won't go ya bail,
word's on the street that he's got ya girl.

Now ya days are dull, at night ya can't sleep,
ya gotta be careful where ya plant ya feet.

Chapter 3

Killing Democracy;
or, How the Drug War Drives
the Prison-Industrial Complex

Daniel Mark Larson

On June 9, 1930, President Herbert Hoover signed H.R. 11143 into law, creating the Federal Bureau of Narcotics (FBN) and entrusting the Secretary
of the Treasury, Andrew Mellon, with the responsibility of establishing the
first federal organization whose sole purpose was to rid the nation of illegal
narcotics. When the bureau opened its doors on July 1, 1930, Mellon named
former vice counsel with the State Department and recently displaced assistant commissioner of Prohibition, Harry J. Anslinger, as the FBN's acting
commissioner. Two weeks into his new position, the heat of this new charge
was already singeing Anslinger, as South Carolina Senator Coleman Livingston
Blease rose on the Senate floor, waved a tin of opium, and shouted "this was
purchased only one block from where we are now deliberating." The senator's
showboating reminded the new FBN director that "time was running out, if
the newly formed Federal Bureau of Narcotics was to win and hold the respect
of Congress and the public, it would have to act fast." For the following thirty
years, Anslinger was indeed fast and ferocious, as he carried out the mission
of the FBN and turned the fight against drugs into a national obsession. In
fact, Commissioner Anslinger shepherded the passage of a series of legislative bulwarks, spanning the 1937 Marijuana Tax Act up to the 1956 Narcotics Control Act. In addition, he provided spectacle-hunting authors with the
juicy anecdotes that fueled Hollywood's notorious 1936 drug exposé, *Reefer
Madness*, which avows that "women cry for it, men die for it"; and he dabbled
in his own forms of cultural production by writing fear-mongering articles
such as "Marihuana: Assassin of Youth," which linked "marijuana fiends"
with "murder (and) degenerate sex attacks." Thus, through more than thirty
years of service, Anslinger pushed antidrug legislation and both supported and
produced countless horror stories spread throughout the American public—as

much as any figure in our national history, Anslinger was the godfather of our current drug war.[1]

Nearly six decades after Senator Blease challenged Anslinger from the floor of the Senate, a similar event unfolded in our nation's capital. In 1986 President Ronald Reagan declared that "today there's a new epidemic: smokable cocaine, otherwise known as crack. It is an explosively destructive and often lethal substance, which is crushing its users. It is an uncontrolled fire." Within a few years, Reagan's dutiful vice president, George H. W. Bush, rose to the Oval Office, where he promptly recreated Senator Blease's compelling episode by staging a symbolic extinguishing of the "uncontrollable fire" announced by his predecessor. And so, on September 5, 1989, President Bush addressed the nation from the Oval Office and introduced the latest antidrug initiative: "This is the first time since taking the oath of office that I felt an issue was so important, so threatening, that it warranted talking directly with you, the American people. All of us agree that the gravest domestic threat facing our nation is drugs." During his speech, the president held up a bag of crack cocaine that he claimed was purchased in Lafayette Park, across the street from the White House. He pointed to the bag and asked, "Who is responsible? Let me tell you straight out, everyone who uses drugs, everyone who sells drugs, and everyone who looks the other way." The embarrassing secret behind the president's righteous theater was revealed shortly thereafter, when the *Washington Post*'s Michael Isikoff reported that upon the president's requesting a bag of crack as a stage prop for his speech, Drug Enforcement Agency (DEA— the new and improved FBN) agents had to set up the drug buy in Lafayette Park by luring a drug dealer to the area. Like Anslinger and Reagan before him, President Bush was warning the nation of an impending drug epidemic, one so virulent that it reached even to the immediate neighborhood of the White House, yet drugs had to be imported into the neighborhood to support the president's point. The president's staged event illustrates one of the critical rhetorical strategies of the government's response to drugs: arguing that drugs are not only ever-present but ever near, not only lurking within the nation but within your neighborhood. Like communists during the Cold War, when Senator Joe McCarthy and his allies forwarded claims that Reds were not only omnipresent but local, worming their way into the government itself, so the president's ability to purchase crack across the street from even his vaunted residence means that drugs are not only omnipresent but proximate. Pointing out that President Bush's drug claims were staged (or that McCarthy's Red claims were false) suggests that when the facts got in the way, drug warriors from Anslinger to Bush would not hesitate to manufacture fear.[2]

Although separated by a half-century, these two events demonstrate the continuation of the U.S. government's hysterical response to illicit narcotics, which, stretching from Anslinger up to the present, has been based on the assumption that some drugs (but not all) and some users (but not all) are so dangerous that they require the mobilization of the legislative, executive, judicial, penal, intelligence, and military institutions of the United States. This supposed threat has rallied the government and the public to support various campaigns against drugs, some of them so extreme that we have been taught to refer to them as part of a larger drug war. Much as recent foreign wars have relied upon the media's breathless representations of smart bombs and nationalism-pumping portrayals of heroic troops, so the drug war has produced an onslaught of media spectacles. In fact, the drug war has been waged largely by producing dramatic, made-for-television moments. Whether it was DEA agents posing atop a small mountain produced by a one-thousand-pound marijuana bust in 1982, Nancy Reagan and a live television crew accompanying the police on a warlike drug raid in South Central Los Angeles in 1985, or two eggs crackling in a frying pan in 1987—*this is your brain on drugs*—the drug war has been fought, in large part, by marshaling fear-mongering images meant to cower Americans. While these spectacles target individual fears about how drugs and drug users assault your neighborhood, your children, and your brain, the drug war has also relied on suggestions that it somehow defends the national security as well. Linking the fight against drugs to defending the nation has thus created another platform from which elites stir up nationalism to distract the citizenry from other issues, all while consolidating the power of the state. Indeed, during an era when the threat of communism was declining, and rendered before the tragedy of 9/11, the drug war filled a gap in our national consciousness by offering Americans a new series of enemies to be feared and pursued by the military, and to be punished and incarcerated by the prison-industrial complex.[3]

Contrary to the habitual fear-mongering driving the drug war and the prison-industrial complex, I argue that it is our civic responsibility to try to peer behind drug war spectacles to make sense of how the drug war has turned from a campaign against illegal drugs into a campaign for the mass incarceration of particular segments of America. Moreover, I argue that part of the collateral damage of this drug war is democracy itself. Indeed, the loudest media voices, intricate government-sponsored campaigns of panic and propaganda, strict draconian laws, and a new vocabulary of the dismissive now mute one of the fundamental principles of our modern democracy: honest debate. For almost any discussion of drugs in Washington or among the mass media is often ended before it starts by the shouting of a litany of pejorative terms, such as "pothead," "soft on crime," "crack whore," "drug fiend," "violent criminal," "drug lords," "gang bangers," and the like. These dismissive rhetorical terms are meant to eliminate all discussion of alternatives to mass incarceration and to portray select Others as beyond redemption or rehabilitation, hence pushing public policy and sentiment toward either the imprisonment or military eradication of the dreaded source of fear. And so, since President Reagan's announcement of a crack epidemic, prisoners serving drug sentences have become 53 percent of the federal prison population and 20 percent of state prison populations. Thus driven largely by the drug war and its corresponding rhetoric of dismissal—forget redemption, rehabilitation, or second chances, drug users must be dismissed as monsters—America's prison population has ballooned to more than 2 million citizens.[4]

At the same time as this domestic rush toward mass incarceration, the United States escalated a series of international antidrug campaigns in Central and South America. Initiated under the Clinton administration as Plan Colombia, and continued under the George W. Bush administration, including a 2007 budget request of $721 million for the Andean Counterdrug Initiative in Colombia alone, these efforts have led to the further militarization of the region, skyrocketing drug prices, and no discernable drop in drug usage in the United States. These investments have produced spectacles abroad as well. In March 2008, two particularly gruesome murders of leaders of FARC (the Revolutionary Armed Force of Colombia) were hailed as victories in the war. The first victim, Raul Reyes, believed to be FARC's second-in-command, was gunned down in a raid on the guerilla's camp in Ecuador, setting off a week of diplomatic stalemate and sovereignty boasts between Colombia, Ecuador, and Venezuela. The murder of the second victim, Manuel Jesus Muñoz, recalled the gangster mythology of yesteryear, as Muñoz's severed hand was turned in to authorities by one of his own men, who deserted the brigade. In addition, in a stunning move in May 2008, Colombian President Álvaro Uribe signed the extradition papers of fourteen paramilitary soldiers who were bound to face drug charges in the United States, while also attempting to hide the political scandal of his party's ties to drug warlords (such charges have engulfed his cabinet and family) while simultaneously negotiating a free-trade agreement with the United States. Like most wars, then, the drug war is metastasizing, leaping across national borders, encircling an ever-widening network of allies and enemies. Critics have argued that plans like Plan Colombia are less of an effort to stop drug production than covert means of funding a string of human-rights-abrogating regimes that, in the name of fighting drugs, use SWAT-like special forces and paramilitary hit squads to curtail oppositional parties and grassroots organizing by those opposed to U.S. interests. Both at home and abroad, then, the rise of a new punishing democracy is directly related to the drug war.[5]

This chapter responds to this domestic and increasingly international crisis by unpacking the rhetorical history of our approach to illegal drugs in the United States, thus enabling readers to understand how the prison boom of the last twenty-five years is driven largely by arrests stemming from the drug war. Moreover, I demonstrate how drug-related punishment strategies influence our national conversations on poverty, social justice, race, class, gender, incarceration, and education. Because these critical conversations are too often clouded by the hysteria caused by our drug warriors, this chapter attempts to reclaim a voice in this conversation, hence both enabling readers to rethink the drug war and the norms of democracy more broadly. Ultimately, I argue that abolishing the prison-industrial complex depends in large part on ending the disastrous and now decades-long war on drugs.

Governing Through Fear; or, The Drug War as the Engine of the Prison-Industrial Complex

The August 8, 2005, cover of *Newsweek* blared "The Meth Epidemic: Inside America's New Drug Crisis." The headline was imposed over the shadowy silhouette of a young man, baseball cap turned slightly to the right, who held a glass pipe to his lips as an orange flame cooked the end of the pipe and a single billow of smoke rose up. Inside the magazine, a collection of stories focused on the personal narratives of "lives destroyed" by methamphetamine, the institutional responses to "combat" this enemy, and the societal fears of the meth "plague" and its "widening path of destruction." While the ominous image on the front cover and the use of terminology like "war" and "epidemic" in the magazine are of keen interest, for the purpose of this chapter, the choice of "new" on the cover provides an entrance into my argument. For a critical component of the history of the drug war is this question of its recurrent "newness": as each fresh decade finds the nation overrun by a "new" drug menace (marijuana and psychedelics in the 1960s, heroin and speed in the 1970s, cocaine powder and crack-cocaine in the 1980s, and methamphetamine in the 1990s and beyond), so the nation succumbs to an imposed cultural amnesia and aggressively forgets the past as it succumbs to the "new" menace. In contrast to this habitual forgetting, this chapter will recount the rhetorical history of the drug war, which, throughout the generations, has depended on what I have called dismissive rhetoric and also an impregnable rhetoric, whereby the nation is constructed as a homogeneous entity whose boundaries must be defended against alien invaders. Indeed, drugs and their users have been constructed as much-loathed Others and as threats to national security, hence justifying both mass incarceration and more militaristic responses. Marshaling both dismissive rhetoric and impregnable rhetoric, each new generation of drug warriors has used the war on drugs to define alliances, recruit partisans, unite interests, and establish enemies to be either imprisoned or eliminated.[6]

In fact, over the past thirty years the drug war has become one of the major routes for building what can only be considered a parallel government, a shadow world where fighting drugs and drug users serves as an avenue for amassing governmental power. For example, ever since the most recent version of the war on drugs was instigated by the Nixon administration, this shadow world has relentlessly picked up momentum, enabling new generations of drug warriors to tap into an ever-increasing pool of federal money. Consider the growth of the National Drug Control budgets over the last thirty years: the Nixon administration spent $43 million in 1969, the Ford administration spent $382 million in 1977, the Carter administration spent $855 million in 1981, the Reagan administration spent $1.65 billion in 1982, the Clinton administration spent more than $17.9 billion in 2000, and the Bush administration spent more than $20 billion in 2004. When combined with state and local monies, the 2006 expenditures for the drug war exceeded $40 billion—that is *$40,000,000,000.*[7]

These ballooning budgets correlate with a population explosion in our local, state, and federal penal institutions. According to the Bureau of Justice Statistics, between 1982 and 1999 the percentage of defendants in U.S. district courts who were charged with a drug offense almost doubled, increasing from 18 to 32 percent. During this same time, and empowered by the passage of the Sentencing Reform Act in 1984, the proportion of time spent in prison for a federal drug offender rose from 47 percent of his or her sentence if convicted in 1982 to 87 percent in 1999. Likewise, the enactment of the Anti-Narcotic Drug Abuse Acts of 1986 and 1988 established mandatory minimum sentences for drug traffickers, hence removing judicial oversight, raising critical questions of constitutionality, and institutionalizing longer prison terms. Because of this increase in drug prosecutions and longer federally mandated prison terms, the state and federal prison population leapt from 400,000 in 1982 to nearly 2.3 million by 2008. This unprecedented explosion in the penal population was accompanied by the opening of more than 650 state and at least 54 federal correctional facilities. The number of local jail inmates also tripled, rocketing from approximately 200,000 in 1982 to 600,000 in 1999, while the number of adults on probation increased from more than 1.3 million to nearly 5 million persons. This explosion in the number of prisoners has been good for business, especially for private companies like Corrections Corporation, which manages more than 60 state and federal detention centers in 19 states. "It's as if they run high-occupancy hotels where people can check in but they can't check out," cracked Paul J. Rasplicka, manager of the AIM Capital Development Fund, which first added the stock to its portfolio in 2003. "State and federal governments' need exceeds available beds," Rasplicka cooed, "and [this] company has them." Although levels of violent crime and property crime remained the same over the last twenty-five years (and in some cases even decreased), the prison population and the industry that maintains it grew at an alarming pace—and the imprisonment of drug users and traffickers makes up a significant portion of this growing population. Indeed, the systematic intensification of the drug war has contributed mightily to building a nightmare scenario in which 7 million citizens are under the direct supervision or surveillance of state and federal law-enforcement agencies. In short, the prison-industrial complex is fueled largely by the drug war.[8]

From its central role in filling the cells of the prison-industrial complex, citizens might at least expect the drug war to have produced some discernable benefits for the health of the nation. For a heavily funded, government-sanctioned, military-planned operation of such massive scale—costing *$40 billion a year*—should produce a reduction in the availability of drugs and their rate of usage, eventually leading to a diminished need for imprisonment. Nevertheless, hundreds of thousands of families are in peril because of an ever-expanding (and ever-shifting) network of drug manufacturers and dealers. Eradication, interdiction, and elimination have been a stated goal of the U.S. government since Anslinger, yet illegal drugs are still readily available to meet consumer demand. Indeed, on the premise that any social policy should be evaluated based on its effectiveness, we can conclude that our national drug war is a failure. No less than the father of modern neo-conservatism, Milton Friedman, concurs in this conclusion; in a recent editorial about the drug war, he asked the following hard question: "can any policy, however high-minded, be moral if it leads to widespread corruption, imprisons so many, has so racist an effect, destroys our inner cities, wreaks havoc on misguided and vulnerable individuals and brings death and destruction to so many countries?" After decades of zero-tolerance policies and increasingly harsh criminal penalties, we have more than half a million people behind bars on drug charges—more than the total prison population in all Western Europe—yet drug use continues unabated. We are spending billions of dollars to keep fellow citizens locked up, and more billions militarizing the drug war effort at home and abroad, yet the federal government's own research demonstrates that drugs are now purer and more readily available than before the escalation of the drug war. Radicals, liberals, and even (some fiscally responsible) neoconservatives agree: the drug war is a catastrophe.[9]

Nonetheless, while the drug war is a failure in terms of stemming drug usage, it has become a profound success in terms of offering politicians a series of rhetorical tools for preempting discussions about alternative modes of public health. Thus, the ease with which questions of hospital rehabilitation for imprisoned users, decriminalization of narcotic use, or even legalization are pilloried in Washington as repudiations, according to President Reagan, of "everything America is." The vast totality of that statement indicates how the drug war's meanings are elastic enough to come to stand as metonymic condensations of America itself: to fight drugs is, simply, American; to think otherwise is, simply, un-American. Such simplistic generalizations dovetail with the purported national security implications of drugs, thus enabling drug warriors to speak, like former Cold Warriors, in a warlike, siege vocabulary, invoking precisely the everything-we-believe-in-is-under-attack hysteria that has enabled leaders since Nixon to speak of a drug war. Writing about our longstanding national need for enemies, Bob Ivie has argued that "the image of a threatening Other [waiting] for a chance to destroy America's freedom and democratic form of government" has always served useful political functions for those who want to govern through fear. As Ivie observes, such enemies fuel "a polarizing rhetoric of political demonization, which reduces difference to deviance and evil." Thus, although a failure in terms of public health, the drug war has proven rhetorically productive for those who find "a polarizing rhetoric of political demonization" useful for distracting the masses and justifying extreme governmental actions. The drug war is therefore less about ending America's longstanding addiction to various drugs than about providing political, military, and penal elites a useful set of terrifying images and loathed Others for governing through fear.[10]

From Temperance to War:
The Scapegoating of Drugs and Their Users

From as early as the antebellum period of U.S. history, when temperance activists advocated against the deleterious effects of the "demon rum," hence driving what came to be known as the "cold water frenzy," Americans have been worried, even obsessed, with the powers of alcohol and drugs. For example, Elizabeth Cady Stanton declared in 1852 that alcohol was "the unclean thing . . . to taste, see, smell or touch it, polluted female virtue." In his 1882 *Opium-Smoking in America and China*, Dr. H. H. Kane noted that "smokers coming East were constantly making converts, so that in a few months' time small and large towns, like Carson, Reno and many others, each had their smoking dens and their regular customers. Each new convert seemed to take a morbid delight in converting others, and thus a standing army was daily swelled by recruits." A 1902 pamphlet from the American Federation of Labor warned "there are hundreds, aye thousands, of our American boys and girls who have acquired the deathly habit and are doomed, hopelessly doomed." Speaking of cocaine in 1910, U.S. diplomat Dr. Hamilton Wright, one of the leading advocates for the passage of the forthcoming Harrison Act, declared "this new vice, the cocaine vice, the most serious to be dealt with, has proved to be a creator of criminals and unusual forms of violence, and it has been a potent incentive in driving the humbler negroes all over the country to abnormal crimes." Late twentieth and early twenty-first century constructions of the threat posed by drugs and its addicts appropriated and refigured these early flourishes to produce an amalgamated monster consisting of both individual corruption ("the unclean thing") and collective threats to national security ("a standing army"). Within such constructions, the infected self and an allegedly treacherous anti-society of users are drawn toward dangerous forms of deviance ("unusual forms of violence" and "abnormal crimes"). Finally, such portrayals depict all drug users as beyond care (they are "hopelessly doomed") and as racialized (as "humbler negroes" gone wrong).[11]

While the nation has thus been haunted by various manifestations of drugs and drug users since its inception, the United States had no significant federal control of drugs until the Harrison Anti-Narcotic Act of 1914. Upon acquisition of the Philippines in 1898, at the end of the Spanish-American war, the United States took a keen interest in controlling the burgeoning opium traffic out of the Philippines. Much as drug use among soldiers in and veterans of Vietnam became a lightning rod in the late 1960s, so drug-using troops and merchants returning from the conquest of the Philippines helped fuel a growing awareness that Americans were importing and using opiates. Thus wrapped up in one of the early moments of U.S. imperialism, the Harrison Act generated revenue by requiring anyone dealing in opiates or cocaine to register with the government, purchase tax stamps, and keep records of all transactions. As the act stated, "It shall be unlawful for any person required to register under the terms of this Act to produce, import, manufacture, compound, deal in, dispense, sell, [or] distribute, any of the aforesaid drugs without having registered and paid the special tax provided for in this section." At this stage of U.S. history, then, the concern was not in eradicating drugs and criminalizing drug users, but in taxing them. This question of taxation recalls the Whiskey Act of 1791 and the subsequent Whiskey Rebellion, which prodded Secretary of the Treasury Alexander Hamilton to describe the protested legislation "as a measure of social discipline" deployed, as Michael J. Graetz and Deborah H. Schenk noted, "to advance and secure the power of the new federal government." From its earliest moments, then, the U.S. government's claims for enforced moral righteousness and its attempts to legislate against vice have been entwined with the deeper motives of managing taxes, controlling commodities, and thus consolidating state power. While the Harrison Act neither outlawed the habitual use of opiates nor mentioned addicts, and while it avoided the mass opposition that followed the Whiskey Act, it aimed to limit users' access to drugs, for it was assumed that by applying a tax on users, thus raising the cost of a fix, recreational use would be curbed. If its terms were violated, the act called for a maximum sentence of five years imprisonment. Hardly the opening shot in a "war" against drugs, the Harrison Act seems in retrospect to be less about eradication than about management.[12]

In fact, soon after its passage, a number of cities, including New York, New Orleans, and Atlanta, opened narcotics clinics to monitor users, manage their habits, and wean addicts off their habit. This medically driven response outraged the Treasury Department, which interpreted the Harrison Act as trying to prevent this type of drug maintenance for the user; and so revenue agents of the Narcotic Division of the Prohibition Unit launched "visits" to these clinics and even began arresting doctors and druggists. The years following passage of the Harrison Act were thus witness to a rigorous argument among physicians, state health departments, and Treasury agents, often held before judges, over whether physicians had the right to prescribe opiates for addiction recovery and maintenance. In the midst of this confusion, Dr. Jin Fuey Moy of Pittsburgh was arrested for "supplying one addicted to the use of opium." Initially, a federal district judge agreed with the doctor, as did the Supreme Court in *U.S. v. Jin Fuey Moy* (1916), where Justice Oliver Wendell Holmes noted that "if opium is produced in any of the States[,] obviously the gravest question of power would be raised by an attempt of Congress to make possession of such opium a crime." Thus, the Supreme Court disagreed with the government's assertion that possession of a narcotic was evidence of a violation of the Harrison Act. For a moment, then, America seemed to understand that addiction was a medical issue best handled by doctors and clinics, not police and prisons.[13]

By 1920, as war hawks used World War I to trigger a new round of national security hysteria, the Harrison Act was interpreted from a much less progressive perspective. Indeed, federal powers on surveillance and punishment were enhanced by the wartime 1917 Espionage Act and the 1918 Sedition Act, which together gave the government unlimited authority to prosecute those who present a "clear and present danger that will bring about the substantive evils that Congress has a right to prevent." In *U.S. v. Doremus* (1919), the Supreme Court modified its 1916 opinion by ruling that "Congress, with full power over the subject [drugs, drug users, and responses to them], short of arbitrary and unreasonable action which is not to be assumed, inserted these provisions in an act specifically providing for the raising of revenue. Considered of themselves, we think they tend to keep the traffic aboveboard and subject to inspection by those authorized to collect the revenue." In the same year, the Court went on to note in *Webb v. United States* that prescribing narcotics solely for maintaining a patient's habit and avoiding withdrawal was not within the scope of legitimate medical practice and was therefore a violation of the law. The Court noted that "to call such an order for the use of morphine a physician's prescription would be so plain a perversion of meaning that no discussion of the subject is required." The notion that "no discussion is required" indicates an accelerating trend toward what I have called *a rhetoric of dismissal*, where certain subjects, in this case how to respond to drug users, are framed as beyond the pale of enlightened debate. Informed give-and-take, the foundation of democracy, is here replaced by dismissal and the creation of an abject Other worthy only of prosecution. Moreover, while the *Webb v. U.S.* decision maintained the revenue-raising powers of the Harrison Act, thus maintaining provisional market control over drugs, it also, for the first time, appropriated the power to pass judgment upon the medical questions of addiction—henceforward, addiction would be handled not by doctors but by police. These paradigm-shifting decisions led to the closing of legal narcotics clinics, which in turn led to an expanded black market for the now illegal substances. Thus, by criminalizing addicts and their fixes, these World War I–era decisions produced a new underworld of criminal drug dealers, middlemen, and users.[14]

These unfortunate legal decisions were matched by a rising culture of fear over the allegedly swelling ranks of addicts. These fears were triggered in large part by widely circulated government reports in 1918 and 1919 (both relying on imprecise data and fabricated World War I draft statistics) claiming that the addict population stood between 750,000 and 1,500,000 (a 1924 report would more accurately place the addict population at 110,000). Although A. G.

DuMez, the primary author of these reports and the chief expert for the U.S. Public Health Service, soon acknowledged that his numbers were erroneous, his inflated figures were nonetheless quoted routinely by both politicians and reformers like Captain Richmond P. Hobson, president of the International Narcotic Education Association and the World Narcotic Defense Association. Relying on the outrageous numbers of DuMez, Hobson delivered a now infamous address on the evening of March 1, 1928, via NBC's radio network, wherein he warned listeners that "upon the [drug] issue hangs the perpetuation of civilization, the destiny of the world and the future of the human race." Hobson described America's exploitation by dealers who would profit from this deadly, viral drug traffic, and he portrayed the effects of addiction in terms that sound straight out of a science fiction film: "so hopeless is the victim and so pitiless the master," intoned Hobson, "that heroin addicts are known as the Living Dead." Like later drug warriors, Hobson imagined the living dead as criminals "who constitute the primary cause of our alarming crime wave." Hobson drew upon medical terminology as well, arguing that the problem of drug use was "likened to a contagion" that transformed addicts into a menace that was "marching to the capture and destruction of the whole world." By the end of the radio broadcast, Hobson warned listeners that "narcotic drug addiction has become one of the major factors endangering the public health," and that the United States was "in the midst of a life and death struggle with the deadliest foe that has ever menaced its future." The threat was so dire, in fact, that Hobson saw it endangering "all the continents, the welfare of the peoples of today and the survival of generations unborn." Hobson thus expands what I have called *the rhetoric of proximity*, wherein drugs are portrayed as both omnipresent and local, to include a now universal claim, "all the continents," thus globalizing the threat. Moreover, he expands the threat of drugs from the temporal present into the indefinite future—*the destiny of the world and the future of the human race*—thus, like President Bush's Global War on Terrorism, opening the door to an infinite struggle, to what one critic has called "the forever war."[15]

Hobson's hysterics provided a blueprint—including viral metaphors, claims of both proximity and global consequences, indefinite warfare, and national security threats—still in use for the rhetorical construction of the drug problem and the drug user. His pathos-laden hyperbole was constructed in large part by employing that cornerstone of all appeals in moral politics: the false dilemma. Richard Lanham notes that this rhetorical device of division provides the appearance of choice, yet the choice is a stark binary where the alternative is unacceptable. Following the logic of this rhetorical fallacy, we are left with one choice, Hobson's choice, to fight for good in this "death struggle with the deadliest foe that has ever menaced [our] future"; to not fight this struggle, and to not fight it on Hobson's terms, thus amounts to treason. *You are either with him or against him.* Such argument strategies make appeals, then, not to informed discussion and deliberation but to governing through fear and intimidation. Indeed, like similar charges that faced the French in 1798 during the "half-war" with the United States, or that harassed socialists during the Great War, Hobson both creates an enemy/Other and attempts to scare his listeners into unquestioning compliance. Moreover, Hobson draws upon viral metaphors of contagion to portray *an enemy that is infectious*, most often attacking teenagers, especially young girls. The chronic repetition of this argumentative pattern—false dilemmas plus hyperbolic fear plus viral assault—escalated the national mood to dangerous and irrational heights, where the production of fear, rather than reasoned discourse, dominated the conversation. In fact, Hobson's fear-mongering was so persuasive that after his speech various new citizens' groups were formed and existing civic organizations were mobilized to help combat this "evil." These groups were active throughout the 1920s and 1930s. Then, in the wake of Hobson-like reports linking marijuana use with crime in the early thirties (mostly among Mexican and black youths in the south and southwest), there was renewed agitation for the regulation of marijuana. By 1935 marijuana was called America's newest drug menace; the Marihuana Tax Act was then passed in 1937, with restrictions and penalties modeled on the Harrison Act. The state surveillance and punishment of those miscreants Hobson called the living dead was thus expanding in lockstep with new cultural discourses that justified increasingly harsh, even military, responses to drugs and their users.[16]

Indeed, part of Hobson's and other antidrug reformers' successes stemmed from their ability to modernize the language of earlier temperance movements, calling upon longstanding images and narratives in the national memory and redeploying them to fit changed historical circumstances. Within the temperance tradition, dating from as early as the American Revolution, one of the most effective tools of persuasion was the memoir or testimony, which often told heartbreaking tales of drug- or alcohol-induced declines into ruin followed by heroic struggles to break the habit. Beginning with Dr. Benjamin Rush in the early Federalist era, these firsthand stories of addiction, often rendered in deeply religious tones, were supplemented by medical tracts wherein physicians noted that drunks and addicts tended to conceal their habits and would lie or steal to support them if necessary. By the late 1800s, morphine and laudanum addicts were characterized as contemptible as a consequence of their addiction.

Opium smokers, including many Chinese immigrants, had a darker reputation of vice and decadence and aroused hostility precisely as they entered the new labor markets of the rapidly industrializing West. By 1910, several accounts, both testimonial and medical, began linking "cocaine mania" to delinquency and crime perpetrated by urban youth. As David Courtwright demonstrates, by 1890 drug usage changed demographically, moving away from an addict population of middle-class medicinal users to lower-class and recreational users. With this shift, the connection between drug use, vice, crime, and particular populations circulated more potently in the public sphere. Thus, whereas the national narrative of addiction began around the time of the Revolution as a deeply religious script about sin and redemption, by the early twentieth century it had morphed into a discourse primarily about racial fear, economic uncertainty, and threatened national security.[17]

These longstanding national narratives and the World War I–era work of Hobson and others would crystallize under the leadership of Harry J. Anslinger, whom many consider the first federal drug czar of the United States. With the end of Prohibition, young Anslinger was out of a job as assistant commissioner of Prohibition, but he found his new crusade in 1930 with the formation of the Federal Bureau of Narcotics. An astute student of the national mood, Anslinger updated temperance story lines for the twentieth century by shifting their weight from religious concerns to racialized fears of uncontrollable youth expressed in mass-media-friendly scenes of carnage. For example, in an editorial run in *American Magazine* soon after his appointment, Anslinger shared stories from his "gore file," a collection of police-blotter narratives—most with little or no substantiation—causally linking marijuana usage with graphic violence:

> An entire family was murdered by a youthful addict in Florida. When officers arrived at the home, they found the youth staggering about in a human slaughterhouse. With an axe he had killed his father, mother, two brothers, and a sister. He seemed to be in a daze. . . . He had no recollection of having committed the multiple crimes. The officers knew him ordinarily as a sane, rather quiet young man; now he was pitifully crazed. They sought the reason. The boy said that he had been in the habit of smoking something which youthful friends called "muggles," a childish name for marijuana.[18]

Anslinger's sensational rhetoric strives to create hysteria with the rhetorical trope of *exemplum*, where a single startling anecdote represents a larger social dilemma; in this case, the graphic illustration of one allegedly drug-caused scene of violence works to generate an omnipresent fear of a lurking drug menace. The story is therefore not exceptional, a case of extreme behavior, but representative, an index of widespread danger. Moreover, in describing how the young man is possessed by the demon "muggles," thus converting him into a dazed killing monster, the story eschews any sense of tragedy, or sympathy for the victims, instead creating an anger-driven froth of retribution—readers are meant, then, to respond not with concern or caring but with righteous violence, or at least with enthusiastic support for heightened government intervention.

Anslinger's nationwide campaign of gory spectacles produced both the national prominence he had long coveted and created widespread panic about a new villain: the drug-addled young male running rampant through the streets of the country. In most instances, this enemy was colored by the racism of the day. For example, in 1937, in testimony before the Senate, Anslinger declared that "those who are habitually accustomed to the use of the drug are said to develop a delirious rage after its administration, during which they are temporarily irresponsible and liable to commit violent crimes. This narcotic is said to produce mental deterioration. Among some people the dreams produced are usually of an erotic character, [the drug] operates to destroy the will . . . its use frequently leads to insanity." For Anslinger's "gore file," this user, this destroyer, was often characterized by his dark skin (whether black, Chinese, or Latino), by his listening to jazz, and by his nefarious attempts to corrupt innocent white girls. Anslinger also introduced a scapegoat that would last for decades: popular culture (in this instance, it is the "satanic music" of jazz, in the future it will be heavy metal, rap music, and R-rated movies). As Thomas Szasz has noted, a *scapegoat* is similar to the Greek *pharmakos* (which described the person sacrificed in certain state rituals and ceremonies); on the scapegoat "all evil is loaded, [and] instead of being let loose and driven into the desert, is completely destroyed, together with its evil burden." Szasz continued, the pharmakos is an "expendable person, an object or thing: he or she was an effigy or symbol—the scapegoat—in a purification ceremony." The modern American pharmacological scapegoat, according to Szasz, shares this trait with the Greeks, but is also "an agent, participant in a counter-ceremony celebrating a substance tabooed by society's dominant ethic." Even as jazz was revitalizing American culture, building one of the great lasting traditions of our national heritage, Anslinger was depicting it as a hotbed of drug-spawned vice and miscegenation. It stands as a startling testament to our national addiction to racism that Anslinger's peers found such absurd claims persuasive—as if jazz and grass produce "human slaughterhouses" filled with "delirious rage"—yet his scapegoating tactics were well received by his contemporaries. In fact, Anslinger's unrelenting narrative of racialized fear led to a series of laws, including the Marihuana Tax Act of 1937 (which continued the revenue principle and punishments established via the Harrison Act, while also classifying marijuana as no different from cocaine or heroin), the Boggs Amendment of 1951 (which increased the punishments outlined in 1937 four times over, while establishing mandatory minimum sentencing), and the Narcotics Control Act of 1956 (which increased the punishments established in 1951 eight times over and included a separate penalty of ten to forty years for distribution to a minor, and from ten years to life, or death when a jury so recommended, if the drug was heroin)—these Anslinger-driven acts built the groundwork for the drug war-fueled prison boom that would soon follow.[19]

Ever attuned to the interweaving of legislation and culture, Anslinger capped his thirty year-long career as director of the FBN and chief architect of U.S. drug policy for the first half of the twentieth century by publishing his 1961 memoir, *The Murderers: The Story of the Narcotic Gangs*. The book introduced Frank Gin, a fantastic and diabolical character who stood as the symbolic condensation of the drug-induced evils Anslinger had committed his career to eradicating. An embodiment of "the living dead," the super-addict Gin was characterized as "wily, crafty, evil, and beyond redemption," a wayward Asian hurtling down the drug spiral and culminating in uncontrolled violence and ultimately homicide. Anslinger argued that the death penalty was the only reasonable response to Gin's crimes. Indeed, in *The Murderers* Anslinger concluded a career dedicated to the conviction that drug use was an act of both moral repugnance and political subversion; Gin and his kind required an unforgiving response, one that would, beginning with the presidency of Richard Nixon, soon be referred to as a war.[20]

Nixon's Declaration of War

Following the Anslinger precedent, President Richard Nixon arrived in the White House in 1969 intent on stomping out those who were "wily, crafty, evil, and beyond redemption." In response to the turbulent 1960s, which witnessed the dismantling "of a national order by the civil rights and anti–Vietnam war movements" and widespread drug use among multiple populations, Nixon and his followers boasted that they would reestablish law and order. With the nation reeling from the tumult of the decade, and with public discourse dominated by the language of war, Nixon used the occasion to transform crime control from a local issue addressed by traditional police into a national campaign that would be waged by new and increasingly militarized forces. And so, six months into his first term, Nixon announced his war on drugs by identifying drug trafficking as "public enemy number one." Nixon told Congress that "Within the last decade, the abuse of drugs has grown from essentially a local police problem into a serious national threat to the personal health and safety of millions of Americans. . . . A national awareness of the gravity of the situation is needed: a new urgency and concerted national policy are needed at the federal level to begin to cope with this growing menace to the general welfare of the United States." While speaking of national security, and hence implicitly linking the war against drugs to the fight in Vietnam, White House tapes reveal that Nixon understood the "abuse of drugs" in more domestic terms; in fact, one Nixon White House insider later reported that for the president, this "whole problem is really the blacks. The key is to devise a system that recognizes this while not appearing to." Nixon thus launched a drug war by appropriating Vietnam-era concerns over national security, by playing to a post–Summer of Love backlash politics that viewed American culture as spinning out of control, and by believing in private, although not saying so publicly, that the root of the problem was African Americans. Militarism, fear, and racism would thus drive the drug war for years to come. As Bob Ivie has noted, presidential war rhetoric "perceives [the] situation as a moral crisis, a challenge to American ideals"; indeed, by alluding to the Constitution ("the general welfare of the United States"), President Nixon argued that drugs and their users—especially "the blacks," now empowered by the Civil-Rights movement—challenge the very foundations of America and thus require a military response.[21]

The legislative buttress for Nixon's war would come in 1970, first with the passage of the Comprehensive Drug Abuse Prevention and Control Act, which included $220 million for enforcement, scheduled drugs into five rankings, and granted police the right to "no-knock" searches. The second plank in this new offensive was the Racketeering Influence and Corrupt Organizations Act, which produced the first secret "special grand juries" and relaxed the regulations for using illegally attained evidence for prosecutors. The same year, Congress doled out $3.55 billion to the Law Enforcement Assistance Administration to support state agencies with their drug efforts; as addressed by Julilly Kohler-Hausmann in this volume (see chapter 2), these funds encouraged the use of military expertise and hardware in the domestic fight against drugs. Three years later, the Rockefeller drug laws, named after then-governor Nelson Rockefeller, and signed on May 8, 1973, outlined a drastic increase in the penalties for selling two ounces or more of heroin, morphine, "raw or prepared opium," cocaine, or cannabis, including marijuana, or for possessing four or more ounces of the same substances. These acts made punishments for possession and sale the same as for second-degree murder: a minimum of 15 years to life in prison, and a maximum of 25 years to life in prison. The passage of the Rockefeller drug laws gave New York State the distinction of enforcing the toughest mandatory-minimum laws in the Unites States, but this approach was soon imitated by sixteen other states, including Michigan, which in 1978 enacted a "650-Lifer Law," calling for life imprisonment, without the possibility of parole, for the sale, manufacture, or possession of at least 1.45 pounds of cocaine or any Schedule I or Schedule II opiate. Thus following the lead of Anslinger and Nixon, federal and state authorities began a remarkable campaign: drug laws were toughened, prison sentences were lengthened, and the possibility of appeals and parole were reduced—and so America's prisons and jails began to swell with the fresh harvest of the war on drugs.[22]

As Nixon's drug war and the nascent prison-industrial complex were thus interwoven, so the American publicity machine again focused its attention on the drug problem. At the White House, on April 9, 1970, surrounded by executives from the major television networks, production companies, and advertising agencies, Richard Nixon somberly asked his audience for their support to help "warn our youth constantly against the dangers of drugs." Nixon declared, "drug traffic[king is] public enemy number one domestically in the United States . . . [therefore] we must wage a total offensive, worldwide, nationwide, government-wide, and, if I might say so, media-wide." A decade later, Ronald Reagan would remind the same audience that "the newsrooms and productions rooms of our media centers have a special opportunity to send alarm signals across the nation"; he then promised an "unshakable commitment to do what is necessary to end the drug war." Reagan's successor, President George H. W. Bush, then declared during his first televised address as president that "the gravest domestic threat facing our nation today is drugs." By this time the corporate mass media had learned that drug war imagery was good for sales, and so the nation was hit not only with presidential warnings but with offerings such as "American Vice: The Doping of a Nation," "48 Hours on Crack Street," and "Cocaine Country." Television and print media produced several stereotypical tropes in this era, notably the "crack house," "crack mother," and "crack baby," to scare the reading and viewing public into demonizing the crack user as a diabolical criminal. In fact, the three major networks and the *New York Times* and *Washington Post* quadrupled their news coverage of crack between 1983 and 1986; at the height of this frenzy, in April of 1986, public opinion polls found 2 percent of the population who considered drugs to be the nation's number-one problem, but six months later, in September, 13 percent of Americans polled by the same New York Times/CBS news poll said drugs were the number-one problem facing the country. The same month, ABC released its own poll that found 80 percent of respondents believed the U.S. faced a national drug crisis. Despite this hysteria, crack use was primarily isolated to just a few metropolitan areas, like Los Angeles and New York. Still, the message from the media and the White House screamed of a crack tide flooding across the shores of the United States. Jimmie Reeves and Richard Campbell have studied this period of media bombardment, concluding that it produced a "siege paradigm" in which the drug user was "treated as an alien Other on the order of a space invader." This otherworldly invader was of course made proximate by drawing upon longstanding racial stereotypes, thus producing a "color-coded mob of dehumanized inner-city criminals threaten[ing] the suburbs, small towns, schools, families, status, and authority of middle America." From Hobson's and Anslinger's theatrics to Nixon's "total offensive" to Presidents Reagan's and Bush's White House pronouncements to the mass-mediated fantasies of the 1980s, the drug war thus merged fears of national security with longstanding racial hatreds.[23]

Presidents Reagan and Bush did not leave it up to the media to monitor their war, as key pieces of legislation at home, and covert action abroad, escalated the stakes once again. With the nation symbolically under siege, Reagan imposed greater authority for Executive Branch regulations by establishing thirteen federal task forces from 1982 to 1984. These task forces marshaled the resources of countless assistant district attorneys and agents from, among others, the DEA, U.S. Customs, the FBI, Alcohol Tobacco and Firearms, the Internal Revenue Service, the Coast Guard, and the U.S. Marshals Service. At a special gathering in the White House for representatives of these task forces on June 24, 1982, President Reagan boldly declared that "we're rejecting the helpless attitude that drug use is so rampant that we're defenseless to do anything about it. We're taking down the surrender flag that has flown over so many drug efforts. We're running about the battle flag. We can fight the drug problem, and we can win." To win this battle, Reagan's signature legislation was passed, the Anti–Drug Abuse Act of 1986, which once again intensified the governmental response to drugs, most notably by instituting the formal classification of drugs as a national security problem, which in turn gave greater latitude to the use of military power. In addition, for the first time, a mandatory minimum sentence was assigned for a federal conviction for simple possession of any scheduled narcotic, thus aligning federal mandatory minimum sentencing policies with existing state policies and so again legislating longer prison terms. Two years later, a new cabinet position was created by the passage of the Anti–Drug Abuse Act of 1988, which also established a governmental epicenter for drug policy, the Office of National Drug Control Policy (ONDCP). Its primary objective was to "restore order and security to American neighborhoods, to dismantle drug trafficking organizations, to help people break the habit of drug use, and to prevent those who have never used illegal drugs from starting." These government initiatives were matched on a local scale by the growing neighborhood crime watch movement; at the same time, a major educational push was made in public schools to "D.A.R.E." kids to stay off drugs. And so, by 1988, drug warriors wielded a formal seat in the president's cabinet, a massive institutional apparatus of support, a series of legislative victories, a growing network of military and policing task forces, and an increasingly vitriolic public relations arm.[24]

By the summer of 1989, the newly sworn-in President George H. W. Bush was ready to deploy these new tools in the ever-expanding drug war. In his September 6 address to the nation, he proposed that "we enlarge our criminal justice system across the board [and] when requested, we will for the first time make available the appropriate resources of America's armed forces." Defense Secretary Dick Cheney soon ordered the military to develop plans for "operational support" to ensure a "more aggressive and robust" U.S. presence in Latin America. The dramatic arrest of General Manuel Noriega, during the invasion of Panama at the end of the year, clearly demonstrated the "more aggressive and robust" nature of U.S. interdiction efforts, in which protecting imperial interests and fighting drugs were now linked. At home, President Bush warned that "American cocaine users need to understand that our nation has a zero tolerance for casual drug use. . . . [We must] face this evil as a nation united, victory over drugs is our cause, a just cause." The president's first "drug czar" of the ONDCP, William Bennett, knew where to locate this evil: in the "criminogenic communities—where the social forces that create predatory criminals are far more numerous and stronger than the social forces that create decent, law-abiding citizens." Even while President Bush waged his drug war by invading foreign nations and threatening Americans who broke the law, and even while the newly formed ONDCP was weaving together private corporations, research institutes, and government officials into a massive new institutional apparatus for fighting drugs, so the drug czar invoked nineteenth-century notions of biological determinism to explain how some communities were genetically incapable of producing the right kinds of citizens—like Noriega, the monsters populating these "criminogenic communities" would need to be locked up in the name of protecting the nation and fighting drugs.[25]

Conclusion: Taking the Fight to the Enemy
by Militarizing the Drug War

On September 20, 2002, the sounds of teenage laughter and the flash of video game guns and lasers in an arcade in Soacha, a town outside Bogotá, Colombia, were interrupted as seven masked men stormed in and announced the commencement of a "cleansing operation." Brandishing handguns and Uzis, the men opened fire, killing Andres Salazar (13), Fabio Bayona (16), and brothers Hernán (19) and Henry González (22). As the men cavalierly walked out of town, they shot up several homes and promised more death if silence was not maintained. Although the United Self-Defense Forces of Colombia (AUC), the leading right-wing paramilitary group of Colombia, officially denied responsibility, several of the shooters were later identified as members of the AUC. To date, no arrests have been made, and many Soacha residents, following a steady stream of Colombians over the last ten years, have packed up their belongings and fled their homeland. This tragic event demonstrates one of the many paradoxes of the U.S. drug war: in the name of defending democracy at home by targeting drug dealers abroad, the United States has funneled billions of dollars to the Colombian government, which has (depending on your sources) either armed or turned a blind eye to the murderous actions of paramilitary outfits like the AUC. Alongside these legal federal subsidies for carnage in Colombia, American dollars that go to the purchase of cocaine and crack return to Colombia as support for both the right-wing paramilitaries, like the AUC, and their enemies, who include equally murderous leftist guerrillas such as the Revolutionary Armed Forces of Colombia (FARC). No one knows how many illegal drug-derived dollars have flowed south, but since 2000 the total U.S. aid to the Colombian government has exceeded $6 billion, making Colombia the fifth-largest consumer of U.S. aid (behind only Israel, Egypt, Iraq, and Afghanistan). Thus, as both drug consumers and drug warriors, Americans are funding a decades-long civil war in Colombia. And while neither the United States-led drug war nor the Colombian civil war has seemed to slow the flow of drugs into consumers' hands, the murdered youth of Soacha testify that U.S. interdiction efforts are failures, for in this war, as in all others, the victims are drawn largely from the innocent.[26]

The botched U.S. engagements in Colombia flow from Plan Colombia, a ten point agenda signed into law on July 13, 2000 (P.L. 106–246). The plan was meant to end Colombia's civil war be reviving its economy, streamlining its fiscal situation, modernizing its military, supporting its counter-narcotics efforts, advancing respect for human rights, seeking alternative modes of economic development, increasing social participation, accelerating human development, pursuing domestic peace, and linking these goals to larger, international initiatives. Since its passage, however, the military has received most of the U.S. aid sent to Colombia, and the economic and fiscal stimulants not tied to the military have been managed by the International Monetary Fund and World Bank to coincide with U.S. economic interests. Less of a Marshall Plan than a military agreement, Plan Colombia has thus outraged critics both in the United States and abroad. Consider how the money is spent: in its first year, the Plan Colombia aid package totaled $1.3 billion, of which $860.3 million was marked for Colombia, $180 million went to neighboring countries' counter-narcotic efforts, $223.5 million was used to increase budgets at various U.S. agencies, and the remaining $55.3 million was classified. Of the hundreds of millions of dollars sent to Colombia, more than 80 percent was earmarked for an upgrade of military resources, including the purchase of 16 UH-60 Black Hawk helicopters at a total cost of $208 million, 30 UH-1H Super-Huey II helicopters at a total of $40 million, 18 UH-1H Huey II helicopters for the Colombian National Police at a total of $40 million, and support and maintenance for the new helicopter fleet at $40 million. Plan Colombia thus included a wideranging list of social goals, with fighting drugs and revitalizing local democratic practices standing as leading parts of the proposal, yet its implementation has led to one major result: the further militarization of the region with hardware purchased from U.S. weapons manufacturers.[27]

Officially, the plan's military aid is assigned for the eradication of Colombia's coca and poppy fields; unofficially, the weaponry destroys leftist guerillas. By proxy, some of Plan Colombia's aid finds its way into the coffers of the AUC and other right-wing paramilitaries, who sometimes work under the direct supervision of the Colombian military. Senator Patrick Leahy concluded, "We give more aid to the military, [and] they give more aid to the paramilitaries." And, in a cruel historical irony, as reported by the RAND National Defense Research Institute, most of the more than 3 million illegal arms in Colombia are the recycled remains of U.S. Cold War–era weapons pilfered from stockpiles in Nicaragua, Honduras, and El Salvador—the current civil war is thus fought both with new weapons purchased with U.S. tax dollars and used weapons that amount to the spoils of President Reagan's Iran-Contra Affair.[28]

The amnesia-fueled "new"-ness that greets each reinvention of the drug paradigm is not isolated inside the United States, as Plan Colombia has been repackaged as the Mérida Initiative, a 2007 agreement between the United States and Mexico that responds to issues escalated since the passage of NAFTA. For the free-trade promises of NAFTA, which is openly referred to as the

North American Drug Trade Agreement by U.S. Customs and DEA agents, have largely backfired, as more than 50 percent of all illegal drugs cross the border on the free-trade highways between Mexico and the United States, and have produced an explosion of drug-related industry and mayhem at our southern border. In May 2008, Edgar Eusebio Millán Gómez, the public face of Mexico's response to illegal drugs, became the highest-ranking law enforcement official killed since the launch of Mexican president Felipe Calderón's renewed efforts to combat his country's drug cartels (he was not the first, however, for six other high-ranking law-enforcement officers were killed the week before Gómez's death). Many observers are concerned that this assassination will give renewed confidence to drug cartels blamed for 6,000 killings in the past two and a half years. "This could have a snowball effect, even leading to the risk of ungovernability," Luís Astorga, a Mexico City–based sociologist, said in an interview. "It indicates terrible things, a level of weakness in our institutions—they can't even protect themselves." In response to this escalating crisis, the Mérida Initiative called for the United States to provide an initial $500 million to Mexico over the first twelve months ($1.4 billion over three years) to provide training for the police and tools to dismantle drug cartels, including helicopters, surveillance planes, drug-sniffing dogs, and computer software to enhance surveillance and tracking capabilities. Secretary of Defense William Gates urged a reluctant Congress to see the big picture: "It has to do with counter-narcotics, but it also has to do with protecting national air space and maritime boundaries." And so, even while the drug war fails at home, in Colombia, and in Mexico, its supporters return again and again to the same solutions, the same rhetoric, and the same tragic results.[29]

In short, while Plan Colombia, the Andean Initiative, and now the Mérida Initiative are sold to the public in the name of fighting the drug war, their real goals are to protect the interests of U.S. weapons manufacturers and other global economic elites. Consider, for example, the staggering fact that multinational corporations control 80 percent of Colombia's economic activity, including its lucrative petroleum and mineral industries. Moreover, the Colombian army provides security for oil-drilling sites in return for cash, essentially turning the nation's armed forces into postmodern Pinkertons, hired guns charged with protecting the privileges of the rich. Meanwhile, the FARC rebels hold much of the south of Colombia, which may contain billions of barrels of oil beneath its farms and forests. Oil giants like BP and Occidental covet that oil, meaning it is difficult to discern whether efforts against the rebels are being launched in the name of fighting drugs, energizing the democratic process, or opening up new oilfields to multinational expropriation. While the international political and economic stakes of the situation are both significant and confusing, it is clear that Plan Colombia, the Andean Initiative, and the Mérida Initiative amount to a form of drug-war-justified corporate welfare at home. For example, from the 2000 Plan Colombia budget, most of $750 million in military assistance was spent on contracts with U.S. corporations—it is called foreign aid, but the money ends up back on Wall Street. Private corporations join in the frenzy as well, by supplying the spray planes that spread tons of Monsanto's Roundup (glyphosate) on suspected drug fields (devastating the surrounding ecosystems), and leasing surveillance planes that come bundled together with ongoing maintenance, logistics, and training contracts. Such dealings are so lucrative that at least six U.S. military specialty companies have set up operations in the region. Two Virginia-based companies, DynCorp and Military Professional Resources, Inc., or MPRI, are completing contracts related to logistical support and training of Colombian police and counterinsurgency forces. Like the boondoggles in Afghanistan and Iraq, then, where fighting terrorism justifies a wide range of corporate-enriching actions, so the drug war has produced a situation in which Colombia, and soon Mexico, has become a feeding trough for U.S. interests. The drugs continue to flow, but so do the contracts—thus, like that other "forever war," the drug war has become a permanent funding channel for military contractors.[30]

Meanwhile, back at home, the political capital gained by the continued demonization of the drug user is employed by political elites of both parties to restrict civil liberties, to increase the state's surveillance of the population, to ensure greater reliance upon the military-industrial complex for defense, to scapegoat the user as a spectacle useful for distracting attention from larger social issues, and to further expand the prison-industrial complex. Since interdiction efforts have proven to be failures ever since Anslinger's time, why does the public continue to support these efforts? This chapter has sought to answer that question by showing how, for most of the twentieth century and now twenty-first century, illegal drugs and their users have been considered the enemy of a "war." The critical purpose of the declaration of war is to sow fear, for this simple word eliminates nuance and context; environments of fear and danger, whether real or imagined, are not conducive to broad discussions of complicated crises and their possible solutions, instead leading the nation to engage, again and again, in the rhetoric of dismissal. Instead of neighbors in need of care, then, we are taught to see loathsome Others, "the living dead," a veritable army of racialized monsters. Because these Others are beyond concern, and because the nation is supposedly under threat from them, Americans have been taught since Hobson and Anslinger that to speak out against the drug war is to risk being labeled a traitor. And so unity is maximized while dissent is minimized, marginalized, or even eliminated altogether. The effect of this drug-war-induced language of dismissal and fear and mandatory patriotism is to foster conformity, dispel dissent, and banish doubt. The stunning success of this strategy may be seen in the fact that the prison-industrial complex and drug war continue to grow, even while the war in Iraq garners increasing opposition. Indeed, as this chapter has demonstrated, it may well be the case that the "living dead" targeted by the drug war stand as our longest-running and most feared national enemy, albeit one we are not likely to defeat with mass incarceration or other military responses. In summary, if we hope to transform our punishing democracy by abolishing the prison-industrial complex, then one good starting place would be to begin questioning the drug war, America's longest-running and most spectacular failure.

Notes

1. Blease and Anslinger's quotations are from Harry J. Anslinger and Will Oursler, *The Murderers: The Story of the Narcotic Gangs* (New York: Farrar, Straus, & Cudahy, 1961), 20; for background on Anslinger and this early phase of the drug war, see Douglas Valentine, *The Strength of the Wolf: The Secret History of America's War on Drugs* (New York: Verso, 2004): 6–189; Melvin L. Hanks, *NARC: The Adventures of a Federal Agent* (New York: Hastings House, 1973): 162–166; Harry J. Anslinger, *The Protectors: The Heroic Story of the Narcotics Agents, Citizens, and Officials in Their Unending, Unsung Battles against Organized Crime in America and Abroad* (New York: Farrar, Strauss, 1964): 6–50; and Maurice Helbrant, *Narcotic Agent* (New York: Vanguard, 1941): 273–281.

2. President Reagan is quoted from his 14 September 1986 "Address to the Nation on the Campaign against Drug Abuse," accessed from the Reagan Library at www.reagan.utexas.edu/archives/speeches/1986/091486a.htm; the president was joined that night by his wife, Nancy, who introduced her infamous "Just Say No" campaign; President George H. W. Bush is quoted from the "Text of the Address by President Bush," *Washington Post* (6 September 1989), A18; Michael Isikoff, "Drug Buy Set Up for Bush Speech; DEA Lured Seller to Lafayette Park," *Washington Post* (22 September 1989), A1; on the elegant tragedy of Lafayette Park, see Stephen John Hartnett, "Walking amidst Heroes: Celebrating the Enlightenment and the Persistence of Democracy," *Cultural Studies <—> Critical Methodologies* 8, no. 2 (2008): 187–223; on the production of fear, see Erica R. Meiners, *Right to Be Hostile: Schools, Prisons, and the Making of Public Enemies* (New York: Routledge, 2007).

3. On the production of drug war hysteria, see Jimmie L. Reeves and Richard Campbell, *Cracked Coverage: Television News, the Anti-Cocaine Crusade, and the Reagan Legacy* (Durham, NC: Duke University Press, 1994); Nancy D. Campbell, *Using Women: Gender, Drug Policy, and Social Justice* (New York: Routledge, 2000); and

Carol A. Stabile, *White Victims, Black Villains: Gender, Race, and Crime News in U.S. Culture* (New York: Routledge, 2006); for discussions of how nationalism requires enemies and thus requires order and security, see Robert L. Ivie, *Dissent from War* (Bloomfield, CT: Kumarian, 2007), Jeremy Engels, "Disciplining Jefferson: The Man within the Breast and the Rhetorical Norms of Producing Order," *Rhetoric & Public Affairs* 9 (2006): 411–35, and *The Morality of Nationalism*, ed. Robert McKim and Jeff McMahan (London: Oxford University Press, 1997); for an overview of the relationships among mass-mediated fear, state security, and mass imprisonment, see PCARE, "Fighting the Prison-Industrial Complex: A Call to Communication and Cultural Studies Scholars to Change the World," *Communication and Critical Cultural Studies* 4, no. 4 (2007): 402–20.

4. Population information from the Bureau of Justice Statistics (hereafter BJS), *Prisoners in 2006* (Washington, DC: U.S. Department of Justice, 2007): 24–26, Appendix tables 9, 10, and 13; according to the Justice Department, 5.3 percent of drug offenders in federal prisons are serving time for possession while 91.4 percent are serving time for trafficking and 3.3 percent are in for "other" drug-related offenses; in addition, 27.9 percent of drug offenders in state prisons are serving time for possession while 69.4 percent are serving time for trafficking and 2.7 percent are in for "other" (see BJS, *Drug Use and Dependence, State and Federal Prisoners, 2004* [Washington, DC: U.S. Department of Justice, 2006], 4); on the rhetorical power of Othering within the drug war, see Stephen John Hartnett, "A Rhetorical Critique of the Drug War and the 'Nauseous Pendulum' of Reason and Violence," *Journal of Contemporary Criminal Justice* 16, no. 3 (2000): 247–71.

5. On U.S. international adventures and expenditures, see Office of National Drug Control Policy (hereafter ONDCP), *National Drug Control Strategy, FY 2007 Budget Summary* (Washington, DC: U.S. Department of State, 2006), accessed from www .whitehousedrugpolicy.gov/publications/policy/ 07budget/dept_state.pdf; Angel Rabasa and Peter Chalk, *Colombian Labyrinth: The Synergy of Drugs and Insurgency and Its Implications for Regional Instability* (Santa Monica, CA: RAND Corporation, 2001): 62–63; *Drug Trafficking in the Americas*, ed. Bruce M. Bagley and William O. Walker III (Miami, FL: University of Miami, North/South Center, 1994); and Peter Dale Scott, *Cocaine Politics: Drugs, Armies, and the CIA in Central America* (Berkeley: University of California Press, 1998); for evidence of the complex drug-war-fueled interweaving of domestic policing and international politics, see Juan Forero, "Colombia's Coca Survives U.S. Plan to Uproot It," *New York Times* (19 August 2006), A1; Simon Romero, "Settling of Crisis Makes Winners of Andes Nations, While Rebels Lose Ground," *New York Times* (9 March 2008), A12; Simon Romero, "Colombia Extradites 14 Paramilitary Leaders to the United States," *New York Times* (14 May 2008), A6.

6. Quotations from David J. Jefferson, "America's Most Dangerous Drug," *Newsweek* (8 August 2005), 41–48; for a global history of illegal drugs, see Richard Davenport-Hines, *The Pursuit of Oblivion: A Global History of Narcotics* (New York: W.W. Norton, 2002); on U.S. responses, see Eva Bertram, Morris Blachman, Kenneth Sharpe, and Peter Andreas, *Drug War Politics: The Price of Denial* (Berkeley: University of California Press, 1996); on the notion of chronic forgetfulness as a key ingredient of U.S. national consciousness, see Michael Rogin, "'Make My Day!': Spectacle as Amnesia in

Imperial Politics [and] the Sequel," in *Cultures of United States Imperialism*, ed. Amy Kaplan and Donald E. Pease (Durham, NC: Duke University Press, 1993), 499–534.

7. For a budget timeline, see U.S. Congress, "Hearings on Federal Drug Enforcement before the Senate Committee on Investigations, 1975 and 1976" (Washington, DC: U.S. Government Printing Office, 1976); ONDCP, *National Drug Control Strategy, 1992: Budget Summary* (Washington, DC: U.S. Government Printing Office, 1992), 214; ONDCP, *National Drug Control Budget, Executive Summary, Fiscal Year 2002* (Washington, DC: Executive Office of the President, 2001), 2; ONDCP, *National Drug Control Strategy: FY 2003 Budget Summary* (Washington, DC: Office of the President, 2002), 6; and National Research Council, National Academy of Sciences, "Informing America's Policy on Illegal Drugs: What We Don't Know Keeps Hurting Us" (Washington, DC: National Academy Press, 2001), 1; on the production of a drug war-fueled parallel government, see Bertram et al., *Drug War Politics*, 102–50; Hartnett, "Rhetorical Critique of the Drug War"; and Scott, *Cocaine Politics*.

8. For more on the relationship between drug arrests and the prison population, see BJS, *Prisoners in 1996* (Washington, DC: U.S. Department of Justice, 1997), 2–9; BJS, *Prisoners in 2004* (Washington, DC: U.S. Department of Justice, 2005), 10; BJS, *Federal Drug Offenders, 1999, with Trends 1984–99* (Washington, DC: U.S. Department of Justice, 2001), 7; BJS, *Substance Dependence, Abuse, and Treatment of Jail Inmates, 2002* (Washington, DC: U.S. Department of Justice, 2005), 6; on the consequences of mandatory minimums, see Federal Bureau of Investigation, *Uniform Crime Reports, 1996* (Washington, DC: U.S. Department of Justice, 1997), 62; BJS, *Sourcebook of Criminal Justice Statistics, 1998 and 2000* (Washington, DC: U.S. Department of Justice, 2001); Department of Health and Human Services, *Preliminary Estimates from the Drug Abuse Warning Network, 1999* (Rockville, MD: U.S. Department of Health and Human Services, 1998), 58; Ernest Drucker, "Drug Prohibition and Public Health: 25 Years of Evidence," *Public Health Reports* 114, no. 1 (1999), 14–29; for information on prison building, see Elliott Currie, *Crime and Punishment in America* (New York: Henry Holt, 1998), 3; Sarah Lawrence and Jeremy Travis, "The New Landscape of Imprisonment: Mapping America's Prison Expansion" (Washington, DC: Urban Institute/Justice Policy Center, 2004), 1–5, 8–10; on the increase in other expenditures associated with the prison-industrial complex, see BJS, *Sourcebook of Criminal Justice Statistics, 1996* (Washington, DC: U.S. Department of Justice, 1997), 20; Executive Office of the President, *Budget of the United States Government, Fiscal Year 2002* (Washington, DC: U.S. Government Printing Office, 2001): 134; BJS, *Justice Expenditure and Employment in the United States, 1999* (Washington, DC: U.S. Department of Justice, 2002), 1; BJS, *Justice Expenditure and Employment in the United States, 2001* (Washington, DC: U.S. Department of Justice, 2004), 2; Rasplicka as quoted in Ian McDonald, "Corrections Corp. Finds Success in Stir," *Wall Street Journal* (25 September 2006), C1.

9. On the futility of the drug war, see James Gray, *Why Our Drug Laws Have Failed: A Judicial Indictment of War on Drugs* (Philadelphia: Temple University Press, 2001); Dan Baum, *Smoke and Mirrors: The War on Drugs and the Politics of Failure* (New York: Little, Brown, 1997); Elliott Currie, *Crime and Punishment in America: Why the Solutions to America's Most Stubborn Social Crisis Have Not Worked—and What*

Will (New York: Owl, 1998); *Drugs, Crime, and the Criminal Justice System*, ed. Ralph Weisheit (Cincinnati, OH: Anderson, 1990); Arnold S. Trebach, *The Great Drug War, and Rational Proposals to Turn the Tide* (Bloomington, IN: Unlimited, 2005); and Ben Wallace-Wells, "How America Lost the War on Drugs—After Thirty-Five Years and $500 Billion, Drugs Are as Cheap and Plentiful as Ever: An Anatomy of a Failure," *Rolling Stone* (27 November 2007): 90–119; Milton Friedman, "There's No Justice in the War on Drugs," *New York Times* (11 January 1998), WK19 (Sunday editorial section).

10. President Reagan is quoted from his 14 September 1986 "Address to the Nation on the Campaign Against Drug Abuse," accessed from the Reagan Library at www.reagan.utexas.edu/archives/ speeches/ 1986/091486a.htm; Ivie, *Dissent from War*, 9.

11. Elizabeth Cady Stanton quoted in Thomas Metzger, *The Birth of Heroin and the Demonization of the Dope Fiend* (Port Townsend, WA: Loompanics, 1998), 91; H. H. Kane, *Opium-Smoking in America and China* (New York: Putnam, 1882), 4; Samuel Gompers, *Some Reasons for Chinese Exclusion: Meat vs. Rice; American Manhood against Asiatic Coolieism: Which Shall Survive?* (Washington, DC: American Federation of Labor, 1902), reproduced in the *Congressional Record*, 57th Congress, 1st Session, 1902, Senate Document 137, quotation from p. 22; Wright quoted in John Helmer, *Drugs and Minority Oppression* (New York: Seabury, 1975), 12; on the history of temperance movements, see Mark E. Lender and James K. Martin, *Drinking in America: A History*, rev. ed. (New York: Free Press, 1987); W. J. Rorabaugh, *The Alcoholic Republic: An American Tradition* (Oxford, England: Oxford University Press, 1979); Joseph R. Gusfield, *Symbolic Crusade: Status Politics and the American Temperance Movement*, 2nd ed. (Urbana: University of Illinois Press, 1986), and Scott C. Martin, *Devil of the Domestic Sphere: Temperance, Gender, and Middle-Class Ideology, 1800–1860*, (Dekalb: Northern Illinois University Press, 2008).

12. *Harrison Narcotics Act of 1914*, Public Law 223, 63d Congress, 3d sess. (17 December 1914), 785–90; Alexander Hamilton quoted on the Whiskey Tax in Samuel E. Morrison, *The Oxford History of the United States, 1783–1917* (London: Oxford University Press, 1927), 182; Michael J. Graetz and Deborah H. Schenk, *Federal Income Taxation: Principles and Policies* (New York: Foundation Press, 2005), 4.

13. On the narcotic clinics and the story of Jin Fuey Moy, see David F. Musto, *The American Disease: Origins of Narcotic Control*, 3rd ed. (New York: Oxford University Press, 1999), 128–182; Davenport-Hines, *Pursuit of Oblivion*; Bertram et al., *Drug War Politics*, 61–77; and *U.S. v. Jin Fuey Moy*, 241 U.S. 394 (1916).

14. For the Supreme Court's "clear and present" danger test to justify the 1917 Espionage Act and the 1918 Sedition Act, see *Schenck v. United States*, 249 U.S. 47 (1919); *U.S. v. Doremus*, 249 U.S. 86 (1919); *Webb v. United States*, 249 U.S. 96 (1919); for more on this early era of drug legislation and legal rulings, see Kurt Hohenstein, "Just What the Doctor Ordered: The Harrison Anti-Narcotic Act, the Supreme Court, and the Federal Regulation of Medical Practice, 1915—1919," *Journal of Supreme Court History* 26, no. 3 (2001): 231–56; Victor V. Anderson, "The Alcoholic as Seen in Court," *Journal of Criminal Law and Criminology* 7 (March 1917): 89–95, accessible at http://heinonline.org; Alfred Lindesmith, *The Addict and the*

Law (Bloomington: Indiana University Press, 1965); Rufus King, *The Drug Hang-Up: America's Fifty-Year Folly* (Springfield, IL: Charles C. Thomas, 1972); and Musto, *American Disease*, 128–41.

15. The extent of opiate addiction during this period is analyzed in David T. Courtwright, *Dark Paradise: A History of Opiate Addiction in America* (Cambridge, MA: Harvard University Press, 2001), 9–34, where Courtwright estimates no more than 250,000 addicts after 1920; for a sample of how the media took up DuMez's claims, see "A Million Drug Fiends," *New York Times* (13 September 1918): 10, "The Drug Menace in America," *American Review of Reviews* (September 1919): 331; for DuMez's updated national figures, see the 1924 report, Lawrence Kolb and A. G. DuMez, "The Prevalence and Trend in Drug Addiction in the United States and Factors Influencing It," *Public Health Reports* 39 (May 1924): 1179–1204; Richmond Hobson, "The Struggle of Mankind against Its Deadliest Foe" (Broadcast 1 March 1928), transcript reprinted in *Narcotic Education* 1 (1928): 51–54; Hobson received the Medal of Honor for his role in the Spanish-American War; upon returning stateside, he was elected a U.S. Representative from Alabama (1905–15) and began a long career of public speaking about and writing against the evils of alcohol and drugs; his books include *Alcohol and the Human Race* (1919), *Narcotic Peril* (1925), *Modern Pirates: Exterminate Them* (1927), and *Drug Addiction: A Malignant Racial Cancer* (1933); for more on DuMez and Hobson, see Susan L. Speaker, "The Struggle of Mankind against Its Deadliest Foe: Themes of Counter-Subversion in Anti-Narcotics Campaigns, 1920–1940," *Journal of Social History* 34, no. 3 (2001): 591–611, and Arnold Jaffe, *Addiction Reform in the Progressive Age* (New York: Arno, 1981), 94–114; on the notion of an endless "forever war," see Mark Danner's "Taking Stock of the Forever War," *New York Times Sunday Magazine* (11 September 2005), available at www.markdanner.com/nyt/091105_taking.htm.

16. On false dilemmas, see Richard Lanham, *A Handlist of Rhetorical Terms* (Berkeley: University of California Press, 1991), 54; for the Othering of the French in 1798, see James Morton Smith, *Freedom's Fetters: The Alien and Sedition Laws and American Civil Liberties* (Ithaca, NY: Cornell University Press, 1956), 1–34, 159–87; for similar attacks against socialists during World War I, see Howard Zinn, *A People's History of the United States* (New York: Perennial, 1980), 314–367.

17. For examples of drug memoirs, see Thomas de Quincey, *Confessions of an Opium Eater* (London: John Taylor, 1826); John H. Hughes, "The Autobiography of a Drug Fiend," *Medical Review of Reviews* 22 (1916): 27–43, 105–20, 173–90; and D. F. MacMartin, *Thirty Years in Hell: The Confessions of a Drug Fiend* (Topeka, KS: Capper, 1921); for an overview of this genre, see H. Wayne Morgan, *Drugs in America: A Social History, 1800–1980* (Syracuse, NY: Syracuse University Press, 1981), 91–93.

18. Harry J. Anslinger "Marihuana: Assassin of Youth," *American Magazine* 124, no. 1 (1937): 18–19, and 150–53, accessed from www.redhousebooks.com/galleries/assassin.htm. This article was one of several key components of Anslinger's campaign, as it was published the same year as the release of the film by the same name; on the rhetorical work of *exemplum*, see Lanham, *Handlist of Rhetorical Terms*, 31.

19. Statement from Harry Anslinger quoted in House Committee on Ways and Means, *Taxation of Marihuana: Hearings on H.R. 6385*, 75th Congress, 1st sess. (April

27–May 4, 1937), 29–30; Thomas Szasz, *Ceremonial Chemistry: The Ritual Persecution of Drugs, Addicts, and Pushers* (Syracuse, NY: Syracuse University Press, 2003), 19–27; *Marihuana Tax Act of 1937*, Public Law 553, 75th Congress, 1st sess. (2 August 1937), 551–56; *Boggs Act of 1951*, Public Law 255, 82nd Congress, 1st sess. (2 November 1951),767; *Narcotic Control Act of 1956*, Public Law 728, 84th Congress, 2nd sess. (18 July 1956), 567–76.

20. See Harry J. Anslinger, *The Murderers: The Story of the Narcotics Gangs* (New York: Farrar, Straus, and Cudahy, 1961): 25; for more on Anslinger's use of the Frank Gin story, see Campbell, *Using Women*, 82, 84–90.

21. "Text of Nixon Message on Plan to Attack Drug Abuse," *Congressional Quarterly Almanac* 24 (1969): 57A; the second Nixon quotation is from Christian Parenti, *Lockdown America: Police and Prisons in the Age of Crisis* (New York: Verso, 1999), 3; Robert L. Ivie, "Presidential Motives for War," *Quarterly Journal of Speech* 60, no. 3 (1974): 337–45, quotation from 343.

22. By 1983, forty-nine states had passed drug laws that included mandatory-minimum sentencing; for information on Nixon's drug and crime legislation, as well as the Rockefeller and Michigan Drug Laws, see Parenti, *Lockdown America*, 10–14; Musto, *American Disease*, 254–56, 273; Baum, *Smoke and Mirrors*, 45–85; Morgan, *Drugs in America*, 149–68; on the Nixon-era militarization of police tactics, see Richard Lawrence Miller, *Drug Warriors and Their Prey* (London: Praeger, 1996), 156–62, and Julilly Kohler-Hausmann's essay in this volume (chapter 2).

23. Nixon quoted in Edward Jay Epstein, *Agency of Fear: Opiates and Political Power in America* (New York: Verso, 1990), 171, 178; Reagan quoted from his 14 September 1986 "Address to the Nation on the Campaign against Drug Abuse"; for more on this media phenomenon and the siege paradigm, see Reeves and Campbell, *Cracked Coverage*, 15–161, and Campbell, *Using Women*, 19–54 and 169–92; on Presidents Reagan's and Bush's use of the drug war as a form of public relations, see William N. Elwood, *Rhetoric in the War on Drugs: The Triumphs and Tragedies of Public Relations* (London: Praeger, 1994), 19–80; on marshalling racism as part of this effort, see Stabile, *White Victims, Black Villains*, 128–74; Clarence Lusane, *Pipe Dream Blues: Racism and the War on Drugs* (Boston, MA: South End Press, 1991), 11–53; and Travis Dixon's essay in this volume (chapter 4).

24. For more on the Reagan legacy, see Steven Wisotsky, *Beyond the War on Drugs: Overcoming a Failed Public Policy*, (Buffalo, NY: Prometheus, 1990), 95–195; the Reagan quotation is from Trebach, *Great Drug War*, 152; despite President Bush's declaration on April 8, 2008, "National D.A.R.E. Day," that for twenty-five years "Drug Abuse Resistance Education has given school children across America an opportunity to gain the skills they need to avoid involvement in drugs, gangs, and violence" (the speech was available via the Bush White House at www.whitehouse .gov/news/releases/2008/04/20080409-3.html), researchers have concluded that the D.A.R.E. program at best contributed to moments of transitory success and at worst to a continuation of inane stereotypes—see Richard R. Clayton, Anne M. Cattarelo, and Bryan M. Johnstone, "The Effectiveness of Drug Abuse Resistance Education (Project D.A.R.E.): 5-Year Follow-Up Results," *Preventive Medicine* 25, no.3 (May 1996): 307–18; Dennis P. Rosenbaum and Gordon S. Hanson. "Assessing the

Effects of School-Based Drug Education: A Six-Year Multi-Level Analysis of Project D.A.R.E.," *Journal of Research in Crime and Delinquency* 35, no. 4 (November 1998): 381–412; Donald R. Lynam, Richard Milich, Rick Zimmerman, Scott P. Novak, T. K. Logan, Catherine Martin, Carl Leukefeld, and Richard Clayton, "Project D.A.R.E.: No Effects at 10-Year Follow-Up," *Journal of Consulting and Clinical Psychology* 67, no. 4 (August 1999): 590–93; and Dennis P. Rosenbaum, "Just Say No to D.A.R.E.," *Criminology and Public Policy* 6, no. 4 (November 2007), 815–24.

25. President George H. W. Bush is quoted from the "Text of the Address by President Bush," *Washington Post* (6 September 1989), A18; Secretary of Defense Dick Cheney is quoted in Scott, *Cocaine Politics,* 6; William J. Bennett, John J. DiIulio, and John P. Walters, *Body Count: Moral Poverty And How to Win America's War Against Crime and Drugs* (New York: Simon and Schuster, 1996): 28.

26. The massacre is described in Cecilia Zarate, "Daily Life in Colombia," *ZNet* (29 October 2003), accessible at www.zmag.org/znet/viewArticle/9632; for context, see Patrick L. Clawson and Rensselaer W. Lee, *The Andean Cocaine Industry* (New York: St. Martin's Griffin, 1998); Dominic Streatfeild, *Cocaine: An Unauthorized Biography* (New York: Picador, 2001), 431–72; Robin Kirk, *More Terrible Than Death: Massacres, Drugs, and America's War in Colombia* (New York: Public Affairs, 2003); Peter Dale Scott, *Drugs, Oil, and War: The United States in Afghanistan, Colombia, and Indochina* (New York: Rowman and Littlefield, 2003), 71–105; Wallace-Wells, "How America Lost the War on Drugs"; and Michael Shifter, "This Plan Isn't Working; U.S. Military Aid Alarms Colombia's Neighbors," *Washington Post* (10 December 2000), B4.

27. See Conference Committee Report 106–710 (Public Law 106–246), June 29, 2000, available at http://thomas.loc.gov/cgi-bin/query/z?r106:H29JN0–78; Duncan Campbell, "Drugs in the Firing Line," *Manchester Guardian* (20 July 2002), 11; U.S. Department of State Fact Sheet, "Civilian Contractors and U.S. Military Personnel Supporting Plan Colombia, Bureau of Western Hemisphere Affairs" (Washington, DC: Author, 15 May 2001), accessible at www.state.gov/p/wha/rls/fs/2001/3509.htm; also see William Aviles, "Institutions, Military Policy, and Human Rights in Colombia," *Latin American Perspectives* 28, no. 1 (2001): 31–55.

28. For a report on the Iran-Contra weapons link and the Colombian situation, see Kim Cragin and Bruce Hoffman, "Arms Trafficking and Colombia" (Santa Monica, CA: RAND National Defense Research Institute, 2003), accessible at http://rand.org/pubs/monograph_reports/MR1468/MR1468.pdf; for more context, see Julian Borger and Martin Hodgson, "U.S. Drug War Aids Colombian Paramilitaries," *Guardian* (17 May 2001), 12.

29. For an overview of the nexus among NAFTA, the border economy, and drug control, see Peter Andreas, *Border Games: Policing the U.S.-Mexico Divide* (Ithaca, NY: Cornell University Press, 2000); William von Raab and Andy Messing, "Will NAFTA Free the Drug Trade? Cocaine Businessmen Too Will Exploit Open Borders," *Washington Post* (15 August 1993), C2; Gwen Florio, "At Busy U.S.–Mexico Border, a 'Real Mess'; While NAFTA Has Increased Traffic at Ports of Entry, Drug Searches Have Slowed It," *Philadelphia Inquirer* (10 February 1999), A3; James C. McKinley, "Bush Asks Congress for $1.4 Billion to Fight Drugs in Mexico," *New York Times* (23 October 2007), F1; Manuel Roig-Franzia, "Drug Trade Tyranny on the Border; Mexican Cartels Main-

tain Grasp with Weapons, Cash, and Savagery," *Washington Post* (16 March 2008), A1; Astorga quoted in Manuel Roig-Franzia, "Mexico's Police Chief Is Killed in Brazen Attack by Gunmen," *Washington Post* (9 May 2008), A1; Oscar Avila, "Echoes of Colombia in Mexico Drug War," *Chicago Tribune* (14 May 2008), A8; Gates quoted in David Morgan, "Gates Urges Congress to Avoid 'Slap' at Mexico," *Reuters Online* (29 April 2008), accessible at www.reuters.com.

30. On the oil politics enmeshed in the drug war, see Thad Dunning and Leslie Wirpsa, "Oil and the Political Economy of Conflict in Colombia and Beyond: A Linkages Approach," in *The Geopolitics of Resource Wars: Resource Dependence, Governance, and Violence* (New York: Frank Cass, 2005), 81–108; Scott, *Drugs, Oil, and War*, 71–105; and Jim Hightower, "The Drug War Isn't All about Drugs," *Colombia Journal* (13 August 2000), accessed from www.colombiajournal.org/colombia23 .htm; on the larger political questions involved in this new stage of globalization, where military contracts are justified in the name of fighting drugs and terrorism, see Stephen John Hartnett and Laura Ann Stengrim, *Globalization and Empire: The U.S. Invasion of Iraq, Free Markets, and the Twilight of Democracy* (Tuscaloosa, AL: University of Alabama Press, 2006), 212–66, and Pratap Chatterjee, *Iraq Incorporated: A Profitable Occupation* (New York: Seven Stories, 2004).

Another Day

Erika Baro

A member of the Writing Workshop at the Denver Women's Correctional Facility, in Denver, Colorado, Erika Baro writes strong poems about survival and moving on in the face of hardship; this poem became an anthem for our workshop, as we all pledged to try to follow its sage advice; the piece was published in *Captured Words/Free Thoughts* 6 (Spring 2009).

Laying in a pool of tears
Hidden by darkness
I wander lost between the hundreds
Of stars that decorate the night sky

As my voice whispers strangely
Driving me deeper into a madness
I cannot escape
I drift farther and farther away
On an infinite path to nowhere

But just as the last drop of hope slips away
A faint ray of light falls on my face
The sunrise dries my tears
And I realize I've survived

I will live another day

Teaching You to Love Fear: Television News and Racial Stereotypes in a Punishing Democracy

Travis L. Dixon

Because I am one of the few African American professors my students have ever met, I am often asked to speak to various student groups about my life and work; one of the questions I address regularly is "why do you study racial stereotypes in the media?" I usually respond that my scholarly work is inspired by my personal experiences, for I grew up in South Central Los Angeles, that Hollywood symbol of projected racial stereotypes and fears, and later attended a college where I encountered white students who had been taught by the media to see me as a problem requiring careful scrutiny, perhaps even punishment. I had grown up fearing the police and the violence of angry white men, but *my classmates were afraid of me.*

While growing up, even though I was a hardly imposing "geek," I was often harassed by police officers who assumed that I was up to no good simply because of my race and my neighborhood. On one occasion I was attending a church barbecue. When it was time to head home, I borrowed my grandfather's truck (with his permission, of course). I was soon pulled over and confronted by two white police officers with their guns drawn; although I was a good kid returning home from a church function, they thought I was a violent predator. It turns out that I was dropping off a friend who lived near a store that had been burglarized earlier that day, and so the Los Angeles police were on a manhunt, looking for a black man, any black man. One inappropriate move, including any verbal protest against my mistreatment, and I might have been beaten, arrested, or even shot. And so my childhood unfolded in South Central, where, on more than a dozen occasions, I faced profiling behavior, was handcuffed, or was pulled over for no reason other than the color of my skin. I thus learned to be careful around the police, to know when to shut up, and both to recognize and fear the inarticulate fury of those who had been trained to see the world through the lens of mass-mediated racial stereotypes.

Later in life, I came to realize that the same fear and misunderstanding that drove some white police officers to target me also encouraged many of my teachers and then professors to expect little from me in the classroom. When I was a freshman in college, I recall a mathematics professor who talked down to me when I attended his office hours and who seemed to be systematically rude to all the women and people of color in his class. While pacing in front of the class during the final exam, a black student turned in his exam somewhat early, prompting the professor to exclaim: "Now I know this test is too easy!" Perhaps he thought he was being funny, but many of us heard the comment as yet another racial slur. While walking across campus, I remember the familiar question posed by my classmates: "Are you an athlete?" This was a question I would have never been asked while attending my predominantly black high school, where I was known as a geek, not a jock—I was not an athlete; it was self-evident that I was the nerd, not the sports star. Nonetheless, mediated stereotypes led my classmates to believe that black people are either criminals or athletes, not scholars.

I eventually overcame this institutionalized racism to obtain a Ph.D. and become a professor. As I pursued my degree, I was dogged by a persistent question: "Why do people use stereotypes to guide their decisions?" As I read others' research and undertook my own investigations, I became convinced that support for policies that hurt the life chances of young black men is tied to either a tacit or explicit endorsement of racial stereotypes. Furthermore, because we live largely in a segregated society, many of these stereotypical conceptions are perpetuated not by individuals reflecting upon their interpersonal contacts with others, but by the mass media. Unfortunately, these mass-mediated racial stereotypes may be teaching us to love fear by prodding us to support a punishing and racist democracy rather than an empowering one. Neil Postman famously worried that we Americans have fallen so in love with our televisions that we are "amusing ourselves to death"; in that same vein of thought, I fear that we may have become so inundated by mass-mediated racial stereotypes that we are losing the ability to see past our racialized fears. What if the mass media are, in effect, teaching us to see the world in ways that will, ultimately, lead to disaster?[1]

To begin answering that question, this chapter outlines what we know about the content and effects of mediated racial stereotypes on black male criminality. I focus on television news shows because people tend to view them as accurately reflecting reality and therefore use them as a basis for constructing both their personal worldviews and their positions on public policy. Given this premise, I offer two claims about the news media and racial stereotypes: First, the news media misrepresent black men as criminal suspects; second, exposure to this misrepresentation perpetuates the stereotypical belief that African Americans comprise the bulk of threatening criminal suspects and therefore need to be incarcerated in order to protect white society. I argue, therefore, that watching television news leads to implicit racism, and that unconscious racism underpins support for a punishing democracy that treats black men as criminals rather than as citizens. In short, television news is teaching us to love fear.[2]

The Stereotypical Content of News Programming

The majority of research suggests that news programming perpetuates stereotypical crime imagery focused on the monstrous deeds of black men. These findings hold true for both local and national news coverage. To help readers understand the crushing implications of these claims, I offer overviews of the racializing content expressed in local and national television news shows. Studying these sources enables me to map two of the main paths of indoctrination into a world driven by racial stereotypes and hence prone to accepting the mass incarceration of young black men.

The Black Criminal Stereotype on Local Television News

Communication scholars, political scientists, and psychologists have studied the effects of the entertainment media in perpetuating stereotypes for decades, but substantial attention to the role of the news media in depicting stereotypes and reinforcing stereotypical thinking did not occur largely until the 1990s. One of the first and most important investigations was undertaken by Bob Entman and his colleagues, who analyzed 55 days of local television news in Chicago; the study indicated that black men accused of a crime were much more likely than similarly accused white suspects to be shown in the grip of a restraining police officer. At some deep visceral level, then, the news media tended to portray black men as needing restraint, as requiring state intervention, as predators to be feared. Entman also found that black men accused of committing a crime were less likely than white suspects to be identified by name in news stories. Entman interpreted such differences as evidence that when African American and white suspects are accused of similarly serious offenses, black suspects appear to be treated in a more dehumanized manner. Thus, whereas white suspects have individuating names, black suspects are anonymous, more nameless evidence in the long-standing narrative claiming that black men are criminals. Moreover, Entman maintained that those black suspects who were most dehumanized were portrayed as being the perpetrators of violence against white victims. These images appear to suggest that while crime is always a terrible event, it is even worse when committed by a black man against a white victim. Although limited to fifty-five days of coverage in Chicago, Entman's findings suggest strongly that the television news perpetuated a series of stereotypical depictions in which black suspects were violent, nameless, and perpetually attacking white victims.[3]

Although Entman limited his investigation to local Chicago stations, such stereotypical depictions are not confined to Chicago news. For example, Daniel Romer and his colleagues analyzed the 11:00 p.m. news broadcast for three stations in Philadelphia over fourteen weeks. In each of the stories, Romer and his associates coded the ethnicity of primary actors (i.e., "person of color" or white) and they recorded their roles (i.e., victim or perpetrator). Echoing Entman's conclusions for Chicago, Romer's study found that black Philadelphians were more likely to be shown as perpetrators than as victims in the news. In addition, Romer and his team found evidence that white Philadelphians were overrepresented as victims, and that these portrayals of white victims were matched by an overrepresentation of black perpetrators. Indeed, although crime reports indicate that only 10 percent of white victims are murdered by black offenders, the Philadelphia television news shows studied by Romer and his colleagues depicted a world in which 42 percent of white victims were murdered by black thugs—*this amounts to an overrepresentation of black-on-white murder by more than 400 percent*. In short, the television news studied by Romer distorts reality by creating a nightmare world driven by fear-based racial stereotypes.[4]

Whereas Entman, Romer, and their colleagues have made a substantial contribution to our understanding of race and the news in Chicago and Philadelphia, other research on racially biased depictions in local news programming has addressed Los Angeles. Much of this work has been undertaken either by me and my colleagues or by Franklin Gilliam and his colleagues. These studies reveal several consistent findings. First, in relation to actual crime reports, African Americans are overrepresented as criminal suspects in Los Angeles news programs. On average, crime reports indicate that African Americans make up about 21 percent of actual perpetrators in the Los Angeles area, yet they appear as perpetrators about 37 percent of the time on Los Angeles area news. I should note as well that this overrepresentation of black criminal suspects on local television news is likely even more egregious than these numbers suggest, for the crime reports I am using for my baseline figures likely include disproportionate numbers of black men who are arrested because of racist police practices. This means, then, that the discrepancy between television news depictions of black criminals (37 percent of suspects) and crime reports (21 percent of actual suspects) is most likely even larger than what I am reporting here. As in Chicago and Philadelphia, then, the television news in Los Angeles is systematically filling our heads with racist images that do not report the facts faithfully but that perpetuate the stereotype of the young black man as a violent threat to society.[5]

Second, my and my colleagues' research has shown that African Americans are generally associated in television news shows with negative roles. For example, we found that African Americans are more than twice as likely to appear as criminal suspects than as officers on news programs—put simply, the television news depicts black men as criminals, not as law-protecting police officers. As in the Romer study, we also found that black men are more likely to appear as perpetrators than as victims in the news in Los Angeles area news programs. In fact, in proportion to crime reports, African Americans are underrepresented as homicide victims on local television news: whereas black Angelinos represent about 23 percent of the victims portrayed in television news, they account for almost 30 percent of the actual victims in the Los Angeles area. Because being a victim of crime puts one in a position of sympathy in most viewers' eyes, this underrepresentation of black victims amounts to yet another subtle way that African American experiences are downplayed, as if our pain is less newsworthy than that experienced by white victims. Finally, African Americans are twice as likely as white suspects to have negative pretrial publicity aired about them in the news. For example, if you are a black suspect on television news, then the news story is more likely (than if you are a white suspect) to air the fact that you have committed crimes in the past. This reporting of past deeds is important because the American Bar Association has identified negative pretrial publicity as a hindrance to the constitutional principle of a fair trial. The bedrock commitment of our justice system, the belief that one is innocent until proven guilty, is thus jeopardized by the mass circulation of racial stereotypes.[6]

As a corollary to these findings about media bias in its depictions of black men, we have also found a consistent pattern in the portrayal of white suspects and victims. For example, we found that white Angelinos are underrepresented as both violent and felony perpetrators. One of the things we have been taught to forget is that a significant number of crimes (in Los Angeles, almost 28 percent) are committed by white criminals; however, our research indicates that white men make up only about 20 percent of the perpetrators shown on Los Angeles television news. By overemphasizing the crimes committed by African Americans and underportraying the crimes committed by white Californians, the Los Angeles news media racializes crime, showing it not as a communal dilemma to be addressed by all of us, but as a specifically racial problem in which predatory black men victimize innocent white citizens. This systematic pattern of racializing news stories about crime depends in part on showing white Angelinos as the upholders of law and order. For example, white suspects are underrepresented as the perpetrators of crime, and white Angelinos are simultaneously overrepresented as police officers: They account for 69 percent of police officers on television but only 59 percent in fact. This stereotypical local news depiction suggests that law and order is the province of white police officers, whose job is to defend white victims from black villains. When inundated with such images, day in and day out, year after year, there can be little wonder that so many Americans support the prison-industrial complex, for the mass media are indeed teaching us to be racists, to clamor for more arrests of young black men, to surrender our hopes for justice and racial equality to the hysteria of a punishing democracy.

The Black Criminal Stereotype on National Television News

Network news is important to study because national news programs often air information about the laws and policies on crime and violence. Whereas local news shows tend to sensationalize local events, national news shows tend to run stories that position African Americans within the larger context of law and policy. I should note, however, that network news spends less time discussing crime than local news; instead, several studies have noted that network television news tends to address stories that link African Americans with other social issues, including welfare and education, which tend to associate black Americans with stereotypes such as being complainers, loafers, and underachievers. For example, Jimmie Reeves and Richard Campbell have provided an insightful analysis of network news coverage during President Ronald Reagan's so-called "war on drugs." They found that the media was complicit in supporting a type of new racism that falsely overassociated black youth with the then-booming cocaine drug culture; according to Reeves and Campbell, the news media produced a cocaine narrative that "took shape around social conflicts and cultural distinction related to the contemporary politics of race, class, gender, sexuality, region, religion, age and taste. At various moments during the narrative the meaning of cocaine would be inflected by gender issues, it would take on racial overtones, and it would animate myths about the sanctity of small-town life in middle-America." As these narratives trumpeted the threat of black male aggression against white middle class values, so this overarching racial theme became a ubiquitous refrain of network news coverage. Thus, whereas the local news stories analyzed above tended toward sensational (and factually inaccurate) portrayals of black men as violent criminals preying on local white victims, the national news stories addressed here tended to link African Americans with larger social issues, such as welfare or education or drugs, thus subtly depicting us as the cause of social decline. In short, black men were shown on national news not only as criminals but as the cause of a host of other social crises. The national news would thus have us think this way: if America is falling apart, then it is *my fault*; as a black man, *I am the problem*.[7]

Moreover, when national news shows did address victims of crime and upholders of law, they tended to do so in ways that repeated the stereotype-reinforcing patterns deployed in local news. For example, while African Americans make up 48 percent of crime victims nationally, we account for only about 30 percent of the victims shown on network television; similarly, whereas black officers total 17 percent of the police forces nationally, only 3 percent of the officers portrayed on network news are African Americans. As in local news shows, this network news pattern communicates the false impression that blacks are perpetrators of crime but are not its victims and definitely not the police officers trying to stem the tide of crime.[8]

To summarize my argument thus far, the best available data on both local and national news coverage suggest that when television news shows address crime and other crime-related issues, black men are overrepresented as criminals but underrepresented as police officers and agents of the law; we are overrepresented as attacking white victims but underrepresented as the victims of crime; we are often depicted in ways that are likely to prevent receiving a fair trial; and, in keeping with cultural narratives originally derived from slavery, we are portrayed as the root cause of a host of other social problems that require heavy-handed responses.

From Media Content to Daily Life:
How Biased News Depictions Reinforce Stereotypes

The content analyses offered above include strong evidence of how the media produce and perpetuate racial stereotypes; however, they cannot tell us much, if anything, about the effects of consuming such mass-produced racist content. In order to understand whether news viewing contributes to an individual employing racist stereotypes in his or her daily life, I would like now to consider a field of research known as systematic effects investigations. There are two kinds of tools used by social scientists to tease out these effects. The first involves laboratory experiments in which viewers are asked to watch certain programs in a controlled environment and then to record their impressions, hence enabling scholars to study the flow of ideas from a given show to a particular viewer. As critics have noted, such contrived experiments are not very naturalistic—they do not reflect typical viewer patterns or practices—and so some experts question whether such experiments are generalizable across diverse populations and situations. The second study technique is the survey wherein viewers watch television at home and then report their responses to scholars. Such surveys are more naturalistic, but even when well conducted they cannot tell us definitively about causation, just about relationships (for as in exit-voting reports, most Americans are loath to admit that race influences their thinking, even when answering in anonymous surveys). Because both research methods have limits and strengths, I report on both kinds of studies, thus hoping to provide the best understanding of whether distorted race and crime imagery influences support for the mass incarceration of black men. I should note as well that many scholars agree that even the most egregiously racist news programs could appeal to and hence influence only viewers who are already predisposed to consuming such images; this means, in short, that stereotypes must somehow be fulfilling, they must somehow provide a sense of understanding and meaning. And so, before diving into an analysis of the experimental and survey research on media effects, I need first to discuss the psychological reasons that enable stereotypes to be appealing.[9]

The Psychology of Mediated Stereotyping
of Black Men as Criminals

From a psychological standpoint, stereotypes are cognitive structures that help us understand the world around us: in the face of confusion, stereotypes provide a sense of stability and order, they anchor meaning to certain assumed truths. Moreover, psychologists tend to agree that because stereotypes fulfill these sense-making roles, the more they have been used in the past, the more likely they are to be used in the future—in short, stereotypes tend to be both self-fulfilling and self-perpetuating precisely because they help us explain the world. The technical concepts describing this process are *chronic activation* and *chronic accessibility*. Chronic activation denotes the ways consistent exposure to stereotypical images triggers chains of associations in the brain; chronic accessibility denotes how, after years and years of chronic activation, we learn to draw upon stereotypes to explain the world, thus accessing meaning by activating stereotypes. The two processes interlock to form a cycle of stereotype-producing thought: If a stereotype has been repeatedly activated in prior and multiple contexts to make sense of situations, then the stereotype becomes a source of meaning likely to be more and more readily accessible. Chronic activation leads to chronic accessibility and then back again, creating a loop of stereotype-driven sense-making that is difficult to break—and so thinking in a stereotyped way becomes almost addictive. The crucial questions, then, are how do stereotypically racist television news shows contribute to this cycle, and how can we measure the effects of this process in daily life?[10]

Experimental Research on Stereotype Reinforcement Via the News

A growing body of research suggests that exposure to biased media portrayals activates stereotypes that associate black men with criminality. This stereotypical association then leads to biased judgments that may be made even without the perceiver's conscious awareness. For example, in one of her experiments, Mary Beth Oliver tried to study how viewers respond to news stories, and how their choices may reflect stereotypical racial biases. She exposed participants to a series of similar news stories, with different versions of the story featuring suspects of different races; she then asked the participants to identify the race of the suspect portrayed. She found that people tended to pick the black suspect, even after having watched a news story identifying someone else as the suspect. Confronted with a hard choice, participants, almost by default, relied upon stereotypical thinking and assumed the suspect was black. Oliver then brought participants back into the laboratory several months later and found that many of those who had been shown an image of a white suspect now identified a black suspect as the assailant they had seen several months earlier—their memory was overridden by racist stereotypes. Oliver later repeated the study using newspapers and varied whether it was violent or nonviolent stories that people read. Here again she uncovered a similar process of participants relying upon racializing stereotypes to try to make sense of the stories they had read. In short, participants' mistakes in reporting what they had seen or read were driven by relying upon racial stereotypes. Chronic activation theory thus suggests that repeatedly seeing black suspects in the news will encourage people to unconsciously use a black criminal stereotype to make sense of news clips, even when they have just witnessed images of white suspects.[11]

Pursuing this same line of research, Franklin Gilliam and Shanto Iyengar conducted a series of experiments in which they exposed thousands of participants to either a black, white, or racially uncoded criminal suspect (in some cases even showing participants stories that were not about crime). Afterward, they asked participants about their endorsement of subtle racism and their support for punitive crime legislation. Their studies produced two notable conclusions. First, as in Oliver's studies, they found that participants tended to falsely recall the race of unidentified suspects as black. Second, they found that white participants, but not participants of color, were more likely to express subtle racism by supporting punitive crime policies after exposure to either an unidentified or black criminal suspect, but not after being shown a story about a white suspect. Specifically, white participants exposed to an identical crime story in which a black rather than a white suspect was shown were six times as likely to express support for three-strikes legislation and other punitive measures for crime. Witnessing a white criminal produced one response and witnessing a black criminal produced a harsher response explicitly linked to punitive crime policies; and so we can conclude that racially biased stereotypes do indeed have a direct impact on our attitudes on crime-related social policy.[12]

Critics of this argument will raise the question of cause and effect: Are racist stereotypes more accessible because we live in a racist culture or because people repeatedly watch racist news programming? Which factor causes which result? To address this concern, my colleagues and I conducted a series of experiments designed to understand the potential impact of repeated viewing of stereotypical news coverage on stereotype activation and use. We suspected that frequent viewing of newscasts that overportray black criminality would lead to the development and reinforcement of a cognitive association between black men and lawbreaking. In other words, we tried to develop a method for measuring whether and how watching biased news coverage of black criminality contributed to the chronic activation of the black criminal stereotype, and whether and how such viewing increased the accessibility of the stereotype when relevant policy judgments needed to be made. And so we exposed participants to a news program featuring either a majority of black suspects, a majority of white suspects, a number of unidentified suspects, or noncrime stories. We also asked participants about how much news they watched daily. We found that heavy news viewers were more likely than light news viewers to believe, when exposed to images of black suspects, that the world is a dangerous place and, as a result, to experience emotional discomfort when witnessing such images. In addition, heavy news viewers were more likely than light viewers to assume, when exposed to either black or unidentified criminals, that a subsequent race-unidentified perpetrator was culpable for his offense. This study suggests that heavy news viewing perpetuates fear of black offenders and a willingness to assume that black suspects are guilty. Moreover, it suggests that by chronically activating racializing stereotypes, some of our participants in turn found such images more accessible as a means of explaining the stories we showed to them—each racializing moment fed the next.[13]

I want to emphasize that some of our experiments involved the assessment of exposure to news images of unidentified suspects. We thought that assessing or reacting to unidentified suspects might be a particularly powerful way of demonstrating whether and how news programming reinforced stereotypical cognitive links between black men and criminality. For if reactions to black suspects and unidentified criminals were similar or connected, then we thought it would illustrate the strength of the stereotypical link between African Americans and lawbreaking. In short, we thought it might be convincing if we could demonstrate how viewers, even when shown a suspect of nondescript status, tended to assume that the offender was a black man. In many cases, we found that participants misremembered unidentified persons as black suspects, that they became equally punitive when exposed to black and unidentified suspects, and that their support for the black community declined as a result of exposure to unidentified suspects. Apparently, the association between African Americans and criminality is so strong that simply thinking about crime, even when shown a suspect of nondescript characteristics, causes many perceivers to conjure visual images of black criminals.[14]

While viewers' responses to crime news reveal assumptions about race and its impact on the guilt or innocence of suspects, I have also wondered about viewers' responses to questions about the deeper social causes of success or failure in contemporary America. For example, in one study we found that heavy news viewers were less likely than light news viewers to believe that African Americans face structural limitations to their success in life. This study echoes a growing body of research providing evidence that watching television news makes you more likely to believe that black Americans are an irresponsible group of loafers rather than a people who have been oppressed for hundreds of years by institutionalized racism. While television news thus overrepresents black Americans as violent criminals, and underrepresents us as the victims of crime, this more recent line of research has perhaps even more far-reaching implications, for it suggests that television news is pushing a storyline in which the legacies of slavery have been transcended, the playing field is even, and talk of racism is just bad nostalgia.[15]

The "New Racism" and Stereotype Reinforcement in the News

Scholars are in fact beginning to understand that racism in the twenty-first century has taken on a dangerous pattern wherein most white Americans no longer speak openly about race—they even deplore racism when asked about it directly—yet they refuse to support the social programs that might redress the damage caused by hundreds of years of racism, and they offer rabid support for penal policies that reinforce those same patterns of disenfranchisement. Paul Street has thus argued that the combination of media stereotypes and the prison-industrial complex has launched "the new racism"; Eduardo Bonilla Silva has called this a condition of "racism without racists." To support the findings of these cultural critics with social-science-based research methods, scholars are trying to craft surveys to measure how television news influences how we think about race and crime and their causes and consequences in the twenty-first century. In one such study, Gilliam and Iyengar tested whether exposure to local news programming in Los Angeles would be associated with old-fashioned racism (e.g., the belief that black Americans are inherently inferior beings) or the new racism (e.g., lack of support for policies designed to assist African Americans); moreover, they tried to assess support for punitive crime policies such as three-strikes legislation and the death penalty. They found that overall exposure to local news programming was associated with higher "new racism" scores and also with greater support for punitive crime measures.[16]

But we are still left with the question of cause and effect. One possibility unexamined by Gilliam and Iyengar is that those who already endorse stereotypes about black criminality are more likely to watch the news, perhaps because the news reflects their racist thinking. I therefore became interested in repeating and extending their survey work. My goal was to assess whether television news created racial stereotypes in viewers' minds or rather reinforced already-lodged biases. As in the previous studies discussed above, I found that even after controlling for prior racial attitudes, attention and exposure to crime news was positively correlated with a general concern about crime. In short, the more news you watch, the more afraid of crime you become. In addition, crime news exposure was also positively correlated with hypothetical culpability ratings for black and unidentified criminals, but not with white criminals. So the more news you watch, the more likely you are to assume that black suspects are guilty. Finally, and most telling, respondents with heavier exposure to local news content that overrepresented black men as criminals—even those respondents who denounced racism when asked directly—had a stronger perception that all African Americans are violent. This means that independent of one's prior racial attitudes, the more you witness black men portrayed as criminals in the news, the more likely you are to hold negative racial perceptions of all African Americans. In other words, even people who tend to be consciously sympathetic to African Americans can unconsciously stereotype black men if they watch extensive amounts of television news portraying black criminality.[17]

Conclusion: Television News, Crime, and the Production of Racial Fear

Taken together, the experimental and survey work discussed in this chapter provides a consistently disturbing picture of the effects of exposure to racially biased crime news. Specifically, this research points to three incontrovertible patterns. First, crime news exposure increases the accessibility of a black criminal stereotype that associates African Americans with criminal behavior. This has the consequence of encouraging news viewers to associate crime stories, even those devoid of direct racial references, with African Americans. In short, exposure to racist television news leads to *chronic activation* of racist stereotypes. Second, crime news exposure leads viewers to harbor an elevated fear or concern about African Americans and leads to a greater perceived danger and concern about becoming a victim of crime. This includes creating a perception in viewers that black men are violent or intimidating. Over time, this pattern means that viewers come to *chronically access* stereotypical narratives about and images of black men, hence creating a foundation of racist thinking. Third, heavy news exposure encourages viewers to endorse punitive measures to address the so-called problems with African American crime. This support for punitive crime measures comes in the form of culpability judgments of suspects, support for tough prison terms, and flagging support for affirmative action and the other social programs meant to heal the wounds of hundreds of years of institutionalized racism. In short, the television news teaches you to be a fear-filled racist who supports the most brutal policies of the prison-industrial complex—the media are indeed teaching us to love fear.

I will leave the macro-analysis of the political economy of the corporate media to others who can better articulate the impact of market consolidation on media content. As I have noted elsewhere, however, we need to be clear that the profit motive encourages the corporate media to emphasize coverage of the kinds of crimes poor black men are more likely to commit while ignoring those crimes more likely to be committed by wealthy white offenders. In other words, because of poverty and structural racism, black men have a higher likelihood of committing blue-collar crime (e.g., robbery) rather than white-collar crime (e.g., embezzlement). And because the former are easier to cover and depict in graphic ways, the media target them, hence appealing to viewers and hence keeping advertising profits as high as possible. Indeed, whereas street crime can be covered by an intrepid reporter in a van with a camera, reporting on corporate malfeasance requires several things, including: (1) a whistleblower, (2) the will to offend a powerful company or advertiser, (3) the funds to cover a story long-term, and (4) the ability to make an intricate story of corporate intrigue interesting to the average person. These are not insurmountable hurdles (for example, consider the success of the documentary *The Smartest Guys in the Room*, a blistering exposé of the Enron debacle), yet they make it almost impossible to cover such stories in the nightly television news. Rather than covering rampant corporate crimes committed by white executives, then, the profit motive leaves television news viewers inundated with gruesome depictions of gangland slayings—and so rich white criminals go unreported while poor black criminals are splashed across the television screen each and every night.[18]

To help reverse these patterns, we can pursue a few political and personal strategies. First, we can demand that the Federal Communications Commission and Congress require broadcasters to report fair and balanced news coverage using a standard similar to the now-defunct fairness doctrine. The news wing of a station should no longer be seen as a profit center or propaganda machine for the network; instead, news should serve the greater good of providing information to the public. Second, as citizens, we should discourage the loosening of restrictions on conglomerate ownership of media outlets. In other words, as long as profits are the primary goal of networks, then they will rely on stereotypes to tell their stories. Third, at an individual level, television viewers could be encouraged to become more conscientious about the media choices they make, thus enabling them to distinguish between news and racializing hysteria. One way to achieve this goal is for news consumers to expose themselves to diverse media sources and to actively pursue media outlets run by, working with, or at least addressing the concerns of people of color—for scholars have shown that one of the best ways to break down stereotypes is to present viewers with multiple exemplars of the stereotyped group, thus illustrating that the group or character type formerly thought to be monolithic is in fact diverse, complicated, and full of individuals. There are many nonprofit organizations working to facilitate this process, especially on the subject of stereotypical representations of crime and race, including BeyondMedia Education (www.beyondmedia.org), Paper Tiger TV (www.papertiger.org), the Prison Radio Project (www.prisonradio.org), the Thousand Kites Project (www.thousandkites.org), and others. Visiting these groups and other local alternative media outlets can indeed help viewers to move beyond the numbing pattern of chronic activation and chronic access of stereotypical images of black men and crime. I only hope that we can spread this message and hence begin breaking the cycle of racism before it is too late.[19]

Notes

1. Neil Postman, *Amusing Ourselves to Death: Public Discourse in the Age of Show Business* (New York: Penguin, 1986); for more on media-produced racism and the prison-industrial complex, see Marc Mauer, *Race to Incarcerate* (New York: New Press, 1999), 118–41 and 171–77; Erica Meiners, *Right to Be Hostile: Schools, Prisons, and the Making of Public Enemies* (London: Routledge, 2007), 81–112; and Carol Stabile, *White Victims, Black Villains: Gender, Race, and Crime News in U.S. Culture* (London: Routledge, 2006), 128–89.

2. Shanto Iyengar, "Television News and Citizens' Explanations of National Affairs," *American Political Science Review* 81 (1987): 815–31, and Shanto Iyengar and Don Kinder, *News That Matters* (Chicago: University of Chicago Press, 1987).

3. Robert Entman, "Blacks in the News: Television, Modern Racism, and Cultural Change," *Journalism Quarterly* 69, no. 2 (1992): 341–61; see pages 350–51 for a discussion of how black suspects may be dehumanized and undifferentiated from one another in news coverage.

4. Daniel Romer, Kathleen Hall Jamieson, and Nicole J. de Coteau, "The Treatment of Persons of Color in Local Television News: Ethnic Blame Discourse or Realistic Group Conflict?" *Communication Research* 25, no. 3 (1998): 268–305.

5. My work in this area includes Travis L. Dixon and Cristina Azocar, "The Representation of Juvenile Offenders by Race on Los Angeles Area Television News," *Howard Journal of Communications* 17 (2006): 143–61; Travis L. Dixon and Daniel G.

Linz, "Overrepresentation and Underrepresentation of African Americans and Latinos as Lawbreakers on Television News," *Journal of Communication* 50, no. 2 (2000): 131–54; and Travis L. Dixon and Daniel G. Linz, "Race and the Misrepresentation of Victimization on Local Television News," *Communication Research* 27, no. 5 (2000): 547–73; Gilliam and his colleagues' work in this area includes Franklin D. Gilliam, Shanto Iyengar, Adam Simon, and Oliver Wright, "Crime in Black and White: The Violent, Scary World of Local News," *Harvard International Journal of Press/Politics* 1, no. 3 (1996): 6–23; Franklin D. Gilliam and Shanto Iyengar, "The Superpredator Script," *Nieman Reports* 52, no. 4 (1998): 45–46; and Franklin D. Gilliam and Shanto Iyengar, "Prime Suspects: The Influence of Local Television News on the Viewing Public," *American Journal of Political Science* 44 (2000): 560–73.

6. For information on prejudicial pretrial information, see the American Bar Association, "Model Rules of Professional Conduct" (first adopted in 1983, accessible at http://www.abanet.org/cpr/mrpc/rule_3_6.html); monopolizing the subject position of aggrieved victim has become crucial for proponents of the death penalty and other "get tough on crime" measures. In this regard, see three essays by Jennifer K. Wood: "In Whose Name? Crime Victim Policy and the Punishing Power of Protection," *National Women's Studies Association Journal* 17 (2005): 1–17; "Justice as Therapy: The Victim Rights Clarification Act," *Communication Quarterly* 51 (2003): 296–311; and "Refined Raw: The Symbolic Violence of Victims Rights Reforms," in *Un-Disciplining Literature: Literature, Law, and Culture,* ed. Kostas and Linda Myrsiades (New York: Peter Lang, 2000), 72–93; on the question of pretrial publicity and race, see Travis L. Dixon and Daniel G. Linz, "Television News, Prejudicial Pretrial Publicity, and the Depiction of Race," *Journal of Broadcasting and Electronic Media* 46 (2002): 112–136.

7. Jimmie L. Reeves and Richard Campbell, *Cracked Coverage: Television News, the Anti-Cocaine Crusade, and the Reagan Legacy* (Durham, NC: Duke University Press, 1994), 15; for more information on racialized drug coverage, see Clarence Lusane, *Pipe Dream Blues: Racism and the War on Drugs* (Cambridge, MA: South End Press, 1991), and Daniel Larson's essay in this volume (chapter 3).

8. For my study on network news, see Travis L. Dixon, Cristina Azocar, and Michael Casas, "The Portrayal of Race and Crime on Television Network News," *Journal of Broadcasting and Electronic Media* 47, no. 4 (2003): 495–520; for other important studies of biased network news programming, see Robert Entman, "Representation and Reality in the Portrayal of Blacks on Network Television News," *Journalism Quarterly* 71, no. 3 (1994): 509–20; on racialized portrayals of welfare, see Martin Gilens, "Race and Poverty in America: Public Misperceptions and the American News Media," *Public Opinion Quarterly* 60, no. 4 (1996): 515–41, and Martin Gilens, *Why Americans Hate Welfare: Race, Media, and the Politics of Antipoverty Policy* (Chicago: University of Chicago Press, 1999).

9. For more information on the methodological claims for the power of surveys and experiments, see Earl Babbie, *Survey Research Methods,* 2d ed. (Belmont, CA: Wadsworth, 1990), and Earl Babbie, *The Practice of Social Research* (Belmont, CA: Wadsworth, 1992).

10. For more information on chronic activation and stereotypical processing as-

sociated with news programs, see Robert W. Livingston, "What You See Is What You Get: Systematic Variability in Perceptual-Based Social Judgment," *Personality and Social Psychology Bulletin* 27, no. 9 (2001): 1086–96; Travis L. Dixon, "Psychological Reactions to Crime News Portrayals of Black Criminals: Understanding the Moderating Roles of Prior News Viewing and Stereotype Endorsement," *Communication Monographs* 73, no. 2 (2006): 162–87; and Travis L. Dixon and Cristina Azocar, "Priming Crime and Activating Blackness: Understanding the Psychological Impact of the Overrepresentation of African Americans as Lawbreakers on Television News," *Journal of Communication* 57, no. 2 (2007): 229–53.

11. See Mary Beth Oliver, "Caucasian Viewers' Memory of Black and White Criminal Suspects in the News," *Journal of Communication* 49, no. 3 (1999): 46–60.

12. See Franklin D. Gilliam and Shanto Iyengar, "Superpredator Script," *Nieman Reports* 52, no. 4 (1998): 45–46, and Gilliam and Iyengar, "Prime Suspects."

13. See Dixon, "Psychological Reactions to Crime News Portrayals of Black Criminals"; Dixon and Azocar, "Priming Crime and Activating Blackness"; and Travis L. Dixon and Keith B. Maddox, "Skin Tone, Crime News, and Social Reality Judgments: Priming the Stereotype of the Dark and Dangerous Black Criminal," *Journal of Applied Social Psychology* 38, no. 8 (2005): 1555–70.

14. See Dixon, "Psychological Reactions to Crime News Portrayals of Black Criminals"; Dixon and Azocar, "Priming Crime and Activating Blackness"; and Travis L. Dixon and Keith B. Maddox, "Skin Tone, Crime News, and Social Reality Judgments"; these conclusions are echoed in Oliver, "Caucasian Viewers' Memory of Black and White Criminal Suspects in the News."

15. See Mary Beth Oliver and Dana Fonash, "Race and Crime in the News: Whites' Identification and Misidentification of Violent and Nonviolent Criminal Suspects," *Media Psychology* 4 (2002): 137–56; Mark Peffley, Todd Shields, and Bruce Williams, "The Intersection of Race and Crime in Television News Stories: An Experimental Study," *Political Communication* 13, no. 3 (1996): 309–27; and James D. Johnson, Mike S. Adams, William Hall, and Leslie Ashburn, "Race, Media and Violence: Differential Racial Effects of Exposure to Violent News Stories," *Basic and Applied Social Psychology* 19, no. 1 (1997): 81–90.

16. Paul Street, "Color Bind: Prisons and the New American Racism," in *Prison Nation: The Warehousing of America's Poor*, ed. Tara Herivel and Paul Wright (New York: Routledge, 2003), 30–40; Eduardo Bonilla Silva, *White Supremacy and Racism in the Post–Civil Rights Era* (Boulder, CO: Lynne Rienner, 2001), and *Racism without Racists: Color-Blind Racism and the Persistence of Racial Inequality in the United States* (Boulder, CO: Rowman and Littlefield, 2003); on "racism without racists" in the prison-industrial complex, see PCARE, "Fighting the Prison-Industrial Complex: A Call to Communication and Cultural Studies Scholars to Change the World," *Communication and Critical Cultural Studies* 4, no. 4 (2007): 402–20, and Gilliam and Iyengar, "Prime Suspects."

17. Travis L. Dixon, "Crime News and Racialized Beliefs: Understanding the Relationship between Local News Viewing and Perceptions of African Americans and Crime," *Journal of Communication* 58, no. 1 (2008): 106–25.

18. See *The Smartest Guys in the Room*, dir. Alex Gibney (Los Angeles: Magnolia

Pictures, 2005); for an introduction to white-collar crime, see the resources posted by the FBI at www.fbi.gov/whitecollarcrime.htm; for macro-analyses of the media, see Robert W. McChesney, *The Problem of the Media: U.S. Communication Politics in the Twenty-First Century* (New York: Monthly Review Press, 2004), and Robert W. McChesney, *Rich Media, Poor Democracy: Communication Politics in Dubious Times* (Urbana: University of Illinois Press, 1999); for my analysis of these misrepresentations, see Dixon and Linz, "Overrepresentation and Underrepresentation of African Americans and Latinos."

19. For background on FCC policy and lobbying, see Pat Aufderheide, *Communications Policy and the Public Interest* (New York: Guilford Press, 1999); on news culture and producing change, see Don Heider, *White News: Why Local News Programs Don't Cover People of Color* (Mahwah, NJ: Erlbaum, 2000); for research on how counter-stereotypical depictions can thwart stereotypes, see Juanita Covert and Travis L. Dixon, "A Changing View: Representation and Effects of Women of Color in Mainstream Women's Magazines," *Communication Research* 35, no. 2 (2008): 232–56; for further suggestions on media activism, see Robert McChesney, Russell Newman, and Ben Scott, eds., *The Future of the Media: Resistance and Reform in the 21st Century* (New York: Seven Stories Press, 2005); on media activism and prisons, see PCARE, "Fighting the Prison-Industrial Complex."

In Search of Salvation

William T. Smith

A member of the Writing Workshop at the Champaign County Jail, in Champaign, Illinois, William T. Smith writes poems full of religious imagery and a wry sense of personal responsibility; this piece was published in *Captured Words/Free Thoughts* 1 (Summer 2006).

O Lord, you say *Far too long*
have I been absorbed with
the destructive manners of man
for the spirit stands willing
but the flesh is weak
and though I am covered with sin
you peer beneath to see
the lost child running wild
running from truth salvation
and the purity of thy word
running headlong into oblivion
as if I had never heard your truths

I constantly take disastrous routes
that lead to nowhere
and sit on the bottom steps of negativity
with head hung low
pleading begging demanding
that you rescue me O Lord
like I have a right to demand anything!

Yet always when I fall
through devices of my own making
I assume you'll be there O Lord
to pick me up
dust me off
and send me about
my merry, destructive way
time and time again
until one day
it will be too late

Chapter 5

Diagnosing the Schools-to-Prisons Pipeline: Maximum Security, Minimum Learning

Rose Braz and Myesha Williams

In the course of 24 hours in May 2007, without holding a single public hearing, much less a public vote, the California state legislature passed the largest prison-expansion plan in U.S. history. The law, AB900, will add 40,000 new prison beds and 13,000 new jail beds and will cost the state $15 billion for construction and debt service; that stunning price tag is deceptive, however, for it does not include future operating costs, which will amount to hundreds of millions of dollars for generations to come. Of this $15 billion, interest payments on the bonds that will be sold to finance the new prison construction will amount to as much as $330 million per year by 2011. Readers may wonder why California purportedly needs to embark on this unprecedented prison expansion, for it already warehouses more people in its prisons than any other state in the Union (with roughly 12 percent of the nation's population, the state was responsible for 20 percent of the total increase in the number of people imprisoned during the twelve-month period ending June 30, 2006). In fact, the proposed increase of 40,000 prison beds surpasses the number of existing prison beds in 41 states. And so California, a state confronted by annual budget shortfalls, and already locking up the nation's largest prison population, has embarked on the astronomically expensive construction of 53,000 new beds for prisoners not yet captured, all to be paid for with taxes not yet collected—leading experts such as Ruth Wilson Gilmore to wonder whether the Golden State is becoming a "Golden Gulag."[1]

While California and other states shift their resources toward mass incarceration, the nation's schools face a funding crisis that affects the already curtailed educational opportunities of the poor, and especially poor people of color. For example, Gary Hopkins reports that "one-half million of the 9.5 million students enrolled in school [nationwide] leave without completing a high school program"—that is a dropout rate of roughly 6 percent. Among the nation's so-called dropouts (a term we will take exception to later), students classified as Hispanic are more likely to leave school than black or white students, and students from low-income families are six times as likely to leave school as students from high-income families. These are alarming trends, for leaving school dramatically escalates the likelihood of incarceration; in fact, the Bureau of Justice Statistics (hereafter BJS) reports that as of 2003, approximately 75 percent of the people incarcerated in state prisons had not received a high school diploma. We are therefore witnesses to a disastrous cycle wherein prison spending rises, educational spending declines, the number of students pushed out of school in at-risk communities rises, and then those students disproportionately end up imprisoned, hence helping to fuel the call for more prison spending, which in turn curtails education spending, which leads to more students pushed out of school, and on and on it goes. California's AB900 will turn this self-defeating cycle into an institutionalized funding imperative, for because of that bill's guidelines, spending on the state's prison budget is projected to rise by 9 percent annually, while spending on the state's already beleaguered postsecondary educational system is projected to rise by only 5 percent over the same period. Thus, by fiscal year 2012–13, California is projected to spend $15.4 billion on locking people up and $15.3 billion on higher education. As our title suggests, then, we believe the schools-to-prisons pipeline is fueled by persuasive yet delusional policies by which students are offered maximum security while receiving minimum learning.[2]

To pursue these charges, this chapter analyzes the connections between the prison-industrial complex and America's educational crisis. We argue that increases in prison funding are devastating educational opportunities for many students and that the policing technologies of the prison-industrial complex are increasingly migrating into classrooms; as a result, many students report that when they go to school, they are not being challenged, inspired, and treated as future leaders, but placed under surveillance, conditioned to accept second-class lives, and treated as future prisoners. To support these claims, we document how our education system increasingly uses juvenile prisons, detention, policing in schools, metal detectors, surveillance cameras in the classrooms, and zero-tolerance discipline policies to respond to larger social problems within our schools and communities. We are particularly committed to demonstrating how the Bush administration's No Child Left Behind Act is an outgrowth of so-called zero-tolerance policies that have, in invoking law and order, actually accelerated the number of youths caught up in the schools-to-prisons pipeline. The term *dropout* is therefore misleading, for we argue that the combined forces of increases in prison spending, the No Child Left Behind Act, legacies of racism, and schools that function more like juvenile detention centers than youth empowerment zones are actually pushing students into the juvenile and adult prison systems—activists have therefore begun to refer to these students not as dropouts but as pushouts. We accordingly argue that reversing the devastating effects of the schools-to-prisons pipeline requires addressing the educational needs of pushouts and, ultimately, abolishing the prison-industrial complex.[3]

"A Budget Is a Statement of Priorities"; or, How Rising Prison Spending Produces Underfunded Public Schools and Abandoned Communities

When a reporter asked him about state spending on imprisonment, Bill Shiebler, the president of the University of California Student Association, responded that "a budget is a statement of priorities. I think our state's got its priorities wrong. . . . It seems they're more interested in locking people up than in giving people an opportunity in life." While Shiebler's analysis is correct, it is important to remember that California's skewed priorities did not begin with AB900—the crisis has its roots (at least some of them) in the budget crisis of 2002. At the time, the general fund's shortfall over the next year and a half was projected to top $34 billion. In response to the dilemma, Democratic governor Gray Davis proposed a budget for 2003–2004 that, as the state's independent Legislative Analyst's Office highlighted, "identifies major proposed reductions in all areas of the state budget except criminal justice. It includes major reductions in K–12 and community college funding." Indeed, because of the proposed $14 billion cut in K–12 education funding, approximately 30,000 teachers, nurses, counselors, and school administrators were sent layoff warning notices, class-size reduction programs were on the chopping block, the San Francisco Unified School District was forced to cancel summer school for elementary school students, and the rural Clovis School District canceled 135 school bus-route stops. At the community college level, tuition was slated to double under the proposed budget; estimates showed that more than 100,000 community college students would likely not be able to afford to return to school—they too would become pushouts. And so the state's educational system was slated to be gutted while prison spending would rise.[4]

Indeed, the same budget that proposed to cut $14 billion from education sought to spend $40 million more on existing prisons, to continue plans to build a new $595 million state prison, and to add 965 new death cells (at a cost of an additional $220 million), all while cutting funding for academic and vocational training programs for prisoners. This prompted the California Teachers Association's John Hein to complain: "I don't know what happened to the governor who said that education was his first, second, and third priorities. Maybe now he is the governor who believes corrections is his first, second, and third priorities." While Davis may have been trying to position himself as a "Get Tough on Crime" candidate capable of standing tall against Republicans, his budgetary priorities clearly violated the wishes of those who elected him, for a December 2001 poll found that four times as many surveyed Californians preferred to reduce the state's prison budget as preferred to cut higher education. Such sentiments reflected Californians' longstanding pride in what was once one of the great public education systems in the world: in 1964, the golden state ranked fourth in the nation in per-pupil spending, yet forty years later, by budget year 2003–2004, California had risen to first in the nation in prison spending while dropping to forty-fourth in the nation on state government expenditures for education per $1,000 of personal income. It would be a mistake to place all the blame on Governor Davis's 2003–2004 budget—there were many factors contributing to the political sea changes we are discussing—yet the figures cited here make it painfully evident that, as Shiebler argued, California has "got its priorities wrong." In fact, between 1984 and 2005, California built twenty-four new prisons and only two new universities. This is a disastrous trend, for slashing educational funding while feeding the prison system can only produce two results: worse schools and more prisoners.[5]

While Governor Davis's 2003–2004 budget illustrates how California was choosing to invest in becoming a "golden gulag" rather than a leader in education, many other states were also diverting funds from education to incarceration. For example, between 1977 and 1999, total state and local expenditures on corrections increased by 946 percent, roughly two-and-a-half times the rate of increase in spending on education. Thinking proportionally, between 1980 and 2000, corrections' share of all state and local spending grew by 104 percent while higher education spending dropped by 21 percent. This remarkable drop in education spending and escalation of state and local spending on prisons has resulted in an incarceration nation where, according to the National Association of State Budget Officers, total state expenditures on corrections were projected to reach $45.7 billion in fiscal year 2006. Even professionals who work in the prison-industrial complex recognize the consequences of this spending pattern. As Michael Jacobson, director of the Vera Institute in New York and the former head of the New York State Department of Corrections notes, "budgets are a zero-sum game. . . . The money for corrections comes from other places. . . . When you think about some of the alternatives for spending that kind of money, there are much better things you can do for public safety that would be a lot more effective." Unfortunately, schools are not only being forced to function with smaller budgets, but the prison system that is hedging in on their resources is, as we discuss below, increasingly migrating into classrooms and hence turning many schools into Lockdown High.[6]

Lockdown High; or, How the Prison-Industrial Complex Harms the Classroom

According to a report released in 2000 by the U.S. Congress's Bi-Partisan Working Group on Youth Violence, "statistically speaking, schools are among the safest places for children to be." In fact, the Justice Policy Institute's *School House Hype: School Shootings and the Real Risks Kids Face in America* observes that "99% of the times a youth is killed in America, it is outside of a school." Nonetheless, Bernardine Dohrn reports that "between 1990 and 1995, while juvenile homicides dropped 13 percent, related coverage on network evening news programs increased by 240%"—so what the public believes about violent crimes at school is not based on material facts but on mediated fantasies. As Barry Glassner argues in *The Culture of Fear*, our collective anxiety grows "proportionate to our unacknowledged guilt. By slashing spending on educational, medical, and antipoverty programs for youths, we adults have committed great violence against them. Yet rather than face up to our collective responsibility we project our violence onto young people themselves." One result of this projection of fear onto young people, and especially young people of color, is that the policing strategies of the prison-industrial complex are increasingly being implemented in our schools. Arising from frightening but statistically rare and isolated incidents of schoolyard violence, juvenile crime and education laws have increasingly focused on suspension, expulsion, curfews, zero-tolerance policies, and harsh law enforcement responses to school-based misconduct. We argue that these policies have not made our schools or communities safer; rather, they have turned many of our schools into auxiliaries of the prison-industrial complex. To prove this charge, we offer below a series of observations on how the prison-industrial complex is harming the educational promises and priorities of our schools.[7]

Zero Tolerance in the Schoolhouse

The term *zero tolerance* was coined by the Reagan administration during its so-called war on drugs, but, as a response to much-publicized incidents of school yard violence, it was soon applied to classrooms as well. The Clinton administration then escalated the crackdown on the alleged (but factually inaccurate) rising tide of school violence when it implemented the Gun Free Schools Act in 1994. The act marked a significant milestone in education's response to harm, for while the act mandated that the punishment for any student found on school property with a firearm is expulsion, the act also called for the application of zero-tolerance policies across a wide range of other actions in the schoolhouse—and the results have been disastrous. For example, in 2000 the Justice Policy Institute and the Kentucky Children's Law Center issued a report outlining the following cases:

» A seventeen-year-old junior was expelled after he shot a paper clip with a rubber band at a classmate, missed, and broke the skin of a cafeteria worker.

» A nine-year-old on the way to school found a manicure kit with a one-inch knife, brought the object to school, and was suspended for one day.

» In Louisiana, a twelve-year-old diagnosed with a hyperactive disorder warned fellow students not to eat all the potatoes, or "I'm going to get you." The student was suspended for two days, then referred to police by the principal and charged with making "terroristic threats." The student was imprisoned for two weeks while awaiting trial.

» Two ten-year-old boys in Virginia were suspended for three days for putting soapy water in a teacher's drink. Police charged the boys with a felony, carrying a potential twenty-year sentence; the case was eventually dismissed months later.

» In Texas, a class assignment asked a thirteen-year-old to write a "scary" Halloween story, and so a student wrote about an imagined school shooting. He received a passing grade but was referred to the school principal's office. School officials called the police, and the child spent six days in jail before the courts confirmed that no crime had been committed.

» In Florida, a fourteen-year-old disabled student was referred to the principal for allegedly stealing $2 from another student. The principal called the police, who charged the student with strong-armed robbery. The student was held for six weeks in an adult jail. In response to local media criticism about his decision to file adult felony charges, the prosecutor criticized the media, alleging that "depicting this forcible felony, this strong-arm robbery, in terms as though it were no more than a $2 shoplifting fosters and promotes violence in our schools." Charges were eventually dropped.[8]

In each of these stories, overzealous zero-tolerance guidelines escalated low-level schoolhouse incidents into allegedly criminal actions requiring suspension, or expulsion, or even police intervention. In the name of getting tough on crime, the delicate give-and-take of student-teacher relationships and the intricate dance of student-student interactions were turned into adversarial battles wherein students were shamed, heavily disciplined, and in some cases imprisoned. This is not a good pedagogical model; this is no way to inculcate a love of learning and a healthy respect for self and others.

Moreover, a host of scholars, activists, parents, and educators have demonstrated that zero-tolerance policies disproportionately affect students of color. For example, a 1999 study by the Applied Research Center found that while African American students composed 16 percent of students in the San Francisco Unified School District, they received 52 percent of its suspensions. A national study that same year surveyed ten school districts and found that black students, already suspended or expelled at higher rates than their white peers, faced even harsher disciplinary treatment under zero-tolerance policies. The nationwide study concluded that black students total 17 percent of the public school population but account for 34 percent of all out-of-school suspensions and 30 percent of all expulsions; by contrast, white students, who account for 62 percent of the student population, received 48 percent of all out-of-school suspensions and 49 percent of all expulsions. In short, under zero-tolerance policies, black and Latino students are 70 percent more likely than white students to be disciplined, and between 200 and 300 percent as likely to be suspended. Summarizing these findings, a report by the Advancement Project concluded that zero tolerance means that black and Latino students tend to be pushed out of the schoolhouse faster than their white peers—zero tolerance thus means diminished educational opportunities, and therefore hope, for children of color. This pushing away of some children has dire consequences, for states with higher school suspension rates are more likely to have higher juvenile incarceration rates. The schools-to-prisons pipeline is therefore greased with policies such as zero tolerance.[9]

For an example of how racial biases and racially driven responses to social conflict fuel community tension and lead some students to imprisonment, consider the recent train of events in Jena, Louisiana. White students hung nooses from a tree in front of Jena High School after a black student asked permission to sit under a tree that had traditionally been regarded as the territory of white students only. To protest the display of nooses—a clear reference to Jim Crow–era lynchings, and hence effectively a death threat—nearly every black student in the school stood under the tree. When the town's district attorney and some police officers arrived on the scene, they advised the black students to stop making such a fuss over the nooses, which school administrators deemed a "harmless prank." After this initial round of controversy, when some white students admitted to hanging the nooses, they were not severely punished; when white students beat up a black student at a party, they were not severely punished; when a white former student threatened two black students with a shotgun, he was not severely punished. But when six black students got into a fight with a white student, they were charged with attempted murder and threatened with long prison sentences. The "Jena 6" have subsequently received massive media attention, worldwide outpourings of support, and legal counseling, but their case indicates how zero-tolerance policies are applied according to longstanding racial biases.[10]

As is often the case in America, race is closely affiliated with class in the thinking about the effects of zero-tolerance policies. For example, *Equity or Exclusion,* a 2003 report by the National Center for Schools and Communities at Fordham University, found an overwhelming correlation between high suspension rates and schools that were both racially segregated and underresourced. Schools with the highest suspension rates were also the most overcrowded, staffed with the least qualified teachers, hosted the fewest extracurricular activities, housed the worst libraries, and offered the fewest functioning computers—and were servicing the highest percentage of black and Latino students. Zero-tolerance policies thus seem to be pushed upon students of color who attend the least affluent schools, yet even while flagging the unequal application of zero-tolerance policies, we need to emphasize that suspension and expulsion are not effective deterrents of violence, regardless of where they are applied. Indeed, the Justice Policy Institute found that although suspensions have doubled since the 1970s, the level of violent crime in schools has remained constant. Rather than making our schools safer, then, racially driven and class-based suspensions and expulsions function as social reinforcers, as powerful lessons that reduce a student's excitement about school, that foster disciplinary rather than learning environments, and that create a self-sustaining culture of low achievement. In sum, a school environment enmeshed in and even grounded upon prison-style punishments, and driven by zero-tolerance policies, impedes the promises of constructive pedagogy and social justice, hence fueling the rise of our punishing democracy.[11]

Police and Security Guards Replace Counselors

As a part of this disastrous turn to zero-tolerance policies, schools, especially those located in moderate to high-poverty areas, have increasingly been prodded to turn to police rather than teachers, counselors, and mediators to address harm. For example, in New York City, initially under the direction of then-mayor Rudy Giuliani, school security has been taken over largely by the police. The Division of School Safety was formally transferred from the Board of Education to the New York Police Department on December 20, 1998. Susan Amlung, a spokeswoman for the United Federation of Teachers, hoped at the time that "maybe the New York Police Department knows something the schools don't. They have an expertise the school system just lacks." In contrast, Carl Haynes, representing Local 237 of the International Brotherhood of Teamsters, gave a statement titled "Schools Are Not Jails/Keep Cops Afar," wherein he argued that "cops do not belong in the schools." But they are now there in unprecedented numbers; it is not surprising that, as critics feared, the transfer of authority from the Board of Education to the Police Department resulted in a tremendous growth in the number of school security personnel (formally called School Security Agents, SSAs) and budgetary dollars devoted to security. Indeed, prior to the 1998 transfer, the New York school safety division employed 3,200 personnel; by the start of the 2005–2006 school year, New York City had increased the number of SSAs to 4,625 and had deployed an additional 200 armed New York City policemen and policewomen to patrol the hallways of New York City's public schools. As Julie Drew and William Lyons argue in *Punishing Schools*, such heavy-handed tactics "construct students as either potential victims in need of protection, or as criminals in need of punishment. . . . [E]ither option is predicated on a lack of agency."[12]

Drug Testing

Another way the prison-industrial complex has invaded our classrooms is through the pervasive use of mandatory drug testing, which is now a regular occurrence in middle and high schools in approximately 1,000 districts across the country. Federal officials estimate that an average of one school a month adds testing programs, with school drug testing spreading even more rapidly since the events of September 11, 2001. When drug testing was first implemented widely in schools, some parents complained about the invasive practice, especially when required for students who participate in extracurricular school activities, but the U.S. Supreme Court ruled in 2002 that testing students involved in such programs, as long as it does not affect their right to an education, does not violate their Fourth Amendment rights. This legal hair-splitting misses the point, however, since such drug testing is, we believe, teaching students the norms of a life of perpetual surveillance and suspicion. Moreover, one of the largest studies on school drug testing, conducted by three scholars at the University of Michigan Institute for Social Research in 2003, and questioning 90,000 students at 900 schools nationwide, found essentially identical rates of drug use in schools that used drug tests and those that did not—*mandatory drug testing made no difference in usage rates*. For this reason and others, the California State Parent Teacher Association, the American Academy of Pediatrics, the National Education Association, the National Council on Alcoholism and Drug Dependence, and the vast majority of the nation's school districts oppose school-based drug testing. In addition, few physicians support school-based testing of adolescents for drugs, as a national survey of physicians (pediatrics, family medicine, and adolescent medicine) found that 83 percent disagreed with drug testing in public schools. Drug testing in schools is therefore an example of bad pedagogy, ineffective criminology, and heavily opposed medical practice.[13]

Furthermore, while mandatory drug testing does not reduce school drug use, experts increasingly fear that the policy actually impedes other school programs and policies that do work. For example, the Academy of Pediatrics notes that "our experience—and a broad body of relevant research—convinces us that a policy [of random student drug testing] *cannot* work in the way it is hoped to and will, for many adolescents, interfere with more sound prevention and treatment processes." Likewise, Elizabeth J. Clark, executive director of the National Association of Social Workers, writes that "social workers, concerned with a child's well being, question whether [drug testing] will do more harm than good." In her dissenting opinion in *Board of Education of Pottawatomie v. Earls,* U.S. Supreme Court Justice Ruth Bader Ginsburg argued that the Oklahoma drug testing policy under consideration "falls short doubly if deterrence is its aim: It invades the privacy of students who need deterrence least, and risks steering students at greatest risk for substance abuse away from extra-curricular involvement that potentially may palliate drug problems." These experts agree, then, that mandatory drug testing puts children under surveillance, and likely drives possible drug users away from the very activities that might give them reasons to believe in themselves, their schools, and their communities. Instead of addressing underlying social crises, mandatory drug testing imports the policing techniques of the prison-industrial complex—with the predictable bad results.[14]

Metal Detectors

As technology advances and becomes increasingly accessible and mobile, so we have witnessed a tremendous expansion of the use of prison-related technologies in the schoolhouse. For example, in 2003, nearly all surveyed students between the ages of twelve and eighteen reported the presence of one or more technological security measures at their school. In some facilities, metal detectors are the first thing greeting any student, parent, teacher, or visitor; in other schools, the hallways are lined with surveillance cameras. Like other manifestations of the prison-industrial complex in the classroom, these mechanisms are not working; in fact, U.S. Department of Education researchers concluded that using such prison-related technologies in schools is "not likely to be effective" and even potentially harmful.[15]

Indeed, while get-tough-on-crime proponents argue that stocking the schools with police, SSAs, surveillance cameras, and metal detectors makes our schools safer, the facts do not support that position. Consider the proliferation of SSA-staffed metal detectors in New York City, where they have been deployed ostensibly to catch students smuggling guns and other weapons into schools. The NYCLU's *Criminalizing the Classroom* documents 17,352 "confiscated items" turned up in roving metal-detector searches conducted between April and December 2006—and "not a single gun was found." *Not a single gun.* So the only guns making their way into New York City's schools are those bouncing upon the hips of the police. Rather than protecting the schools by snaring weapons, such roving searches netted immense piles of the electronic paraphernalia of a new generation's communicative devices and gaming toys. While millions of dollars are spent arming the schools with metal detectors and a massive force of SSAs (there are more SSAs in New York City schools than police officers in Boston, Detroit, San Diego, and Phoenix), the educational budgets of many of the affected schools are dismal. In fact, whereas New York City spends an average of $11,282 per year per high school student, those schools with permanent metal detectors spend only $9,602 per year per student, only 85 percent of the citywide average. Those schools with more than 3,000 students and permanent metal detectors spend only $8,066 per year per student, 71 percent of the citywide average. So the most heavily policed students receive the least educational funding. In fact, of those schools with permanent metal detectors, *only 53 percent even have librarians*. This means that some of New York City's schools are treating their poor students like prisoners-in-waiting: they are subject to constant surveillance, they are accosted by belligerent police and SSAs, they receive less educational funding than other students, and many of them have no access to librarians. These young people are being taught to fail, taught that they are expendable, taught that they are permanent members of a second-class caste. The situation has become so dire that Jonathan Kozol, the celebrated historian of America's public education system, has argued that we are witnessing "the restoration of apartheid schooling."[16]

Big Brother Is Watching: Surveillance Cameras

Along with metal detectors, police in schools, and drug testing, America's schools increasingly rely upon surveillance cameras. For example, in 2002, approximately 950 new public schools opened in the United States; architects estimate that three-quarters of those new schools were equipped with surveillance cameras. The Biloxi, Mississippi, public school district leads the nation in schoolhouse surveillance technology: It uses cameras not only in corridors and common areas but in all 500 of its classrooms. Steve Lillienthal, director of the Free Congress Foundation, believes that "putting cameras on children trains them to believe that being watched every minute of the day is O.K. But they should be teaching students to behave not because a camera is on them, but because it is the right thing to do." Indeed, like drug testing for students who want to participate in extracurricular activities, it seems to us that relying upon surveillance cameras misses the point: We are not made safe because we are watched by technology, but by inculcating values of respect, solidarity, and good communication. Indeed, we believe that a school environment where students are constantly being watched has grave implications for learning and development. For rather than learning how to think creatively, how to solve problems, and how to communicate across social divisions—that is, rather than being taught the skills necessary for becoming successful adults—students today are too often taught to think of themselves either as suspects or as potential victims whose safety depends on a machine. Moreover, we suspect that knowing that every discussion in class, every flirtation in the hallway, every casual exchange between student and teacher, *every single interaction is being recorded*, must have dire consequences on students' and teachers' lives.[17]

No Child Left Behind: Pushing Students into the Schools-to-Prisons Pipeline

In the preceding section we argued that the prison-industrial complex is harming America's schools by encouraging local administrators to implement disastrous zero-tolerance policies, to contract school safety to armed police and police-managed SSAs, to use mandatory drug tests, to deploy metal detectors, and to rely upon surveillance cameras, all purportedly deployed to ensure the safety of students, teachers, and administrators. These five steps, each a reflection of the creeping influence of the prison-industrial complex in our nation's schools, have not made our schools safer, yet they have helped to foster a culture of fear, one where students, and especially students of color, tend to feel that they are treated less like future leaders and more like suspects. This is why we do not use the term *dropout,* for we believe the policing-in-schools strategies addressed here are leading some students to the door, literally inviting them to leave school. As argued by Steve Orel, the founder of World of Opportunity, "I have yet to meet a single student who woke up one morning and consciously chose to leave school. My experience has been that the school system left them."[18]

Perhaps the most glaring example of how America's schools have abandoned our children, the Bush Administration's No Child Left Behind Act (NCLB) encapsulates many of the issues we have been addressing here. Indeed, we think of the NCLB as the legislative embodiment of zero-tolerance policies, for at its disciplinary core, the NCLB enforces a zero-tolerance mandate on schools and students: When schools do not improve their rankings on standardized tests, lower dropout rates, reduce absenteeism, and raise the percentage of students who graduate in four years, the NCLB mandates automatic state takeover and reorganization. But rather than enabling schools to raise their performances in these crucial criteria—by supporting creative pedagogical practices, providing the funds for new hiring, and encouraging extracurricular activities—the threat of NCLB-ordered takeover as a consequence of failure has created new pressures for schools to push out students whose performances lower their school's overall ranking. As Mark Soler of the Youth Law Center stated, "Zero tolerance is fed less by fear of crime and more by high-stakes testing. Principals want to get rid of kids they perceive as trouble." In fact, Title V of the No Child Left Behind Act, "Safe Schools for the 21st Century," empowers teachers "to remove violent or persistently disruptive students from the classroom. In order to receive funds from this program, states must adopt a zero-tolerance policy for violent or persistently disruptive students." The problem with this strategy, however, as we demonstrated in our previous section, is that the bar of what counts as violent or disruptive behavior has been lowered to the point of threatening the presence of many children in our schools. Moreover, expecting already overcrowded and underfunded schools to live up to unreasonable expectations on standardized tests is a virtual recipe for failure. The NCLB's version of zero tolerance functions, then, not as an encouragement but as a threat, not as empowerment but as criminalization.[19]

These unproductive transformations in how America manages its schools have been accelerated by fear of terrorism. For example, in a U.S. Department of Education fact sheet on the NCLB, the DoE lists reasons it believes NCLB will make schools safer and drug-free. Among those reasons: "America has learned important lessons from September 11. One of the most important lessons is that we must be prepared for the worst. . . . The president believes the first job of government is to protect its citizens—whether the threat is terrorists abroad, criminals at home, or predators or drug dealers in or near schools." The DoE fact sheet goes on to state that NCLB makes schools safer by protecting "teachers, principals and other school professionals from frivolous litigation when they take reasonable actions to maintain order and discipline in the classroom." The NCLB thus invokes the specter of terrorism while offering teachers new legal protections in the event of lawsuits, but it does little in the way of encouraging creative pedagogy rooted in the needs of local communities. Rather, by implementing zero-tolerance policies, metal detectors, drug testing, police in schools, surveillance cameras, and standardized tests, the NCLB actually discourages some students from coming to school while leading some administrators to perceive low-achieving students as hampering school standings in standardized student achievement test scores. The students who require the most attention are therefore penalized, marginalized, treated not as individual learners with specific needs but as collective administrative failures. We therefore applaud the conclusions of a 2005 study conducted by researchers at Arizona State University's Education Policy Studies Laboratory, which called for a moratorium on NCLB's high-stakes testing practices.[20]

Our critique of the NCLB as a harsh extension of prison-related policing strategies and technologies is driven by the assumption that *students cannot be coerced into learning*. Rather, good pedagogical practices (such as those illustrated in part 2 of this book) find ways to make learning fun, to encourage both risk-taking and responsibility, and to inculcate trust and friendship among students and teachers—students must feel that learning is in their best interest, and they must feel that teachers are figures of respect and wisdom. Turning teachers into faux-police, turning schools into surveillance zones, and turning lesson plans into rote learning for the purposes of passing standardized tests—thus turning schools from places of wonder into zones of discipline and fear—are therefore virtually guaranteed to fail, especially in neighborhoods with long histories of underfunded schools. For example, the *New York Times* reports that at the Abraham Lincoln High School in East Los Angeles, a historically poor neighborhood, only seven out of one hundred students perform at grade level in mathematics or English; at the Woodrow Wilson High School, only four out of seven do so. Statewide, "all 6,063 public schools serving poor students will be declared [by NCLB rules] in need of restructuring." We argue that what these schools need is not NCLB-mandated "restructuring"; rather, they need more teachers, better facilities, more creative arts and musical offerings, more sports programs, and more opportunities and support for meaningful parent involvement—in short, they need our care and attention, not NCLB-driven threats.[21]

Conclusion: Abolishing Prisons, Rebuilding Democracy

What message does it send our children when we tell them that in order to go to school, they must be searched, probed, tested for drugs, and watched at all times? What does it say about the competency of our school system when we resort to treating students as if they will commit a crime every time they go to school? How does it affect learning to go to school under the heavy burden of possibly being removed from school either temporarily or permanently for minor infractions, or of being arrested for petty school offenses? How can learning be imaginative and fun when it is pegged not to individual growth and communal values but to standardized tests? As we have argued here, these questions point to a culture that penalizes the poor and especially poor students of color, who, because of zero tolerance and other prison-related disciplinary maneuvers, are being pushed from the schoolhouse and into the schools-to-prisons pipeline. In short, the atmosphere created by these policies has resulted in a maximum-security but minimum-learning environment.

Rather than continuing to pursue prison-related disciplinary measures, we have argued that we must instead focus on empowerment: that means revoking NCLB, removing police and metal detectors and surveillance cameras from schools, and returning the power of making lesson plans to teachers freed from the threat of standardized tests. To fund this renewed commitment to our children's futures, we propose shifting resources away from mass incarceration and back to education; we thus urge the defunding of the prison-industrial complex by reducing the number of people in prison and closing prisons, with these steps leading to the reinvestment of those funds into our communities. We are calling, then, for redirecting the billions of dollars poured into the prison-industrial complex into a "peace dividend" committed to enhancing our schools. Indeed, closing the schools-to-prisons pipeline by rebuilding and reinventing our nation's schools is a necessary first step toward abolishing the prison-industrial complex and thus reclaiming hope and justice from our punishing democracy.[22]

Notes

1. The details of AB900 are discussed in James Sterngold, "Prisons' Budget to Trump Colleges': No Other Big State Spends as Much to Incarcerate Compared with Higher Education Funding," *San Francisco Chronicle* (21 May 2007), A1, available at www.sfgate.com/cgibin/article.-cgi?f=/c/a/2007/05/21/MNG4KPUKV51.DTL; incarceration figures are from Bureau of Justice Statistics, *Prison and Jail Inmates at Midyear 2006* (Washington, DC: U.S. Department of Justice, 2007), 3; the closing phrase is borrowed from Ruth Wilson Gilmore, *Golden Gulag: Prisons, Surplus, Crisis, and Opposition in Globalizing California* (Berkeley: University of California Press, 2007)—and see 97–102 for her analysis of the long-term implications of the funding choices noted here.

2. Gary Hopkins, "Who Are Today's School Dropouts?" a 2006 report posted by Education World, available at www.educationworld.com/a_admin/admin/admin026 .html; additional data along these lines is available from the National Education Data Resource Center, accessible at www.nces.ed.gov/partners/nedrc.asp; prisoners and graduation rates as reported in BJS, *Education and Correctional Populations* (Washington, DC: U.S. Department of Justice, 2003); for a powerful argument that better schooling reduces crime rates and recidivism, see *Saving Futures, Saving Dollars: The Impact of Education on Crime Reduction and Earnings*, a 2006 issue brief released by the Alliance for Excellent Education, available at www.all4ed.org/files-/savingfutures .pdf; funding figures reported in Sterngold, "Prisons' Budget to Trump Colleges.'"

3. Examples of student testimonies supporting these claims can be found in Meredith A. Browne, *Derailed! The Schoolhouse to Jailhouse Track*, a 2003 report posted by the Advancement Project, accessible at www.advancementproject.org, and in *Criminalizing the Classroom: The Over-Policing of New York City Schools*, a 2007 report posted by the New York Civil Liberties Union, accessible at www.nyclu .org; for an overview of these claims see William Lyons and Julie Drew, *Punishing Schools: Fear and Citizenship in American Public Education* (Ann Arbor: University of Michigan Press, 2006); regarding the politically loaded assumptions that make dropout an inaccurate word for describing the children mentioned here, see "Why We Use the Term 'Pushouts' Instead of 'Dropouts,'" a handout posted by Education Not Incarceration, available from the editor; and see the Dignity in Schools Campaign

Statement, "Children Are Being Pushed Out of School" (2008), available at http://www.dignityinschools.org/summary.php?index=158.

4. Shiebler quoted in Sterngold, "Prisons' Budget to Trump Colleges'"; the governor's budget, 2003–2004, is accessible at www.dof.ca.gov/html/Budgt03–04/BudgetSum03-/BudSum_Web.pdf; the consequences noted here are reported in Ray Delgado, "Budget Squeeze: Elimination of Summer Programs Leaves Parents Scrambling for Day Care," *San Francisco Chronicle* (17 March 2003), B1; "Clovis Schools to Cut 135 Bus Routes," *Fresno Bee* (13 February 2003), A1; Jamilah Evelyn, "California Governor Seeks Deep Budget Cuts and Doubling of Tuition at Community Colleges," *Chronicle of Higher Education* (24 January 2003), A22.

5. Hein quoted in Evan Halper and Mitchell Landsberg, "Davis Budget of 'Hard Choices' Spreads the Pain," *Los Angeles Times* (11 January 2003), A1; the poll numbers are taken from a December 2001 field poll, "California Opinion Index: A Digest on How the California Public Views a Variety of Matters Relating to Taxes and Government Spending," available at www.field.com/fieldpollonline/subscribers/COI-01-Dec-Taxes.pdf; the figures on California's education spending are from the National Education Association, "Rankings and Estimates: Rankings of the States 2006 and Estimates of School Statistics 2007" (December 2007), p. 52 of the text available at www.nea.org/edstats/images/07rankings.pdf; prison building figures from Gilmore, *Golden Gulag*, 7.

6. The first set of figures are from Bruce Western, Vincent Schiraldi, and Jason Ziedenberg, *Education and Incarceration,* an August 2003 report posted by the Justice Policy Institute, accessible at http://www.justicepolicy.org/images/upload/03-08_REP_EducationIncarceration_AC-BB.pdf and from the BJS, *Justice Expenditure and Employment in the United States, 1999* (Washington, DC: U.S. Department of Justice, 2000); the phrase incarceration nation is from Stephen John Hartnett, *Incarceration Nation: Investigative Prison Poems of Hope and Terror* (Walnut Creek, CA: AltaMira, 2004); $45.7 billion is from the National Association of State Budget Officers' "2005 State Expenditures Report" (Fall 2006), p. 56 of the text available at www.nasbo.org/Publications/PDFs/2005%20State%20Expenditure%20Report.pdf; Jacobson quoted in Sterngold, "Prisons' Budget to Trump Colleges.'"

7. U.S. House of Representatives Bipartisan Working Group on Youth Violence, *Final Report of the Bipartisan Working Group of Youth Violence* (106th U.S. Congress, March 2000); the Justice Policy Institute's *School House Hype: School Shootings and the Real Risks Kids Face in America* (1999), as quoted in "Schools and Suspensions," a September 2001 policy brief posted by the Justice Policy Institute at www.justicepolicy.org/images-/upload/0109_REP_SchoolsSuspensions_JJ.pdf; Bernardine Dohrn, "'Look Out Kid, It's Something You Did': Zero Tolerance for Children," in *Zero Tolerance: Resisting the Drive for Punishment in Our Schools,* ed. William Ayers, Bernardine Dohrn, and Rich Ayers (New York: New Press, 2001), 89–113, quotation from 90; Barry Glassner quoted in Lyons and Drew, *Punishing Schools,* 1; also see Browne, *Derailed! The Schoolhouse to Jailhouse Track.*

8. These stories are culled from Kim Brooks, Vincent Schiraldi, and Jason Ziedenberg, *School House Hype: Two Years Later,* an April 2000 report posted by the Justice Policy Institute, available at www.justicepolicy.org; similar incidents are discussed

in the NYCLU's *Criminalizing the Classroom*; for overviews of these questions, see Erica Meiners, *Right to Be Hostile: Schools, Prisons, and the Making of Public Enemies* (London: Routledge, 2007); Lyons and Drew, *Punishing Schools*; and Ayers, Dohrn, and Ayers, *Zero Tolerance*.

9. The Applied Research Center report cited here is discussed in *Education on Lockdown: The Schoolhouse to Jailhouse Track*, a March 2005 report posted by the Advancement Project, accessible at www.advancementproject.org; the figures cited here are culled from Russell Skiba, "Zero Tolerance, Suspension, and Expulsion: Is School Discipline Fair and Effective?" a July 2007 presentation before the University of Pittsburgh Summer Institute of the Center on Race and Social Problems, available at www.crsp.pitt.edu/downloads/institutes/Skiba.pdf; and from Annette Fuentes, "Discipline and Punish: Zero Tolerance Policies Have Created a 'Lockdown Environment' in Schools," *Nation* (15 December 2003), available at www.thirdworldtraveler.com/Education/Discipline_Punish.html; also see "Opportunities Suspended: The Devastating Consequences of Zero Tolerance and School Discipline," *Proceedings of the National Summit on Zero Tolerance* (Washington, DC: June 15–16, 2000), available at www.eric.ed.gov/ERICWebPortal/custom/portlets/recordDetails/detailmini.jsp?_nfpb=true&_&ERICExtSearch_SearchValue_0 =ED454314&ERICExtSearch_SearchType_0=no&accno=ED454314.

10. Among the teeming reviews of this case, see Jordan Flaherty, "The Struggle to Free the Jena 6," *Countercurrents* (27 August 2007), available at www.countercurrents .org/flaherty220807.htm, and Associated Press, "Last of Jena 6 Teens Pleads Not Guilty," *New York Times* (7 November 2007), available at www.nytimes.com/aponline/us/AP-Jena-Six.html?_r=1&oref=slogin. Editor's note: we should recall that hanging nooses has been employed since the early nineteenth century as a death threat. For example, when William Lloyd Garrison was speaking against slavery in antebellum Boston, proslavery thugs sought to intimidate him by decorating his front porch with a noose. The threat was reported in the *Boston Advertiser* (12 September 1835) and is discussed in James Elbert Cutler, *Lynch-Law: An Investigation into the History of Lynchings in the United States* (New York: Longmans, Green, 1905), 102.

11. Annette Fuentes discusses the *Equity or Exclusion* report in "From Schoolhouse to Jailhouse: Doing Hard Time in Public Schools," *Black Commentator* (8 April 2004), accessible at www.blackcommentator.com/85/85_guest_schoolhouse .html; the characterizations of underfunded schools are taken from Skiba, "Zero Tolerance, Suspension, and Expulsion"; the Justice Policy Institute, "Schools and Suspensions"; and the NYCLU, *Criminalizing the Classroom*; for a success story recounting how a South Bronx Junior High School has improved its offerings, not by treating students as future prisoners but by respecting their academic talents, see Elissa Gootman, "In Bronx School, Culture Shock, Then Revival," *New York Times* (8 February 2008), A1, 14.

12. The quotations are reported in Maria Newman, "Giuliani Chides Cortines for Resisting Use of Police," *New York Times* (1 June 1995), available at http://query .nytimes.com/gst/fullpage.html?res=9C07E2DE1639F932A35755C0A963958260; the statistics and a grueling version of this argument, complete with stories of the consequences of flooding New York City's schools with SSAs, are offered in

NYCLU, *Criminalizing the Classroom*, 5 and passim; Drew and Lyons, *Punishing Schools*, 46.

13. See Ryoko Yamaguchi, Lloyd Johnston, and Patrick M. O'Malley, "The Relationship Between Student Illicit Drug Use and School Drug-Testing Policies," *Journal of School Health* 73, no. 4 (2003): 159–64; additional information in this paragraph is drawn from David Kocieniewski, "Is This the Answer to Drug Use?" *New York Times* (25 March 2007), available at www.nytimes.com/2007/03/25/nyregion/nyregionspecial2/25RDRUG.html?_r=1&oref=slogin, and Marsha Rosenbaum, "No Quick Fix," *USA Today* (8 May 2007), accessed at http://blogs.usatoday.com/oped/2007/05/post_11.html; the physician survey is discussed in Sharon Levy, Sion Kim, Lon Sherritt, Michelle Angulo, and John R. Knight, "Drug Testing in General Medical Clinics, in School and at Home: Physician Attitudes and Practices," *Journal of Adolescent Health* 38, no. 4 (2006): 336–42.

14. See the American Academy of Pediatrics' Committee on Substance Abuse and Council on School Health Policy Statement, "Testing for Drug Abuse in Children and Adolescents: Addendum—Testing in Schools and at Home," *Pediatrics* 119, no. 3 (2007): 627–30; the Clark quotation is taken from a National Association of Social Workers press release: "Social Workers Disagree with Supreme Court Decision to Test Students for Drug Use," *NASW* (27 June 2002), available at www.socialworkers.org/pressroom/2002/062702.asp; Ginsburg quoted from *Board of Education of Pottawatomie v. Earls,* 536 U.S. 822 (2002).

15. This information and the DoE quotation are from Bill Dedman, "Does Every School Need a Metal Detector? Experts Say Schools Rely Too Much on Physical Security," *MSNBC* (3 October 2006), available at www.msnbc.msn.com/id/15111439; while these policies make for ineffective schools, they do lead to enrichment for certain corporations—for an overview, see Tara Herivel and Paul Wright, eds., *Prison Profiteers: Who Makes Money from Mass Incarceration* (New York: New Press, 2007).

16. NYCLU, *Criminalizing the Classroom*, 10, 19, 21; Jonathan Kozol, *The Shame of the Nation: The Restoration of Apartheid Schooling* (New York: Crown, 2005); for a historical analysis of "apartheid schooling," see James D. Anderson, *The Education of Blacks in the South, 1860–1935* (Chapel Hill: University of North Carolina Press, 1988).

17. See "U.S. Schools Resort to Security Cameras," *International Herald Tribune* (25 September 2003), available at http://blogs.usatoday.com/oped/2007/05/post_11.html; more broadly, see Christian Parenti, *The Soft Cage: Surveillance in America from Slavery to the War on Terror* (New York: Basic Books, 2003).

18. Orel is quoted in Steve Light, "US 'School Reform' Throws Students into the Street," *World Socialist* website (13 August 2003), available at www.wsws.org/articles/2003/aug2003/push-a13.shtml.

19. The information in this paragraph is from FairTest, National Center for Fair and Open Testing, "'No Child Left Behind' after Six Years: An Escalating Track Record of Failure" (25 January 2008), available at www.fairtest.org/NCLB-After-Six-Years, and from a White House Overview Report, "No Child Left Behind: Transforming the Federal Role in Education" (Washington, DC: 2002), available at www.whitehouse

.gov/news/reports/no-child-left-behind.pdf; Soler is quoted in Fuentes, "Discipline and Punish."

20. Department of Education, "Facts about School Safety" (last modified 03/30/2007), available at www.NoChildLeftBehind.gov; and see Peter Sacks, *Standardized Minds: The High Price of America's Testing Culture and What We Can Do to Change It* (New York: DaCapo Press, 2001); Joe Smydo, "No Child Left Behind Has Altered the Face of Education," *Pittsburgh Post-Gazette* (28 August 2006), available at www.post-gazette .com/pg/06240/716932-298.stm; and D. Meier and G. Wood, eds., *Many Children Left Behind: How the No Child Left Behind Act Is Damaging Our Children and Our Schools* (Boston: Beacon Press, 2004); the call for an NCLB moratorium is from Sharon L. Nichols, Gene V. Glass, and David C. Berliner, *High Stakes Testing and Student Achievement: Problems for the No Child Left Behind Act* (Tempe, AZ: Arizona State University Educational Policy Studies Laboratory, 2005), 6, available at http://edpolicylab.org.

21. Quotations from Diana Jean Schemo, "Failing Schools Strain to Meet No Child Law," *New York Times* (16 October 2007), A1, 21.

22. The notion of a "peace dividend" is discussed in Paul Street, "Color Bind: Prisons and the New American Racism," in *Prison Nation: The Warehousing of America's Poor*, ed. Tara Herivel and Paul Wright (New York: Routledge, 2003), 30–40, quotation from 38.

PART II

Practical Solutions,
Visionary Alternatives

Frankie Davis, *The 911 World Trade Center Buildings,* 2007. Davis brings us into a world that is like ours but seen through a remarkable lens. By creating a tapestry of intricate, interlocking patterns, he records a wealth of descriptive detail in each piece and then binds them into a meditative and dazzling rhythm.

Nancy Jean King, *Stressed,* 1997. King creates pencil drawings of children separated from their mothers and portraits of women filled with stress, anxiety, anger, and fear, thus reminding us of the suffering of women serving disproportionately long sentences. Because her work speaks to and for the millions of families whose lives have been torn apart by the prison-industrial complex, it stands as an indictment of recent laws that permanently take children away from their mothers.

Opposite, top: **G. English, *Halloween: Fall Fun-Time,*** 2008. English transcribes remembered events with astonishing detail. His complex compositions contain narratives in which we can lose ourselves and feel the immediate texture of well-being. He has also used his closely observed visual language to construct paintings about the darker sides of life in prison and the story of his own path there.

Opposite, bottom: **Dara Ket, *Why My Baby,*** 2009. Unlike any other country in the world, the United States sentences minors to life in prison without the possibility of parole. Michigan is second only to Pennsylvania with more than 300 cases. In his *Why My Baby* he portrays the emotional reality of this barbaric law, including the sadness and the trauma of the child, the anguish of the mother, and the depravity of sentencing children to life sentences.

Fred Mumford, *Prisoner Industrial Complex,* 2007. Mumford practiced his watercolor technique so that he could create landscapes that took him back to the places he loved in the rural landscapes of Michigan. Then he began to turn his technique toward picturing prison realities, sometimes evocative, like a bush flowering in front of a barbed-wire fence, and sometimes more direct, like this image of the prison-industrial complex.

Bryan Picken, *Confiscated Goods,* 2009. Picken's early works offered vivid colored pencil drawings of rural life; they focused on details like the pattern on an old woman's sweater, the quilt in her lap, and the wrinkles on an old man's face. This year he turned his impressive skill at rendering space, light, and form to this depiction of the horrifying reality of prison warehousing, thus showing us what the prison-industrial complex does in its daily routine.

Martin Vargas, *Prison Death Scene,* 1996. Vargas has participated in the exhibition since its inception in 1995 and has explored a wide range of media and subject-matter, including landscapes, wildlife, and people. This wrenching image depicts a death scene that he witnessed at Jackson Prison. While emerging from his individual observations, the piece speaks to the endemic violence of the prison-industrial complex.

Opposite, top: **Wynn Satterlee, *Free My Daddy,*** 2005. Satterlee creates a world peopled by characters in strange and haunting situations that we recognize on some instinctive level: People holding their heads and looking at a disturbing spiderlike hole in the ground, a crowd of people at a funeral of the artist, men with wings, hundreds of hats sitting on buildings. We chose to include this image because it powerfully expresses the pain of children whose parents are in prison.

Opposite, bottom: **Kinnari Jivani, *Emancipation,*** 2009. Jivani is an accomplished poet as well as a visual artist; in both genres, she creates haunting images expressing suffering, longing, and hope. Many of her paintings evoke her own and other women's struggle to maintain dignity in a hostile environment. Her work blends the richness of her East Indian artistic heritage with a strong and lyrical sense of color and design.

Virgil Williams III, *Tarbaby's Obsession,* 2000. Imprisoned in the Upper Peninsula where he had no access to art materials, Williams's passion for art and strong faith fueled his drive to create work using only what he could find in his cell. To make this image, he cut shapes out of discarded cardboard boxes and then layered them in various heights to make the body parts. He constructed the surface with glue and pen and made the hair from toilet paper covered with shoe polish.

Chapter 6

"A Piece of the Reply":
The Prison Creative Arts Project
and Practicing Resistance

Buzz Alexander

Nate Jones passed away the evening of May 31, 2007. On April 25 I had helped him celebrate his fifty-eighth birthday by bringing him a huge cake—his doctors had ordered him to eat a lot of rich food—and taking him out to breakfast, where he devoured a waffle covered with strawberries and cream. I knew him as a prisoner, an actor, a writer, a student, a teacher, a social worker, an associate of the Prison Creative Arts Project (PCAP), and a friend. Once a week during his last months, we met for breakfast or lunch, and amid tears, uncontrollable coughing fits, and his spirited, funny interchanges with the waitresses, we shared intense discussions, we laughed, and once, during our final breakfast, he burst into song.

When I arrived at his apartment in Romulus, Michigan, half an hour after his death, and saw him on the bed, hands over his chest, a bruise on his forehead where he had fallen when his heart burst from the stress of not breathing, his face was peaceful, and I remembered a dream he had told me a month earlier. He had been in his casket in a large room, mourners walking all around, and suddenly his eyes sprang open, he leaned up in the casket, and he cried "I'm alive! It was wrong, it wasn't true, I wasn't sick!" Then I noticed what appeared to be a twinkle at the corner of his eye, and I waited, for long minutes, believing, knowing that he might in fact pull it off.

Later, thinking about this curious moment, I realized that for so many of us, that was Nate Jones: Nate dancing suddenly, Nate taking us seriously but also making us laugh, Nate somehow always coming back from whatever destruction had taken him on—he was a spiritual resource, an inspiration for our hard times. We all had various experiences of Nate. He was one of the creators of the play "When Can We Talk?" put together in 2002 by Gillian Eaton, some formerly incarcerated actors, and a few of us from PCAP, but he had disappeared on us, pulled back into his addiction and all its desperate circumstances. Toward the end of the play I stood behind an empty chair and talked about how I was both angry at Nate and angry for him, yet I also stressed that I admired his strength, imagination, creativity, laughter, and resilience. He came to one of our last performances and, after my monolog, sprang to the stage to deliver his own dramatic response. He was back again, alive and vibrant—Nate is both in and at the heart of the work of the Prison Creative Arts Project.

The Prison Creative Arts Project

Although we did not know it at the time, PCAP was born in early 1990. Mary Glover and Joyce Dixon, lifers at the Florence Crane Women's Facility in Coldwater, Michigan, had enrolled in my (University of Michigan) English 319, a guerrilla and action theater course creating plays on social justice issues, working often with local organizations. Throughout the semester, three students and I traveled the 180-mile round trip to talk theater and prison with Mary and Joyce and to cocreate improvisations, scenes, and characters. One day I brought in an exercise I had first used in a video project in Huaycan, a shantytown outside Lima, Peru: I asked Mary and Joyce to sit aside and take twenty minutes to brainstorm questions they had for us. Their first question was "What the hell are you doing here?" and then "Why are you interested in prisoners?" We answered honestly, and then responded as best we could to questions about how we would handle the difficult situations that they faced in prison. At the end of the session they looked at each other and said, "We have to open this up to the entire prison." We received the warden's permission, 120 women signed up, 60 came, and 30 remained after I foolishly started with "Vampire," a game involving closed eyes and shrieks as participants transform into vampires. We promised the thirty who stuck around that we would return every week without limit, several women asked if we could scream every time, and so the Sisters Within Theater Troupe, now on its twenty-fourth play, was born.[1]

Our first play, *The Show,* in 1991, was a series of monologs, dialogs, and scenes. We received a standing ovation, but we also portrayed corrections officers in a comic light and so were promptly fired. Dean Eugene Nissen and I wrote to Warden Carol Howes, who, after a discussion in her office, allowed us to continue. In 1992, English 319 added workshops at three men's prisons, and in 1994 we began our first workshops in juvenile facilities. Since 1990 I and my students have been bringing video and theater projects to Detroit's Dewey Center for Urban Education, a K–8 school that served the local housing projects, and in 1994 we switched our project to Henry Ford High School. Later that year I created English 310 as a vehicle for working with the arts in high schools and juvenile facilities. Then, in January 1996, Janie Paul added Art and Design 310 (Art Workshops in Prisons). As of February 2008, high school youth, incarcerated youth, and prisoners, working with English 310 and 319 and in other PCAP workshops, have created 463 original plays, have given 154 readings of their creative writing and, through English 310 and Art and Design 310, have participated in more than 80 art workshops. In 1996 we held the first Annual Exhibition of Art by Michigan Prisoners, and in the summer of 1997, because for years students had continued going into the prisons after taking the courses and in effect had become an organization, we officially became the Prison Creative Arts Project. In 1999 we held our first annual exhibition of art by incarcerated youth. The year 2001 brought the Portfolio Project, in which we work one-on-one with incarcerated youth, who create portfolios of their art and writing to show judges, employers, teachers, and others, and the Linkage Project, which connects formerly incarcerated people to arts mentors in their home communities. Thus, over eighteen years of growth, heartbreak, and joy, PCAP has evolved into a community arts organization dedicated to practicing resistance to the prison-industrial complex.[2]

The Workshops

I
"In the yard, I am like this!"
Hollis-El shows a clenched fist.
"In here like this . . ." he opens a tiny space
between forefinger and thumb.
"Then I return to the yard,"
and he clenches again.

II
"In California I loved to walk the beaches
and redwood forests," says Dell, a Native American lifer,
adopted and beaten by his Polish family,
runaway, now forever resident in a Michigan prison.
"The theater workshop is like that."

III
At the university
a circle of stiff classroom chairs
we unbend with our minds.
"The men at Ryan and I
come to the workshop," Chris says,
"for the same reason:
something is missing in our lives,
and we come there to find it."[3]

Children and youth, incarcerated youth, and prisoners, working with English 310 and 319 students and with PCAP members, have presented their plays, poetry, and other work in primary schools, in a rural high schools, in urban day-and-night high schools, in girls' and boys' juvenile facilities, and in men's and women's prisons. The youth have been members of special education class-rooms and standard classrooms, of sex offender halls or pods, of cottages or halls for severely damaged youth, of geographically organized units, and of groups segregated according to crime or problem. The adults come from the general population in low-security and medium- to high-security prisons, from the prison mental hospital, from residential treatment units, and from prisons or parts of prisons assigned to youth sentenced as adults. My University of Michigan students, mostly from affluent backgrounds, thus cocreate with youth and adults from this country's most beleaguered neighborhoods—working together, they try to cross the barriers of class and race.

Their audiences have been as small as four and as large as two hundred, perched on bleacher seats in a prison gymnasium. The performers have pre-sented in classrooms so crowded with desks that they could hardly move, in juvenile facilities, in prison chapels and recreation rooms, in halls full of echoes, in gymnasiums where their voices sank at their feet, in large spaces requiring fifteen microphones, and in a tiny patio just off the living quarters in the women's prison mental health unit as the sun went down and their voices carried to the actress who had provoked a fight in the yard the night before and so ended up in segregation. Our shortest play was five minutes. It was created in desperation an hour before it was time to perform: we had the youth go around the circle talking about the source of a ring, earring, necklace, or bracelet they wore, and they imagined a story about a stolen ring. Our longest plays, rehearsed for months, last an hour and three quarters, or until the facility closes down for the night and sends us home. Some of the plays are silly, some are poorly done, some are rich in character and mean-ing, some are complicated, even sophisticated—all the plays are successes.

We spend the first two meetings of a new theater workshop playing and talk-ing, getting comfortable. In the third meeting we might do a conflict exercise for which we choose a partner, create a conflict based in our experiences, and perform it for a minute or more, without resolving the conflict. Then we choose one conflict and elaborate it with new scenes or characters, thus introducing our method of building upon an original scene and characters. In the fourth meeting, after listening to ideas, we choose the two or three that are most thoughtful and developed and ask those who have proposed them to choose as many other actors as they need, then to go into a corner and in five minutes come up with the scene they have in mind, which need not be the opening scene of a play. When they show their scenes, we discuss them, perhaps probe them further, and decide upon one or two as the starting point for a play. Often several ideas merge into a single plot or into subplots. Because the authors and actors live in the same building or neighborhood, go to the same school, or are confined in the same prison, the creative process often extends beyond our classes, hence triggering other discussions in spaces often rendered silent.[4]

Continuing workshops (those PCAP offerings not linked to a specific University of Michigan class) do not need to go through the same process. Members of these groups often already have ideas for the next play and are already comfortable with each other. Either way, once the workshop group makes their choice, the rest of the play's development is a matter of patient week-by-week exploration of plot, character, story, and meaning. Our character interviews are often generative moments; in this exercise, each character describes him or herself and is then grilled by the other actors/characters. Each actor has to tell stories, share memories, and think about his or her conflicts, needs, and relations; out of their responses to their classmates' questioning, their character becomes more interesting. Sometimes, as part of this inventional process, we build new relationships, scenes, and characters. After a while, we begin compiling a list of the scenes developed so far, and then we describe each scene, sometimes with a few pieces of dialogue we wish to remember. This is as much text as we have, and the scenes continue to be improvised as we rehearse them. The actors review the scene before they go on stage and are generally true to it, but the element of improvisation continues into the performance itself, sometimes bringing new comedy, emotion, and power. Thus merging structure and improvisation, order and chaos, we try to balance the need for coherence with the power of impromptu creativity.

It is seldom easy—and I cannot emphasize this enough—because we are working in constantly disrupted environments. For example, in the high schools, attendance is often spotty, especially in the early-morning classes. Holidays, teacher conferences, school closings because of inclement weather, crowded classrooms, fifty-minute sessions rather than the hour and a half at our other sites, and normal adolescent inattention and chaos wreak havoc. These complications are compounded in the juvenile facilities by the painfully unresolved experiences and issues of individual youths and of the groups that live together twenty-four hours a day. In the prisons, some challenges to continuity are emergency counts, monthly simulated mobilization rehearsals that close the prison down, heavy fog or other extreme weather that makes yard movement hazardous for prisoners and officers, uncountable disciplinary measures, something as simple as one of us forgetting our identification, corrections officers randomly sitting in on a session, workshop members getting transferred to other prisons, actors missing sessions for cherished family visits, or some other form of creativity-hampering environmental stress. In any of the workshops, the participants may decide before a performance that they do not want to do the play anymore or that it needs major revisions, sometimes at the last minute. Individual participants might choose to fade back into the prison, where we have no opportunity to talk with them, find out what is happening, and encourage them to return. We make art under duress.[5]

Nonetheless, at their best, our plays lead from disrupted communities and individual conflicts to adjustments, resolutions, and a sophisticated reestablishment of balance. For example, the plot of a 1999 play, "The Genie and the Hood," begins with the thousand-year-old Dr. Krasenknopf and his younger genie, Hasan, opening a pawnshop in the ghetto. They are aided by a younger accomplice, a woman, who is cooperative as long as she is well lubricated with alcohol. When three men see the magic lamp in the window, they enter the store, touch the lamp, and Hasan appears, speaking in rhyme, to offer them three wishes. Hasan and Dr. Krasenknopf then twist the men's wishes to divide and destroy the ghetto. Eventually some women in the ghetto, including the accomplice (the evil pair have made a mistake and let the community go dry), figure out that they can defeat Dr. Krasenknopf and Hasan by marshaling the power of women's laughter. They teach it to the community and march on the pawnshop. Krasenknopf and Hasan, defiant and nearly victorious at first, melt away under the power of the laughter. The community has resisted, come together, learned, and asserted new values. While this is at least a temporary victory for the community, the final scene depicts Krasenknopf and Hasan standing in their new pawnshop in Kansas City, Missouri, as some townspeople peer in eagerly at the lamp. And so the struggle continues elsewhere and always. "The Genie and the Hood" thus performed collective decision making in action, perhaps enabling the actors and audience to see that democratic action, like good theater, is always collaborative and often improvised.

The Roles of the University Facilitators

Although we usually come from some degree of affluence and academic success, although most but not all of us are white and female, although at the end of every session we are able to return to the comfort of our apartments and homes in Ann Arbor, and although it is because of us that these creative spaces have opened, in a very crucial sense we are no different from the others in the workshop: We are there to play games, to take risks, to be vulnerable, to brainstorm, to discover, to cocreate, to act, and to codirect. We bring our particular backgrounds, personalities, talents, and skills and throw them into the mix; along with everyone else, we get down to the task. This cannot be emphasized enough: Our work is not about talk, theory, or instructing—it is about collaboration and praxis.

In English 310 and 319, in Art and Design 310, and in the PCAP workshops we emphasize that the play (or poetry or art or dance) is theirs, that we do not bring in a text, that we are not teachers with lesson plans, and that the product will rise from the dynamic of the workshop. Some University of Michigan students understand this to mean that we are passive and that they will make it all happen. These students do not recognize that most workshop participants have not done this before, that they are uncertain, likely to flounder in the open-ended discovery process, that they may think of us as teachers even though we have refused the role, and that they need the kind of guidance we, with our training in the courses, can provide. And so, even while refusing the role of teacher, we must be willing to call the group to focus (a great challenge in the youth facilities), provide games, exercises, and improvisations, move the process along, make sure the character interviews are challenging, engage the whole group in feedback on the scenes, and contribute our own ideas and feelings about both story and process. In most workshops, others quickly join us in all these roles. We are equal members of the workshop in most ways, which means that if we have a different vision of the play, it is our responsibility to contribute it, even to fight for it, but not to insist that it go our way.

When students or PCAP members feel too young and inexperienced, or too privileged, or lacking in street experience, or mercifully free from abuse and pain—when they feel these things and hold back, they let down their workshop. A moment everyone in English 310 in the fall of 2006 will remember is when Grace Pan, suddenly in tears, urged her classmates to make demands on the youth they were working with, because to do so—to challenge them, to push hard, to ask for so much—was to offer them the respect they deserve. When PCAP members Emi Kaneko and Katie Craig, because they felt their experience was elite and their poetry amateur, did not take risks and step forth boldly as writers, they were disrespecting the men at the Parnall Correctional Facility and holding back the workshop. We identified this problem in a group meeting, and when Kaneko and Katie returned to Parnall the next week, they took risks, stepped forth boldly, and brought a new respect to the process—and so the quality and honesty of the writings at Parnall rose to a new level.

Because we have access to resources denied to our imprisoned collaborators, we have certain responsibilities, and so we bring notepads, pens, and paper, costumes and props, scene lists, programs, flowers for the high school and youth facility curtain calls, and refreshments when the facility lacks the budget to provide them. We stay in touch with the liaison, we phone ahead to make sure everything is in order, we enter the facility with positive spirit and respect, and we adhere to the facility rules and regulations. When rules and regulations are stifling, we invent within the limits imposed. For example, if we are not allowed, at a particular prison, to shake hands with the prisoners, then together with the prisoners we develop a symbolic gesture that signifies shaking hands; if we are told the women may not dance in a play, we create sculpted images with our bodies, which then shift from image to image. We do all we can to make everything go smoothly and to protect the workshop.

Protecting the workshop can also mean struggling for significant meaning. Although the plays move toward resolution, the nature of the resolution can be problematic. In a play at Maxey Boys Training School, a boy about to hit another boy is taken into the future and shown two outcomes: to end up in a mental institution or to live in a luxurious house with his wife and children enjoying his success as a corporate giant. He chooses the latter and does not strike the other boy. But the boys did not imagine other ideals, like becoming a social worker, a teacher, a public health worker, or a member of Doctors without Borders, and the team working with them did not offer such options for discussion and acceptance or rejection. The play thus reinscribed a narrative in which the unquestioned goal of life is wealth and privilege. Struggling for significant meaning therefore implies working toward a consciousness of social values and economic injustice, as well as an awareness of what is at stake for every participant in the workshop, yet neither university students nor participants in the workshops necessarily have such consciousness and awareness. A more alert team would have offered but not imposed other narrative options. For example, facing the dilemma posed by unyielding "young thugs" in the community, the actors creating "In the Ghetto" at the Western Wayne Correctional Facility, in 1997, advocated arrest and incarceration. But some of us suggested the option of a meeting addressing the "thugs" and their view of the community. The two actors playing the "thugs" described what was wrong in the community so powerfully that they convinced their elders to make necessary changes, and so the play ended with a fund-raising gathering accompanied by the neighborhood band (with original music for the occasion played by prisoners). While I and my fellow facilitators thus proposed this alternative ending, the actors agreed to improvise the meeting scene—together, we made collective, democratic decisions about what values we wanted our play to represent.

Protecting the workshop can also mean struggling for its very existence. Toward the end of the Sisters Within Theater Troupe's residence at the Florence Crane Women's Facility, the women, Pilar Anadon, and I were faced with increasing hostility from the warden and the regional prison administrator. Perhaps they identified us with Mary Glover and Tracy Neal, former Sisters who were lead litigants against the Michigan Department of Corrections, even though we had always known better than to discuss the lawsuits with the women or to get involved with their court case. In the fall of 1999, the warden notified us that our next play must be from a written text. We asked to discuss this with the women and were given a half hour in the muster room. In that half hour we recalled a title we used to joke about, "Y2K and the Wicked Stepmother," and imagined a basic plot and characters. The next day the women met in the yard, elaborated the plot, and sent us what they had. We developed it into a full-length story and submitted it in outline form to the warden and regional prison administrator, only to be told it had to be a line-by-line text. At this point we might have quit, but instead agreed to submit such a text when the time came. Then each week we improvised the play, as usual, but with Pilar writing down the lines. Our original text was then approved. Although the hostility continued—we were denied outside guests, were limited in our choice of props and costumes, received glares from prison officers, were told after the performance that the promised refreshments were locked up and couldn't be accessed, and were harassed on the way out—we gave two spirited performances of that wonderful play. Our celebration after the second performance was enhanced by our sense of solidarity in refusing to yield in the face of so much opposition, for we were making art, building community, and practicing resistance.[6]

Walls and the Fight for What Is Missing

We frequently use an exercise called "Magician." Someone stands on a chair and hollers, "I am a magician, and I turn you all into angry red rabbits" (or "into your father" or "into bees on my left and people afraid of bees on my right" or "dancing mummies"). When that person has finished several transformations of the group, he or she cries out, "I am a magician, and I turn Pedro into a magician." Pedro then ascends to the chair and repeats the process. In a variation on this exercise, each boy in Lauren Rubinfeld's and Myrna Vaca's workshop at Maxey, in 2001, would shout, "I am the magician and I give my power to _____." On one occasion, Terry gave the power to De'Aries, then De'Aries gave it to Ricardo, but when Ricardo was ready to hand off his power, he shouted, "I am the magician and I give my power to these walls." Lauren was "speechless." As she wrote in her final paper,

> Ricardo recognized that his power was being replaced by the power of the walls and the fences that surround him. When I drive away from Maxey, I can't just snap right back into the outside world. After hearing the voices of my boys, their screams, their ideas, their cartwheels, their imaginations yelling, it is so difficult to drive out of the gates of Maxey, where even with my windows rolled down, I cannot hear even one sound escape from the fences. They are being silenced. And their silence screams to me louder than the loudest shrieks Ronnie has placed in my eardrum. They are my shrieks. They are the shrieks that sustain my anger—and my anger propels me. My anger [is directed] at the neighborhood (that we are all a part of) that surrounds Maxey, and that is comforted by the silence of boys' voices. It is comforted by the silence of my boys' futures.[7]

Lauren's use of "my boys" is interesting. Although it might imply some power dynamics and possessiveness, what I think she is expressing is her deep connection to and affiliation with the boys. She is expressing, then, how PCAP enables its participants to cross the barriers of class and race to begin forging new bonds of solidarity, bonds that empower us to try to break through the imposed silences that so enrage Lauren (and all of us who have shared similar experiences). As I describe below, however, this work is never easy, for we are separated by walls of many sizes and shapes.

Indeed, the walls incarcerating our bodies and minds are constructed from many materials. Alienated and overcrowded homes, dangerous streets, ragged, rotting schools and demoralized teachers, lack of medical access, hunger, illiteracy, physical and sexual assault, environmental pollution, helpless rage, low expectations, daily degradations, accumulated insults to the spirit, everyday violence, the rat in the corner, the rat in the crib, gangs, the color of one's skin, the color of one's class, guns and drugs, the police car, the jail garb, the shackles, the voices of others in the courtroom, rotating poorly paid counselors, inadequate psychiatric attention, haunted minds, chaos, cuttings, suicide attempts, screams, running, state uniforms, the humiliations of count time, of arbitrary orders, of lost control in almost every aspect of one's life, of health care that neglects and kills, of food that bloats, of constant noise, constant boredom, of stabbings and rape, of having to watch one's back, of having no choice about one's company, of parole board denials, of knowing the public hates you, of being imagined as a person without loved ones or aspirations or creativity, of attending funerals under guard, of missing a child's graduation, a child's marriage, a chance to care for a dying parent.

Our imprisoned neighbors are not the only ones incapacitated by such conditions. In *The Night Is Dark and I Am Far from Home*, Jonathan Kozol demonstrates how the high schools most of us attend train us to be "good citizens," to be smart, imaginative, intelligent, well-intentioned adults who, while we may volunteer and donate to charity, are ethically indifferent to the sufferings and struggles of others, unconscious of the everyday violence that surrounds us, or, if conscious of it, not inclined to or not capable of doing anything about it. Through fragmentation of our learning, through the group recitations of the Pledge to the Flag, through elimination of "I" from our essays, through the emasculation and taming of the major rebellious figures we study, through softening, diminishing, and managing our inclinations to righteous anger or action, through celebrating individual achievements, such schooling diverts our force into safe channels. In fifth grade, my son brought to show-and-tell a story of human-rights abuses in Chile. His teacher was moved and asked all the children to write "world wishes." They all wished for a better world, and it was taken care of. In seventh grade the art teacher asked him to draw a picture of freedom. He had lived with us in the mountains of Peru, had visited peasant communities, and had listened to our talk. His picture was of a man speaking at a podium, wearing a black beret, and below him men stood with their rifles raised in the air in response. His art teacher refused to accept the drawing—he had, according to my son, accepted a drawing of a man in a white sheet—and asked my son to think of something in America he liked to do. Totally unsure now, my son said he liked to camp; when that topic was approved, he drew a picture of a tent in a campground.[8]

This is all typical enough, for schools reproduce the social order; some of them even do so in ways that are sophisticated, that allow for individuality, self-criticism, intelligence, imagination, creativity, and the other characteristics that enable some of us to become vital citizens who can advance science, develop markets, cure patients, write important books, make art, and so on. But even in these schools, the best schools, students are taught to consent to the absence of such schooling for others—*it has always been this way; there have always been rich and poor; that's just the way it is*—or to be compassionate and activist in limited ways. My students at the University of Michigan, so many of them lively, deeply intelligent, wonderfully creative individuals, are at risk of crossing an invisible line into numbness, of having the light of concern and action for justice that was taught them in some of their churches and synagogues and in American history books, go out. When

I was growing up on the North Shore of Chicago, no one told me, no one in my family, no one in my schools, no one in the Sunday school at the Wilmette Methodist Church—no one even hinted that there was anything problematic about the world as it was, and no one needed to tell the kids from Chicago that they weren't welcome on our beach. I was being primed for numbness.

The Missing

Chris says something is missing for all of us and that we come to the workshops to find it. Hollis El opens a tiny space between thumb and forefinger; Dell remembers the beaches in California; Wilson-Bey storms out of a workshop at the Southern Michigan Correctional Facility, angry about something, but then storms back in to proclaim: "I don't need to cater to any of you. I don't need to cater to you. My brother is in the hospital paralyzed from the neck down, my niece was in a coma, and my wife was buried today, my daughter is out there with no parent, and I need this workshop, I need its focus, I need to keep my mind off these other things." Wilson-Bey *needs* the workshop; Robin's daughter was killed and she needs the workshop; Suzi is reliving her abuse, her crime, and she needs the workshop; Valeroso had vowed he would never become close to someone again after Vietnam and after he watched a buddy blow his brains out in the Veterans hospital, but he became close to Pilar, Maria, Janie, and me; Nate says he found in me his first real friend through the workshop; Sammarah Fine wrote in her journal in 1999 that if they closed her workshop, then they would take away the only place in the prison where one of her men said he felt human. In the Poet's Corner, in 2001, Mike challenged me to write a poem about what the workshops mean to me. In "For Mike, Because You Asked," I began with the three verses quoted above, and then continued:

> IV
> Antonio comes to extend what he knows of love
> and anger
> Gucci comes seeking new families through finding
> his old,
> Chi comes to find the stories and voice that will let him
> pass wisdom on
> Co-Pilot comes to tame his whirling thoughts into
> powerful renderings of his time
> Mike, you come to find rhymes for your hard past
> and for the discipline and insight that motivate you now
> Sarah comes for the composite person and comes to delight and surprise us

with her lyrical twists, her quick laugh
Phil comes out of a commitment to us and to himself
And I come, like you all, to find justice

V
I find it in our unusual laughter
I find it in our challenges and risks
I find it in the gasps I hear when someone reads a powerful poem
or finds a right line
I find it in the safety of our space and in our liking for each other
I find it in our generosity
in our forgiveness for what we have not done well
in the voices we discover as they lift up out of us,
like smoke and fire,
singing
I find it in our attempts to understand why we are here,
in our anger when it rises
I find it in Co-Pilot's desire to write poetry like cutting quick right
for a jump-shot and passing off, spontaneous,
I find it in Chi's assignment not to revise
in Gucci's photographs
in Phil's mantra
in Sarah's many names
in Antonio's family and Co-Pilot's cohesiveness
in the insistence of the podium
And Mike, I find it in your direct, penetrating questions
and in our answers

VI
Prisons are about *No*, the workshops are *Yes*
Prisons are limits, blocks, barriers,
workshops are openings, doors, dances, breakings through
Prisons are about poverty and poor opportunity,
boarded houses and rotting schools,
a system that leaves so many children out,
Workshops are a piece of the reply,
they are about the strength of our stories,
about our voices, our songs, our laughter, our resistance,
about our families
our neighborhoods,
our communities,
ourselves,
about what might and may be.

Of course we are not often conscious of what we are looking for, of our hopes
for what might and may be. In fact, many of us entering the workshops—

youth, prisoners, professors, and students—are often scrambling to write a poem or create a character or draw something that isn't in the room, and that isn't always easy to do. Sometimes, one of us will have a beef with the person across the table or at the podium, or we'll feel chaotic and like we are getting nowhere, and we may feel that what is being created—and we are often right—is shallow, undeveloped, not fully formed or articulated. As in other workshops and classrooms, many of us are preoccupied with other facets of our lives. Yet I think for most us, there is always a sense of the potential for something being found between us, among us, perhaps a piece of the reply.

In an English 310 exercise, I number my students off into groups of three, then have them decide which two will play incarcerated youth and who will play the new earnest student facilitator from English 310 who comes to work with them. I send the facilitators out of the room and tell the students playing the roles of incarcerated youth to make everything extremely difficult. What happens is sometimes agonizing to watch: the facilitators face inattention, chaos, individuals acting out or closing down, youth storming out, and hard challenges and questions. Afterward, we debrief. One year, Jessica Anthony, who had played a Maxey youth, had kept pushing the facilitator, because she needed him to be the right person and to say the right things, to be the person she, from an abused, neglected background, needed more than anything. But he wasn't able to give her that: He wasn't ready, he couldn't focus on *her*, and so his words were nice but conventional. I'm sure he also desperately wanted her to understand who he was, what brought him there, his needs, what was authentic in him. And this too is a part of the work: not understanding, missing connections, talking past each other, recognizing how hard it is to create meanings together.

Nate Jones was in that English 310 class. A few years earlier, incarcerated, at the end of *Inside Out,* the PCAP video play he and others had created at the Western Wayne Correctional Facility, he had spoken to youth in danger of going to prison. In what he says, we can feel what was happening between the men in the process of making the play:

> I had learned after coming here, from group therapy, that I could take a risk and say things about my life that would help me. And I had to take that risk so I could make an initial change in my life. It was up to me to make that choice; I couldn't allow no one else to do it. It seemed it was more meaningful to me. And I'm learning that even more through drama club. . . . Sometimes it's like I'm right there and it's like a healing process for me. And the guys in the group, I sense sometimes that they want to touch me and hold

me and say it's okay, and I can appreciate it. I really appreciate it, but even then I find myself shunning them off or pushing them away or going into a silence or something, but I still know that it's something good coming from it. We go through a lot of angry times and a lot of happy times, sad times, a lot of tearful times, and everything that we say and all our feelings manifest themselves in . . . the play.[9]

What I am missing when I work with the Western Wayne Players or the Poets Corner or the Sisters Within Theater Troupe may be different from what Chris seeks or from what Shar or Wilson Bey or Hollis-El or Ricardo or Nate seek, but all of us have been cut off from each other, all of us have been malnourished. While we are all full of experience, talent, and history and are rich, problematic persons, we have all been deprived by the walls that have been built within and between us. But at some level, even when voiced clumsily or sometimes angrily, we all want connection and community. What is so exciting about the workshops is that connection and community are in the air, in the process. Each of us is challenged to find within ourselves what we have to show or say, what we have to give to ourselves and others, and for a moment, at least, we penetrate the walls, the doors open. Whether we know it or not, the workshops are charged with this possibility. Most of the time we fail—we don't often get the words right—but when a session turns electric, even for a moment, we find what we are looking for, and this in turn can prod us to seek out and create such moments in our relationships beyond the workshop.

Remembering Nate Jones

Nate grew up on Legrand and Varney, in downtown, pre–Civil Rights Detroit, where he was poor and black and surrounded by a sea of white kids. The local toughs would run up to him and issue swaggering challenges: "Nigger, what you doin' walkin' down our street?" One time, an elderly white woman looked at him scornfully and asked, "What are you doing looking in my eyes? Boy, look at the ground, don't look at me." Nate and the neighborhood's children walked to school in bunches for protection. But the violence was not only imposed from outside, for it lurked in Nate's home as well. Shorty, Nate's father, watched his father shoot his mother and then turn the gun on himself. Shorty was passed from family member to family member until his uncle came home from the war, took him in, and beat him every day. Shorty never made it out of elementary school and couldn't read, Shorty didn't go to work, hung out with women, and beat Nate's mother. Here's how Nate remembers those days: "An uncle came by with four leeches. He purchased them from the drugstore. Ma was lying on the couch on her back. My uncle took the leeches and placed them around my mother's eyes. The leeches laid there sucking blood from the enormous black eyes caused by the beating she took from my father. I remember crying every time I saw the leeches sucked up against her eyes. The fights were always one-sided. Ma never had a chance, but she never gave up. She would argue to get her point across. 'Shorty, we have to feed the kids.'" As his uncle had beaten him, so Shorty beat Nate brutally. Nate's little brother was killed by a passing car, Nate's cousin sexually abused him, Nate wet the bed, Nate was always in fights, Nate ran away from home, Nate ended up in juvenile facilities. He joined the army and volunteered for Vietnam, and then four white men in a Georgia barracks tried to stab his eyes out and kill him; Nate was given an honorable discharge and disability, but no one ever investigated the incident. Like his grandfather and father, Nate was violent in his own marriage. His drugs of choice were cocaine and heroin. He was convicted of armed robbery. When he came home from prison, he attempted suicide, was convicted again for a second armed robbery, and again served a lot of time. Nate never fully got over any of this, yet he tried to make sense of it by writing his thoughts with the help of an old computer someone gave him in the final month of his life. His family and friends buried him in the national cemetery in Battle Creek. The brief ceremony, before they took the flag off his coffin, included a rifle salute by aged veterans from the four branches of the service. As souvenirs, the former soldiers offered us the empty shell casings.[10]

The Classes, Trust, and "How Unlikely It Is"

Before students can join PCAP, they must take any one of three classes, my English 310 or 319, or Janie Paul's Art and Design 310 ("Art Workshops in Prisons"). The required entrance interview for 310 and 319 consists largely of me describing the course and being very firm about what is expected: The students will follow facility rules and policies, they will not jeopardize the workshops, they will respect and believe in the participants, they will not exploit the incarcerated for their own academic or résumé purposes, they will not be "teachers." I am clear about the challenges and the pain that students will face. If they pass the interview and wish to take the course, they are in. So that students can build a sense of each other and can choose partners wisely, the first week is demanding and highly interactive: We read a book, hold a three-hour evening workshop, engage in intensive discussion, and spend all day, the first Saturday of the semester, in a retreat at which students introduce themselves and explain why they wish to go to places most of their family and acquaintances consider to be dangerous, filled with scum, and not worth their time. At the end of the retreat, having by now formed a good sense of each other, they choose partners.

During the next two weeks, besides regular on-campus class time, the students twice meet with me in groups or teams, go to their site for an orientation, and (in English 319) have a second evening workshop. In the first team meeting, they share questions, anxieties, and aspirations; I take notes and then talk again about what I expect of them at the site. I remind them that they will make mistakes, and that that is okay, for I have made mistakes too. I remind them that I am their support person, and that they need to tell me immediately whenever something happens so that I can troubleshoot. I talk about what males working in female institutions and what females working in male institutions might face, and we go over how we handle the situations that arise when desire flares. In the second meeting, we talk about what they will do to make their first session lively and engaging. I tell them not to lecture, not to sit together, to listen carefully, and to indicate from the start that the work is fully collective and participatory. I tell them warning stories about past teams, and stress that they must communicate with each other, and that if they have a partnership problem, then they must communicate with me, for the youth and adults deserve teams who like each other and bring high spirits into the space each week. The second evening workshop gives them more exercises and begins to acquaint them with our improvisational method of building plays.

And that's it; that is all the preparation they get. I have not given them texts nor lectured on crime, criminal lives, prison culture, the streets, or poor urban neighborhoods. It is only fair: I have not given the high school youth or incarcerated youth or adults texts or lectures about university students. I prefer that everyone enter the workshop on the same footing. Most students will enter the workshops self-conscious about their limited, even pampered backgrounds, their lack of street smarts, worrying that the prisoners and youth will see them as rich, pretentious, naïve brats. Sometimes they are right. While on the whole the high school youth don't worry much about how they will be perceived, prisoners and incarcerated youth often enter the workshops expecting students to fear them as "hardened criminals," or to patronize them while instructing them in the arts. Sometimes they are right. The students are mostly white, mostly female, and mostly affluent; the prisoners are a mixture of African American, Hispanic, Native, and white, usually male, always poor.

When we enter a facility, we are usually opening a creative space where none existed before, so we do not know what will happen in that space. We bring our ability to make the space happen and to maintain it through negotiation with officials, and we bring our ability to get everyone focused. We bring in some exercises and our own skills, whatever they may be, in acting, art, or writing. We also bring the need of all creative people to be vulnerable and to take risks. And we bring our willingness to listen, to work collectively, and to struggle to get the work done. The youth and adults who walk into the space from their neighborhoods and classrooms, their rooms and cells, bring their own abilities, experiences, skills, vulnerabilities, and their willingness to struggle to get the work done.

Despite our differences, I know that the vast majority of our participants will work together to create a play; my knowing this enables them to know it. PCAP is built on such trust. Although for many people this question of trust is too difficult to understand—they have too many reasonable doubts—it is at once the simplest and most necessary element. As Jesse Jannetta, who became PCAP's first full-time administrator, wrote in a booklet of tribute and analysis:

> From my 319 journal: "At the potluck, after Buzz left, Leslie Neal said something that really struck me. She said that she couldn't understand why the work that we're doing works. The results show that it does, but the weight of her experience tells her that it shouldn't. She thinks it's a little dicey that a bunch of college kids are sent into the prisons to do the workshops with only two or three weeks of training behind us." When you're up close to the prison workshops, and PCAP, it can be easy to forget how amazing, how unlikely it is. Rereading my journals from that class brings me back to that time, when nothing seemed less likely than that I would be driving out to a prison every week, working with a group that was a new thing to each other, creating a play that was also a new thing. Why did I think I could do it? Because Buzz thought I could do it, trusted me to do it. So I did.[11]

At the outset, workshop members may experience some suspicion, awkwardness, hard questions, and other challenges based on what is true in the stereotypes they have of each other. Yet negotiating the cultural and political divides between us and inherent within the creative space unfolds quickly: normally the fears and stereotypes have vanished by the end of the first or second session. Entertaining, wacky, low-risk acting, drawing, and writing exercises in which everyone participates lead quickly to a space of vitality, risk, and respect where everyone begins to deepen their participation and their struggle to bring forth their own stories, images, and ideas. The collective task of creating a quality public performance further draws everyone together across both superficial and real barriers.

The university classroom is also a democratic, collaborative, struggling space. I don't lecture. And I seldom initiate the questioning. Students have interviewed for the course, they are going into hard, new places, and the texts are challenging. The retreat, which is inevitably emotional and personal, shows them that they are in a class of amazing people. They might not like or agree with each other, but it is a great start. And so I expect them to bring energy and tough questions into the classroom, where I wait, listen, let the conversation stir, and refuse to dominate. It is essential that I am interested in what individuals are saying or trying to say, and that I know that any one of them can give me a story, an insight, a trigger, something that frightens me or makes me question myself. I try to embody the trust that shows that the group can take itself and me to places we had not thought of before, and that I know that the class is a story being told, a play being written, with the outcome in suspense. And a lot is at stake in the outcome. We live in a country of massive incarceration that has destroyed countless human beings and neighborhoods. We are governed by people who have chosen to perpetuate violence at home and abroad, who carry out mass murder with weapons of mass destruction. PCAP thus asks us to wonder *Who are we going to be?* As individuals, of course, but more important, as a group that has a remarkable opportunity to think and learn and commit together, *Who are we going to be?* [12]

It is essential that I am not outside the stories answering this question, that I am one of the characters, that I am *in* the discussion and that I believe something is at stake in being there, including our souls, the lives of urban youth and the incarcerated, a struggle for justice, our futures, an emerging community. It is essential that I do not have in mind something that must be asked, said, or known in a given session, that I never begin with questions to which I know the answers and to which my students must make their way, and that we start from students' brainstorming and from what they write on the board, from their questions, issues, and challenges. When I speak, it is important that I speak authentically, that I know how to provoke and tolerate chaos, that I don't intervene when things get rough, that I am not automatically protective, and that I know how to provoke community. It is essential that I am not only a teacher who sends them out to have an experience that I will later help them analyze, or that I am the administrative figure who comes once to their workshop and then to the performance and is the contact with the liaison, or that I am an older scholar who reads their journals and papers, but that I myself am committed to doing the work, that I founded PCAP and am a member of theater and poetry workshops in two different prisons, that I speak publicly and bear witness to the voices inside and to the economic practices that have put them there, that I participate in guerrilla theater, lobby, devote hours and hours to the annual prison art exhibition, and go to bat for my students and for the incarcerated.

Part of the challenge for me, then, is in remaining open to the question "who are we going to be?" while also maintaining a commitment to certain personal values and pedagogical criteria. For example, because students occasionally won't read through to the end of Paulo Freire's *Pedagogy of the Oppressed*, I sometimes give a quiz. In the fall of 2005, students were given seven minutes to answer the following question: "Give Freire's likely analysis of the following story: A man walks along the beach and sees that thousands of starfish have been washed up on the shore. He comes to another man who is throwing fish back into the ocean one at a time. He says, 'You are wasting your time: There are thousands of dying fish, and throwing back a few does nothing useful.' The second man replies: 'You are wrong: even if I save only a few fish, those fish are alive.'" The question is meant to tease out the students' understanding of the language of consent. Those who thought Freire would praise this familiar, celebrated story did poorly; those who understood that he would recognize it as a deceptive individualist myth intended to stifle collective action did well. Because the story is so favorable to the remark of the second man, the reader is impressed and does not notice that the second man does not ask the first to join him, nor does he ask him to run to town (or pick up his cell phone) to summon others to join the effort. Those people who believe in individual acts of charity as the way to intervene in the world find the story inspiring, whereas those who think our actions should not be so limited find the story deceptive; the class, as always, is open to disagreement on these matters, but the answer to the quiz question is clear: Freire, who believed in collective action, would find the story problematic. In short, the story is on the side of the devil, albeit disguised as a story on the side of the angels.

Over the next month, intrigued, the students spontaneously elaborated on the story. One of them argued that the two men (and the men and women who join them) should investigate the deaths of the starfish and find out who is responsible. Others added that they should also look into the effects caused by the local fishing industry. One student insisted the man should plunge into the water and join the starfish in their effort to resist. This in turn led to a question: Should they, driven by what they had learned from the class readings and their workshops, devote their lives, skills, and careers to struggling together with people in the economic situations of the members of their workshops? A troubling, highly conflicted, potentially alienating dialogue ensued. If someone only facilitated a strong workshop with incarcerated girls, for example, then left it behind, had they merely dabbled? Should they disdain and be disdained by those who made a radical plunge? What they figured out was that all of them had crossed a border, had been challenged by what they met, had engaged creatively with urban youth and the incarcerated, and that they valued each other for that and could be allies. Those who did not plunge could stay in touch, advocate, help with connections, and raise funds; those who plunged would respect those who had not and would recognize the breadth of the work that needs to be done.

Participating in this conversation reminded me again of the ways our classrooms can offer spaces of growth, reflection, and giving. Indeed, the 310 class the following fall received an unusual gift. For our final session, we decided on a talk circle. One at a time, without interruption, we spoke what was on our minds, reflecting, offering each other words, thinking about what the youth we worked with might need from us now. Alison Stroud, who cofacilitated a poetry workshop with incarcerated boys, is profoundly deaf. Her stenographer, Katie Miller, had typed away all term, the words appearing on a screen, so that Alison could see in detail what we had said. First Alison spoke, and then she turned to Katie and said "now you talk!" I encouraged her, "yes, please do, you've been with us all term." Katie replied, "I'm sorry, but it is policy that I do not speak in classes." She paused, then: "But the children . . ." She paused again, and then said: "I have two children, and I want them to grow up to be like all of you." The students were visibly moved. Several, when it was their turn to speak, thanked her. She had been our reader and taken in our story. She had seen the students' struggles with each other, their outbursts and tears, their contentious and subtle arguments over the value of their work, and the hard personal questions they had asked about different kinds of generosity. She had heard the urban and incarcerated youth integrated into their voices and words as they talked about the workshops, and she had heard their growing commitments to each other and to those who had been granted so much less. And so Katie was able to tell us that we had become powerful together and that children's lives would be different because of our efforts.

The Annual Exhibition of Art by Michigan Prisoners

In 1995 Janie Paul and I sent out a letter to the twenty-two prisons within a 200-mile radius of Ann Arbor, asking wardens and staff to announce to prisoners that we would exhibit two-dimensional art by Michigan prisoners at the University of Michigan for eight days in February, that the work would be for sale, that the income would go to the artists' prison accounts, that we would take responsibility for matting and labeling, and that we would deliver unsold art to family members and other artist contacts. We thought we would give it a try. We had no idea what was out there. We were stunned when more than seventy artists from sixteen of the prisons responded. One of them, J. Anthony Jones, challenged us: *Who are you? Will the exhibition be sensationalist, or exploitative of prisoners?* We replied: This is an exhibition of *artists* who happen to be in prison, not an exhibition of the work of *prisoners*. Satisfied, he entered his work and for the next five years was one of the best artists we would ever have the privilege of exhibiting. When he came home in 2000, he served for several years as a member of our National Advisory Board.

We had no idea of the breadth and quality of art we would encounter. Rick Ward's "Basement Apartment," "Cadillac Bill," and "When I Was Young" were painted with a mixture of instant coffee and glue. Virgil Williams built his bas-relief "Tarbaby" out of layer upon layer of toilet paper. Tracy Neal's brilliant untitled collage consisted of fragments of cloth, including her panties, and documentation of the sexual assaults she had suffered in prison. Martin Vargas painted and framed a small rendering of a man bleeding in the snow surrounded by legs in prison blue, hence depicting a murder he had witnessed at the Huron Valley Men's Facility some years before. (Readers may see these and other pieces in the Appendix.) At the Ionia Maximum Facility, we met Herschell Turner, a man who would become one of my heroes. An all-American basketball player at the University of Nebraska, and later a Harlem Globetrotter, he was a Michigan Department of Corrections art instructor who taught level-six (highest security) prisoners through the windows on their cell doors; he taught level-two artists in a studio space he had carved out of the prison. So many of the excellent artists we would exhibit in the years to come benefitted from his tutelage. He fought for them, he fought for prisoner art, and he fought for the integrity of his teaching against the constraints of prison. Herschell would continue to fight and negotiate over the next ten years until one day his patience finally wore out and he quit.

In 1995 we selected seventy-seven works by fifty prisoners. We looked for work with some kind of edge in design or content, and we tried to be as inclusive as possible, for we knew what it would mean to incarcerated artists with disrupted childhoods and little or no access to art in their homes and schools to exhibit at the University of Michigan. The exhibition was free to the public and was made possible by hundreds of hours of dedicated volunteer work, including students who engaged in flyering, gallery sitting, and hanging and taking down the show. We invited the artists' family members and friends to the opening reception and to the closing receptions, where they and purchasers could pick up unsold work. Janie Paul spoke at the opening reception, as did Herschell Turner and installation artist and prison activist Richard Kamler, who had brought a piece of his "Table of Voices," which would later appear at Alcatraz. During the eight days of the exhibition, 462 visitors passed through the gallery; 33 of the 45 artists (73 percent) who wished to have their work sold were successful, and 43 of the 69 works for sale (62 percent) were sold at prices set by the artists. Total sales, every dollar of which went to the artists' prison accounts, came to $2,267.50. But more than raising money, the show raised consciousness and hope. Indeed, we had no idea that this exhibition would catch on and go on to affect so many people. In 2007 we completed our Twelfth Annual Exhibition of Art by Michigan Prisoners. At that exhibition 280 artists submitted more than 1,100 works of art, 224 artists from 42 prisons exhibited 347 works of art, 3,526 visitors came to the gallery over two weeks, 57 percent of the works for sale sold, and 63 percent of the artists with work for sale sold at least one work. The total artist income was $17,974.[13]

The general public is content with the highest incarceration rate and the longest sentences in the world. The national tone is punitive, full of stereotypes: Prisoners are rapists, killers, child molesters—dangerous, scruffy, isolated people behind bars who have no love of family, no creativity, no commitments other than crime. A first-time visitor to the gallery expects "prison art": rudimentary images of violence and the dark places of prison. Instead they encounter what one of them called "the most exciting contemporary art I have seen in a long while," a rich range of images and forms, including landscapes, family portraits, abstractions, humor, intriguing analyses of prison life, rich interpretations of the current political scene, and the vitality and pain of our cities. Gallery visitors write in the show's guest book "This is magic"; "A tremendous show of courage and emotion, a surprising and enlightening experience"; "This work is amazing, it wakes you up." Each year we provide a series of speakers and panels that further enrich the public understanding of the politics of incarceration, the complexity of prisons and prisoners, and those who work in the prisons. Our speakers have included Jimmy Santiago

Baca, Ellen Barry, Bell Chevigny, Bernardine Dohrn, Liz Fink, Lenny Foster, Stephen John Hartnett, Michael Keck, Lateef Islam, Phyllis Kornfeld, Terry Kupers, Dorsey Nunn, Tony Papa, Christian Parenti, Sister Helen Prejean, Beth Richie, Raul Salinas, Edmond Taylor, and other leading figures in the prison arts, education, and abolitionist community. In addition to our invited guests, former prisoners talk about prisoner art and parole, and their family members talk about the experience of having loved ones in prison. We host panels on the death penalty, mandatory minimums, prisoner health and mental health, the Michigan Battered Women's clemency project, restorative justice, and much more. In short, we do all we can to bridge inside and outside communities. Formerly incarcerated artists speak at the opening reception, and a videotape of the opening, which includes takes of each work in the gallery and takes of gallery-goers looking at the art, goes out to each participating prison, where it is shown to the artists and often to the prison population at large—we hope as an influence on artists to continue developing their work. Artists contribute autobiographical and artistic statements, which appear in a gallery book that visitors can carry about with them. Visitors write responses to individual artists, to contributing artists as a whole, and to the exhibition in a gallery book, and their responses, along with fliers, reviews, and a list of all the artists and their work, goes in a packet to each artist. In short, we try to marshal every communicative tool at our disposal to raise community awareness, empower the artists, and change public perception about the prison-industrial complex.

For the artists, the exhibition means visibility, respect, and stimulus. That we walk into the space where they are warehoused and respect them, talk with them about their art and their lives, and select what they submit validates their talent and commitment. The public despises them, the prisons humiliate them, and they have left damage behind in their communities, yet we are there to exhibit their work at a prestigious university. And so an important and growing piece of them is acknowledged. Hidden away in prison, they learn that thousands of people will witness their expression of self, their images, their ideas, their art. The exhibition also means stimulus; in fact, because of the exhibition, art has proliferated in Michigan prisons. New artists apprentice to old, workshops spring up, the word spreads, prisoners spend the entire year preparing for the exhibition. In 2004, faced with a space crisis because of the amount of art being submitted, and needing new selection criteria without sacrificing inclusiveness, we asked the artists in our October letter to strive for original art, "work that comes from the heart, that is unexpected, that we have not seen before," work where we can "see the imagination of the artist

. . . your unique skill, your unique vision." In a postexhibition evaluation, one artist talked about how this request worked for him and others:

> I know how hard it is to be on this side of the fence. I see people who are very well meaning doing their best to help. Most of them fail to be true to their mission. They seem to think that they can make us more to their kind of people. Your team tries to let us be ourselves. Asking us to tell people who we really are. . . . Perhaps the best service anyone could give a man in prison is to make him think. . . . It seems the best service anyone could give a man in prison is to let him know it is okay to think. It is sure most of the artists in prison will never get the chance to show anyone what they can do. They are not encouraged to think. It is discouraged more than anyone out there can ever understand. Your exhibition encourages us to think. I thank you for that.[14]

The exhibition therefore offers an opportunity to begin constructing a new image of oneself, of new possibilities and responsibilities. Echoing this point, another exhibition participant wrote us, just before leaving prison, about her artistic growth and about our Linkage Project, which will hook her up with a community artist:

> I just don't know how to describe how all this has made me feel. I guess if you consider a woman who felt like she was nothing, who felt she had no potential for anything, and would never be anything, then maybe you can understand just a little, what this has done for me. I now have a talent that I can utilize to support myself, and give people pleasure, at the same time, it is so amazing to me! Then, to incorporate my art with my skills in Graphic Arts, eventually own my own business, and hire displaced women, train them, give them a skill, that they can use to support their children, and hopefully never end up in here, or in a Domestic Violence situation, well, it means the world to me.[15]

As these two testimonies witness, the exhibition can mean survival. Indeed, for some artists, just knowing that their work will be viewed by the public provides them with an emotional jolt of purpose and confidence. For example, here is how Danny Valentine wrote about that first exhibition in 1995:

> Totally shut off from the outside world, I had no other stimuli than what existed inside the prison walls; as a result, I became a zombie, numb to reality—all hope lost. Today, however, I can say without reservation, that the U of M art exhibit for prisoners has *restored my human spirit*. Prior to my experience with the U of M, I was doing basic drawings that depicted a prison mentality boasting of criminal concepts (drugs, gang insignia, etc.), but after the first exhibit, the U of M provided the institutions of the participants with a video. The video allowed the artists to see their work on television. That one

single element of the whole process caused us to feel worthwhile again. . . .
I personally witnessed the ambiance of restored humanity filling the souls of
the other prisoners. Tears of joy welled in my eyes for the first time in many
years. A man crying in prison may not seem like a big deal, but a man in
prison whose soul becomes hard and bitter, soon forgets *how* to cry. I guess
that you would have to be here to really know what that is like.[16]

While Danny spoke about restoring his soul by making art for a larger public, F. Mumford wrote to us to say that for him, the exhibition and workshops
create spaces for pursuing "a kind of forgiveness." "My soul was wounded,"
he wrote, "as I went thru the process of police interrogation, arrest, jailing,
the court experience, and finally imprisonment. The smiles and conversations
with art student volunteers act as a balm for my wound. They are all held
in high esteem. The letters written to all the artists, and particularly to me,
make me cry! I feel filled with gratitude and happiness after the show and
read them thru and all the other things there in the packet." For Valentine,
Mumford, and the two anonymous witnesses quoted above, PCAP's efforts
opened up spaces of self-discovery and redemption.[17]

More than just personal growth, however, the workshops and exhibitions
also enable multiple forms of resistance to the prison-industrial complex. For
example, Janie Paul describes the conditions under which the artists work:

> Prison artists work in difficult conditions with many challenges. Some are
> bunked with five other people in a 12' by 16' cubicle. With people sleeping
> at different times, it is hard to find space and light to work. Some work at
> a small desk. Some may work in the pool/gambling/TV room with bad light,
> smoke and people watching and asking questions. For most, materials are
> hard to come by either because the cost is prohibitive or the materials are
> not allowed in prison. While there is often support from other inmates and
> staff, art sometimes gets intentionally destroyed. There is hardly any storage
> space, so it is not possible, as it is for artists outside, to view the history and
> breadth of one's own work.

Despite these conditions, our artists commit to their work, hence fighting
against the dehumanizing process of incarceration; in so doing, Paul argues
(and our letters confirm) that they "find sustenance" and engage in "resistance to the deadliness of prison." Making art, then,

> is a form of resistance to the oppressive conditions of prison life. In resis-
> tance to the barrenness of prison, artists create images of beauty, joy, and
> celebration. In resistance to poverty of resources, there is inventiveness with
> materials. In resistance to uniformity, there is idiosyncrasy and freshness of
> vision. In resistance to the hidden devastation and violence of prison, art-

ists depict harsh realities that we need to know about. In resistance to the coldness of prison, artists create images of love and tenderness. And in resistance to invisibility, artists create images of themselves.[18]

For these artists, practicing their craft amounts not only to resistance to the conditions of prison, but resistance to what they were given at birth: lousy health care and housing and schools; little access to employment; dangerous neighborhoods; unemployed, angry, negligent, absent, struggling, addicted, punitive parents; malnutrition; the seductions of the streets, of drugs, gangs, prostitution; the heritage of violence. To become an artist, or an actor or a poet, to grow into articulation and originality and dignity, means resisting what has been done to them and what they have done to themselves and others. Although the odds are great, participating in the art-making process described here makes further kinds of resistance more possible.

Goodbye to Nate Jones

During the street dances on Legrand, when the block was closed down and people cooked whole pigs and there were hot dogs and hamburgers for the children and no one fought, the kids would come to the mike to sing their favorite songs. Nate was known for his rendering of "You Ain't Nothing but a Hound Dog." During his second bit in prison, Nate took college classes and got an associate's degree, he joined a therapy group and learned to talk about what was inside and to cry, he wrote for the prison paper, and he became the prison ping-pong champion. Nate joined a writing group and contributed his prose memories to *Gittin' Down*, including his experience of attending his father's funeral in handcuffs, and poems like "The Runaway":

in my
furniture box home
rats scurry around my
run from cruelty
from home to home
prospective man
hunts sparrows
to eat and
feels safe
in the box.

Nate joined the Western Wayne Players and was a great spirit, honest, challenging, the witty elusive comic lead in "The Carpool," a play we never finished; through *Inside Out* he spoke with incarcerated youth and with gang members at Henry Ford High School; he maintained his independence and didn't get caught up, he was on track, he seized an opportunity to take classes through the University of Michigan, he came home and entered the University of Michigan and in my courses went to Maxey and Henry Ford High School and worked with youth; he became a robust friend and mentor to his peer students, he went on to the University of Michigan School of Social Work, he graduated and worked in an assisted living center and at Boysville with incarcerated youth; he liked people so much that he gave out free doughnuts at Dunkin' Donuts and lost his job; he would jump to his feet and act and dance and sing; he met me at the bank to get a loan to rent a home for his little daughter and her sister, whom he had adopted away from a desperate situation, and at the end, after his diagnosis, he fought to get them to a safe place, into a family where they would never fall into the life. He crashed and came back, crashed and came back; gasping for breath, he painted his face and led a parade in Battle Creek during his final weeks—he was always, one way or another, alive again.[19]

Nate is in our hearts and is at the heart of what we all do. He is F. Mumford and Danny Valentine and Mary Glover, he is Chris Lussier, who adopted Nate's daughters and seeks what is missing in his life, he is the students in English 310, who carry the voices of the urban and incarcerated youth in them, he is Jesse Jannetta, being trusted and trusting himself enough to take risks in a new environment, he is the artists and actors and writers who resist, against terrible odds, what has been given them and done to them and what they have become, he is the creative spaces where we improvise and laugh and go inside ourselves and emerge to seek each other out.

Notes

1. Mary and Joyce were receiving University of Michigan credits for their work in this course, which they paid for with a scholarship from the university. Prior to enrolling at the university, they had used Pell Grant money to help pay for courses at Washtenaw Community College and Eastern Michigan University. Mary eventually earned her bachelor of arts degree; Joyce also graduated and went on to earn a master's degree in social work. By cancelling Pell Grants, the U.S. government has made it even more difficult to reproduce such success stories; on the pulling of Pell Grants, see Jon Marc Taylor "Pell Grants for Prisoners," *Nation* (25 January 1993), 88–91, and Stephen John Hartnett, "Cell Block Grants," *In These Times* (17 April 1995): 6–7.

2. For more information about PCAP, or to order our poetry, art books, or videos, go to www.prisonarts.org.

3. These verses are from "For Mike, Because You Asked," by the author.

4. For introductions to the methods discussed here, see Augusto Boal, *Games for Actors and Non-Actors*, 2d ed. (New York: Routledge, 2002); Paulo Freire, *Pedagogy of the Oppressed* (1977; New York: Continuum International, 2007); Miles Horton, with Herbert Kohl and Judith Kohl, *The Long Haul* (New York: Teachers College Press, 1997); Augosto Boal, *Theatre of the Oppressed* (New York: Theatre Communications Group, 1995); and Hernan Kesselman and Eduardo Pavlovsky, *La Multiplicación Dramática*, 2d ed. (Buenos Aires, Argentina: Ediciones Ayllu, 1991); on the concept of workshops serving as "outreach" within prisons and other disadvantaged communities, see Stephen John Hartnett, "Lincoln and Douglas Engage the Abolitionist David Walker in Prison Debate: Empowering Education, Applied Communication, and Social Justice," *Journal of Applied Communication Research* 26, no. 2 (1998): 232–53.

5. In Michigan, the presence of an officer or special activities staff person is required only in level-four prisons; in a 1996 play titled "Seasons," turnover was so high that our lead character ended up being a composite of three actors' experiences.

6. When Florence Crane ceased being a women's facility in 2000, the Sisters within Theater Troupe continued at Western Wayne; when that facility was closed in 2004, we continued at the Huron Valley Complex for Women; on May 10 and 12, 2008, we performed our twenty-fifth play, "Arsenica Titanium Plutonium Noodler; or Two Rosary Peas."

7. Lauren Rubinfeld's statement, and all other quoted passages from PCAP members, is used with permission of each author.

8. Jonathan Kozol, *The Night Is Dark and I Am Far from Home* (Boston: Houghton Mifflin, 1975), quotation from 27, with themes from pages 2, 4, 7, 8, and 12.

9. Nate Jones, speaking in the video *Inside Out* (Ann Arbor: Victor/Harder Productions, 1994).

10. Nate's words here are from unpublished material he was working on just before his death; some of the memories shared here are depicted in *Inside Out*.

11. This passage is from p. 5 of an untitled 2006 booklet, edited by Suzanne Gothard and Megan Schuchman, including brief essays addressed to the author by his students and former students on the occasion of his receiving the 2005 Professor of the Year Award from the Carnegie Foundation for the Advancement of Teaching and the Center for the Advancement and Support of Education.

12. While the texts for English 310 and 319 have varied over the years, here are the written texts assigned currently: William Ayers, Bernardine Dohrn, and Rick Ayers, *Zero Tolerance; Resisting the Drive for Punishment in Our Schools* (New York: New Press, 2001); an unpublished essay and poem by Lizzy Baskerville, PCAP Associate; Nell Bernstein, *All Alone in the World; Children of the Incarcerated* (New York: The New Press, 2005); Boal, *Games for Actors and Non-Actors*; Freire, *Pedagogy of the Oppressed*; Horton, *Long Haul*; Edward Humes, *No Matter How Loud I Shout; A Year in the Life of Juvenile Court* (New York: Simon and Schuster, 1996); Herbert Kohl, *36 Children (New York: Plume, 1988)*; Kozol, *Night Is Dark*, and Kozol, *Savage Inequalities: Children in America's Schools* (New York: HarperCollins, 1992); Marc Mauer and Meda Chesney-Lind, eds., *Invisible Punishment; The Collateral Consequences of Mass*

Imprisonment (New York: New Press, 2002); Peter Sacks, *Standardized Minds; The High Price of America's Testing Culture and What We Can Do to Change It* (New York: DaCapo Press, 1999); and Judith Tannenbaum, *Disguised as a Poem; My Years Teaching Poetry at San Quentin* (Boston: Northeastern University Press, 2000).

13. The Annual Exhibition of Art by Michigan Prisoners is funded in part by the generous support of many units within the University of Michigan, including the Office of the Provost; the College of Literature, Science and the Arts; the Rackham School of Graduate Studies; the School of Art and Design; the Department of English Language and Literature; and the Program in American Culture. It has also been funded with an access grant from the National Endowment for the Humanities, a PACT Grant from the Rockefeller Foundation, a grant from the Kellogg Foundation, and the generous donations made by its many patrons. Richard Kamler's "Table of Voices: Conversations on the Criminal Justice System: An Interactive Installation with Community Conversations," opened on Alcatraz Island in 1996; for information on Kamler and his long history of engaged art, go to richardkamler.org. As the show has grown, we have had to become more fiscally sophisticated: for example, the Michigan Department of Corrections now takes 15 percent of the show's profits for the Inmate Benefit Fund, and we must report 6 percent as a sales tax—in response to these pressures, we have encouraged the artists to raise their prices accordingly.

14. Evaluation statement from the 12th Annual Exhibition of Art by Michigan Prisoners, April 2007.

15. Anonymous letter to the author (14 April 2007).

16. Danny Valentine, undated letter to the author.

17. Fred Mumford, letter to the author (June 2007).

18. These are from an untitled essay in *Doing Time, Making Space; 10 Years of the Annual Exhibition of Art by Michigan Prisoners*, ed. Janie Paul (Ann Arbor: PCAP, 2005), no pages, available from PCAP.

19. This section comes from discussions with Nate, from his writings toward the end of his life, and from passages in *Gittin' Down; Profiles from Michigan Prison Writers*, ed. Lolita Hernandez (Brighton, MI: ArtsGrowth Opportunities, 1991), 18–23.

The Poet's Corner

George Hall

Founded by Buzz Alexander, the Poet's Corner is a long-running group of writers who gather once a week in the Jackson Prison, in Jackson, Michigan; in this poem, the seventy-three-year-old George Hall celebrates how the Poet's Corner offers him a space of redemption; the piece was published in *A Crack in the Concrete: Writings and Art by Michigan Prisoners for World Environment Day*, ed. Buzz Alexander, Jean Borger, Mica Doctoroff, Thylias Moss, and Rachel Nelson (Detroit: LeAdfooT Press, 2005).

The times I have been at peace
are almost beyond my memory's reach
and sometimes I ask myself
have I ever really been there in here?
Or am I merely borrowing
from what I imagine it might be
but have never been able to see?

As I look back through my mind
in an attempt to find
the thing inside me that instills in kind
I keep coming back to where I am right now
standing here in front of you.

When I am up here reciting a poem
I feel as if I am standing upon a pulpit
and my poem is the sermon
I am trying to preach
because I don't always know
why I write what I write.
It begins with a thought veering away
off toward an idea

and ends up flowing, going,
tossing about like a boat without oars
caught in the eddies of my emotions.

And then it dawns on me,
a time when I have felt at peace?

Right now, right here this moment
reading this poem to you
and what has been stuck inside me
and kept me going
beyond the call to end it all,
what has overridden the anger
and the pain and the hate
is my need to feel human and still alive.

And so when I come here to be with you
and listen to your poems
and read mine to you,
that is what you help me to feel,
that I am still alive,
that I am still a human being.

And that is as close to peace
as I will ever be again.

Chapter 7

Each One Reach One: Playwriting and Community Activism as Redemption and Prevention

Robin Sohnen

As Santos lay bleeding to death in the public bathroom where he had been shot, he scrawled "open your eyes" on the floor with his own blood. When told of his deathbed command, most of his gang members thought he was telling them to nail the crazy *vato* who had gunned him down—they thought his final wish was for revenge, for more blood, for another hit in the endless cycle of ghetto violence. But the play's hero, Solo, believed the blood-scrawled message meant something else: He thought it was a desperate call to open his eyes to life's possibilities, to change his hoodlum ways, to stop killing and dying for a few square blocks of hell in the middle of a bombed-out city. Santos had come to this realization too late, but Solo still had a chance to turn his life around; he could, with Herculean effort, wrench himself free from the death cycle and begin building a different life. So argues Mario Rocha in a play he wrote while awaiting trial in the Los Angeles County Juvenile Detention Center. One of hundreds of imprisoned young men and women who are learning new means of self-expression and self-commitment though play-writing workshops run by Each One Reach One (EORO), Rocha embodies the hopes of EORO, for during his ten years of wrongful incarceration (he was finally released in 2007) he wrote plays, poems, editorials, and stories, literally writing his way to self-respect, national prominence, and ultimately freedom.[1]

Taking our cue from Mario's bravery and Solo's life-saving realization—*open your eyes*—EORO is dedicated to enabling incarcerated youth to explore life's possibilities by using writing as a means of self-discovery, group art making, and sometimes political organizing. We struggle to fan the small flame of hope in youngsters whose lives have been difficult, sometimes even tormented. By helping them to learn new means of self-expression and group art-making dynamics, EORO hopes these youngsters realize that they are precious people who can change their lives and their communities. EORO is not content to work inside juvenile detention centers exclusively, however, and so we work in our communities as well, where we argue that the youth filling the prison pipeline are not irredeemable monsters but *abandoned children*—and like all children, they need our love and care to help them grow into happy and healthy contributing members of our communities. Ultimately, then, EORO works in juvenile detention centers to help youngsters find their own redemptions through art, and we work in communities to try to prevent another generation of urban youth from getting sucked into the prison-industrial complex.[2]

I founded Each One Reach One in the San Francisco Bay area in 1997 with the mission of diverting incarcerated youth from a life in prison; I thought I could accomplish this task by relying upon the transformative power of the arts and education. Ten years and many hard lessons later, EORO has evolved into a collaborative network of paid office staff, professional artists, and an ever-changing supporting cast of volunteers. Together, we conduct playwriting workshops, academic tutoring, and reentry preparation programs inside juvenile detention facilities, we organize the community to participate in reforming the juvenile justice system, and we promote cooperation and collaboration among the many stakeholders involved both in and in combating the prison-industrial complex. The primary population that we serve is teenage boys and girls, many of whom are imprisoned in the maximum-security units of short-term juvenile facilities and detention camps. And while the vast majority of our workshop participants are still teenagers, they are on the fast track to the adult prison system and lifetimes of incarceration—we therefore try to divert these youngsters while it is still possible, before it is too late, before they become institutionalized into prison life, their souls crushed, their horizons receding.[3]

In the following pages, I outline how EORO tries to accomplish this dual task of using the arts as both redemption and prevention. We call our program ADAPT (A Dream and Plan for Tomorrow); it begins with a one-on-one creative arts program based on playwriting; the second step is a weekly after-school study hall program that provides one-on-one academic tutoring, with an emphasis on preparing for the GED and exploring life goals; it concludes with reentry planning and support for the youth as they return to our local communities, ideally now empowered with a new sense of themselves and their possible futures. Indeed, the ADAPT program hopes to enable incarcerated youth to find their inner voices, to encourage them to assess their lives, and to empower them to make choices that will divert them from a future life in prison. I am proud to say that in our first ten years of work, more than 630 youth have enrolled in the playwriting program and completed a one-act play. More than 4,000 family members, probation officers, corrections staff, teachers, mental health workers, judges, and interested community members have attended performances of these plays, which have been staged by more than 1,500 volunteer actors and directors. More than 400 youth have participated in the after-school academic tutoring program, and more than 65 of them have successfully passed all five of the tests necessary for completing the GED; an additional 160 students successfully completed three of the five necessary tests before being transferred from their institution (whereupon EORO brokered links to outside agencies that could help them complete their GEDs). These are small numbers and humble successes to be sure, but they are a start, and they suggest that EORO's three-step ADAPT plan works—we need now to expand it, to broaden our goals, and to begin reclaiming hope and justice from our punishing democracy.

My hope in describing the Each One Reach One model is that others may choose to replicate it, hence joining the fight to shut down the schools-to-prisons pipeline and the prison-industrial complex. To reach this goal, we will need to honor the transformation described by James, an ADAPT veteran; if we are successful, then such comments will reflect not a unique reclamation of a lost soul but the baseline of self-discovery and exploration to which all young people are entitled:

> I have undergone a complete mental transformation from an undisciplined drug user to a driven, hard-working student. I knew it was time to change—all I needed was a reason. The ADAPT program was that reason. While incarcerated, the ADAPT program allowed me to spend my time on creative self-reflection and improvement, and the program forced me to realize that I could have a future if I wanted one! My presence in the ADAPT program, the realization that I was doing something to improve my future on my own volition, was an extremely powerful motivational force. In jail, it is difficult to find opportunities to educate and express yourself emotionally and intellectually, but the program did that for me, and the result has been invaluable. In retrospect, the program has done more for me than I could ever do for myself, not just for my educational future but for the rest of my life.[4]

The First Step: Playwriting Workshops and Bearing Witness to "The Block of Death"

Monty is a seventeen-year-old African American male who was incarcerated on the maximum-security boys unit in San Francisco; he wrote a play titled *The Belly of the Beast* featuring two characters: Stuck, the pigeon, and No Love, the street block. As the play opens, No Love is trying to dissuade Stuck from making a mistake that might end up getting him killed, but it's too late for Stuck, for he has lost all hope—life has ground him down into the state of "despair and dread" described by Cornell West in the introduction to this book, where we saw him argue that young men in hard-hit communities are facing the "monumental eclipse of hope, the unprecedented collapse of meaning, [and] the incredible disregard for human (especially black) life." While he cannot be bothered to ponder ways to make a more meaningful life, death does not scare Stuck, for like many of our young men and women who are involved in the activities of the street, he suspects he won't live much longer anyway—nobody does in his world, so why should he try to make a change, what's the point? But when asked to describe his neighborhood, to chronicle the tragedies that litter his childhood, Monty/Stuck discovers a sense of outrage, and this leads from merely witnessing pain to taking a stand against it. This is how Stuck puts it, in all capital letters:

> MY WHOLE LIFE'S BEEN UP AND DOWN
> AND IT'S BEEN MORE DRAMA THAN SITCOMS
> AND TO BE A WITNESS IS TORTURE.
>
> THE BELLY OF THE BEAST IS WHERE WE COME FROM,
> A CORNER OF DEATH, GREED, AND STRUGGLE.
> NO LIGHT, JUST A DARK VALLEY.
>
> YOU SEE MOVEMENT IN THE SHADOWS;
> YOU HEAR WHISPERS AND CRIES FOR HELP,
> BUT THEY ONLY GO SO FAR.
>
> ONCE YOU GO THROUGH THE BLACK HOLE,
> TO THE BELLY OF THE BEAST,
> DEATH'LL BE THE LEAST OF YOUR WORRIES.
>
> GET UP AT 0–600
> PUT ON YO GEAR; DON'T FORGET YO WEAPON;
> GO TO THE BLOCK OF DEATH.
>
> YOU WALK THROUGH PUDDLES, TRASH, AND PEOPLE
> CRUMPLED ON THE FLOOR IN BUNDLES OF BLANKETS.
> ARE THEY DEAD?
>
> YOU WOULD THINK SO
> IF THEY WEREN'T SHAKING
> FROM THE COLD AND RAIN AND ANGER.
>
> A DANK AROMA FLIES FROM A GROUP OF YOUNGSTAS.
> A BOTTLE IS PASSED AROUND.
> THIS IS WHERE DEATH IS SOLD AT A LOW PRICE.
>
> WHAT CAN YOU ASK FOR IN THE BELLY OF THE BEAST?
> HARD TIME GOT MY PEOPLE DOWN IN THE TRENCHES,
> FIGHTING FOR ELBOW SPACE AND A PLACE TO CALL THEIR OWN.

AND IT'S SUCH A COLD, COLD WORLD.
WHERE WE'RE BORN IN THE BELLY OF THE BEAST
AND ONLY ONE OR TWO MAKE IT OUT.[5]

Imagine being seventeen and having witnessed these horrors; imagine being seventeen and possessing the talent to convey them in powerful verse; and imagine the amazement of Monty's friends, family, fellow detainees, and his jailers when these words were performed by professional actors who could bring the scenes to life. I don't want to overreach here and claim that writing *The Belly of the Beast* singlehandedly saved Monty's life, but if you believe in the power of art and public performance, and if you believe in the power of wanting to change your life, then it would be almost impossible to see this play without knowing that something significant has just occurred: a young man has moved from being a silent victim to being an eloquent witness. EORO is driven by the belief that the composure gained in making that life change, the hard-earned confidence in himself built up through the writing process, the teamwork skills learned in staging and rehearsing his play with others, and then the public thrill of having others acclaim his new command of words—small miracles in themselves—will serve Monty well as he tries to build a new life, one where he can "make it out" of the belly of the beast.[6]

As suggested by the revelatory tone of Monty's play, in which he seems to be seeing his world for the first time, EORO's playwriting workshops attempt to assist incarcerated youth to recognize and change their self-destructive behavioral patterns, to encourage them to find their inner voices through self-expression, and to empower them to make choices that will divert them from a future in prison. The playwriting workshops intervene in the participants' lives by employing professional theater artists, who not only teach incarcerated youth playwriting skills, but also engage them in an examination of their life choices and goals. It would be hard to overstate the importance of the creative bond formed between our incarcerated young playwrights and their professional mentors/actors, for in many cases the young prisoners EORO works with have never had anything approaching a tutor or mentor, let alone an attentive parent. In fact, for many of our workshop participants, the one-on-one care and respect they receive from their mentors/actors is some of the first sustained attention from adults that they have ever received.

Once a partnership has been formed between a playwright and a mentor/actor, the playwriting workshop unfolds in three-hour sessions held every workday for two weeks—the workshop thus offers an intense immersion in the playwriting process. Each of the ten sessions focuses on a different aspect of the creative process, including how to tell a dramatic story, how to weave a narrative, how to explore conflict through dialogue, how to create consistent characters, and how to resolve the problems implicit in their stories. Because participants write about their own life experiences, the script development process serves as a springboard for encouraging the young playwrights to examine their own and others' values, opinions, feelings, and attitudes. Once participants decide what to write their plays about, their professional mentors/actors guide them through drafting and other improvisational acting exercises to assist them in developing characters and scenes. All the creative stages mentioned here overlap with each other, so the process is not linear—characters come and go, narratives change from session to session, scripts evolve and sometimes blow up only to resurface in new forms. Compressing the entire process into two intense weeks therefore serves both logistical and pedagogical functions: It is wise logistically because we often do not have long to work with these young playwrights before they are shipped out to other facilities; it works pedagogically because when they are faced with a short-term goal and an impending deadline, these youth often respond by building a sense of a team working on a shared mission.

Another unique aspects of Each One Reach One's playwriting workshops is that we ask our young authors to write their stories with characters that are animals, objects, forces of nature, or emotions—like Monty's telling his story through the voices of Stuck and No Love. Asking our playwrights to speak through such characters provides them with a protective mask for conveying what are often deeply confessional materials. For example, in one play, an imprisoned young girl staged a conversation between a dog and a cat. They are archetypal enemies, but in this play the animals learn to trust each other, with the big strong dog eventually confessing to the smallish cat that his deepest wish is simply for companionship. He doesn't want to bully anyone or chase anyone; rather, he confesses in a performative wail: "Iiiiii want a frieeeennnnd." To describe the scene in this way makes it sound childish or simple, yet in a room full of youth on probation, incarcerated youngsters, and their families, and when performed by a professional actor, these lines called forth a thunderous round of applause mixed with tears. To confess feeling vulnerable, to ask for help, and to share such honesty struck the audience like a thunderclap. Especially for our young playwrights, approaching their core concerns through the voices of animals or objects enables them to address the fear, loneliness, rage, betrayal, and abandonment that they might feel too close to if they were asked to address them in their own voices. Whether the characters are dogs or cats or the wind, our young playwrights often circle around a shared set of wishes: to be loved, to be safe, to build friendships, to have or to make their own family—everyone is sick and tired of being alone.

As would be expected of youngsters in almost any setting, EORO's playwriting workshop participants seem especially concerned about their relationships with their parents. This makes obvious sense, for the prison-industrial complex ruins families. In 1999 the Bureau of Justice Statistics reported that 1.5 million children nationwide had a parent behind bars. At the time of imprisonment, nearly half these imprisoned parents ran single-family households, meaning their children were sucked into child services upon the imprisonment of their parent. (I should note that these numbers are ten years old, meaning they underrepresent the breadth of the current problem.) The production of a culture of children suffering from a lack of parenting is thus one of the devastating consequences of the prison-industrial complex. Moreover, the location of many penal facilities leaves imprisoned parents sequestered at great distances from their children, extended family, and friends, leaving their children lonely and their families fractured. The prison-industrial complex therefore plays a central role in perpetuating a cycle of broken families that is likely to create more prisoners. EORO's young playwrights reflect this damage.[7]

An example is "Thinking of You," a dialogue between a baby bird named Tiny and her mother. The author, Casandra, is a fourteen-year-old willow, barely 90 pounds, just 4' 6", she is a beautiful girl with bright brown eyes and long, braided pigtails—the picture of youthful energy and vulnerability. In her play, Tiny's mother has made "a very bad choice" by repeatedly buying the "bad stuff" from an intimidating lion. The mother needs the "stuff" and wants to go see the lion for another fix, which launches a familiar battle between mother and daughter. "Why bring a child into the world and not take care of it?" cries Tiny, in a heart-wrenching wail, before offering this glum question: "Maybe you don't love me!" After heavy negotiation, Tiny lets the mother bird go see the lion, but only if she leaves all her money with Tiny. The mother returns safely, but Tiny says, "When you went to see the lion, I felt like I had lost you again." The mother replies, "You're my reason to stop using the bad stuff, Tiny," and the play comes to a happy ending. Casandra thus used the theater to create a different reality, a world that reflects both her deepest wish and her most painful loss. After the play's conclusion, tears welled up in her father's eyes as Casandra's smiling face beamed out to the audience while taking her "playwright's bow," hand in hand with her actors and mentor. Regretfully, her mother was not able to attend—she was still out with the Lion.[8]

Because our work often touches upon these complex family dramas of loss and redemption, of hopes shattered and loves lost, EORO strives to create public occasions for praising the hard work of our workshop participants—these kids have had too little public acknowledgment and encouragement in their lives. And so the public staging of plays functions not only as the culmination of our workshops but as a group celebration of accomplishment. For many of our workshops begin with the young participants convinced that they cannot write a play, that they do not have anything to say, or that no one will listen anyway. EORO helps such youngsters realize that they were wrong: They can write plays, they do have something to say, and we will not only listen to but cheer their words. Finally, each workshop includes a "closure circle," where the participants, their mentors, and their families join hands, offer final comments, and collectively acknowledge the group's success. These are tear-filled occasions at which parents see their children in a proud new light and incarcerated writers bask in their newfound confidence and friendships—it sounds hokey, but these events are living testaments that we can shut down the prison-industrial complex, for these children are proof that with a little love and care, the youngsters we choose to imprison can be creative, hardworking, successful members of our community.[9]

The Second Step: Academic Tutoring and "This Tool to Keep Me Going"

The second step in Each One Reach One's three-step ADAPT plan (A Dream and a Plan for Tomorrow) involves an academic tutoring program offered in the maximum-security boys unit in San Francisco and in the boys and girls units of the Youth Service Center in San Mateo, California. These are the Bay Area's first afterschool one-on-one academic tutoring programs conducted inside a short-term juvenile detention facility. The goal is to assist the youth in envisioning a future life as a contributing member of society and to take the initial steps in that direction while working closely with a tutor. By engaging college students and community volunteers to staff our study halls, we hope to provide imprisoned youth with positive role models; indeed, all mentors are trained to challenge the participants to perform beyond their self-expectations—excellence is not a hope but a demand.

The study hall aspect of ADAPT responds to what can only be called the disaster of California's public schools, especially as regards the opportunities offered in certain devastated communities. The laws of California mandate that all youth under the age of eighteen must attend high school classes five days a week for anywhere between five and six hours a day, with individual student class loads that may include work credit and independent study. These requirements apply to all schools, including those inside youth detention centers and mental institutions, meaning even imprisoned youth are owed, by law, the right to an education. I should note as well that some of the educators and administrators working in these schools in carceral settings are nothing less than saints, for creating and facilitating meaningful learning plans inside these facilities is a daunting task requiring profound patience. Nonetheless, the conditions in most of these learning environments are dire at best. On any given day inside these schools within detention centers, educators are asked to work with youth between the ages of twelve and eighteen, who speak multiple languages, who carry various special education needs, who sometimes have learning disabilities, and whose reading and writing skills range anywhere from first grade to college level. Pedagogically, such classrooms require exceptionally talented teachers.

In addition to these pedagogical challenges, the students in these classrooms often suffer from attention deficit disorder (ADD) and, in many cases, exhibit the symptoms of posttraumatic stress disorder (PTSD), just one of the results of living in environments suffused with violence. Indeed, affiliates of the American Bar Association have found that 28 to 60 percent of imprisoned juveniles suffer from an educational disability: within that group, 11 percent have learning disabilities, 20 percent have severe emotional disturbances, 18 percent have some kind of attention deficit disorder or attention deficit hyperactivity disorder, and 3 to 10 percent have cognitive disabilities. Making the situation even more difficult, the classrooms in juvenile detention centers are often full of youngsters suffering from mental illnesses, drug addictions, and hopelessness—but even the best teachers cannot function as therapists, medical doctors, and spiritual healers. Kick in the fact that the average length of stay for a detainee in juvenile hall is less than two weeks, and you begin to catch a glimmer of an almost impossible educational situation. So even while California law mandates offering classes to imprisoned youths under the age of eighteen, the children placed in these situations almost universally fail to achieve academic excellence; of course the teachers asked to work with them are frustrated—it would not be cynical to argue that the system is structured to produce failure.[10]

Responding to this dilemma, the ADAPT afterschool educational tutor and life-skills program attempts to disrupt the downward academic spiral that has contributed to many youths' truancy, their getting pushed out of school, or other self-destructive behavior by enabling the participants to envision a career/life plan and to take the first steps toward implementing that plan. The program comprises weekly two-hour study halls, at which community volunteers and college students conduct individual academic tutoring. ADAPT's study hall manager facilitates these weekly sessions and assembles transcripts of each student's academic history, thus identifying what the youth must achieve to graduate or to meet GED requirements. Using the information compiled by EORO's staff during an intake interview, the tutors identify each participant's individual skills, aptitudes, and needs; the tutor then emphasizes these strengths and interests to engage the teenager in the formulation of a postrelease plan for achieving success. Once participants envision a "dream," they work with their mentor to express it in an essay. (These essays serve obvious pedagogical purposes, but they also often end up in the hands of counselors, lawyers, and judges, for whom these essays serve as strong evidence of the will to succeed—they stand then as an advance payment against recidivism.) EORO thus merges rigorous academic training with exploratory idea testing, enabling students to envision a new future while providing them with the tools to succeed.

During the first hour of each tutoring session, the participants work on practice exercises meant to prepare them for the GED test's five sections: essay writing, reading comprehension, mathematics, science, and social studies. During the second hour, participants complete assignments that enhance their academic, vocational, and critical-thinking skills. These assignments might include composing essays that identify career goals; discussing current events or important social issues; learning independent living skills; reading the want ads; developing and submitting résumés; or completing application forms for jobs and admission to job-training programs, drug-treatment programs, and counseling services. Ideally, students in the study halls will have participated in, witnessed the performance of, or at least heard about the playwriting workshops before they join the study halls—this means the youngsters come to study hall already convinced that they can succeed, for the plays have shown these children that they have talents the world has ignored or even repressed. Artistic and pedagogical excitement is infectious, so EORO hopes the playwriting workshops feed and energize the study halls. Unlike the ten-week playwriting workshops, however, study hall mentors meet one-on-one with their chosen youth every week for as long as the student is incarcerated and willing to learn, thus continuously encouraging them to take steps that will facilitate their transition back into society.

Our student surveys indicate that the youngsters involved in the program understand the long-term goals that lie behind our pedagogical philosophies. One question on the EORO survey asks, "If given the opportunity, would you be willing to give up your free time to study and prepare to take the GED exams while incarcerated?" Angelo's answer, representative of many of his study-hall classmates, was "Yes, I would. Just so I can show myself I can do it, and to show my family and the judge that I'm still willing to learn, even in my position. . . . Because without a high school diploma or a GED, you can't really get a good job." In that same line of thought, Julia observed how "being in juvenile hall, I tended to lose track of the bigger picture by drowning in my room about all the things I feared." Julia started to overcome this sense of fear-driven drowning first by writing a play, after which she was thrilled to report that "it was a touching moment for my father and me when my play was performed. For the first time, I felt we really bonded." Fueled by that positive experience, Julia entered one of our study halls, of which she said: "These two hours per week are far from as many as I would like, but they add up and are greatly appreciated! The possibilities are endless now that I have this tool to keep me going. I've come to the conclusion that I can get out whatever I put in." Julia thus allowed herself to write in a new voice, to build a new relationship with her father, and to build productive study habits—and these, surely, are skills that will serve her well as she leaves imprisonment to reenter the free world. Perhaps more than anything else, EORO sought to help Julia reconceive herself not as a criminal but as a promising young woman who can achieve excellence. As she wrote, "this program [EORO] accepted me and many other inmates with open arms, unlike most you didn't judge me by my file, you judged me by my attitude and optimism to set higher standards for my life—thank you so much, you have changed my life."

The Third Step: Reentry Preparation Services and the Fight against "Labor Market Disenfranchisement"

Once released, even highly motivated youth have few resources to assist them to keep moving forward—they too often return to broken homes in broken communities haunted by broken dreams. In the past, this gap in services meant ADAPT program participants received little attention at the very moment when they most needed support. (This is true of adult prisoners as well.) The goal of the Reentry Preparation Program is to close this care gap by linking youth to community-based employment, career development, and educational programs, and to use their self-identified dreams as a roadmap for guiding their transition back to freedom. In this capacity, EORO has partnered with JobTrain, a Bay Area group offering a range of opportunities, such as full-time vocational training, after-school classes, summer internships, GED preparation, ESL workshops, and child care. EORO's academic tutors help imprisoned participants to prepare application forms seeking admission to one of JobTrain's training programs, which include classes in basic education, culinary arts, digital video, nurse assistants, construction, electronics, office skills, medical billing, computer coding, and Web design. If a participant's dream is to pursue a professional career as a teacher, or another career that requires a college degree, mentors assist youth in enrolling in community college courses as well as in JobTrain's education program. Thus, to help EORO break the cycle of recidivism, we work with JobTrain to make sure that our playwrights and study-hall participants leave juvenile detention with renewed self-confidence, a life plan for fulfillment, and the practical contacts and mentoring they need to succeed.[11]

I need to note that this final aspect of our ADAPT plan marks the far edges of reform, for this is where our best practices and hopes as educators and activists crash into the harsh realities of neoliberal capitalism. Indeed, in an increasingly networked and wired marketplace that depends upon technological savvy and interpersonal skills, the formerly incarcerated face daunting challenges. For while languishing in prisons and juvenile detention centers obviously means the incarcerated are not advancing their job skills, some observers have also noted how prisons teach behavior patterns almost guaranteed to cause friction in any workplace. As Paul Street has argued, "the alternatively aggressive and sullen posture that prevails behind bars is deadly in a job market where entry-level occupations increasingly demand 'soft' skills related to selling and customer service." Former prisoners are thus among the least successful in the new economy; they suffer unemployment rates as high as 50 percent; those who do work tend to make low wages, to receive scant benefits, and to fall off the ladder of upward mobility. Former prisoners are thus subject to what Street calls "labor market disenfranchisement," for they are literally taught how not to succeed. EORO has partnered with JobTrain to try to fight this new form of labor-market disenfranchisement, but any long-term success in this regard will depend on pushing dramatic changes in local, national, and even international economics, and that, to be practical, is outside the feasible purview of what Each One Reach One can accomplish.[12]

Nonetheless, we do what we can, we hope for the best, and we celebrate the hard work of those who fight for a better life. Consider the story of Tatanisha, a young woman who enrolled in our study-hall program at the Youth Services Center in San Mateo. She was working toward her GED when she was released; she then continued to prepare for her GED with our partners at JobTrain. But when Tatanisha's family situation became unbearable, she was forced to move to San Jose to live with her grandmother; unfamiliar with our program, not accustomed to a young woman with big hopes, and struggling financially, Tatanisha's grandmother made living with her conditional upon Tatanisha taking a full-time job. And to her credit and our great pleasure, Tatanisha not only found a full-time job at a K-Mart but also kept working at night with JobTrain counselors who continued to help her prepare for the GED. Having found the gift and power of knowledge in an EORO study hall, Tatanisha is now committed to getting her GED, entering community college, and studying for a nursing degree. All the cards are stacked against her, yet Tatanisha is unstoppable—she will break the cycle of recidivism by becoming a nurse, and in learning to care for others she will reclaim her life.

From Working inside the Prison-Industrial Complex to Abolishing It

I have thus far described Each One Reach One's three-step ADAPT plan—our playwriting workshops, our afterschool study halls, and our reentry preparation services. Our hope is that by offering incarcerated youth these programs, we can enable them to turn their lives around, ideally diverting them from the prison-industrial complex and toward a sense of self-respect, community involvement, and art-making as a way of being in the world. But working with youngsters who are already incarcerated is not enough, and so the final component of EORO's mission is to lay the groundwork for a broad-based community response to the prison-industrial complex. As part of this larger plan, EORO currently conducts ADAPT in collaboration with two counties' juvenile probation departments and their institutional staffs, two unified school districts, one local college and two universities, and professional Bay Area theater workers, nonprofit service providers, and community members and activists. Thus, in addition to working inside the prison-industrial complex, EORO works in local communities, where we hope to build the political alliances, working groups, art-making collectives, and other interpersonal and interorganizational bonds that will help us continue to dismantle the schools-to-prisons pipeline and the culture of hopelessness that keeps our prisons bursting with youngsters.

To illustrate how EORO works in communities, I will discuss here our efforts on Assembly Bill 622, which responds to what we see as a major gap in California's education policy. In the 2005–2006 school year, 12,300 students enrolled in California's juvenile court schools, but the state's juvenile courts are not required to offer instructional services to these students after age eighteen. Shuffled in and out of various juvenile institutions, often bouncing from courtroom to courtroom, and thus virtually prohibited from completing regular high school requirements before they turn eighteen, this policy amounted to a virtual ban on successful education for imprisoned youths. To enter the juvenile justice system meant, in short, that students would never graduate from high school or pass GED tests—disenfranchised from the public school system, these young people were essentially doomed to lives of crime. This policy also crippled educators, for it is almost impossible for teachers to motivate imprisoned students who know *they will never graduate*. Yet under-eighteen incarcerated students are required by state law to attend classes all day long that will have no tangible educational outcome. Imagine the scene: You are an imprisoned youth, and you are required to go to classes meant to lead to a degree that *you know you will never earn*. In this situation, it can be no surprise that students do not work hard and that teachers are frustrated. Indeed, many imprisoned youth perceived the situation as a cruel joke.

To rectify this self-defeating situation, EORO and JobTrain met with staff members of California state assemblyman Gene Mullin, who had been an educator for thirty-two years. We eventually circulated several bill ideas on the academic needs of and challenges faced by incarcerated youth. After many rounds of negotiation and revision, Assemblyman Mullin introduced Assembly Bill 622 in February 2007. The original bill read as follows:

> Existing law requires the Superintendent of Public Instruction to issue a California high school equivalency certificate to any person who passes a general educational development test approved by the State Board of Education and administered by an approved testing center, is a California resident or a member of the armed services and assigned to duty in California, and is either 18 years old or would have graduated from high school if he or she had remained in school and followed the usual course of study toward graduation. This bill would, in addition, include a person who is at least 17 years old, has accumulated certain units of high school credit, and is confined to a state or county hospital or to an institution maintained by a state or county correctional agency, to the persons who may be eligible to receive a high school equivalency certificate.

> Existing law authorizes the Superintendent to provide for the administration of the general educational development test to persons confined in certain hospitals or correctional institutions. This bill would authorize the Superintendent to grant a waiver to a county office of education to provide a general educational development test preparation program during the regular school day to a person who is at least 17 years old, has accumulated certain units of high school credit, and is confined to a state or county hospital or to an institution maintained by a state or county correctional agency.

In short, AB 622 sought to change the law so that GED preparation classes would be available to all incarcerated youth, regardless of their ages. When presented on the floor of the state legislature, California's assembly and senate voted unanimously to support the bill (one legislator was absent, all present voted *yea*). After the senate and assembly's unanimous votes, we had one more stop: Our bill needed to be vetted by an independent committee that reviews all bills before they hit the governor's desk. At this point, the committee responded that if we did not change the bill to indicate that such GED-preparation classes would be offered for "no more than one hour per day," then the governor would kill the bill. Somehow, the committee thought that schools might make money on the proposed changes, and so they sought to limit class time. We thought this concern was ludicrous, but were in no position to argue. And so, with the change included in the bill, we went forward to Governor Arnold Schwarzenegger, who signed the revised bill on October 5, 2007. Having cut our teeth on working in juvenile detention centers, many of us were stunned to experience the rough-and-tumble world of politics in Sacramento. Nevertheless, we took what we could get, we learned our lessons, and we will go back again for more. In the classroom as on the assembly floor, even small victories can open the doors for big changes.

A Closing Cautionary Caveat: or, A Wonderful Success versus the Tragedy of Another Youngster Lost in the Battle

When Malcolm first showed up in an EORO playwriting workshop, he was not only a mess but a representative mess: He was angry, sullen, full of rage, lacking all hope, a bottle rocket waiting to explode. He refused to join in the workshop exercises, and when he did, he made everyone's life difficult. He suffered from ADD and other emotional traumas from a life that read like a trip into hell, and so he told us from the beginning that he was not going to open up or let us in because we would just leave. Everyone else in his life had left, why wouldn't we? But thanks to the dedication of our playwriting instructor, Dave Garrett, and Malcolm's mentor, Anna Maria Luera, this young man eventually wrote a play that enabled him both to express his pain and explore his talents—in doing so he surprised us and himself.

In Malcolm's play, the characters were Phoenix the Sun, Ocean the Ocean (his sister), the Volcano that is Always Erupting (his father), and the Dolphin that Eats All the Salt (his mother). Phoenix opens the play by speaking to Ocean, to whom he literally begs: "Sis, I got something to tell you. I need you to listen right now! I burn a lot of things because mom ain't there for us and dad is always erupting. I'm distracted a lot. I don't concentrate. I'm frustrated and I get stressed a lot." After describing why he "gets stressed," Phoenix makes the important step of asking for what he needs: "We are supposed to be on the same page. I need help. I need help. Show love instead of getting mad." I should note that Malcolm is a giant young man: more than six feet tall, he is a strapping 240-pound African American youth, and so showing what some might consider weakness—by asking for help and care—was a huge developmental step for him. Through his play, he learned that he was strong enough to show vulnerability; instead of playing the street tough, Malcolm used the character of Phoenix to explore a new way of being in the world. When the night's plays were finished, we formed our traditional feedback circle, and as usual we asked one of our volunteers to start us off, but Malcolm shouted out "I will, I will." And then the newly expressive young man said, "I want to thank my mentor Anna for hanging in there with me and never giving up. I know I gave her and everyone else a hard time during this program, but you never gave up on me. What I really learned from this program is that I need somebody to love me. And so I am going to work on letting people in and on letting people love me." For a youngster trained in the ways of violence and machismo, a young man literally given up on by almost everyone in his life, this was a tremendous, transformative moment. Realizing the immensity of his growth, and feeding off of his positive playwriting experience, Malcolm enthusiastically entered the ADAPT study hall and tutoring program, where he worked with an EORO mentor for the next six months, during which time his previously repressed talents began to blossom. When he was finally released from the detention center, Malcolm was not the same angry and sullen young man who had entered the hall nine months earlier. Now, for the first time, Malcolm was hopeful, he had earned some confidence—the world suddenly appeared to him full of options and opportunities.

We work toward successes like this every day—they fuel our program, keep us inspired, and remind us that change is possible. But we also feel the brunt of tragedy. For Malcolm's wonderful journey began in a playwriting workshop that he shared with a young man named Allen. In his preprogram evaluation form, Allen was asked "What would be helpful for you to know or to learn to make your life better?" Allen answered: "How to stay off the streets." When asked about his plans for the future, Allen wanted "to finish college with an MBA, get a real-estate license, and be a broker, eventually getting my own business and teaching the kids in the 'hood how to get out without baseball or rap." And so, from his first day in our workshop, Allen was a young man on a mission; he had a vision. His political goals were expressed clearly in his play, where we find two dogs talking about community issues:

> **Ruff, a dog:** Damn it Toby! You sound like a poodle! I'm tired of bein' a house dog! I don't give a damn about the park. When we're free, we can go to any park any time we want. You talkin' bout goin' to that park with fences around it, with D, while he got our leashes in his hand and these collars on our necks! That ain't freedom, Toby! I'm talkin' 'bout really bein' free. But before we can make that happen, you got to get the collar from around your mind, then we can get 'em off our neck.

> **Toby, another dog:** And how am I supposed to do that Ruff?

> **Ruff, the dog:** First you gotta stop waggin' yo damn tail and open ya eyes! Look at what's really going on, bro, and think about our ancestors. In some places we're worshipped like kings, but here we're animals. You need to look inside yo-self and have a critical mind!

For Allen, building "a critical mind" meant learning how to examine his own life, and thus learning how both to identify his emotional needs and how to express them in political terms. Malcolm needed to learn how to voice his needs; Allen needed to explore a voice of urgency and motivation—and so both men wrote plays that left us beaming with joy. Malcolm then entered the EORO study-hall program, and Allen was released back to the free world, where we lost track of him. When an EORO mentor ran into him on the street a few months after his release, Allen was upbeat, inspired, still committed to fulfilling the mission that Ruff called for. And then, on November 19, 2007, the *San Francisco Chronicle* ran the following story: "San Francisco police are investigating four apparently unrelated shootings that happened over the weekend in San Francisco, leaving two dead and injuring eight others, according to law enforcement officials. No arrests have been made, and no suspects have been identified. . . . The weekend's first city shooting occurred around 1:30 a.m. Saturday on Polk Street, near McAllister Street. A man was shot in the hip and later died at San Francisco General, police said. He was identified by the San Francisco medical examiner as Allen Bow."[13]

Notes

1. Mario Rocha's story has been chronicled in Susan Koch's and Jeff Weaver's award-winning documentary, *Mario's Story* (Cabin John, MD: Cabin Films, 2006), and in Stephen John Hartnett, *Incarceration Nation: Investigative Prison Poems of Hope and Terror* (Walnut Creek, CA: AltaMira, 2004), 135–53; for examples of his work, see his "Liberation," *Broken Chains* (Summer 2001), 17–24, and the other pieces posted on his blog: http://mariostory.typepad.com/marios_blog.

2. For additional information about EORO, see our website, www.eoro.org; for similar arguments about reclaiming the lives of a lost generation, see Michael Wald and Tia Martinez, *Connected by 25: Improving the Life Chances of the Country's Most Vulnerable 14–24 Year Olds,* a William and Flora Hewlett Foundation Working Paper, presented November 2003, at Stanford University, and available at www.hewlett.org/Archives/Publications/connectedBy25.htm; for additional groups seeking to shut down the prison pipeline by employing art, see Buzz Alexander's chapter in this book (chapter 6), and marvel at the miracles chronicled by Tori Samartino's group, Voices Unbroken, available at www.voicesunbroken.org.

3. Most experts agree that locking up juveniles only produces future prisoners; along these lines, see "States Adjusting to Influx of Adolescent Prison Inmates," a 25 July 2001 brief posted by the National Center for Policy Analysis, available at www.ncpa.org/sub/dpd/index.php?-Article_ID=8011; on the dire circumstances of youth in prison, see Ronnie Greene and Geoff Dougherty, "Kids in Prison," a two-part article in the *Miami Herald* (18–19 March 2001), which I accessed by using the search function at www.tgorski.com; on the madness of treating adolescents who need schooling as if they are criminals who need incarceration, see Bernardine Dohrn, "'Look Out Kid, It's Something You Did': Zero Tolerance for Children," in *Zero Tolerance: Resisting the Drive for Punishment in Our Schools*, ed. William Ayers, Bernardine Dohrn, and Rich Ayers (New York: New Press, 2001), 89–113, and Rose Braz's and Myesha Williams's chapter in this book (chapter 5).

4. This and all other comments by ADAPT members, quotations from plays, and transcribed conversations are from my personal notes and EORO records; these materials appear with the permission of the authors, some of whose names have been changed.

5. Cornell West, *Race Matters* (Boston: Beacon Press, 1993), 12. Editor's Note: The title of Monty's play echoes the title of Jack Henry Abbott's classic, *In the Belly of the Beast: Letters from Prison* (New York: Random House, 1981); the book was published with the strong support of, and included an introduction by, Norman Mailer; but after Abbot was released from prison in 1981, it took but six weeks before he murdered a man, thus landing himself back in prison, where he committed suicide in 2002—Abbott's life thus illustrates the same cyclical struggles depicted in Monty's play. For further discussion of how America's inner cities are treated like war zones, see Julilly Kohler-Hausmann's essay in this volume (chapter 2).

6. For studies supporting this notion of bearing witness as a route to self-discovery and community building, see Judith Tannenbaum, *Disguised as a Poem: My Years Teaching Poetry at San Quentin* (Boston: Northeastern University Press, 2000); Stephen John Hartnett, "Lincoln and Douglas Engage the Abolitionist David Walker in Prison Debate: Empowering Education, Applied Communication, and Social Justice," *Journal of Applied Communication Research* 26, no. 2 (1998): 232–53; and Patricia Yaeger, "Editor's Column: Prisons, Activism, and the Academy—a Roundtable with Buzz Alexander, Bell Gale Chevigny, Stephen John Hartnett, Janie Paul, and Judith Tannenbaum," *PMLA* 123, no. 3 (2008): 545–67; this same issue contains another ten articles on prisons, education, and activism.

7. Bureau of Justice Statistics, *Incarcerated Parents and Their Children* (Washington, DC: U.S. Department of Justice, 2000), 1, available at www.ojp.usdoj.gov/bjs/pub/pdf/iptc.pdf; for grueling visual evidence of these claims, see *What We Leave Behind*, a documentary film from Beyondmedia Education, available at www.beyondmedia.org, and the materials about how the prison-industrial complex harms families posted by Families against Mandatory Minimums, available at www.famm.org.

8. My re-creation of this scene is taken from my own notes and includes quotations from Melody Ermachild Chavis, "Grown Up Too Soon," a 15 August 2000 posting to Prisonwall.org, where she too described Casandra's play; for Chavis's moving account of how these issues played out in her neighborhood, see her *Altars in the Street: A Neighborhood Fights to Survive* (New York: Harmony/Crown, 1997).

9. For additional evidence of this claim, that we can in fact teach these children to excel, both as scholars and artists, see Garrett Albert Duncan's essay in this volume (chapter 8); for additional resources along these lines, see the materials posted by the American Bar Association's Commission on Youth at Risk, available at www.abanet.org/youthatrisk; and see the resources available in *Radical Teacher, A Socialist, Feminist, and Anti-Racist Journal on the Theory and Practice of Teaching*, which is archived at www.radicalteacher.org.

10. The figures listed here on learning-challenged students are from "Special Ed Kids in the Justice System: How to Recognize and Treat Young People with Disabilities That Compromise Their Ability to Comprehend, Learn, and Behave," ed. Lourdes M. Rosado (New York: American Bar Association/Juvenile Justice Center, 2000), available at www.njdc.info/pdf/maca5.pdf; the argument that the prison-industrial complex has been organized so that its "failures" serve the political needs of the state was popularized by Michel Foucault, who argued that "for the observation that prisons fail to eliminate crime, one should perhaps substitute the hypothesis that prison has succeeded extremely well in producing delinquency" (*Discipline and Punish: The Birth of the Prison*, trans. Alan Sheridan [New York: Vintage, 1995], 277).

11. On recidivism, see the data available from the Bureau of Justice Statistics, at www.ojp.usdoj.bjs/reentry/recidivism.htm; for more information on JobTrain, see the materials posted on their website at www.jobtrainworks.org.

12. Paul Street, "Color Blind: Prisons and the New American Racism," in *Prison Nation: The Warehousing of America's Poor*, ed. Tara Herivel and Paul Wright (New York: Routledge, 2003), 30–41, quotations from 34, 32; on the relationship between neoliberal economics and the prison crisis, see Ruth Wilson Gilmore, *Golden Gulag:*

Prisons, Surplus, Crisis, and Opposition in Globalizing California (Berkeley: University of California Press, 2007), and Stephen John Hartnett, "The Annihilating Public Policies of the Prison-Industrial Complex; or, Crime, Violence, and Punishment in an Age of Neo-Liberalism," *Rhetoric & Public Affairs* 11, no. 3 (2008): 491–533.

13. Delfin Vigil, "4 Weekend S.F. Shootings Result in 2 Deaths, 8 Injuries," *San Francisco Chronicle* (19 November 2007), D2, available via the archive search engine at www.sfgate.com.

Devil Talks

Robert "Chicago" McCollum

A member of the Writing Workshop at the Champaign County Jail, in Champaign, Illinois, Robert "Chicago" McCollum writes hard-hitting poems about the violence and betrayal that marked his life as a young man growing up in one of Chicago's toughest neighborhoods; this piece was published in *Captured Words/Free Thoughts* 2 (Autumn 2006).

It's as if he seen my ability ta get dough radiate off me
as he drove by in his cheap but expensive car
He said MOE I know you like shinin'
cause I see that spark in ya right eye
Cum Fuck witcha boy—'n you could be making stacks right now!
You know where my spot at right?
meet me there at 4:30 NAW make it 5

I remember it like it was yesterday
when I walked through dat door
'n seen dem two 38s in his shoulder holster
'n in his waist band was dat PHAT AZZ 4-five
He said be4 I get started po' yoself a drink
an roll a few blunts of dis strawberry 'n kiwi lime

As I inhaled the weed smoke he stared in my eyes 4 a second
be4 he said, I know you young MOE
therefore Ima educate you on Hustle-'n-Grind
First Ima teach you how ta turn soft ta hard,
but most importantly Ima teach you
how ta distribute yo products through yo sell line

Now look, you can do whatever da FUCK u gonna do
wit yo money. But Remember Dat 60% of that shit is mine
'n da first time a piece of my cash gets messed up
that's ah slice ta ya left wrist
but the second time it happens Ima EAT'CHA FACE
wit billy the 38 'n kid that 4-fifth

Fostering Cultures of Achievement in Urban Schools: How to Work toward the Abolition of the Schools-to-Prisons Pipeline

Garrett Albert Duncan

In this chapter I highlight educational reform efforts that show tremendous promise for abolishing the schools-to-prisons pipeline in the United States. I illustrate how parents, teachers, and administrators foster cultures of achievement that promote academic excellence and civic engagement among underserved urban students, thus offering them more promising futures. Such accomplishments are triply remarkable, for they counteract a generation's worth of disastrous zero-tolerance policies, they resist longstanding historical forces that doom poor children to second-class educations, and they counteract the legacies of racism that have turned our schools into race-making machines. Before presenting a case study of such empowering urban school reform efforts, I address the broader role of race-making institutions in the United States; this examination is of paramount importance, for no analysis of the schools-to-prisons pipeline is complete without examining the intertwined histories of public schooling, labor, and the variegated legacies of racism in North America. I should note as well that I believe that the schools-to-prisons pipeline is largely the *unintended* result of contemporary educational policies and practices, including those produced by people with good intentions. Indeed, the race-making processes described herein, and the morally indefensible social conduit that leads so many of our poor children to prison, is supported not so much by active and conscious racism as by widespread societal *indifference* to the race- and class-based disparities that persist in our public schools. While unintended results and indifference have played large roles in shaping the schools-to-prisons pipeline, the historical record also shows how the U.S. federal government has repeatedly used its power over educational policies, labor practices, and the political process to aid white elites and the white middle class—such uneven and race-based efforts have, in effect, thwarted the struggles of people of color to enjoy the full benefits of American citizenship. Each pivotal epoch over the course of U.S. history offered ample occasions for redirecting our course toward achieving a more just and perfect union, yet the record repeatedly shows that promises were customarily broken, opportunities were readily squandered, and the episodic gains made by people of color were typically short-lived. In this sense, the schools-to-prison pipeline amounts to the culmination of centuries of unintended consequences, indifference, and unequal federal action—it is the contemporary manifestation of racism and among the most brutal examples of race-making in America.[1]

The idea that the actions of decent people with good intentions may result in harmful outcomes in the schooling of historically marginalized student populations is not a radical concept in the field of education. This notion inheres in concepts such as "the hidden curriculum" and, more recently, "collateral damage." The hidden curriculum refers to how schools tacitly— and even unintentionally—transmit to students the norms, values, and skill sets that reproduce inequalities and racial prejudice in the larger society. Collateral damage refers to the injurious effects—largely unintended—of ill-conceived educational reform policies meant to hold schools accountable for the education of their students and to eliminate social disparities in academic attainment. These theories suggests that in the realm of education, as in society as a whole, race-making and racism are incredibly complicated patterns with deep histories. W. E. B. DuBois alluded to these intricate processes in 1968, when he paused to reflect on the meaning of his work during the later stages of his life: "not simply knowledge, not simply direct repression of evil, will reform the world. In long . . . the actions of [women and] men which are due not to a lack of knowledge nor to evil intent, must be changed by influencing folkways, habits, customs, and subconscious deeds." Working to build cultures of achievement in our urban schools is one way to contribute to the hard work of changing these race-based "folkways, habits, customs, and subconscious deeds." Indeed, I argue that shutting down the schools-to-prisons pipeline stands as part of a new civil-rights movement, as part of the long effort to end racism in the United States.[2]

Race-Making and the Legacies of Slavery

The "folkways, habits, customs, and subconscious deeds" noted by DuBois have not always been a part of the nation's moral fabric; rather, they emerged over centuries while advancing certain social, economic, and political interests.

But contrary to conventional wisdom, people of African descent have not always occupied a subordinate social position in American society. During the colonial period, for instance, persons of African descent were viewed—as we commonly view people of European descent—as a multiform population of individuals from different geographic regions, religious traditions, cultural norms, and linguistic and political histories. These early African Americans established autonomous communities and often formed multiracial townships where they engaged in interracial relations. Africans of diverse backgrounds possessed enough autonomy during the early colonial period to establish Wolof as their *lingua franca* in the New World. Further, many owned property and were highly learned; by the Revolutionary period, such figures had established enduring and influential institutions, such as the African Methodist Episcopal Church and the Prince Hall Free Masons. Prior to the Revolution, the masses of Americans of European and of African descent lived and worked under similar circumstances, often oppressive, which created conditions for multi-racial challenges to the elite class, such as Bacon's Rebellion of 1676. The white elite effectively undermined such alliances, though, by passing laws, instituting economic policies, and disseminating cultural imagery and narratives that forged a racial hierarchy and consigned black people to a uniform subordinate class. These processes worked to "make race" in the United States and, moreover, to solidify the status of Americans of African descent as a marked and dishonored group.[3]

Race-making therefore involves political, economic, and cultural processes that sequester certain populations, label them, discipline them, and—prior to the advent of the contemporary prison-industrial complex—extract their labor. These processes "race" certain groups by marking them as inferior, expendable, and, increasingly, as appropriate targets of mass incarceration. We cannot understand mass incarceration in contemporary U.S. society, then, without addressing the legacies of chattel slavery, both as historical starting points for race-making in America and as central components, perhaps even the driving elements, of our current incarceration nation. Indeed, according to Loïc Wacquant, the systems of southern plantation slavery, Jim Crow segregation, post-Reconstruction urbanization, and contemporary imprisonment in the United States are linked by their historical and contemporary race-making functions. As Waquant notes,

> The highly particular conception of "race" that America has invented, virtually unique in the world for its rigidity and consequentiality, is a direct outcome of the momentous collision between slavery and democracy as modes of orga-

nization of social life after bondage had been established as the major form of labor conscription and control in an under-populated colony home to a precapitalist system of production. The Jim Crow regime reworked the racialized boundary between slave and free into a rigid caste separation between "whites" and "Negros"—comprising all persons of known African ancestry, no matter how minimal—that infected every crevice of the post-bellum social system in the South. The ghetto, in turn, imprinted this dichotomy onto the spatial makeup and institutional schemas of the industrial metropolis.[4]

The key step in understanding these race-making processes is realizing that they do not merely reinforce existing color-coded social divisions; rather, they work with other forms of power to build racialized divisions out of other demarcations of group power. For example, over the course of U.S. history, immigrants from Ireland and Italy have moved from being thought of as racial outsiders to being considered "white"; Jews, too, have slipped in and out of being "white" according to other political forces and cultural trends. Ever since the late colonial and Revolutionary eras, however, Americans of African descent have continuously been subjected to forms of oppression that were justified by virtue of their association with the race-making institution of slavery. In other words, by stigmatizing black populations with the institutional brands of "slave" or "felon," race-making institutions, such as plantations and prisons, have provided a public rationale for why certain groups are systematically denied the full rights of citizenship.[5]

In contemporary, post-civil-rights America, public schools also serve a race-making function. They do so by defining what it means to be a citizen and by constructing citizenship's negative corollary: a racialized superfluous population of urban—and sometimes suburban—students of color who are perceived not only as living outside, but also as threatening, the social, economic, and cultural mainstream. Rather than being a recent phenomenon, however, schools have served race-making functions in American society ever since the post-Reconstruction period. For instance, during the first several decades of the twentieth century, race-making in schools was linked to preparing black youth for what James Anderson has called "Negro jobs." According to Anderson, from 1880 to 1930, the express objective of the architects of the Southern public black high school system was "to meet the needs" of black students by equipping them to "move from unskilled to skilled labor" in preparation for "Negro jobs." In practice, these schools met the needs of black students by adjusting their expectations to align with their presumed fixed economic station in society. Such racialized jobs, as Anderson explains, were by default those jobs that remained only after full white employment was achieved. In short, the iron cage of slavery was being replaced with a more flexible yet still racializing mode of social control, one where the brute force of the plantation was replaced by the socializing power of schools.[6]

The post-civil-rights era refers to the period after the 1954 landmark *Brown v. Board of Education* ruling that abolished legal segregation in public institutions such as education, housing, and the workplace. Prior to *Brown*, schooling inequalities were explained as the predictable outcomes of hundreds of years of segregation and discrimination; after the *Brown* decision, however, institutional obstructions to opportunity were purportedly dismantled. So, nowadays, society explains the social inequalities endured by communities of color as their own fault; a generation of Americans proceeds as though hundreds of years of chattel slavery and segregation were erased without leaving a trace—according to this narrative, the Civil-Rights movement was a triumph that forever leveled the playing field. Such ahistorical explanations reinforce the view that black community struggles are not the product of historical factors, including racial cleansing, sundown towns, and governmental neglect, but of individual failings.[7]

Post-civil-rights-era schools are still in the race-making business of preparing students of color for "Negro jobs." In a postindustrial society, however, where jobs are scarce, such students are now shunted not toward low-paying industrial or agricultural production but instead into the schools-to-prisons pipeline. In contemporary America, the new "Negro job" is being a prisoner. Nonetheless, post-civil-rights-era conventional wisdom on race and racism entails such canards as the claims that we should engage in so-called color-blind interpretations of social inequalities and that formal, legal measures are adequate to building social justice. Such conventional wisdom is perhaps the greatest obstacle to engaging in a constructive discussion about the contemporary schools-to-prisons pipeline, even if this conduit is posited as historical in origin and as an unintended effect of educational policy and practice. But instead of engaging in this historically inflected conversation about how the legacies of racism and institutionalized racism have led to the prison-industrial complex, conventional wisdom holds that local community norms and self-imposed factors (such as drug use, criminality, laziness, and so on) are almost exclusively responsible for the academic underperformance of students of color in public schools.

Contemporary educational inequalities, captured in the catchphrase "achievement gap," are indeed evident in academic disparities between black and Latino students and white and some Asian American students, where the latter groups outperform the former groups on various measures of academic attainment. Black students, in particular, bear the brunt of these disparities. Two of the more popular views of their circumstances hold that anti-intellectualism is prevalent in black communities and that parents place little value on education, thus accounting for why their children underachieve in schools. Another common explanation is that black children have oppositional identities that lead them to reject academic achievement on the grounds that it is tantamount to "acting white." Some scholars speculate that such anti-intellectual peer influence is so severe that even high-performing black students who identify with education eventually succumb to pressures from their black peers to underachieve, or become so preoccupied with how others view them that their academic performance suffers as a consequence. What unites these disparate explanations is a failure to recognize that the "achievement gap" also reflects longstanding political impediments within certain communities; that is, many contemporary commentators explain the state of young black students in America's schools without addressing the legacies of slavery and racism.[8]

In contrast to such ahistorical and purportedly "color blind" scholarship, a growing body of work argues that urban students in diverse, post-civil-rights schools are being taught in environments characterized by the still unaddressed damage of slavery. This perspective suggests that although the civil-rights movement succeeded in desegregating black students from supposedly "separate but equal" schools, hence finally supporting their civic and political rights as guaranteed by the Fourteenth Amendment, the exercise of such legal power—so-called first generation rights—can go only so far in creating a culture that expects excellence for black students. This is because forced desegregation does not guarantee *integration*, an idea that presupposes the exercise of equal social and cultural rights, or so-called second generation rights. While the federal government has mandated first generation rights, it has, certainly since the Reagan administration, explicitly rejected calls for upholding second generation rights. This means that black children are legally equal to all others, yet in daily practice they are still subject to second-rate schools and are met with second-rate expectations, even when they are taught in affluent, integrated settings.[9]

A number of observers have noted how the emphasis on legal rights, even though absolutely necessary in the struggle to end racism, has also moderated the possible effects of the *Brown* decision and the ensuing civil-rights agitation. For example, the Reverend Martin Luther King Jr., expressed reservations about the implementation of *Brown*-inspired social policies, especially in light of the early failings of desegregation policy. King lamented that black people were being integrated into American institutions *without power*, and that intransigent notions about their inferior worth as human beings sustained social inequalities even in the face of civil rights legislation. Making these remarks at a rabbinical conference just ten days before he was assassinated, King decried everyday cultural representations that associated "black" with "evil" and "bad," such as in "devil's food cake" and "black lie," and that associated white with "good" and "permissible," such as in "angel's food cake" and "white lie." "What is necessary now is to see integration in political terms where there is a sharing of power," King said. "When we see integration in political terms, then we recognize that there are times when we must see segregation as a temporary way-station to a truly integrated society. There are many Negroes who feel this . . . [and] I must honestly say that there are points at which I share this view. There are points at which I see the necessity for temporary segregation in order to get to the integrated society." In contrast to the forever compromising image to which America holds him captive, King thus concurred with the view that posited self-separation, albeit temporarily, as a means to black empowerment.[10]

Observing the differences between enforced legal rights and the lived experience of daily life, Vanessa Siddle Walker likewise offered that care was the greatest casualty when black children desegregated previously all-white schools, where they were subjected to teachers who were indifferent, if not hostile, to their educational needs. Indeed, Vivian Gunn Morris and Curtis Morris have studied how white teachers never viewed civil-rights-era black students as being as capable as white students; some white teachers were so deeply entrenched in racial stereotypes that when black students exceeded their racially informed expectations, they referred to their students as "unusual Negroes." The notion that achieving academic excellence was "unusual" for "Negroes" reflects the fact that many white educators were aware that segregated schools were offering second-class educations, but it also shows us that these teachers tacitly lowered their expectations, and hence diminished the self-worth of those students they regarded as "usual Negroes." In short, first generation rights enabled black children to enter the schoolhouse, but without second generation rights, achieving political equality and academic excellence would remain "unusual."[11]

Timeworn, racially informed narratives continue to inform the ways contemporary schools sequester and brand certain students as superfluous populations that society invests more on incarcerating than it does on educating. Moreover, the 2001 No Child Left Behind Act (NCLB), arguably the greatest federal intervention into schooling since 1954, has exacerbated rather than ameliorated the educational problems faced by children, especially urban youth of color. Nonetheless, despite the legacies of slavery, the race-making processes described here, and the implementation of NCLB, students, parents, teachers, and administrators across North America have built cultures of achievement that extend to historically underserved students the means to defy both history and their entry into the schools-to-prisons pipeline. In the remaining pages of this chapter, I honor their heroic efforts, for I believe they offer us visionary yet practical means of disrupting the race-making function of public schools and of inspiring those who hope to abolish the schools-to-prisons pipeline.[12]

Fostering Academic Achievement in Post-Civil-Rights-Era Urban Schools

Despite widespread pessimism about the prospects of promoting high achievement among urban students of color, excellent schools for these students have existed in the past, particularly in all-black settings, and they exist today in diverse contexts. Students at these schools are academically engaged and civic-minded and typically achieve scores on high-stakes standardized tests that either meet or exceed those of their peers at more affluent suburban schools. In short, these schools are high-achieving, with the academic performance of urban students far exceeding the minimum standards of effectiveness and adequacy. More important, these success stories provide road maps for educators, researchers, and policymakers who hope to promote high achievement among urban students. Along these lines, Theresa Perry argues in *Young, Gifted, and Black* that "African-American students will achieve in school environments that have a leveling culture, a culture of achievement that extends to all of its members a strong sense of group membership, where the expectation that everyone achieves is explicit and is regularly communicated in public and group settings. African-American students will achieve in these environments, irrespective of class background, the cultural responsiveness of the setting, or the prior level of preparation." For Perry, myself, and a new generation of educators, scholars, and activists, the point is clear: We must demand academic excellence for and from our historically underserved student populations—excellence should not be unusual, but expected.[13]

To support this argument, I turn now to Jim Scheurich's analysis of a select group of high-achieving public elementary schools in Texas, where the schools' core values and cultural characteristics enable poor children of color to pursue excellence. In contrast to teaching driven by the high-stakes testing that is found in schools across America—and that is mandated by the NCLB—Scheurich offers insights into what has been proven to promote high achievement among black students by studying what administrators, counselors, teachers, and staff describe as the "goings on" in their schools. By focusing on such daily "goings on," the minutiae of daily exchanges that build a school's culture, Scheurich points to what the leaders of these schools have come to call the Hi-PASS model of school reform, or high performance all student success. As Scheurich explains, this model "did not come from the reform literature or from the leadership or organizational literatures"; rather, "those who developed the model were not self-consciously developing a model; in their view, they were just developing schools that were successful" for traditionally underserved working-class and poor students of color, students whom they called "their children." Hi-PASS, then, was not a top-down mandate but a grassroots response and the product of deep caring and hands-on teaching that resulted in the creation of an empowering culture of achievement where all students excelled, regardless of their class, racial, or linguistic heritage. In short, what helped these students achieve excellence was not NCLB-enforced testing but caregiving driven by an intense respect for the children's potential.[14]

As expressed when teachers, students, staff, administrators, and parents described their schools, the facilities included in Scheurich's study are characterized by five core beliefs. First, administrators, teachers, and students at these schools believe that all children can achieve at high academic levels—everyone is expected to succeed. Second, they hold that academic work in these schools must be focused on the needs of the child rather than on the demands of the bureaucracy. Third, adults believe that all children must be treated with love, appreciation, care, and respect. Fourth, they believe that the culture of the child's home, including their first language and religious beliefs, must always be valued. And fifth, they hold the unflinching view that the school exists for and serves the community. If the NCLB amounts to a federally driven mode of punitive test-taking, and hence a virtual guarantee that more poor children of color will be herded toward the prison-industrial complex, the five pedagogical and community values described here amount to a locally crafted mode of care-giving, and hence as an invitation to academic success.

Along with these five core beliefs, Scheurich describes seven interwoven, mutually reinforcing features, or "shared meanings," that characterize the organizational structures of the schools he studied. The organizational structures are cultural characteristics that are readily observable by anyone upon entering a school building. Such schools evince a strong, shared vision among all community members and foster loving, caring environments for children and adults. Teaching and learning occur in the schools Scheurich studied in collaborative, familylike environments. Teachers in these schools are innovative, experimental, and open to new ideas. In addition, the teachers are hardworking but are not prone to burning out. Adult leaders at the schools build appropriate codes of conduct into the schools' organizational cultures and communicate them effectively to their students. Finally, a sense of shared responsibility, in which the school staff as a whole holds itself accountable for the success of all children, is clearly evident at schools like these. Remarkably, even though the schools in Scheurich's study had previous histories of chronic underachievement, they were typically transformed in three to five years under the leadership of newly assigned principals. The new principals were student-centered leaders who guided the transformation of their schools from low-performing to high-achieving educational centers while retaining 80 to 90 percent of the teachers and without changing the general socioeconomic demographics of their student populations.

Schools like Scheurich's uphold the first generation rights guaranteed to all citizens under the Equal Protection Clause of the Fourteenth Amendment, yet they also go much further by supporting second generation rights, the more expansive social, cultural, and economic rights affirmed by the Universal Declaration of Human Rights. According to Article 22 of this remarkable document, "Everyone, as a member of society, has the right to social security and is entitled to realization, through national effort and international co-operation and in accordance with the organization and resources of each State, of the economic, social, and *cultural rights indispensable for his dignity and the free development of his personality*." The italicized portion of the article coheres with some of the longstanding positions of the United Nations Education, Scientific, and Cultural Organization (UNESCO), which advocates the centrality of culture in the education of diverse students in multiracial societies. For instance, UNESCO argues that young children learn best through the medium of their mother tongue. This view, shared by the schools in Scheurich's study, anchors various child-centered theories of learning, such as constructivism and culturally responsive instruction, as well as the pedagogies of the likes of W. E. B. DuBois, John Dewey, and Paulo Freire. In contrast to these positions, studies show that when the cultural practices of young learners, including their home language, are stigmatized and demeaned, then the students too will be disparaged and dishonored, almost as a matter of custom in U.S. schools and classrooms.[15]

In contrast to schools that foster empowering cultures of achievement, schools that sustain cultures of prejudice and suspicion often lack consensus among the stakeholders on the long-term goals of and daily practices in their schools. Further, even when teachers and administrators express some semblance of agreement along these lines, their words often fail to materialize in the form of actual practices that promote cultures of achievement. For example, a study that I led in an urban school in Missouri suggested that the presence of core beliefs and cultural characteristics that support high achievement among black students was limited to a handful of classrooms and programs; such beliefs and characteristics were neither systematically held by teachers nor widely supported by administrators. As a result, pedagogical practices that would support a new culture of high achievement among black students were unevenly distributed within the school, all but guaranteeing that they would not be incorporated into the school's general culture.[16]

On the one hand, one-fifth of the teachers at the school in the study accounted for about 90 percent of the positive, empowering pedagogical characteristics that were recorded by the team of researchers—this means that for every teacher explicitly working to close the schools-to-prisons pipeline, four maintained the traditional pedagogical practices that have led us into the current crisis. On the other hand, individual characteristics, such as teacher innovation and openness to new ideas, greatly outnumbered social characteristics, such as shared vision or collaboration. So, while a small group of teachers (roughly 20 percent of the faculty) were responsible for creating pockets of excellence at the school, the larger social climate severely restricted their ability to foster a new culture of achievement for all students. Under these conditions, it came as no surprise to our research team when the data we collected showed that black students at the school chronically underperformed; in fact, shortly after we conducted our research, the school was placed on probation for its academic underachievement. I want to be clear that the educational harm done to the students at this school was not the result of any apparent malicious intent or racism on the part of teachers or administrators. My team and I did encounter incompetent and abusive teachers at the school, but they constituted a small minority of the staff (and unfortunately could be found at most if not all public schools). The fact that this school's pedagogical environment pointed toward almost inevitable failure for so many black students, even in the absence of intentional racism, and despite the best efforts of a small cohort of progressive teachers, points to the sobering complexity of educational reform and suggests how the schools-to-prisons pipeline continues to run its devastating course. In fact, ample evidence suggests that many black and Latino children are shuffled toward the schools-to-prisons pipeline as early as their pre-kindergarten and elementary school years. As I demonstrate below, however, schools with committed leadership and a shared vision can indeed foster cultures of achievement in urban schools.[17]

Reconstructing the Pipeline:
From Incarceration to College

In contrast to the bleak news offered above, exciting pedagogical experiments are flourishing across the United States, many of them with heartening results. To explore one of these schools, I launched a study in an urban community in America's heartland that has taken a novel approach to constructing a new pipeline, one that holds a promising future for all children, without regard to their racial, ethnic, or class backgrounds. It would be misleading, though, to suggest that the community effort that I describe in this section is the result of a conscious attempt by educators and business and community leaders to stem the flow of black and Latino youth into America's jails and penitentiaries—this will be a welcome result of their efforts, but it is not their explicit purpose. I do not mean to suggest, however, that those responsible for the reforms are not guided by noble intentions, for they are; they are also, however, pursued in the name of color-blind and neoliberal practices meant to reform lagging economies. The critical point is that just as the schools-to-prisons pipeline is largely the unintended consequence of bad pedagogical practices that produce racial prejudice, even while implemented by those who decry racism, so it should come as no surprise to learn that nonracial or "color-blind" policies might prove to play a vital role in dismantling it.

The case study considered herein was conducted in Kalamazoo, Michigan, where, in 2005, business, community, and educational leaders announced the Kalamazoo Promise, a scholarship program that, for students who have attended Kalamazoo Public Schools (hereafter cited as KPS), provides four years of tuition and fees at any of the 44 public State of Michigan two-year or four-year colleges and universities. The per-student cost of the scholarship ranges from about $1,700 a year for students who attend a community college to almost $9,000 a year for those who enroll in the University of Michigan. From the first class of KPS graduates who could take advantage of the Kalamazoo Promise, in 2006, approximately 38 percent were black (of 194 graduates, 93 were females and 101 were males); another 9 percent were classified as "other" (of 48 graduates, 25 were females and 23 were males); the remaining 53 percent were white students (of 273 graduates, 126 were females and 147 were males). Out of this cohort, 417 students were eligible for the Kalamazoo Promise by virtue of having attended at least four years at one of the Kalamazoo city high schools. Of those eligible, 73 percent of the students (303) used the Kalamazoo Promise. In terms of the racial and gender makeup of the participating students, 80 percent of eligible black (60), 74 percent of white (81), and 53 percent of other (9) female graduates are currently benefiting from the Kalamazoo Promise, while 63 percent of eligible black (45), 76 percent of white (96), and 63 percent of other (12) male students are doing the same. The total cost to send this first group of KPS graduates to college was approximately $3.5 million.[18]

Unlike other programs that rely on public coffers, which prompts elected officials to place time constraints on students, the Kalamazoo Promise is funded by anonymous private donors. The scholarship allows recipients up to ten years to earn their bachelor's degree and is available until a student receives the B.A. or B.S., until he or she earns the bachelor's equivalent unit requirement of 130 credit hours, or until the ten-year time limit is reached. The ten-year time limit is far more generous than in similar programs, which typically place a four- to six-year limit on their awards. Kalamazoo's generous completion policy is crucial to the success of first-generation college students who, on average, take twice as long as the typical four to six years that it takes their peers to earn an undergraduate degree. Compared with other statewide "promise" programs, which are becoming especially popular among gubernatorial candidates during their campaigns (I describe one such program below), the Kalamazoo Promise makes schools the cornerstone of revitalizing its city's economic, cultural, and civic life. Indeed, rather than standing as a top-down initiative launched by entrepreneurial concerns, the Kalamazoo Promise was initially conceived in 2000 by Janice Brown, a special education teacher who has since become a school superintendent. According to Brown, the Kalamazoo Promise was inspired by her belief that her community "will not rest until every child is educated every time." For Brown, then, the Kalamazoo Promise was an ethical commitment, a pedagogical imperative, a pledge to end America's two-tiered educational system, where the rich go to college and the poor go into the factory or the prison. Because the Kalamazoo Promise's goal is to help cultivate a culture of empowerment, its founders and leaders are far more receptive than other educational reformers to innovative school policies and instructional practices that affirm second generation rights, those human-rights-centered ideals illustrated earlier in Scheurich's study.[19]

The Kalamazoo Promise reaches students across racial, class, and gender lines, it offers a flexible ten-year period during which to use the funds, it bases community growth on education, and it specifically pursues a set of goals that I have described here as second generation rights, those cultural benchmarks that transcend legally sanctioned desegregation in pursuit of genuine *integration with power and knowledge*. Moreover, where some other Kalamazoo Promise–like programs exclude or discourage students by establishing strict conditions for participating in them, the Kalamazoo Promise is based neither on financial need nor on academic merit but simply on location. In other words, any child resident in the community is eligible for the Kalamazoo Promise without respect to her or his financial situation or scholarly record, two factors that typically have race- and class-specific meanings. By extending the Kalamazoo Promise to all members of the community, the program eliminates unhealthy student competition and race- or class-based conflicts that would likely occur in the scramble for limited resources. Promise funds are based on a sliding scale of long-term residence in the city, awarding from 65 percent of college tuition and fees for students who complete at least four years at a Kalamazoo high school up to 100 percent of such costs for students who have attended city schools and who have lived within district boundaries from kindergarten through high school graduation. The sliding scale was implemented to prevent those with the means to do so from exploiting the Kalamazoo Promise by moving to Kalamazoo without having to make a long-term investment in its schools and wider community. Ostensibly color-blind and not concerned with prior academic achievement, the Kalamazoo Promise's across-the-board offer of grants is thus rooted to one chief goal: helping Kalamazoo to build a better present by investing in the leaders of tomorrow. Shutting down the local access points to the schools-to-prisons pipeline is therefore a welcome, albeit unintentional, consequence of this bold attempt at urban renewal.

According to the U.S. Census Bureau, the 2006 population estimate for Kalamazoo City is 72,161, of which 71 percent is white and 24 percent is black. As the census and the student data reported above indicate, Kalamazoo schools are much more diverse than the general population, suggesting that in the near future a proportionately greater percentage of black and Latino youth (relative to the total number of black and Latino residents) stand to benefit from the Kalamazoo Promise. Indeed, the Kalamazoo Promise has heightened the hope among potential first-generation college students and their families by creating an asset base that ensures future possibilities—it has offered hope to the hopeless. And such hopes for the future foster tangible effects in the present, as parents, now confident in their ability to send their children to college, can communicate and reinforce an achievement ethic to their children. For example, Superintendent Brown recalled the following story as evidence for what she saw as the Kalamazoo Promise–inspired transformation of not only the system but also the students in her district: "A first grader [came] up to me saying, 'I'm going to college. I don't know what it is, but I'm going.'" And so a child enters first grade already knowing that she is going to college—the benefits of this knowledge are immeasurable, but we can assume that such confidence will help this child succeed in school, steer clear of crime, and achieve excellence in the field of her choosing.[20]

I was attracted to the Kalamazoo Promise because of its clear implications for shutting down the schools-to-prisons pipeline, but I must also acknowledge that the Kalamazoo Promise has brought a series of economic benefits to Kalamazoo. For example, the Kalamazoo Promise creates incentives for residents to remain within district boundaries and entices families with children of all backgrounds to move to the city, even those who live outside Michigan, including those who previously lived as far away as Arizona and Hawai'i. By both retaining existing residents and attracting new ones, the Kalamazoo Promise has helped to increase property values, supporting a rising tax base, which, in turn, helps to improve local schools. Indeed, within the first two years of the Kalamazoo Promise, Kalamazoo has attracted 800 new families to the school district, has constructed a $10 million housing development, has experienced rising property values, has added two new schools, and has become extremely attractive for businesses that might invest, expand, or relocate to Kalamazoo to tap into its increasingly well-trained workforce. Contrary to those who see social justice issues as a drain on local economies and government coffers, these impressive results suggest that pursuing the end of race-making and racism-reinforcing pedagogical practices can be both ethically and economically rewarding—doing the right thing is good for business too.[21]

From a long-term educational standpoint, for the Kalamazoo Promise to work, the students who participate in the program must be successful in college. This in turn charges public colleges and universities throughout Michigan to better prepare teachers and the wider Kalamazoo community to support its school district. The stakes are high, for these educational institutions will risk losing millions in tuition fees if they do not prepare Kalamazoo students to succeed in higher education. Because the program is so new, it is too early to amass any comprehensive data pointing to the Kalamazoo Promise's impact on college graduation rates. As is the case with all education reform, however, schools can go only so far in ameliorating problems that begin and end far beyond the schoolyard. For example, according to the U.S. Census Bureau, in 2006 an astonishing 33 percent of the city's residents lived in poverty, with an astronomical 41 percent of children under eighteen living below the poverty level. In Kalamazoo as elsewhere, then, race and class converge, meaning the city's schools are charged with teaching a significant percentage of the traditionally poor and underserved students who are most vulnerable for being sucked into the schools-to-prisons pipeline. The task of educating students living in poverty is not lost on the superintendent: "They can't think about the Kalamazoo Promise if they're hungry. They can't think about the Kalamazoo Promise if they're angry and lashing out," observed Brown. Her point is obvious but merits repetition: Even the best school reforms cannot succeed if communities do not simultaneously attempt to reduce poverty and create better support networks for those families and children who have, at least historically, been left to fend for themselves.[22]

Nonetheless, even while the founders and leaders of the Kalamazoo Promise cannot change the town's economic situation overnight, I have been encouraged by the fact that racial differences in access to the Kalamazoo Promise during its first two years appear to be slight. At the same time, although Kalamazoo's students appear to enjoy equal access to the program, we do not yet have information to determine whether they have access to the same quality education once they move on to college. For instance, what are the race, gender, and class demographics of students attending two-year colleges and universities compared with those attending four-year colleges and universities? What are the trends when it comes to students' selection of majors? For example, we know that nationally, students of color are woefully underrepresented in mathematics and other science majors that provide the disciplinary underpinnings of much of America's postindustrial economy.[23]

Those of us who have studied the Kalamazoo Promise also anticipate some initial disparities—regarding success in college, the choice of a major, the type of school attended, and so on—that are largely attributable to differences in family educational backgrounds. We hope that such disparities will lessen over the years, especially as diverse families continue to move into Kalamazoo and as more and more college graduates return to the community, which would raise its collective educational achievement. But this point prompts other questions about the likelihood of shutting down the schools-to-prisons pipeline. What, for instance, will be the pattern of economic opportunities for those students who avail themselves of the Kalamazoo Promise and either remain in or return to Kalamazoo after they complete their studies? And what is the impact of rising housing costs on residential patterns in the city? Will we see pockets of gentrification? Also, will all Kalamazoo schools equally benefit from the economic boost stimulated by the Kalamazoo Promise? Perhaps most important, will those schools and students that require additional resources receive them? The answers to these questions are interrelated and may offer systemic and lasting effects on stemming the schools-to-prisons pipeline. Because historical and contemporary forces have forged schools into race-making institutions, we hope that other scholars will tackle these and other questions in future research.

Having posed these questions, it is my view that the Kalamazoo Promise nonetheless offers significant hope for deep school reform because of its systemic approach and its inclusion of a diverse community of stakeholders. At the same time, the greatest obstacle to the benefits of the Kalamazoo Promise being reproduced in districts across the country is the cooptation of the idea by savvy politicians seeking election to public offices and by corporations attempting to remake their public images. With respect to the former, in the state where I live and work, Missouri, the attorney general and democratic gubernatorial candidate Jeremiah "Jay" Nixon has proposed the Missouri Promise. This program, according to Nixon's campaign literature, "will provide a pathway for middle-class Missourians to earn a four-year degree from a state college or university—tuition free." But whereas the Kalamazoo Promise is available to all students who graduate from high school without regard to financial need or so-called academic merit, the Missouri Promise employs racially and class-coded language. This does not augur well for the prospects of the state's students of color, who are largely concentrated in one of the state's two major cities, to take full advantage of this scholarship. For instance, "middle-class Missourians," appears to exclude a sizeable portion of Missouri's black students who mainly live in the economically challenged areas of St. Louis and Kansas City. As is so often the case, then, even while proposing educational reform, Nixon's version of a Promise appears to contain typically racist language that will restrict the Missouri Promise's support for poor students of color. In short, and whether intentional or not, this version of the Kalamazoo Promise will reproduce many of our educational dilemmas and not make an impact on the schools-to-prisons pipeline.[24]

Moreover, students participating in the Missouri Promise are required to complete community college, where they must maintain a 3.0 grade point average, perform 50 hours of community service per year, and stay "out of trouble," according to Nixon's proposal. On the one hand, the proposed Missouri program allows the state to tap into the existing A+ Program, which grants greater access to Missouri's community colleges by the state's residents. On the other hand, the program seems to deny qualified students immediate access to four-year public colleges and universities, which may result in derailing the hopes of especially first-generation college students, many of whom are black and poor and for whom an associate's degree may become their *terminal* degree. While an interesting ideal, a mandatory commitment of 50 hours per year to community service may also impose an additional burden on poor students, who often carry jobs to help support their families; hence, to avoid a chilling effect, additional job counseling and career advising would need to be provided so that students fully understand how to fulfill this obligation.

Finally, according to the proposed measure, students must pledge to "stay out of trouble" and avoid disciplinary problems. Such language takes on particularly raced meanings in the segregated city of St. Louis, which has had a number of highly publicized racial incidents during the past several years, including charges of police brutality and the claim that the city's white mayor has been largely insensitive to the needs and concerns of the predominantly black city. Indeed, as so many of the other essays in this volume make painfully clear, "staying out of trouble" often has little to do with the actions of individuals who, because of their race and class, are swept up in various police actions despite their innocence. This stay-out-of-trouble clause will certainly have ominous meanings for black and Latino students who attend the University of Missouri–Kansas City, where a recent audit has followed other reports accusing the university of fostering a racially charged campus climate. Thus, for a number of reasons, the Missouri Promise holds little promise for making a significant difference in the lives of vulnerable students of color and for stemming their entry into the schools-to-prisons pipeline.[25]

In a similar vein, in the predominantly black community of El Dorado, Arkansas, Claiborne Deming, CEO of the Murphy Oil Corporation, recently announced the "Murphy Oil Promise." According to its homepage, Murphy Oil, a member of the Fortune 200, "is a worldwide oil and gas exploration and production company with refining and marketing operations in the United States and the United Kingdom and crude oil and natural gas exploration and production operations in Canada. Murphy Oil also has an office in Kuala Lumpur to oversee its E&P activities in Malaysia." Its United States-based company operates high-volume, low-cost retail gasoline stations in twenty U.S. states, primarily in the parking areas of Wal-Mart Supercenters. The company's domestic profits are thus largely based upon spending by bargain-hunting consumers who frequent discount box stores—that is, the same population the promise seeks to support. Nonetheless, under the provisions of its Promise, Murphy Oil will spend up to $50 million over the next twenty years to pay $6,000 per year on tuition, for up to five years, for any graduate of El Dorado Public Schools who attends a college or university anywhere (as a point of reference, it costs $6,000 per year to attend the flagship campus of the University of Arkansas). Like the Kalamazoo Promise, the Murphy Oil Promise has had an immediate impact on the town: so far, in 2008 alone, families from twenty-five states have moved to El Dorado and, during the same period, housing costs have risen nearly 33 percent. It is perhaps not surprising that, after the Murphy Oil Promise was announced, one of the several small (and majority white) school systems that encase El Dorado, Norphlet School District, began considering consolidating with the neighboring black school district to avail itself of the scholarship. Generations worth of segregation could possibly end, then, because of the largesse of an oil corporation! While I am loath to dismiss the efforts of Deming and his company to provide a college education to the youth of El Dorado, I cannot help but question the timing of the Murphy Oil Promise, in the current climate of climbing costs of oil and the damage that it is causing in all areas of American life. Still, the residents of El Dorado may concur with the conclusions of CBS News correspondent Richard Schlesinger, who broke the story of the Murphy Oil Promise to the nation on network news: "In El Dorado, a little pain at the pump is the price of admission to a future that might otherwise be beyond reach."[26]

Concluding Thoughts: Little Steps
and the Victory in the Struggle

I devoted much of the previous section to a discussion of the Kalamazoo Promise because, in my view, it holds the greatest promise for sweeping, systemic reform to thwart the race-making functions of urban schools and to abolish the schools-to-prisons pipeline. It bears reiterating that there is no evidence to indicate that the Kalamazoo Promise was inspired by a desire to achieve these ends. Rather, as a pledge to all students in Kalamazoo's schools, the scholarship program creates the conditions that foster an empowering culture of achievement that extends to all children and youth in the district. Regardless of its intentions, because the Kalamazoo Promise is the brainchild of a teacher turned educational leader with a vision of achievement that extends to all children, I argued that the Kalamazoo Promise is likely to prove amenable to other pedagogical reforms and community transformations. Indeed, unlike the other, more restrictive, "promise" programs discussed, the Kalamazoo Promise seems poised to help launch a genuine cultural renewal in a formerly struggling urban community.

While I hope to see the Kalamazoo Promise duplicated across the nation, we need not wait for large-scale programs of this kind to participate in abolishing the schools-to-prisons pipeline. For as I mention briefly below, established and emerging programs across the nation are creating empowering cultures of achievement that enable historically underserved students to flourish. Such piecemeal efforts may seem like little steps when we look at the larger picture of a nation still suffering the damage caused by centuries of racism. Nonetheless, throughout the United States, leaders of these programs work on the front lines in urban schools and under some of the most challenging conditions. These reformers have made differences in the lives of countless children and their families and bear witness that the victory is in the day-to-day work of educating underserved students and in doing their small part in dismantling a piece of the schools-to-prisons pipeline. For instance, students fare extremely well at the all-black Marcus Garvey School in Los Angeles, as do the diverse students who attend the multicultural public Central Park East Elementary and Secondary Schools of New York. These schools feature fairly traditional and rigorous curricula with high performance standards. A new partnership in Buffalo, New York, City Voices, City Visions, also fosters an empowering culture of achievement by providing students with digital video tools for visual and analytic thinking. At an afterschool auto shop program in West Philadelphia, Pennsylvania, high school students and a teacher have created a culture of achievement in which young black men, some of whom had previously been pushed out of school, build high-performance, soybean-fueled sports cars. Finally, an untold number of religious and military academies also have had considerable success promoting high academic achievement among underserved students from urban communities.

Despite their different ideological commitments, the various stakeholders in these schools and programs abide by the belief that, regardless of their backgrounds, all children and youth can meet high standards. In doing so, these settings foster empowering cultures of achievement wherein all students who enter them are encouraged to flourish. Most important, these teachers and students go about the business of flourishing as though to do so is nothing out of the ordinary. Simon Hauger, the auto shop teacher at West Philadelphia High School, perhaps captured this view best: "If you give kids that have been stereotyped as not being able to do anything an opportunity to do something great, they'll step up."[27]

Indeed, I concur with the educator, quoted in *Young, Gifted, and Black*, who argues that "we can, whenever and wherever we wish, teach successfully all children whose education is of interest to us." If this observation is true, and I believe that it is, and if we know what works, and we do, then the only question is whether we really want to live up to the promise of the Equal Protection Clause and promote academic excellence among all our students, thereby abolishing the schools-to-prisons pipeline that leads so many of our neighbors toward lives of incarceration.[28]

Notes

1. For a study of the founding moment in U.S. history, when this pattern of broken promises was initiated, see Stephen John Hartnett and Michael Pfau, "The Confounded Rhetorics of Race in Revolutionary America," in *Rhetoric, Independence, and Nationhood,* vol. 1, in *The Rhetorical History of the United States*, ed. Stephen Lucas (East Lansing: Michigan State University Press, forthcoming in 2011); for longer views, see George M. Fredrickson, *The Black Image in the White Mind: The Debate on Afro-American Character and Destiny, 1817–1914* (1971: Middletown, CT: Wesleyan University Press, 1987); Winthrop Jordan, *White over Black: American Attitudes toward the Negro, 1550–1812* (New York: Norton, 1968); Robin Blackburn, *The Making of New World Slavery: From the Baroque to the Modern, 1492–1800* (London: Verso, 1997); and Alden T. Vaughan, *Roots of American Racism* (Oxford, England: Oxford University Press, 1995).

2. Michael W. Apple, "The Hidden Curriculum and the Nature of Conflict," *Interchange* 2, no. 4 (1971): 27–40; Sharon L. Nichols and David C. Berliner, *Collateral Damage: How High-Stakes Testing Corrupts America's Schools* (Cambridge, MA: Harvard University Press, 2007); Jean Anyon, "Ideology and United States History Text-

books," *Harvard Educational Review* 49 (1979): 361–86; and W. E. B. DuBois, *Dusk of Dawn: An Essay toward an Autobiography of a Race Concept* (1968; New Brunswick, NJ: Transaction, 1997), 222.

3. For historical analyses of the transformation of Americans of African descent from a multi-form population to a uniform subordinate class of slaves during the colonial period, see (in addition to the sources listed in note 1 above) David Lyons, *Unfinished Business: Racial Junctures in U.S. History and Their Legacy,* Public Law and Legal Theory Working Paper No. 02–06 (Boston: Boston University School of Law, 2002) and *Corrective Justice, Equal Opportunity, and the Legacy of Slavery and Jim Crow,* Public Law and Legal Theory Working Paper No. 03–15 (Boston: Boston University School of Law, 2003); Vincent Harding, *There Is a River: The Black Struggle for Freedom in America* (San Diego, CA: Harcourt Brace Jovanovich, 1981); Audrey Smedley, *Race in North America: Origin and Evolution of a Worldview* (Boulder, CO: Westview, 2007).

4. Loïc Wacquant, "From Slavery to Mass Incarceration: Rethinking the 'Race Question' in the U.S.," *New Left Review* 13 (2002): 41–60; Wacquant's essay follows a long line of scholars making a similar argument, including David Barsamian, "Expanding the Floor of the Cage: An Interview with Noam Chomsky," *Z Magazine* 10, no. 3 (1997): 36–43; Garrett Albert Duncan, "From Plantations to Penitentiaries: Race Making and New Century Schools," in *Without Fear: Claiming Safe Communities without Sacrificing Ourselves, A Reader* (Los Angeles: Southern California Library for Social Studies Research, 2007), 26–37; Glenn C. Loury, "Why Are So Many Americans in Prison?" *Boston Review*, 32, no. 4 (July–August 2007); John Edgar Wideman, "Doing Time, Marking Race," in *Burning All Illusions: Writings from the* Nation *on Race, 1866–2002*, ed. Paula J. Giddings (New York: Thunder's Mouth Press/Nation Books, 2002), 183–86; and Stephen John Hartnett, "Prisons, Profit, Crime, and Social Control: A Hermeneutic of the Production of Violence," in *Race, Class, and Community Identity*, ed. Andrew Light and Meck Nagel (New York: Humanities Press, 2000), 199–221.

5. For analyses of race-making in terms of how various European groups have become "white," see James Baldwin, *The Price of the Ticket: Collected Nonfiction, 1948–1985* (New York: St. Martin's Press, 1985); Karen Brodkin, *How Jews Became White Folks and What That Says about Race in America* (Piscataway, NJ: Rutgers University Press, 1999); Jennifer Guglielmo and Salvatore Salerno, *Are Italians White? How Race Is Made in America* (New York: Routledge, 2003); Noel Ignatiev, *How the Irish Became White* (New York: Routledge, 1996); Toni Morrison, *Playing in the Dark: Whiteness and the Literary Imagination* (New York: Vintage, 1993); David R. Roediger, *Working toward Whiteness: How America's Immigrants Became White* (New York: Basic Books, 2005) and *The Wages of Whiteness: Race and the Making of the American Working Class* (New York: Verso, 1991).

6. On race-making in the suburbs, see John Ogbu, *Black American Students in an Affluent Suburb: A Study of Academic Disengagement* (Mahwah, NJ: Lawrence Erlbaum Associates, 2003), and Mary Pattillo-McCoy, *Black Picket Fences: Privilege and Peril among the Black Middle Class* (Chicago: Chicago University Press, 1999); quotations from James D. Anderson, *The Education of Blacks in the South, 1860–1935* (Chapel Hill: University of North Carolina Press, 1988), 187–237; for a contemporary version of Anderson's thesis, see Jason Ziedenberg and Vincent Schiraldi, *Cellblocks*

or Classrooms? The Funding of Higher Education and Corrections and its Impact on African American Men (Washington, DC: Justice Policy Institute, 2002).

7. On the historical factors noted here, see Elliot Jaspin, *Buried in the Bitter Waters: The Hidden History of Racial Cleansing in America* (New York: Basic Books, 2007); Ira Katznelson, *When Affirmative Action Was White: An Untold Story of Racial Inequality in Twentieth Century America* (New York: Norton, 2005); and James W. Loewen, *Sundown Towns: A Hidden Dimension of American Racism* (New York: Touchstone, 2005); on the practices of post-racist racism, see Eduardo Bonilla-Silva, *White Supremacy and Racism in the Post-Civil Rights Era* (Boulder, CO: Lynne Rienner, 2001) and *Racism without Racists: Color-Blind Racism and the Persistence of Racial Inequality in the United States* (Boulder, CO: Rowman and Littlefield, 2003).

8. See John H. McWhorter, *Losing the Race: Self-Sabotage in Black America* (New York: Perennial, 2000); Ruby K. Payne, *A Framework for Understanding Poverty* (Highlands, TX: aha Process, 2003); Ogbu, *Black American Students in an Affluent Suburb*; Signithia Fordham and John Ogbu, "Black Students' School Success: Coping with the Burden of 'Acting White,'" *Urban Review* 18, no. 3 (1986): 176–206; Signithia Fordham, *Blacked Out: Dilemmas of Race, Identity, and Success at Capital High* (Chicago: University of Chicago Press, 1996); and Claude Steele, "A Threat in the Air: How Stereotypes Shape the Intellectual Identity and Performance of Women and African Americans," *American Psychologist* 52 (1997): 613–29.

9. On the differences between first and second generation rights, and the difference between desegregation and integration, see Garrett Albert Duncan, "Beyond Love: A Critical Race Ethnography of the Schooling of Adolescent Black Males," *Equity and Excellence in Education* 35, no. 2 (2002): 131–43; Vivian Gunn Morris and Curtis L. Morris, *The Price They Paid: Desegregation in an African American Community* (New York: Teachers College Press, 2002); Theresa Perry, Claude Steele, and Asa G. Hilliard, *Young, Gifted, and Black: Promoting High Achievement among African-American Students* (Boston: Beacon Press, 2003); Vanessa Siddle Walker, *Their Highest Potential: An African American School Community in the Segregated South* (Chapel Hill: University of North Carolina Press, 1996); and Garrett Albert Duncan, "Race and Human Rights Violations in the United States: Considerations for Human Rights and Moral Educators," *Journal of Moral Education* 29, no. 2 (2000): 183–201.

10. See "Conversation with Martin Luther King," in *Testament of Hope: The Essential Writings and Speeches of Martin Luther King, Jr.* ed. Melvin Washington (San Francisco: HarperCollins, 1987), 657–79; the arguments referenced here are on 663–67; the quoted passage is from 666.

11. See Walker, *Their Highest Potential*, and Morris and Morris, *The Price They Paid*.

12. Regarding the NCLB's disastrous impact on students of color, see *Many Children Left Behind: How the No Child Left Behind Act Is Damaging Our Children and Our Schools*, ed. Deborah Meier, Alfie Kohn, Linda Darling-Hammond, Theodore R. Sizer, and George Wood (Boston: Beacon Press, 2004); Garrett Albert Duncan and Gail Emily Wolfe, "The Education of Black Children Living in Poverty: A Systemic Analysis," in *Child Poverty in America Today,* vol. 4, ed. B. A. Arrighi and D. J. Maume (Westport, CT: Praeger, 2007), 126–45; Dale D. Johnson, Bonnie Johnson, Stephen J. Farenga,

and Daniel Ness, *Stop High-Stakes Testing: An Appeal to America's Conscience* (Lanham, MD: Rowman and Littlefield, 2008); and the essay by Rose Braz and Myesha Williams in this volume (chapter 5).

13. Theresa Perry, in Perry, Steele, and Hilliard, *Young, Gifted, and Black*, 107; and see Deborah Meier, *The Power of Their Ideas: Lessons for America from a Small School in Harlem* (Boston: Beacon Press, 2002), and James Scheurich, "Highly Successful and Loving, Public Elementary Schools Populated Mainly by Low-SES Children of Color: Core Beliefs and Cultural Characteristics," *Urban Education* 33, no. 4 (1998): 451–91.

14. Scheurich, "Highly Successful and Loving," 453.

15. The United Nations and UNESCO documents referenced here are available by using the search engine at www.un.org.

16. For the details of this study, see Garrett Albert Duncan, "Schooling and Inequality in the Post-Industrial United States: Toward a Critical Race Ethnography of Time" (forthcoming manuscript).

17. On the deeply rooted ways that race and racism are embedded in schools, see the Applied Research Center, *Education and Race* (Oakland, CA: Applied Research Center, 1998); Duncan and Wolfe, "Education of Black Children Living in Poverty"; Walter S. Gilliam, *Pre-Kindergarteners Left Behind: Expulsion Rates in State Pre-Kindergarten Systems* (New Haven, CT: Yale University Child Study Center, 2005); and Beth Harry and Mary Anderson, "The Disproportionate Placement of African American Males in Special Education Programs: A Critique of the Process," *Journal of Negro Education* 63, no. 4 (1995): 602–19.

18. For coverage of the Promise, see Neal E. Boudette, "College Tuition Promise Stokes Housing in Kalamazoo, Mich.," *The Wall Street Journal Online* (13 March 2006), retrieved from www.realestatejournal.com/buysell/regionalnews/20060313-boudette .html; for more recent data on the Promise, see the materials available from the W. F. Upjohn Institute at www.upjohninst.org/ promise/index.htm.

19. Brown quoted in "'Kalamazoo Promise' Delivers: Teacher Hatched a Plan for Free College Education for Everyone in Her District," *CBS News Assignment America* (5 February 2007), a CBS news video available at http://cbsnews.com.

20. The anonymous child's words are quoted in "Kalamazoo Promise"; for support for my claim about how knowing college is possible increases academic success, see Margaret S. Sherraden, Lissa Johnson, William Elliott III, Shirley Porterfield, and William Rainford, "School-Based Children's Saving Accounts for College: The *I Can Save* Program," *Children and Youth Services Review* 29, no. 3 (2007): 294–312.

21. Arizona and Hawai'i immigrants noted in Boudette and Naomi Goetz, "In Kalamazoo, a Promise Boosts School Enrollment," *National Public Radio* (29 November 2006), available at www.npr.org/templates/story/ story.php?storyId=6552216; the economic issues noted here are addressed in Gary Miron and Stephanie Evergreen, *The Kalamazoo Promise as a Catalyst for Change in an Urban School District: A Theoretical Framework,* Western Michigan University Evaluation of the Kalamazoo Promise Working Paper, No. 1, 2007.

22. Brown quoted in "Kalamazoo Promise"; for an extended case study of how these questions of poverty, crime rates, local family conditions, and educational

policy affect learning practices, see William Lyons and Julie Drew, *Punishing Schools: Fear and Citizenship in American Public Education* (Ann Arbor: University of Michigan Press, 2006).

23. See Garrett Albert Duncan, "Race, Equity, and the Teaching of Science," in *Teaching and Learning Science: A Handbook*, ed. Kenneth Tobin (Westport, CT: Praeger, 2006), 169–78.

24. For samples of Nixon's rhetoric, see the documents available at www.jaynixon.com.

25. On the troubles at UMKC, see Bryan Noonan, "Invisible Men: Black Studies Professors Say No One Should Have Been Surprised by an Embarrassing Report on UMKC's Racial Climate," *Kansas City Pitch*, 20 July 2006, retrieved from www.pitch.com/ 2006–07–20/news/invisible-men; more broadly, see Noliwe M. Rooks, *White Money/Black Power: The Surprising History of African American Studies and the Crisis of Race in Higher Education* (Boston: Beacon Press, 2006).

26. Information and quotation from "When Big Oil Does Good Things: Murphy Oil Gives Every High School Graduate in One Town $6,000 a Year for College," *CBS News with Katie Couric* (16 June 2008), a CBS News video available at http://cbsnews.com; and see the materials available at www.eldoradopromise.com.

27. Hauger quoted in "Kids Build Soybean-Fueled Car," *CBS News Assignment America* (17 February 2006), a CBS News video available at http://cbsnews.com.

28. Anonymous educator quoted in Perry, Steele, and Hilliard, *Young, Gifted, and Black,* 150.

January 3, 2009

Nicole Monahan

A member of the Writing Workshop at the Denver Women's Correctional Facility, in Denver, Colorado, Nicole Monahan wrote this powerful poem in response to her husband's suicide. When she stood tall to perform the piece for a gathering of writers and friends in April 2009, she received a standing ovation; the piece was published in *Captured Words/Free Thoughts* 6 (Spring 2009).

It all started at the mouths of others: the bad news was delivered like an airplane plummeting to the ground. It hit hard, devastating everything and everyone around it—the pain instantly filled my chest. I felt my heart shatter like a glass being thrown against the wall in a fit of anger. "No, this can't be," I said, trying to find some way to convince myself that this was not real, but I knew inside it was. I found it hard to stand on my own two feet, and as I felt the weight of the news, my tears changed from a stream to a gushing river; for days the river was filled with rapids. Even as the shock settled in, my new reality was clouded by disbelief; I found myself refusing to deal with the grief. But deep inside I know that life will never be the same, for a life has been lost too soon. A young man of only twenty-nine years is gone forever. A mother and father have lost their only child, their only son. Three little girls have lost their beloved daddy; a little boy will never get to play ball with his father. And I have lost my best friend, my soul mate, my husband.

Chapter 9

Humanizing Education behind Bars: Shakespeare and the Theater of Empowerment

Jonathan Shailor

A monk asked Chih Men,
"How is it when the lotus flower has not yet emerged from the water?"
Chih Men said,
"A lotus flower."
Then the monk asked again,
"What about after it has emerged from the water?"
Chih Men answered,
"Lotus leaves."[1]

The lotus flower is the Buddhist symbol of our incorruptible, enlightened nature; the use of the symbol in this koan is provocative because it suggests that our enlightened nature is fully present at all times, no matter who we are, and no matter what our circumstances. A few years ago the imprisoned actors at the Racine Correctional Institution (RCI) adopted this metaphor, naming themselves "The Muddy Flower Theatre Troupe." In 2007, in the rap that kicked off our production of *Julius Caesar,* Rashad (a four-year veteran of the program) made use of the ancient image:

As seventeen plus one
Journey
Individually
From inmate
Offender
Cast mate
Actor
And perhaps even
Friend
Muddy Flowers bloom
To no end

Collectively
Exploring humanity
Growing individually
Showing something
Is bigger than you
You
You
And me[2]

In his performance of this poem before our audience of invited guests, Rashad both acknowledged and transgressed the boundary between prisoner and free citizen. Instead of his prison greens, he wore a suit and tie (his costume for our modern dress interpretation). His self-confident swagger filled the room, even as the wary officers looked on from the perimeter. The "seventeen plus one" in his poem referred to the 17 prisoners plus me—the college professor, the director of the play, and their fellow traveler on this journey. In his admonition that "something/Is bigger than you,/You/You/And me," Rashad made direct eye contact with an individual audience member on each "you," affirming the contact with a nod, and pulling them back to him as he tapped his chest: "And me."

Every word and gesture in Rashad's presentation invoked our common humanity and our common human predicament. Indeed, as the prisoners and I investigate the amazing tapestry of characters created by William Shakespeare, we see that everyone is capable of great wisdom and great kindness, and, at the same time, capable of tremendous stupidity and cruelty—no one is exempt. Partly from individual choices, and partly from circumstances beyond our control, everyone's life is a walk along the boundary between comedy and tragedy. And as we all struggle forward in the best way that we can, we go terribly astray when we respond to each other's limitations, mistakes, and acts of violence with further acts of violence, whether psychological or physical.

I am thinking now of my own son, still a toddler. He is beautiful. I hope and pray that he will grow into a fine young man. If for some reason he becomes a danger to himself or others, I will want him contained and corrected, but I will also want him to be treated with understanding and kindness. I don't want him to become convinced of his own worthlessness, to become a prisoner of his own shame. I don't believe that he would be helped (nor would society be helped) by having him placed in a hostile environment designed primarily to punish him, in part by depriving him of normal opportunities for socialization and education. And so I see my work in prisons as a service to those sons and daughters in our human family who by fortune, formation of character, and incarceration, are now in near-intolerable situations. I am there to do what I can to offer an alternative. What I did not understand at the beginning, and what I am coming to understand now, is that my work is also (for many) a provocation and a challenge to the "normal way of doing things" in prison. As I grow into a fuller awareness of the work that other educators are doing in our nation's prisons, I am beginning to understand how our efforts challenge the dehumanizing stereotypes and daily humiliations of the prison-industrial complex.

The Theater of Empowerment

In 1995 a group of fifteen instructors from the University of Wisconsin–Parkside (UWP) began teaching college-level courses at nearby Racine Correctional Institution (RCI), a medium-maximum security state prison in Sturtevant, Wisconsin. The effort was organized by two people who were passionate advocates of better educational opportunities behind bars. Roseann Mason, then the coordinator of the campus writing center, and John Longeway, a professor of philosophy, already had some history of teaching in prison, and they were now reaching out to their colleagues and asking them to do the same. With the help of a series of grants from the Wisconsin Humanities Council (WHC), we were able to bring in a wide range of courses, including communication, literature, poetry, theater, writing, and economics.

My first course (offered in the fall of 1995) was titled "The Theater of Empowerment." As a communication professor specializing in methods of conflict transformation, I had developed a particular interest in the work of Augusto Boal and other theater activists. Boal in particular has written a great deal about his "theater of the oppressed," which is aimed at helping nonactors become "protagonists of their own lives" by jointly exploring their personal and social problems and then transforming them through "a rehearsal for reality." In a ten-week class, I worked with the dozen or so students to develop a sense of ensemble through theater games and exercises. I asked them to identify situations and relationships that they experienced as oppressive; we developed them into scenes, and those scenes became the starting point for discussion and experimentation with alternative responses. At that time the RCI staff and administrators, in particular the deputy warden and the director of education, were relatively open to innovation and experimentation, so we were permitted to conclude the course with a performance of our "scenes of oppression" before a hundred or so prisoners in the prison gym. Two moments from that evening stand out for me as especially vivid: the scene in which a prisoner reenacted his frustrating encounters with an officer who would not allow him to pick up a package that had arrived in the mail (performed in the presence of said officer, as well as the warden), and the passionate response we received from the audience. At the end of the evening, as the audience members greeted us and thanked us, a rather gaunt inmate with sad eyes and a salt-and-pepper beard grasped my hand. "Thank you," he said. "In all the years I've been here, I've never seen anything like this. It's about time."[3]

I was surprised when Deputy Warden Dan Buchler also responded warmly to that eventful evening. In a letter to our project coordinator, he thanked us for the performance and expressed his "pleasure" at what we had achieved. He also admitted to being "a little shocked, but excited, at the amount of meaningful involvement by the prisoners in the audience." He concluded: "It is always a pleasure to see positive things going on within the institution involving prisoners and different types of activities other than the 'norm.' I hope that this can be thought about for the future and considered for repetition." Thanks to the support of administrators like Buchler, I was able to offer the Theater of Empowerment course in various manifestations for the next nine years (1995–2004). A few highlights from that period are worth visiting here.

In the fall of 1996, twelve instructors from UWP coordinated our teaching efforts at the prison around the question: "What is an everyday hero?" The goal of the project, as identified in our Wisconsin Humanities Council grant application, was "to introduce prisoners at the Racine Correctional Institution to alternative non-violent models of heroism through the study of the humanities. The inmate students will reflect on their own actions, learn to think critically about them, to identify correlations between the heroes' circumstances and their own, and recognize and apply practical lessons of everyday heroism to their own lives." Longeway offered a course on the "heroic wisdom" of philosophers who "established traditions of thought in part through their heroic adherence to their conception of the good despite the hostility and persecution inflicted on them by their own societies." Farida Khan and Roby Rajan taught "The Hero in the Global Economy," which focused on "stories about economic and cultural impoverishment and narratives of individual and cultural survival." Ngure wa Mwachofi centered his course on the life of Malcolm X.[4]

My course was titled *King, Warrior, Magician, Lover,* after the title of a book by Robert Moore and Douglas Gillette. In their book, Moore and Gillette employ Jungian philosophy and invite us to "rediscover the archetypes of the mature masculine." Each archetype has multiple manifestations. The "shadow side" includes both a positive pole (inflation, where the individual becomes overly identified with the archetype) and a negative pole (dissociation, where the individual is cut off from the archetype). The ideal outcome is to achieve integration, where the individual has managed to manifest the archetype in a meaningful and balanced way. The king archetype, for example, appears as appropriately integrated in the lives of visionary leaders like Martin Luther King Jr. The shadow side of the archetype shows itself in the tyrant (inflated leaders such as Idi Amin) and in the weakling (dissociated leaders like General George S. Patton, who feared his own weakness and cowardice to a such a degree that he attacked it in other men).[5]

In the course, we read Moore and Gillette, studied historical, cinematic, and everyday examples of each archetype, and then applied the lessons to our own lives. Once again the men created scenes of oppression based on their life experience. They also used the framework of the archetypes to investigate and reinvent their role enactments. A few months after the course was over, I received this letter from an address in Milwaukee: "Dear Dr. Shailor: My husband, Devarius, took a class that you taught while he was in the Racine Correctional Institution, last fall. I just wanted to thank you for teaching that class. I have noticed a big change in him. He is much more understanding and listens to what we have to say. He cares about us and keeps us together as a family. He credits your class and talks about it often. Thank you again, Henrietta Jackson." The same envelope contained another note, this one reading: "Thank you very much for your class. . . . I use your ways of thinking about the theater of empowerment.—Devarius Jackson." I remembered Devarius well, for during the class he had taken some pride in his reputation as a drug kingpin out on the streets and as the master of his castle at home. In both settings, he saw himself as a king, but when the other men in the class heard his stories of how he conducted himself, they identified him as a tyrant. The distinction led to a series of discussions and role-plays that helped Devarius find ways to integrate all the archetypes in more meaningful ways.

Another version of the "Theater of Empowerment" class focused on an event (originally developed by John Bergman and the Geese Theatre Company) called *la corrida*. After several weeks of work in which the prisoners identified their habitual patterns of conflict, studied the archetypes, and practiced alternative ways of thinking and responding, they were "put to the test" in *la corrida* (the bullfight ring). With the participants sitting in a large circle, each actor took his turn being thrust into a scene that had been specially designed to test his ability to cope with a difficult situation. Richard, for example, was frequently troubled by feelings of loneliness, victimization, and despair. His usual ways of responding included drinking, rageful displays, and other controlling behavior. In the scene we designed for him, Richard called on his ex in an attempt to reestablish a relationship (something that he desperately wanted). His ex listened for a while and then expressed her hurt and anger at how she had been treated. Richard was challenged to remain open, to listen, and to respond in ways that showed his understanding and compassion.[6]

The actors who worked with the prisoners that evening were from Chicago, experienced in improvisation, and had connected with me a few weeks earlier through our common interest in social action theater. Prior to our meeting with the prisoners, I briefed the actors on the scenarios. Each prisoner was equipped with a "posse of archetypes" who stood on the sidelines during their scene—a king, warrior, magician, and a lover (played by classmates)—who were ready and waiting to serve as supporters and advisers when called upon. When a prisoner felt stuck, he would stop the action, move to the sidelines for a consultation with one of the characters, and then return to the action, if possible armed with a new idea or line of action. Four persons sitting ringside served as judges: Dr. Donald Hands, the head psychologist at the prison, myself, and two other members of the class. At the end of each scene, the inmate actor offered a concise self-evaluation, using this as an opportunity to call to our attention elements of the performance that he thought were particularly significant. The judges had the opportunity to question the central actor, as well as the other actors, who remained in character. After a few minutes of open debate, the judges appraised the inmate's performance and rated it as exceptional, satisfactory, or unsatisfactory. The prisoners were very active and vocal at this stage of the exercise. In one case, Dr. Hands commended an actor for being able to express and share his feelings, but a prisoner judge criticized him for talking in circles, failing to examine his own assumptions, and neglecting to consider how his girlfriend might be feeling.

During some semesters, I integrated the Theater of Empowerment course with courses from the university's program in conflict transformation. At those times, both the prisoners and the students in one of my upper-level courses (usually Communication 485: Practicum in Conflict Intervention) would work as separate groups during the initial training and scene development. Then, in anywhere from one to several joint meetings, the two groups presented their scenes to one another. Those sessions were always highly interactive. In one session, a prisoner portrayed his painful estrangement from his girlfriend. This led to a discussion in which several prisoners talked about losing contact with their significant others after they had been incarcerated. The absence of communication left them wondering why they had been abandoned. Most of my university students were women, so the prisoners used this opportunity to ask them how they would respond if their boyfriends ended up in prison. How would they feel about the relationship? Would they maintain contact? Would they remain committed? The women provided the men with a wide range of responses, all thoughtfully articulated. It was clear to me that what had been most painful to these men was the disconfirmation they had experienced in being cut off without explanation. What these women offered was an opportunity for them to experience the dignity of being heard and responded to.

In another session, a Parkside student presented a conflict with her father, who had in some ways abandoned her during her childhood. Now that she was planning her wedding and asking for him to attend, the issue of abandonment was once again in the forefront. During the scene, her pain erupted in a tirade of sarcastic replies and bitter condemnations. When the scene had finished, the prisoners offered their perspectives on the conflict—gently, and with great respect for the young woman's feelings. One of the prisoners explained how it was probably very difficult for her father to hear her and understand her when she used such harsh language to express herself. She acknowledged this, and a discussion of alternatives ensued. What we did in these sessions is something central to all my work in conflict transformation: We worked together to examine conflicts from multiple perspectives, with the aim of enriching our understanding and finding new ways forward. To have this discussion take place in a prison setting, between prisoners and college students, was both poignant and revolutionary. In course evaluations, both the prisoners and the Parkside students highlighted one issue as the most important: The university students had recognized the prisoners' humanity. Such recognition is essential if we are to develop more humane ways of responding to crime, violence, and those who break the law.

In yet another manifestation of the Theater of Empowerment, we focused on the importance of story as a way of creating meaning, a form of self-authorship, a way of sharing and reflecting upon our experiences, and as an aesthetic phenomenon: a recognition and creation of beauty. With these objectives in mind, we devoted a series of class sessions to the creation of stories about our fathers. After working together to develop the stories into a performance, we presented them to prisoners in the Alcohol and Other Drug Abuse Program and to students from UWP. The stories included Ricky's warm recollections of how his father used to attend his Little League games; Theron's visit to his father's deathbed (prison authorities allowed him the option of seeing his father alive, or attending his father's funeral—but not both); Dave's phone call to his dad (in which he asks for help procuring gym shoes and help figuring out whether he is really "in love"). Phil composed his section of the play in three scenes. In the first, he is out on the lake, fishing with his father. The pace of the scene is slow and meditative, with the father giving the son instruction on the finer points of fishing as the son hangs on his every word. The second scene begins with the narrator's announcement that Phil's father has died. Phil continues the scene with the following monologue:

> Well, I'm out here on the lake, Dad. But I don't feel like fishing. I don't understand why you didn't take better care of yourself, Dad. I don't understand why you had to go and die. This is the time in my life that I really need you. This is the time I need you the most, and you're not here. You said you would be here for me. You promised me that you would be here for me, and you're gone. And I won't forgive you for that. You should've took better care of yourself. There's a lot of things going on in my life. I'm starting to notice girls. . . . Who am I going to go to with my questions about girls? I can't go to Ma with that stuff. She won't—I can't go to Ma with that stuff, Dad. You should be here. You shouldn't have left me alone. I want to play ball. Who's gonna teach me how to throw a curve ball? You should've took better care of yourself, Dad. You let me down. You said you'd be here for me, and you're gone—forever. Forever. And you let me down. And I don't know if I can ever forgive you for that. I don't think I can.

The narrator then provides a transition to the final scene: "Phil stayed angry for years. Angry at his Dad for leaving him to fend for himself. Angry at God for taking his Dad. This was the start of a long journey into drugs, alcohol, and crime. A journey marked by anger and resentment. But this story does have a happy ending. Do you like happy endings? I know you do. Now we fast forward, and we find Phil on the lake. But he's not alone—no. He is fishing with his 12-year-old son." In the third and final scene, Phil instructs his son on the subtleties of fishing, explicitly following the same advice that his father had given to him. While this scene has not (yet) taken place in real life, it is an expression of Phil's hopes for the future and an example of how he is using art as a means of exploring his emotions and seeking a place of clarity.

On the day that I announced that the scenes would be about the men's relationship with their fathers, Devon came up to me after class to tell me that he wasn't sure how he would be able to complete the assignment, since he had never met his father. I suggested that he write a story about what might happen if his father suddenly appeared after all these years. Devon developed his scene in part by using the empty chair exercise, which is sometimes used in psychodrama: the client places an empty chair opposite his own, imagines the presence of a significant other, and launches into a monologue. Devon's initial performance was so emotionally raw that it blew us away. He was also surprised with the intensity of the feelings that had come up—but he did not shy away from continuing to work with the scene. In the final version, he meets his father for the first time when he comes to visit Devon at the prison. Once the two are seated together and have exchanged banal pleasantries, the scene continues:

Father: I know my excuses are probably worthless, but I struggled to come up here, and

Devon: Hold on—hold on. First of all, one thing you'll learn about *me*, is when *I* say something, I *mean* it. And second of all, for 25 years all you have been to me is a big-ass "what if." A damn "woo." You know, I don't want that chump change from your pocket. All I want to know is where have you been, why you here, and when you *leaving*?

Father: I've come all this way to see you to try to give you my reasons for leaving. Won't you hear me out?

Devon: What is it? I mean, what? What? Because of my Mom? Because you and her had problems?

Father: I can't explain it, son.

Devon: Let me try to help you out here. Maybe it was the indifference between you and my mother. You and her. You split up with her, not me. You know what I'm saying? And the shady thing is—I done played this moment a million times in the back of my mind—and it always comes out the same. A damn *phony*.

Father: Hold on now, son. I ain't never been a fake or a phony. You know, I was incapable of taking care of myself. Hell, I was a young man! This was long ago. Hell, I was a father before I was a man.

Devon: A damn coward. And now you here looking for that little boy you abandoned—to ease your conscience. Shit, if I could take back half the mistakes I made in life!

Father: Hold on, son. It's not like that.

Devon: Don't call me "son." You gave up that right a long time ago. And I needed you then. I needed you when that drunk-ass bastard kicked my ass for taking up for my momma. I needed you for discipline. I needed you to teach me how to be a man. With five kids and a habit, see, she crumbled like brittle.

Father: Hold it one minute. Hold it one damn minute. It wasn't like that. You don't understand how it was. I loved your mother. But don't blame me for her shortcomings. Don't blame me for the indifference. Don't blame me for your mother's—

Devon: You selfish bastard! If you didn't know, you *still* making mistakes. Any fool with a dick can make a baby, but it take a man to take care of one. You know what I'm saying? I mean, did you hear me?

Father: I hear you, son.

Devon: You walked out on me—so now I'm returning the favor. I'm through with this visit. You know what I'm saying? (*He rises and walks toward the door.*) Go back to where you came from. I don't need you. (*Stopping at the door.*) I was told if you ain't part of the solution, you part of the problem—*black man*. (*He exits and slams the door.*)

In an interesting complement to this piece, Devon wrote a fictional scene for our play on the theme of the prodigal son. In Devon's version of the story, a young man from the country is intrigued by the big city life of Chicago. Against his parents' wishes, he leaves home in search of the high life. Once in Chicago, he falls in with the wrong crowd, becomes involved with alcohol and drugs, loses all his money, is betrayed by his friends, and winds up homeless. He is caught stealing and goes to jail. Upon release, he yearns for the stability and love of family life. He hitchhikes his way back home, where his father greets him with open arms. In juxtaposition with the scene about the son who had been abandoned by his father, this scene raises interesting issues about estrangement and the possibility of reconciliation. In the first (autobiographical) scene, the father's actions are so egregious that the son cannot bring himself to forgive him, yet in the second (supposedly fictional) scene, it is the son who leaves, acts foolishly, and begs forgiveness—and it is the father who welcomes him back with unconditional love. It seems to me that one of the things that Devon might be working out here is the idea that reconciliation among family members is always desirable, but also that adults bear a greater burden of responsibility when relationships become strained. They should be held to a higher standard, both in terms of their conduct, and in their willingness and ability to forgive others.

"Our Fathers" concluded with a simple scene, one that Rick (one of the actors) insisted we use to end the performance. Rick hears his infant daughter crying in her cradle. He goes to her, gently lifts her from the bed, and carries her to his chair. After a few soothing words, he sweetly sings a verse of "Daddy's Little Girl," then carefully returns the sleeping infant to her cradle. As he gazes at his daughter in rapt attention, the other performers gather around him, their eyes also drawn to the infant. After a few moments, the actors turn to the audience and end the performance with an excerpt from Dick Lourie's poem, *Forgiving Our Fathers*:

> how do we forgive our fathers?
> maybe in a dream
>
> maybe for leaving us too often or
> forever when we were little maybe

for scaring us with unexpected rage
or making us nervous because there seemed
never to be any rage there at all

for marrying or not marrying our mothers
for divorcing or not divorcing our mothers
and shall we forgive them for their excesses
of warmth or coldness shall we forgive them

for pushing or leaning for shutting doors
or speaking only through layers of cloth
or never speaking or never being silent

in our age or in theirs or in their deaths
saying it to them or not saying it—
if we forgive our fathers what is left?[7]

The theme of fathers and sons resonates powerfully (and painfully) with these men because so many of them have been abandoned, and so many are now estranged from their own children. According to a recent report published by the U.S. Department of Justice, incarcerated parents of children under eighteen now number more than 350,000—a 79 percent increase since 1991. Moreover, almost 1.9 million children have a parent in prison, and more than a third of them will reach the age of eighteen before their parent is released.[8] The prison system has thus become an institution that both feeds on and exacerbates the fragmentation of families. In response to this crisis, the plays discussed here offer my students opportunities to rethink their family histories, to explore new modes of loving and caring, and hence to begin walking the long road toward building new family dynamics.

The Shakespeare Project

As part of my search for new insights and possibilities for our prison theater program, I attended the Pedagogy and Theatre of the Oppressed Conference in the spring of 2002, in Toledo, Ohio, where I met Agnes Wilcox, founder and director of Prison Performing Arts in St. Louis, Missouri. Agnes was in the final stages of directing the Hamlet Project at Missouri Eastern Correctional Center, and I was eager to learn as much as I could about how she did it. She told me all she could over our relatively brief lunch. What it boiled down to was this: the men were challenged and inspired by the material, and they were also very much up to performing it. Agnes was an experienced theater artist, and she directed classical theater in prison just as she would direct it in any other venue. As I listened, my lifelong passion for Shakespeare was reignited, and I began to contemplate the possibilities for the men at RCI. I knew on the spot that our first play would be that epic tale of family dysfunction, *King Lear.*

Back in Wisconsin, RCI's education director, Jean Thieme, was supportive of the idea, and with her help I gradually developed a formal proposal for the King Lear Project. The most important part of the proposal was a set of learning objectives that would be consistent with RCI's stated mission, which is (in part) to create "positive change" in offenders "through an array of services aimed at the positive development of human learning, growth and meaningful behavior control." With this in mind, I articulated the following objectives for the King Lear Project:

> » *Cultural literacy.* We will develop a sophisticated understanding of Shakespeare's *King Lear,* in terms of its context, sources, plot, character, themes, language, imagery, and performance history.
> » *Performance.* We will develop range, power, creative intelligence, and flexibility in our ability to perform as actors.
> » *Empathy.* We will appreciate the humanity of each of the characters in the play through an exploration of their hopes and fears.
> » *Insight.* We will analyze how each character connects his/her experiences to specific thoughts, feelings, and actions, and we will evaluate the consequences of each character's behavior as she or he interacts with others.
> » *Self-awareness.* We will explore how the characters' personalities and choices are similar to and different from our own.
> » *Teamwork.* We will work together by wholeheartedly committing our individual energies to this project, and by listening, respecting, and supporting each other throughout our time together.
> » *Playfulness.* We will cultivate humor, gentleness, kindness, and creativity in our work together.

A few months after the proposal was submitted, the King Lear Project was approved to begin on July 20, 2004. We were given a $2,500 budget that would help us to purchase scripts, rent costumes and props, and pay a professional fight director to come in and choreograph the sword fights and battle scenes. Prisoners with an eighth-grade reading level and no major conduct reports in the past ninety days would be eligible to participate. To drum up interest, I presented a one-man show in the prison gym titled "The Power of Shakespeare." My performance consisted of some Shakespearean monologues, an overview of the King Lear Project, and a question-and-answer session with the audience. Of the eighty men who attended the event, forty signed up; twenty showed up on the first day of class, and seventeen completed the course.

Although I was working solo as the director, I had plenty of support from friends and colleagues. On the advice of a friend in the Theater Arts Department, I got in touch with Curt Tofteland, founder and director of Shakespeare behind Bars (SBB) at Luther Luckett Correctional Complex in LaGrange, Kentucky. Curt was an accessible and invaluable resource. Among other things, he had plenty of good advice on how to establish a healthy working relationship with the prison administration, as well as technical advice on issues like what kinds of swords were most likely to be approved by prison security (as it turned out, the flat wooden swords used by SBB were too real for RCI—so we ended up with escrima sticks, sections of PVC pipe encased in black foam rubber). Other supporters included my brother Christopher, a high school drama director who ran his own summer Shakespeare program; Jacque Troy, then education director for the Milwaukee Repertory Theater (now in the same office with the Milwaukee Chamber Theater); Shakespeare scholar Andy McLean, and the entire Theater Arts Department at UWP.

I met with the prisoners every Tuesday and Thursday evening in the prison library, from 6:00 to 8:00 p.m., and sometimes as late as 8:30 (by that time, everyone had to be making their way back to their units for the evening head count). Every rehearsal began with "the clearing of the tables" in order to create a performance space. During the final weeks of rehearsal (March–April), we met every day in order to prepare for the performances. Two performances were given in the prison gym to inmate audiences of about 100 each, and one performance was given in the visiting area, where the performers' invited guests (friends and family) were able to attend, along with corrections staff and administration, some of my colleagues from the university, and other members of the public (about seventy all together).

The Muddy Flowers *King Lear* was well received by prisoners, staff, and the community. The production also created something of a media sensation, in that we landed front page stories in the local papers, the *Milwaukee Journal-Sentinel*, and the *New York Times*. The Associated Press also picked up the story, the Milwaukee Fox TV affiliate produced a short feature for the evening news, and we were even contacted by a producer from the *Today Show*. While all the coverage was respectful, the main focus of these stories seemed to be on the sheer novelty of the event. The one exception was a retrospective published by the *Racine Journal Times* on May 29, 2005. Reporter Brent Killackey and photographer Gregory Shaver had followed our process over the final three months, attending several rehearsals, conducting interviews, and attending all three performances of the play. Their two-page spread included numerous photographs and profiles on several of the prisoners. Here is how Killackey described one of them:

Ken Spears was tricked into joining the theater troupe—not an easy thing to do to a long-time inmate. Spears, with his long, white hair commonly tied back and a few tattoos on his arms, thought he was heading to the prison library to get help on a legal issue from fellow inmate William White.

Instead, the library had been converted into the rehearsal site for the future production of *King Lear*. White was the assistant director. Spears, who said he was serving time for vehicular homicide, was a bit angry, but that faded as he watched the group of men interact.

In a prison environment where people congregate in terms of age and race—where there was a constant struggle among the "alpha" males—here was a diverse group working together.

"I saw guys helping each other to deliver a single line," Spears said. "It hooked me," he said. "I've been 18 years locked up and all of it has been negative. This was the first positive energy."

The success of the King Lear Project became the springboard for the Shakespeare Project, an annual repetition of the winning formula we had created in year one. In 2005–2006 the play was *Othello*, followed by *The Tempest* in 2006–2007 and *Julius Caesar* in 2007–2008. Continual media coverage has helped to keep us in the public eye: *Othello* was featured on three Wisconsin Public Radio programs, including *Here on Earth with Jean Feraca*. The idea, then, is twofold: to use Shakespeare to create a space for creativity within prisons and to use the resulting plays as media-friendly occasions for inviting our neighbors to rethink their stance on crime, punishment, and the prison-industrial complex.[9]

To see the Shakespeare Project amplified and refracted through so many different media lenses was in some ways exhilarating and validating, and in other ways troubling. If there was to be a critical examination of the prison system, it would not be led by the media. News stories and commentaries fixed mostly on the sheer novelty of prison inmates (those "men we love to hate") and their surprising ability to perform Shakespeare's plays. The reporting was sometimes tainted with a patronizing air, and I was rankled by coy expressions such as the *Milwaukee Journal Sentinel's* winking reference to "a captive audience." The stories that were "in depth" looked at the rehearsal process over time, and to a very limited extent, the stories of some of the prisoners, but not at all at the larger social-cultural context of the prison-industrial complex. For example, not one story referenced the exponential rise in rates of incarceration over the past twenty years, there were no critically engaged discussions of the current state of prison education programs, and none of the stories addressed the conditions within the prison system itself.

Although the stories were far from hard-hitting critical news journalism, some blowback followed from the publicity, as some people asked why prisoners' punishment was being "softened" by this kind of arts programming. For example, on June 17, 2006, I was interviewed by Jean Feraca on her Wisconsin Public Radio program *Here on Earth: Radio without Borders*. The program, which was titled "Othello Behind Bars," focused on our recent production of the Shakespeare play. During the call-in portion of the program, a woman identified as "Suzette from Madison" called in and, in a voice thick with emotion, said that "I love what you're doing. I think it's a *good* thing. I love how you are getting people to realize about themselves . . . except that: my father was *killed* and those people went to prison, and they got out with an *education*? And *arts*? And everything that you know, that was given to them. Meanwhile . . . our family was torn apart. Now I understand what you're doing, and I'm, I'm happy about it. But when do they *pay*?" After expressing my sincere sympathy for her loss, I told Suzette that I believed that the men I was working with *were* paying for their crimes, and that my role as an educator served a different purpose: to provide them opportunities to become the kind of people that we would welcome back to our communities. Such intense exchanges on the radio, and the slew of generally positive media stories generated excitement and hopefulness for those of us associated with the project—the prisoners, the project facilitators, and myself. The actors felt rewarded for their hard work. They were recognized as men of value, defined as something more than their mistakes, and their families were witnesses to this public confirmation. As the mother of one of the actors explained it to the *Racine Journal Times*: "These are real people in here. . . . These are not throwaway people."[10]

The Principles of the Shakespeare Project

In year three of the project, RCI's education director, Elizabeth Gilbertson, was contacted by the education director at another Wisconsin state prison. The question for Beth was "How can we do this at our institution?" Her answer: "Get yourself a Dr. Shailor." I accepted the compliment, because I agree that a project like this requires the fierce commitment of a passionate individual. But I also believe that the Shakespeare Project can be replicated, and so here are some of the critical components of our success.

First, it is important to understand the institutional culture, to be cognizant and respectful of institutional protocols, and to establish professional relationships with the warden, the education director, the officers, and other corrections staff. Second, it is essential to have a clearly defined structure and a consistent process. Our structure included a syllabus with guidelines, objectives, expectations, and a schedule, with all rehearsal and performance dates locked in a year in advance. Our process consisted of some absolutely consistent rituals, like clearing the tables, circling up, checking in, and warming up at the beginning of every rehearsal. The regular use of theater games and exercises helped the men develop confidence, acting skills, and a sense of ensemble. Third, beyond an understanding of the fundamentals of theater (especially acting and directing), it is helpful to have a framework geared specifically to the study and performance of Shakespearean verse. In this regard, I have found Scott Kaiser's *Mastering Shakespeare* to be extremely useful. (Kaiser is the head of voice and text at the Oregon Shakespeare Festival.) Fourth, the director or facilitator should have an infectious enthusiasm for Shakespeare and an insatiable curiosity about his works. I convey this in part by carefully investigating and debating the text with the men. Every actor works with two texts of the play: a rehearsal text (we have used both the Oxford School Editions and the Folger Editions), and a study text (here, we rely on the Arden Shakespeare). We constantly steer between the Scylla of "one correct interpretation" and the Charybdis of "anything goes." Part of the fun includes a discussion of the play's performance history, and a viewing of several film versions and adaptations.[11]

Fifth, I have the men keep journals, where they reflect on Shakespeare, the rehearsal process, and their own personal challenges. Every few weeks, I collect the journals, read them carefully, and respond in writing. On occasion, the men read to one another from their journals. As the warden has noted, this element of the class has been important in helping me to develop a climate of "trust and understanding" with the men. I also encourage other forms of self-expression, and have found that many of the men enjoy sharing drawings, poems, and other personal creations with the group. One of the men handcrafted a "King Lear Play Set," complete with a miniature stage with changeable scenery, a map, and figures representing each of the characters. Sixth, "The play's the thing": It keeps us focused and moving forward at all times. When unexpected challenges arise, as they always do, we take pride in finding ways to meet obstacles and overcome them. Typical challenges include the loss of a cast member from a disciplinary action or competing program needs, an actor discovering that he is unable to carry the part to which he was originally assigned, and personality conflicts among some of the prisoners. We cultivate an atmosphere in which the men are encouraged to speak up and offer their perspectives, ask questions, voice concerns, and make suggestions. When conflicts emerge, we talk them through.

Seventh, and perhaps most important, we have an ethic of unconditional acceptance of each man in the project. I emphasize the facts that everyone has different gifts to offer and that everyone is at a different place in his personal journey, meaning that our job is to support each other and to help everyone be the best that he can be. The most rewarding element of this work for me has been the opportunity to watch individual men grow. Jayden, who was cast as the Fool in *Lear*, is an amiable young man who enjoyed clown roles, but who also deeply desired to be taken more seriously. He had a lot of difficulty with enunciation and articulation and was also somewhat handicapped by a self-confidence problem—he was never sure whether people were laughing with him or at him, but he suspected it was the latter. Over the course of the four years that I have worked with him, I have seen him grow dramatically in confidence and ability. In *Othello*, his diction had clearly improved, and he played a convincing Roderigo. In *The Tempest*, his mastery of Shakespeare's language was better still, and he showed his gift for comedy in the role of Stephano, the drunken butler. In *Julius Caesar*, he demonstrated a truly astounding power, range, and gravitas as Marc Antony. Those who knew him in year one could hardly believe he was the same person.

While Jayden's story stands out, countless other men demonstrated a growth of spirit in less obvious ways—sometimes in a single word or gesture. Aidan, who played the title role in last year's production of *Julius Caesar*, told us about the turnaround he saw in some of his enemies from his unit. In his journal, he wrote that "after the performance [an] inmate who I didn't get along with shook my hand and told me that they liked my performance and they enjoyed themselves. That was really rewarding and it gave me a sense of pride, conviction and accomplishment because my performance forced them to see me in a different light . . . even though it was a brief handshake or a thank you, that feeling will last for a life time."

While the stories of Jayden and Aiden point out how our program empowers and challenges the individual men involved in any play, I also want to stress that I envision the Shakespeare Project as a conduit between the incarcerated and the outside community. Each year, I have involved teachers, artists, and scholars in our rehearsal process, and I have also reached out to various sectors of the community to attend our public performances. Some of these people have become regulars: our costumer, our fight director, our Shakespeare scholar, and our videographer. Last year, both Lisa

Kornetsky (theater professor at UWP) and Jacque Troy (education director for the Milwaukee Chamber Theater) attended several of our rehearsals and provided special training and guidance in their areas of expertise (voice and movement). Also that year, Baron Kelly (a professional actor and theater professor at Chapman University) ran a special workshop for us on acting Shakespeare. Our audiences have included members of the Monday Shakespeare Club in Green Bay, Wisconsin (they have made the three-hour drive to RCI on two occasions), a circuit judge from Milwaukee (and his daughter), members of the Music Theater Workshop in Chicago, and members of the Prison Creative Arts Project at the University of Michigan. The point here is to make the prison walls more permeable, to make prisoners more visible, to raise public awareness, to raise questions about the prison system, and to encourage challenge and innovation. Every year, so that our momentum carries us forward, I try to increase our network of facilitators, audience members, and supporters.

Learning to Work Together; or, "Squashing the Funk"

I believe that the Theater of Empowerment and the Shakespeare Project have been successful because we have managed to create a *sanctuary* in the prison setting, a place of refuge or protection where prisoners are free to express themselves without fear of ridicule or reprisal. It is a place where they can become vulnerable, where they know that their sensitivity and creativity will be rewarded, not punished. It is a sacred place where the men are invited to imagine, to create, and to honor one another in the process. Damian, who played Regan in *Lear*, put it this way in his poem, *Our Lear*:

> We came here first as a means to escape
> from the many facets of murder and rape
> We found it to be a mental retreat
> A safe haven to conquer our own defeat
> A sanctuary now, a place to rehearse
> For a dozen or so with Shakespearean verse . . .
>
> . . . Kings being Kings and men being men
> For nine months we are allowed to pretend
> That we can escape this shame we are under
> And the physical aspects that keep us asunder
> We have been given a chance and a means
> To release from confinement our thoughts and our dreams . . .

Sanctuary helps to create a context for growth, but an element of challenge is also necessary. To this end, the containment and pressure chamber of the rehearsal space forces the men to confront themselves in unexpected ways. This most often occurs through personality conflicts. Instead of ignoring them or suppressing them, I home right in, seeing them as important opportunities for learning. For example, in our evaluation session for *Julius Caesar*, Drew talked about his conflict with Teddy, which had simmered for weeks and finally come to the surface when Teddy confronted Drew in the kitchen with questions about his ability and work ethic. We spent two hours working through the issues in one of our late rehearsals, and although Drew had formally apologized to Teddy for his part in the conflict, it was still not clear to me where things stood between them. Drew said that he had been thinking of possibly not coming to the evaluation session, when he ran into Teddy in the gym. When Teddy told Drew how much he was looking forward to the meeting, Drew understood that it was important, and that he needed to be there. Drew then tried to explain what he learned by working through his conflict with Teddy: "I learned that just because I want it in a certain way—it doesn't mean it's going to be that way. When I get into a conflict, I can step back and say, 'Let's see. What can *I* do to help address this situation?' I can see now that conflict stifles creativity. So I don't need him to be my enemy. I want him to be my friend." As Drew spoke, I looked over to see that Teddy was leaning forward and listening intently. His face was calm, and at moments the hint of a smile appeared. Drew continued: "You know, I see a parallel with all this and the controversy over Obama saying he's willing to talk to Hamas. I mean, what's the big deal? Of course you've gotta talk to your enemies. On the street, we call fighting 'funkin.' And talking to each other instead of fighting is called 'squashing the funk.' Ever since I squashed the funk with Teddy, good things have been happening to me. I got some money in the mail. My daughter came to visit me." In reflecting upon the significance of resolving his conflict with Teddy, Drew demonstrated his capacity to express empathy, insight, and self-awareness. The cultivation of these qualities, as well as enhanced cultural literacy, performance skills, a teamwork ethic, and playfulness, are all central to the Shakespeare Project.

Arts in Corrections: Building Social Capital

For me, the question of the moment is this: How can we, as artists, educators, and activists, build the institutional structures and social networks that will strengthen our efforts to open up, humanize, and ultimately transform the prison system? In my work at RCI, I have endeavored to strengthen our prison theater program by maintaining good relations with corrections officials (in 2006, I received the DOC's "Friend of Corrections" award), by raising community awareness, and by involving artists and educators who understand and value our work. Our success has been documented in glowing reviews from prisoners, community members, and experts like the founder and director of the Prison Creative Arts Project (Buzz Alexander, the Thurnau Professor of English Language and Literature at the University of Michigan), Laura Bates (associate professor of English at Indiana State University, and a twenty-year veteran of teaching Shakespeare in prison settings, including prisoners in solitary confinement), and Dr. Donald Hands, director of psychology for the Wisconsin State Department of Corrections (among many others).

In order for the work to remain viable, it is important to make it integral, even central, to my life as an academic. At UWP, I have successfully argued to my departmental executive committee that my prison theater work should receive recognition under the categories of teaching and service, as well as substantial weight under the category of research and creative activity. This has required some extraordinary effort on my part, in that the committee (rightfully) requested that I justify my argument with documentation and research and a proposed framework for the evaluation of my work. This meant that my annual report this year, in addition to the usual ten or so pages of summary of the year's activities, was supplemented by a fifty-four-page portfolio documenting my efforts with the Shakespeare Project. As a result, my department's executive committee now counts each iteration of the Shakespeare Project (rehearsals, peer-reviewed performances, and associated theoretical reflections) as a contribution to research. And so, as my prison theater work develops, I repeatedly find myself in the process of challenging and sometimes transforming the institutional boundaries of university life as well.

To try to further this process of transformation, and in hopes of connecting with other prison educators, artists, and activists, I attended the first (and so far only) Arts in Criminal Justice Conference, a national gathering held in Philadelphia in October 2007. This proved to be an invaluable opportunity for me to see and to be seen by artists and academics who had developed theater, music, and art programs in prisons and jails across the country. I shared news of my own work (displaying a large poster and running video on a continuous loop), and I also learned a great deal about what others were doing. The time seems right for us to share this work with larger audiences, and so I proposed an anthology titled *Performing New Lives: Prison Theatre* (London, England: Jessica Kingsley, forthcoming) The book will consist of a collection of fourteen essays by artists, academics, and other practitioners who create theater with incarcerated men, women, and youth in U.S. prisons and detention centers. Each chapter will explore the genesis and structure of the practitioner's work, followed by a tale from the field that focuses on a particular issue, challenge, or moment of transformation. A special concluding chapter will feature a dialogue among the practitioners, with the focus on what we have to learn from one another, and where we might go from here.

Epilogue

Despite our high profile and consistent success, the Shakespeare Project was not renewed by the RCI for 2008–2009. The warden's decision was supported by three considerations: (1) RCI's priority was now on preparing prisoners for reentry and reintegration, and this required a reallocation of staff and resources; (2) prisoners who had been a part of the Shakespeare Project for more than two years would no longer be able to participate because of an institution policy that does not allow a prisoner to be assigned to a position for more than two years; and (3) my proposal to use multiple facilitators for the program in 2008–2009 posed "a security risk." In my appeal of the decision, I argued that I could run the program on a zero budget (I should also have noted that the program is excellent preparation for prisoners' reentry and reintegration into society); that although the loss of program veterans would hurt the program and run counter to our ethics of teamwork, commitment, and leadership, I would be willing to continue the program under his enforcement of the "two years and out" policy (a policy that is not enforced with AODA and other programs); and that the three facilitators who would be joining me in the fall were highly qualified educators with a long history with the Shakespeare Project and who would receive the same volunteer training and security clearances as all other RCI volunteers. This issue in particular indicates how starkly different my perspective is from the warden's. What I saw as the most promising innovation in the program—in that it would move us away from a one-man show and toward a broad-based educational effort—is precisely what he saw as the greatest liability.

My appeal was denied—no reason was given other than that "the decision had already been made." Nonetheless, I hope that the men who have been a part of the Shakespeare Project will continue to carry inside themselves the confidence, the hope, and the enlarged sense of possibility that was engendered there. A recent letter from one of the participants encourages me: "What you have done has really given me direction in my life. You have helped me discover my bliss. I occasionally go back through my script, sometimes when I need a pick-me-up, other times just reflecting on great memories. Sometimes even just going over certain speeches and/or roles. People's comments I always go back to. One sticks out from someone who knows me better than anyone, who has known me a long time. Near the end of her comments, she captured everything the process has meant to me, in seven words—'You have found yourself. Go be happy.'" The prevalence of this kind of feedback tells me that I must continue this work, and so I will be seeking another prison where I can establish a sanctuary for prison theater. In the meantime, I will reflect, write, and strengthen my ties with those other artists, educators, and activists who are passionately committed to humanizing education behind bars.[12]

Notes

1. *The Blue Cliff Record*, trans. T. and J. C. Cleary (Boston: Shambhala, 1977), case 21, p. 139.

2. Rashad is a pseudonym, as are the names for the other prisoners represented in this essay; all quotations of their work are used with permission of each author.

3. Augusto Boal, *Theater of the Oppressed,* trans. Charles A. and Marie Odilia Leal McBride (New York: Urizen, 1979); Boal, *Games for Actors and Non-Actors,* trans. Adrian Jackson (New York: Routledge, 1992), 2.

4. John Longeway, *Studying Humanities for Practical Applications: What Is an Everyday Hero?* Grant application to the Wisconsin Humanities Council, 1996.

5. See Robert Moore and Douglas Gillette, *King, Warrior, Magician, Lover: Rediscovering the Archetypes of the Mature Masculine* (San Francisco: HarperCollins, 1990).

6. Bergman's work is described in Alun Mountford and Mark Farrall, "The House of Four Rooms: Theatre, Violence, and the Cycle of Change," in *Prison Theatre: Perspectives and Practices,* ed. J. Thompson (London: Jessica Kingsley, 1998), 109–26.

7. This version of the poem was narrated in the 1998 film *Smoke Signals* (Chris Eyre, director); the original poem can be found in Dick Lourie, *Ghost Radio* (Brooklyn: Hanging Loose Press, 1998), 48.

8. Lauren E. Glaze and Laura M. Maruschak, *Bureau of Justice Statistics Special Report: Parents in Prison and Their Minor Children* (Washington, DC: U.S. Department of Justice, 2008).

9. Brent Killackey, "Come, Let's Away to Prison: Prisoners at RCI Staged *King Lear*," *Racine Journal Times* (29 May 2005), A1; the story can be accessed at www.journaltimes.com/photo_galleries/KING_LEAR.HTM; Jean Feraca's Wisconsin Public Radio show, "Othello Behind Bars," is archived at www.wpr.org/hereonearth/archive_060617j.cfm; *Julius Caesar* was featured in *Wisconsin Trails* (September/October 2008); for other media coverage, see Associated Press, "Dysfunctional Fam-

ily in 'Lear' Hits Home for Inmates," *Chicago Sun-Times* (26 April 2005); Associated Press, "Inmates Stage King Lear: Producer Says Schemes, Struggles in 'Bleak' Play Resonate in Prison," *St. Paul Pioneer Press* (26 April 2005); Greg Berg, "The Morning Show: Interview with Jonathan Shailor on 'King Lear' at Racine Correctional Institution," WGTD (91.1 FM) at Gateway Technical College, Kenosha, WI, broadcast 29 April 2005; Terry Flores, "Night with the Bard: Racine Inmates Take on Roles, Challenges of 'King Lear,'" *Kenosha News* (28 April 2005), 1; Fox 6 (WITI-TV, Milwaukee), feature story: "King Lear Prison Production," broadcast (26 April 2005) at 9:00 pm and 10:00 pm; Meg Kissinger, "Captivating Theater: Inmates at Racine Prison to Stage Production of 'King Lear,'" *Milwaukee Journal Sentinel* (25 April 2005), 1; and Jodi Wilgoren, "In One Prison, Murder, Betrayal, and High Prose," *New York Times* (29 April 2005), A13.

10. The mother is quoted in Killackey, "Come, Let's Away to Prison," A1; the radio exchange is archived at www.wpr.org/HereOnEarth/archive_060617j.cfm.

11. Scott Kaiser, *Mastering Shakespeare: An Acting Class in Seven Scenes* (New York: Allworth Press, 2003).

12. For more on the Shakespeare Project, see Jonathan Shailor, "A Professor's Perspective: The Shakespeare Project at Racine Correctional Institution," in *Creating behind the Razor Wire: Perspectives from Arts in Corrections in the United States,* ed. Krista Brune (independently printed, 2007), 38–41, and "When Muddy Flowers Bloom: The Shakespeare Project at Racine Correctional Institution," *PMLA* 123, no. 3 (2008): 632–41.

Anger

Kenneth Sean Kelly

A member of the Writing Workshop at the Champaign County Jail, in Champaign, Illinois, Sean Kelly responded to the challenge to write a poem of self-improvement by taking responsibility for quelling his anger. This piece was published in *Captured Words/Free Thoughts* 5 (Summer 2008).

Anger
It's a demon that haunts
My heart and soul
Anger
I would love to tie it up
And dump mercy all over it
Then when it's dried, peel it like a banana
Anger
You mother fuckin' son-of-bitch
You cost me countless jobs
And relationships all because
You decided to push my buttons
But when I see myself in the mirror
I see the one person
Who's at fault for getting angry
So, Sean, please calm down

Chapter 10

Breaking Down the Walls: Inside-Out Learning and the Pedagogy of Transformation

Lori Pompa

In 1985, I stepped behind the walls of a prison for the first time. I remember being overwhelmed that day by a sensory cacophony of stale sweat, old sneakers, clanging bars, crumbling cement, deafening announcements over the P.A. system, and the palpable alienation of hundreds of men who seemed to be locked in a bizarre dance, trapped in a listless fugue arrested in time. Twenty-five years later, we are still locking people in cages; mass incarceration remains our default response to crime. If we had the political will, we could use our resources and creativity to address the social issues that lead to crime—but we continue to use cages instead.

As a host of scholars, critics, activists, and incarcerated men and women have observed, the massive incarceration employed in the name of justice compounds the brutalizing effects of crime and punishment on society. In venturing behind the walls of America's prisons, we immediately confront the difference between popular political rhetoric (about rehabilitation, law and order, keeping society safe) and the undeniable fact that we are, in fact, putting our fellow human beings in cages. Meet some of the men and women who have been isolated from society through imprisonment and the situation becomes clear: We are deepening the very problem that we claim to be addressing. If we think about it, anyone kept in this kind of dehumanizing situation for months or years at a time will emerge much worse for the experience.

The Inside-Out Prison Exchange Program (www.temple.edu/inside-out/) is dedicated to stopping this absurd cycle and is based on the belief that by engaging in dialogue, people on both sides of prison walls can discover new ways of thinking about ourselves, our society, and the systems that keep us all imprisoned—some of us literally and for excessively long periods. If we are ever going to abolish this disturbing reality, we need to build relationships across class and race and other social barriers; we need to connect with each other through the walls, both literally and figuratively. This is why I take my college students to jails and prisons. Before describing how that process works, however, allow me to explain how I came to this project, and then how it is implemented through what I call the pedagogy of transformation.

I have been going in and out of prisons and jails for twenty-five years and, in the process, have worked with thousands of men and women behind the walls. Through this work, I have learned much of what I know about crime, justice, incarceration, and the many social issues that are entwined in the prison-industrial complex. I began going into prison in 1985 as a volunteer. This was followed by several years of work with the Pennsylvania Prison Society and, eventually, teaching at Temple University. Throughout the years, my understanding of these problems and the people most directly affected by them was built, literally, from the inside out. In time, I and many others on both sides of the prison wall built The Inside-Out Prison Exchange Program, and over the years, its educational model evolved organically, intuitively, serendipitously, and democratically. Unfortunately, in this same period, the prison system has become increasingly punitive and isolating, mirroring America's retrograde notions about incarceration and education. In particular, two crime-related pieces of legislation—the Violent Crime Control and Law Enforcement Act (1993) and the Higher Education Reauthorization Act (1994)—virtually eliminated access to higher education for incarcerated women and men by, among other restrictions, abolishing Pell Grant eligibility for imprisoned students. For many adults and young people serving time in prison, being cut off from their educational birthright began even earlier; as Erica Meiners (chapter 1), Rose Braz and Myesha Williams (chapter 5), and Robin Sohnen (chapter 7) have demonstrated herein, their futures were sacrificed when resources were diverted from the education system in order to pay for the corrections system of which they are now a part.

At a time when secondary and postsecondary education is becoming a less-achievable goal for many people, especially those who are imprisoned, and while recidivism remains high, The Inside-Out Prison Exchange Program has developed a unique way to reinvigorate mainstream higher education and to return educational opportunities to incarcerated students, thereby changing individuals and institutions on both sides of the prison wall. The inclusion of college students not only widens the audience and impact of the program, but also is the key to the program's financial feasibility. In the absence of significant funding for prison education, the college or university essentially covers the cost of an Inside-Out course, with the possible exception of books for the incarcerated students. In this way, Inside-Out can leverage its work within one institution—the university—in order to pursue change within another—the prison.[1]

The program is guided by the fundamental principles of democracy, uses its model to explore the boundaries of democracy, and employs education to restore the basic tenets of democracy to a severely underrepresented voice in America. In so doing, the program has begun to create change in both academic and correctional institutions around the country. In fact, our model of inside-out pedagogy seems to operate like a wave of change lapping through the system. As it engages incarcerated individuals in a unique and challenging educational experience that can change their postprison trajectory, so it educates the next generation of corrections professionals and social justice activists, who garner a unique perspective that transforms their approach to the prison-industrial complex in particular and to their roles as citizens more broadly. Simultaneously, the program influences the overall environment of the prisons in which we work, as the administration and staff are affected by their tangential participation in Inside-Out. Finally, many instructors trained in the Inside-Out method report experiencing transformations in their approach to education and in their advocacy roles within their academic environments and their communities. The impact of Inside-Out thus steadily washes over every sector of society that it touches, impelling those involved toward a change in both personal choices and future policy. This is just one program, and our resources and staff are minimal, yet we aspire to building a new pedagogy of transformation and, in time, abolishing the policies and beliefs that underlie our punishing democracy.

Education in the Exchange:
"More Than Can Be Read in a Book"

The first intimations of the Inside-Out model grew out of the many trips my students and I made to prisons and jails to augment our classroom learning. During one such trip, to a state prison three hours outside Philadelphia, fifteen students and I engaged in a roundtable discussion with four men serving life sentences. The men were passionate and eloquent, the students were enthralled, and the conversation was complex, nuanced, and full of urgency, as some of the political, racial, economic, gendered, social, psychological, and philosophical dimensions of crime and justice were discussed. Toward the end of our session, Paul, an incarcerated participant, proposed to hold these kinds of conversations over an entire semester, as a formal class. His concept was given form and, two years later, became The Inside-Out Prison Exchange Program.

Inside-Out thus began as a single course that was hosted by Temple University and taught in one of the Philadelphia jails in the fall of 1997. The class was initially developed with a focus on what the undergraduate students would be able to learn about crime and justice by going behind the walls. We were to meet at the jail every other week and on campus during the alternate weeks to debrief the experience. However, during our first debriefing on campus, the students strongly suggested that this approach was flawed: They indicated that by meeting separately we would remain two isolated groups, and that this separation embodied differences in our positions that would lead to a sense of the on-campus students "studying" the imprisoned men on the inside. Such segregation, my students argued, would reproduce one of the problems we hoped to address. Persuaded (and humbled) by their observations, I immediately changed the syllabus and we began holding class inside the jail for the rest of the semester. Each week, fifteen to eighteen undergraduate students went behind the walls to hold class with a comparable number of men incarcerated in the facility.

In the combined group meeting each week, we would address some dimension of crime and justice: What are prisons for? Why do people get involved in crime? What are the myths and realities of prison life? What do we understand about victims and victimization? What are the distinctions between punishment and rehabilitation? The "outside" students brought different understandings to the readings than the "inside" students, yet neither group was ever homogeneous—alliances, conflicts, agreements, and disagreements flourished in all directions (as they do in any well-run class); everyone involved quickly learned to think beyond any inside/outside split. In short, the learning process helped the group transcend stereotypes; we were, together, engaged in a mutual process of discovery. As one student described that first class: "Most college courses are lectures and readings which, later on, we are supposed to apply to real-life situations. But this class was a real-life situation itself. The readings gave all of us facts, statistics, and the opinions of the 'experts,' but the class itself was what gave the course an additional meaning and another dimension. The students in the class gave it life—we taught each other more than can be read in a book." What stands out from this comment is not only the obvious sense that the student enjoyed the experience, but that she, a student at Temple, did not distinguish between anyone being an "inside" or an "outside" participant—her classmates were all just "students in the class." Along with the traditional educational accomplishments of the class, then, this student finished the semester having learned to see past someone as a person in prison, to recognize him instead as a fellow student, a fellow learner. This transcending of stereotypes may be one of the most important results of The Inside-Out Prison Exchange Program.[2]

Indeed, because Inside-Out challenges traditional college students to contextualize and rethink what they have learned in the classroom, they often gain insights that help them to better pursue the work of justice and social change. At the same time, because the course challenges imprisoned students to place their life experiences in a larger social context, it often rekindles their intellectual self-confidence and interest in further education. At its best, then, the process challenges everyone involved to work through their assumptions about others and their imposed limitations on themselves, to form new kinds of connections, to be open to each other, and hence to begin the long road of working toward social justice.

It is important to emphasize that outside participants are not studying their incarcerated classmates; they are not serving in a counseling or teaching or advising capacity vis-à-vis the men and women on the inside. In addition, the outside students do not know the specific charges for which the inside students are incarcerated, as it is neither the focus of the discussion nor anyone's business. Ironically, asking all students to achieve a high level of classroom trust and confidentiality is based in part on developing a boundary based on semianonymity in the classroom space: Only first names are used in class, no other identifying information is shared, and contact between inside and outside participants beyond the classroom is prohibited. These guidelines are one of the most challenging dimensions of the program, but they have helped to keep the fragile nature of Inside-Out and what the program is trying to achieve protected over the years. With more than twelve years of experience, we realize that if these guidelines were not in place, the program would probably no longer exist. Along with these logistical concerns, the parameters are meant to encourage honesty and trust and thus enable the classroom reciprocity and authenticity that makes The Inside-Out Prison Exchange Program experience so unique.

Ideally, the experience triggers a new way of seeing the world, in which everyone involved shares an opportunity to work through their stereotypes and myths. One of the inside students described the experience this way: "When you spend hours in a room with strangers on a weekly basis, those barriers that surround you and me crumble with the wonder of communication and the gratitude of someone accepting you as you, not because of your situation." While there are always individuals who have a more difficult time accepting differences, it has been a continual source of amazement that, by bringing people together in an atmosphere of trust and equality, the vast majority of participants begin to look at issues—and one another—in new ways.[3]

Moreover, while participants learn to look at the issues addressed in the class from new perspectives, a major goal of the program is to encourage participants to see themselves as actors in relation to these issues, and hence as potential agents of change. According to one outside student, "It was extremely empowering to have agency, to know that our opinions not only mattered, but could possibly effect positive change in our community and our criminal justice system." This sentiment is echoed by an inside student in describing his experience of Inside-Out: "It made me feel that I was making something happen that truly mattered, even if it was only in the boundaries of our classroom." The notion of "making something happen" is crucial to our program; in fact, over the years, many of our classes have developed projects (to which I refer below) that have moved from the prison classroom into the public. While institutional constraints cramp the learning and life possibilities of those on the inside, we continue to be inspired by the many incarcerated men and women who, on fire about the issues, figure out ways to make change within both their institutions and their home communities.

Expanding the Program, Realizing the Mission

Thus launched in 1997, The Inside-Out Prison Exchange Program continued for the next three years, all the while exploring the pedagogical and political imperatives discussed above. Then, in 2000, two colleagues from Temple expressed an interest in conducting their own courses based on the Inside-Out model. A professor from the psychology department developed a course, cross-listed with Women's Studies, titled "Parenting from Prison: Mothers on the Inside," which was offered every semester for four years, until her retirement. A second course was developed by a faculty member in the geography and urban studies department, called "Drugs in Urban Society," which has been taught each spring semester since 2002. In that same year, the program was further expanded to the State Correctional Institution at Graterford, a maximum-security prison an hour outside Philadelphia. This class went so well that the group, composed of eighteen inside students (many of whom are serving life sentences) and eighteen outside students (a mix of undergraduate and graduate students), decided to stay together beyond the semester to work on a series of projects focusing on reeducating the public about crime and justice. This group, which came to be called the Think Tank, is still meeting weekly, eight years later, though attrition and addition of new members have caused shifts in the group's composition. The Think Tank's projects have included a set of murals focused on victims and healing, designed in collaboration with Philadelphia's Mural Arts Program, victims, and artists incarcerated at Graterford; monthly theme-based workshops offered to students and members of the community; and original writings by the group that are being collected for publication. The first phase of Inside-Out thus expanded, adding more faculty participants and courses, taking the program into new facilities, stretching the classroom experience beyond the confines of academic semesters, turning classroom experiences into longstanding working groups, and making it possible for the men in the Graterford Think Tank to become core members of the Inside-Out planning team.

The second phase of program expansion entailed launching the program nationally. I began this phase in 2003, when I received a Soros Justice Senior Fellowship. During my fellowship year, I worked in close collaboration with individuals from Temple University, Graterford Prison, and fellow teachers and practitioners from as far away as Oregon. Together, we built an outreach strategy, produced public-relations and pedagogical materials, formulated a training curriculum, and began a fundraising strategy. Then, in July 2004, we held our first Inside-Out National Instructor Training Institute. Expecting to draw the interest of a small handful of professors, the first training instead brought together more than twenty instructors from a dozen states. The success of this first attempt led us to begin offering three training sessions each year. These intensive, weeklong training institutes are notable for their style: The training format mirrors the hands-on, dialogic process employed in Inside-Out classes. As of April 2010, more than 200 instructors from 120 colleges and universities in 35 states and abroad had taken part in an Inside-Out training. As a result of these training sessions, dozens of Inside-Out courses—offered in many and varied disciplines—are now conducted each academic semester in correctional facilities across the country. Courses are held at federal, state, and local institutions, as well as at juvenile facilities and work-release centers, offering titles such as "Regulating Citizenship," "Crisis and Transcendence," "Women and the Penal System," and "Community Organizing: Social Movements for Change Both Inside and Outside." These classes are taught by instructors from major research universities, small liberal arts colleges, and community colleges—in urban, suburban, and rural settings—in the Pacific Northwest, the Midwest, the South, and the Northeast. At this point, at least 7,500 inside and outside students have taken part in an Inside-Out class somewhere in the country.

As the Inside-Out program has expanded nationally, we have seen some important changes within the program. For example, over the years, the Graterford Think Tank has come to play a critical role in the training process; in fact, two days of each instructor training are spent with the Think Tank inside Graterford Prison. During these working sessions with the Think Tank, something unusual happens: College instructors become students who are taught by men serving life sentences. According to those who have taken the training, this component is among the most important parts of the training experience. The intense interaction with, and feedback from, the Think Tank helps instructors both envision and experience how the Inside-Out model works. Consequently, even as we expand our program nationally, our vision continues to evolve: Professors become students, imprisoned students become teachers, students and teachers alike become change agents—and so we continue to work for justice, learn about ourselves, and explore new ways of being and working together.

In 2008 the program began planning for even greater expansion with a comprehensive, three-year, state-by-state growth model. The plan includes a large national mapping project, which will document every academic institution and correctional facility in the nation, helping to facilitate natural linkages and areas of high priority. Inside-Out is also incorporating educators in a wider array of disciplinary fields, thus enabling us to develop a multidisciplinary educational model. This initiative will infuse various disciplines and perspectives into the larger discussion, expose a broader range of outside students to the complex corrections climate, and provide a richer educational experience for inside students. Just as important, we hope this move to broaden our offerings will help to bolster the case for reinstituting credit-bearing education programs inside prisons.

Inside-Out Pedagogy as the Groundwork for Social Justice

The Inside-Out model employs the principles of democracy while pursuing a pedagogy of transformation. Through a process informed by these principles, students participate in lively debate, rigorous coursework, and in-depth analysis of the larger society, as understood through the lens of the prison-industrial complex, or what we refer to as the "prism of prison." This unique pedagogical model could appropriately be called "Inside-Out Learning." The phrase suggests many possible interpretations: education or experiences that turn one's life inside out; inviting out what is inside people (their thoughts, reactions, assumptions, and creativity); enabling the voices of people living inside prison to emerge from behind the walls; taking what is learned on the inside (of prison) out into the world through action; in time, through efforts focused on social change, perhaps even turning society and its structures inside-out; and so on. In short, we could say that the pedagogical model driving The Inside-Out Prison Exchange Program begins to lay the groundwork for social justice and social change. To pursue this claim, the following sections describe in more detail some of the core pedagogical and political commitments of Inside-Out Learning.

Learning with the Whole Self

Traditional college courses often teach students to consume prepackaged information through a routinized process of memorization and test-taking. Paulo Freire famously criticized this kind of learning as "the banking concept of education," wherein ideas, like money, were stuffed into passive receptacles who received their cargo without changing it, challenging it, or considering it critically. In contrast to this banking method, Inside-Out challenges students both intellectually and emotionally; rather than learning "from the eyebrows up," students learn with the whole self in the context of a community of learners. Participants are challenged to consider issues from multiple perspectives and, in the process, often reconsider dimensions of themselves as well. As Alison Cook-Sather recommends in *Education Is Translation*, creative pedagogy enables students to "take up the composed and readable versions of themselves that they have constructed and carried with them" and, through a combination of challenging and empowering exercises, prods them to "translate those versions with the support of teachers and other students." If done well, such translations, such learning-with-the-whole-self, can have a transformative effect on students. Indeed, here is how one outside student evaluated her experience in the program: "Inside-Out was a life-changing experience. It has changed not only the way that I view the criminal justice system and incarcerated people, but also the way that I view society in general. . . . This class has allowed me to work through personal biases. It has done more for me than I ever could have imagined or hoped." This kind of evaluation is common, as students often report that participating in the Inside-Out program changed their lives. For students on the inside, the benefits can sometimes veer into even deeper waters. For example, one inside student reported that, prior to joining the program, "I was becoming hardened by my time in prison and feeling bitter toward a society I felt gave up on me. I did not think I was going to make it." But that student did make it, and he performed admirably in the program, thus finding not only a renewed purpose but multiple reasons to dedicate himself to new academic goals and political hopes.[4]

One reason for such powerful responses to the Inside-Out experience is related to the principle of incorporating the whole self in the learning process. Rather than the atomized, individually oriented, test-taking focus of so much of the traditional educational process, we emphasize learning together through collaboration, dialogue, and engagement. The experience of the face-to-face interaction of inside and outside students draws forth both abilities and responsibilities in those participating in the process, creating a setting that challenges all participants to be accountable for what happens in the learning process. As bell hooks explains: "Making the classroom a democratic setting where everyone feels a responsibility to contribute is a central goal of transformative pedagogy." The classroom then becomes both a microcosm and a beacon of what can happen in the larger world. I should note that the process is neither easy nor comfortable; in fact, the messiness of human interactions is always present, meaning the race, class, political, religious, gender, and other distinctions that are often ignored in traditional college courses are foregrounded in our discussions. The key point, however, is that by employing Inside-Out Learning, these differences are addressed through an open, dialogic process that allows participants to approach conflict in new and creative ways.[5]

What makes the Inside-Out program transformative is the emphasis on learning within a collaborative environment where the subject matter is not only present in books, but in people's lives as well. That is, half the students in any class are living the daily realities of the contemporary U.S. criminal justice system and the other half arrive with any number of assumptions about this system and the individuals involved in it. As inside and outside students begin to share their perspectives and knowledge with one another, the abstract becomes concrete, the concrete is understood within a larger framework, and strangers begin to perceive each other as neighbors caught within the same interlocking systems of power, prejudice, and privilege. Social issues, therefore, become personal and the personal is viewed in a wider social context. This process can be both unsettling and empowering, exciting and deeply disturbing. As one former outside student explained, "I was unprepared for the emotional identification and passion I now feel about the issues." Accustomed to attending classes from which he could leave, his heart and mind unchanged, this student was surprised to find himself identifying with the subject matter so intensely. A former inside student was similarly enlivened by the experience, claiming that "I don't think I have ever felt such a strong change occur inside of me and it will be something that I hold for the rest of my life." The experience leaves some students feeling compelled to shift their focus in fundamental ways, as seen in an outside student's comment that the program "has acted as the catalyst in my passion for life and human rights, and was the pivotal point where I realigned my own path."

At the same time, working collaboratively with others can also reveal to students how they may have cheated themselves in the past. For example, one former inside student admitted that "I've unfortunately never put my mind to accomplishing very much. But by taking this and other classes, I am seeing in action what I've always been told and consequently have always believed, yet never really done. That is, now I know I can be successful." This student had been skating by, doing the least work possible; but here he was, following his immersion in the program, talking confidently of reclaiming his life by dedicating himself to doing his best. For other students, the experience produces, besides a commitment to changing their own work habits and perspectives, the desire to enable others to achieve success. As one former outside student put it, "My experience this semester has not only helped me to shed some light on my own prejudices and misconceptions, but it has also strengthened and reinforced my desire to facilitate the process of growing, changing, and realizing the strength and power that is contained in a voice." While the first student quoted above expresses a renewed commitment to himself, this second student proclaims a new dedication to creating spaces for multiple voices to join a dialogue about social change.

Ideally, this mode of learning-with-the-whole-self nudges students to both understand and embody the difference between power and authority. In *The Courage to Teach*, Parker Palmer suggests that "we often confuse authority with power, but the two are not the same. Power works from the outside in, but authority works from the inside out." Whereas power is imposed from above, "authority is granted to people who are perceived as *authoring* their own words, their own actions, their own lives, rather than playing a scripted role at great remove from their own hearts." In Palmer's model, power is exterior to the self, while authority is what we earn through hard work, self-recognition, and respect shown to others. One of the key moments in grasping this distinction is when students begin to understand that *what they say matters*, and that how we speak, in some measure, defines who we are. In fact, recognizing their unique voices (and, therefore, their different modes of authority) is a precursor to participants beginning to see a vital role for themselves as agents of social change. Hearing the unique voices of others, and being afforded the space to speak their own truths, serves an especially crucial function for imprisoned students, who are locked behind walls meant to produce silence, not exchanges. For example, one former inside student reported that "I've emerged from the Inside-Out experience empowered with an unshakable belief in the human capacity to evolve to a higher state of social consciousness." The Inside-Out model of transformative pedagogy assumes that learning-with-the-whole-self leads to these kinds of epiphanies, thus supporting nothing less than the pursuit of "a higher state of social consciousness."[6]

Students as Producers; Learning as Community Building

The core curriculum of Inside-Out is rigorous, with weekly reading assignments, several analytical and reflective papers incorporating the readings, group discussions, class projects, and a final comprehensive, integrative paper. This coursework serves a number of purposes beyond the normal academic expectations in most classes. First, the readings help to elevate the conversation, as the inside and outside students become equally informed on the basic facts. In this traditional sense, the readings are meant to be both informative and empowering, as they create a shared knowledge base that informs our deliberations. Second, because the course is so dialogue-heavy, doing the readings encourages the students' sense of responsibility to each other and to their shared education. Third, the assigned papers provide an opportunity for all participants to integrate the intellectual and emotional components of their shared experience. These papers help to amplify and facilitate the whole-self learning process. Fourth, instead of the "banking" model of learning, we emphasize that our course readings offer students an opportunity to place their life experiences in a broader context. Rather than just consuming such readings, the students often have personal experiences to bring to the text; in this capacity, they are knowledge-producers, sharers of information, experts in the materials at hand. And while some students come to the texts with knowledge that supplements the arguments of scholars, others find that the texts help them to make sense of their lives by offering a big-picture perspective on experiences that may before have seemed inexplicable.

This mutual transit of information, between assigned readings and classroom participants, can sometimes become so intense that it spills out of the classroom and into the prison. As one inside student observed, "I go back to my cell and think, and two to three days later, I'm still talking about it." We have found over the years that the readings, and the discussions they inspire, provide new topics for conversation and contemplation on the cell blocks where the incarcerated students reside. As a result of these ongoing conversations, it is not uncommon that a sense of community develops on the blocks, where each week's Inside-Out discussion becomes the impetus for debate. In addition, many of the inside students, having abandoned (or been abandoned by) the educational system, come to appreciate what it is like to be in college and to tackle college-level work; this often serves as motivation to seek other educational pursuits.[7]

One of the challenges of this pedagogical approach involves moving from a focus on a canon of knowledge to be imparted by the instructor to a methodology centered on the learners as searchers and creators of new knowledge. As Cook-Sather argues, "I find it imperative that students be as active as possible in their own educational processes. I believe that their being active is, in fact, the only way they will really learn, and that means that I cannot cover as much material or control as much of the process." Similarly, Palmer speaks of the need to "define the course in a way more engaging than engorging, countering my tendency to inundate students with data, and allowing them instead to encounter the subject, each other, and themselves." The emphasis, then, is not on flooding students with materials that they are expected to consume, but rather offering just enough material to help frame conversations that could, ideally, lead to places outside the texts. Readings are prompts to discovery, invitations to dialogue. As one former outside student put it, "I prefer to call the class *an experience*, because while we learned about the criminal justice system, victimization, and restorative justice, we were also able to learn about ourselves. We expressed ourselves freely and respectfully, and through those expressions, we compiled new ways of thinking."[8]

As anyone who has ever taught a class on any subject at any level will attest, students are only likely to "compile new ways of thinking" if they feel safe, if they sense that the classroom is a zone of mutual respect, shared dignity, and equality. Accordingly, a fundamental goal of Inside-Out Learning is to create an atmosphere in which people invite one another to be their best selves. To facilitate this delicate process, several elements of the curriculum are designed to foster equality, genuineness, and mutual respect among participants. For instance, early in the semester, ice-breaker and community-building exercises are used to facilitate participants' beginning to connect with one another, identify commonalities, and build trust. We utilize several activities that serve to reduce the anxiety that is often felt in the first week or two of the course. One example, the Wagon Wheel, adapted from Sidney Simon's *Values Clarification*, asks students to sit in two concentric circles, so that inside students and outside students are paired. An unfinished sentence is provided ("My motto is . . ." or "You would be surprised to know that I . . .") as a prompt for a very brief exchange. After about a minute, the outside circle rotates to the right, each person is paired with someone new, and the group is given a different sentence. It is a simple, nonthreatening, and nonintrusive way for people in the group to quickly meet one another.[9]

These trust-building exercises are crucial for encouraging participants to feel that they can be honest within the classroom. As one former inside student observed, "I must admit I thought we were going to be misunderstood and put under a microscope, but such was not the case." He entered with great caution, but the exercises convinced him that he could come to class feeling like an equal. One place to begin this process of creating trust and mutual respect is by abolishing labels such as "inmate" or "prisoner" or "criminal." Indeed, we spend significant time discussing the power of labels early in the semester; all participants are asked to avoid using labeling language and to strive to see the person beyond the particular characteristics that serve as qualifiers (and too often, definitions) of the person. The pedagogical and political imperatives driving this process are mirrored beautifully in the observations of a former outside student, who explained: "One word or label can never sufficiently qualify the value of a life. *Chick. Woman. Man. Boy. Criminal. Delinquent.* There is power in labels. They are more than classification, they are a caste system. Every paper, I confronted how to address incarcerated people fairly, but the truth is no one can fairly confine an entire population into one word. . . . The important lesson is to focus on the person, not the label or the crime." Eschewing such labels, Inside-Out participants learn to see their classmates simply as fellow agents in a shared learning community. The success of this model was articulated by a former inside student, who noted that "we were just people engaging each other on a basic human level." Of course, the reality is much more complex: At the end of each session, half the class members exit through the prison gate and the other half are locked, once again, in cages. This immutable fact is felt each week by inside and outside students alike. Nonetheless, for the period of time that these two groups become one in the classroom, that distinction fades, allowing individuals to interact with one another in a dignified, empowering, and transformative setting.

Inside-Out stresses that this sort of engagement involves not only speaking clearly and honestly, but listening carefully and thoughtfully. Together, students craft guidelines for dialogue to be followed during the semester and determine together how to hold each other accountable to those guidelines. These guidelines involve ways of listening, responding rather than reacting, and respecting the viewpoints of others. As bell hooks argues, "one of the responsibilities of the teacher is to help create an environment where students learn that in addition to speaking, it is important to listen respectfully to others. . . . [A] focus on student voice raises a whole range of questions about silencing." The issue of silencing and "voice" is especially significant for incarcerated students, many of whom have experienced years of silencing at the hands of forces that have, in large measure, rendered them unable to use the voices they have.[10]

As one simple means of facilitating this attention to voice and listening, all Inside-Out classes are conducted in a circle, allowing everyone in the class to face each other. This arrangement moves power away from the instructor and back to the students, thereby facilitating a sense of shared responsibility for the quality and direction of the discussion. As one former outside student noted, in contrast to sitting in large auditoriums, or in rows, both of which encourage obscurity and a sense of separation, the Inside-Out classroom "is circular, meaning, we all get to see each other's face and not the back of their heads. This method acts as a window for honesty." The basic act of looking at each other, of seeing and being seen while both speaking and listening, engenders a level of intensity not found in traditional classrooms. This circular seating and emphasis on listening opens up new avenues of engagement between students, leading to an interpersonal as well as intellectual experience. As a former inside student observed, "Inside-Out prioritizes the responsibility we have to one another." Acknowledging that responsibility means that students in the Inside-Out program move beyond labels to see each other as individuals, they move beyond being consumers of ideas to acting as producers of knowledge, and they move beyond being silenced and isolated information gatherers to being vocal members of a vibrant community.

Ideally, these transformations merge embodied experiences with heady intellectual inquiry. For example, the concepts of "free" and "unfree" are recurring themes in Inside-Out coursework and discussions, as Inside-Out students experience and explore the complex nature of physical, emotional, intellectual, and spiritual freedom and "unfreedom." This happens when a "free" outside student becomes "unfree" as he or she is temporarily incarcerated during class, or when the "unfree" inside student experiences a measure of freedom when participating in conversations of depth and import in a newly created space that belies the restrictiveness of the context in which the class is being held. Participants free their minds of preconceived notions during class and can see the ways their thinking—about themselves and their society—had been constrained. When both inside and outside students begin to experience the power that stems from an open and engaged mind, they are free to consider alternate paths for their lives and their visions of the world. Indeed, these various elements—the protective guidelines, the empowering circle, the community-building exercises—create a space where it is safe to voice the hopes, fears, and nascent visions imprisoned in each of us. Many students have reported that, in comparison with other group settings, they felt comfortable saying what they really meant, knowing that their words and ideas would be respected, honored, and valued. As educator and philosopher David Hawkins described it, "The most basic gift is not love but respect—respect for others as ends in themselves, as actual and potential artisans of their own learnings and doings, of their own lives; and as thus uniquely contributing, in turn, to the learnings and doings of others."[11]

Reveling in the Unexpected, Finding Commitment

Both inside and outside students are disarmed by their experiences in the Inside-Out classroom; they often find themselves confronting situations described by transformative learning theorist Jack Mezirow as "disorienting dilemmas." For outside students, choosing to enter a prison produces any number of responses, sometimes about their own lives, sometimes about the lives of the individuals warehoused there, or sometimes about the relationships between those who are free and those who are not. One student found himself amazed at the sheer physicality of the prison, the reality of the series of locked doors. He described "that feeling of being locked down as you progressively move through gate after gate after gate, and just being locked in, having somebody open the door in front of you, but having that door, the last door behind you, close." For this student, imprisonment took on physical connotations. For another student, going into prison triggered thoughts about the purpose of these institutions: "The prison itself was a creepy place. . . . Its institutional ambiance reminded me of my days at the Air Force Academy, a place where young adults are treated as children, where every breath they take is regulated by the military structure. It reminded me of the type of brainwashing that went on there. I remembered the days and nights when I wanted to scream, 'What the hell am I doing here?' I remember wanting to escape. The prison's institutionalization made me wonder: 'Can you brainwash [people] into a law abiding life'?" For other students, the "disorienting dilemma" occurred not upon entering the prison but upon leaving it, when the undeniable fact of walking through a door separating their classmates into two distinct groups created moments of cognitive dissonance. As one student confessed, "Walking out of that place every week was hard. It was hard because that was the moment that forced me to face the fact that not all of us were allowed to leave." For this student, the incarceration of her classmates was felt most keenly when she had to leave them behind. In each of the cases noted here, the "disorienting dilemma" of entering or leaving a prison opened up new pathways to learning.[12]

For imprisoned students, the "disorienting dilemmas" occur for other reasons, often stemming from the fact that participating in Inside-Out classes transgresses many of the brutalizing norms of behavior that structure prison life. Indeed, in contrast with the daily horrors of prison life, being treated like a human being and having a space for expression can sometimes be shocking. Ideally, these moments of disruption open up space for growth and change. As a member of the Think Tank (and an instructor in our program) theorized this situation: "If you are a person who has been told your whole life that you're not worth anything, that you've got nothing to contribute, then to have this experience where you are not a liability but an asset—that what you bring to the table is essential—well, that experience can be transformative, transforming oneself both as self and as a member of the community. Suddenly seeing yourself as part of the solution rather than part of the problem is a very powerful thing." For many inside students, this "powerful thing" meant seeing themselves as more capable than they had thought; the class invited them to think in new ways about themselves and their capacities. Inside-Out assumes that such moments of recognizing previously denied self-worth can be the first step toward taking responsibility for building a different life, one in which the student is no longer "not worth anything," but instead "part of the solution."

For some outside students, the reverse is true, and this too can be "a very powerful thing." For example, one outside student observed that "some of the inside students perceived the [outside] students as more intelligent simply because we are in college. This amazed me because some of the most insightful and intellectual comments came from inside students. I felt like the uneducated person, because my education of the justice system had primarily been limited to myths perpetrated by the media." Inside students, taught to think of themselves as useless and voiceless, learn that they are knowledgeable; outside students, taught to think of themselves as well informed, learn that some portion of what they know is nothing more than myth. Both realizations open new doors to better understanding. Such disorienting dilemmas ultimately prod students to ask big questions, not only about their individual learning habits and communication skills, but about their places in society more broadly. It is intriguing that many outside students, ostensibly free, often quite privileged in their class background, express deep frustration with what they perceive as their own powerlessness. Part of Inside-Out Learning is geared toward discussing such frustration and working through it. Here is how one student responded to the experience: "The struggle for me is often frustrating: seeing injustice, trying to change things, sometimes failing and wondering whether anything I can do will make a real difference in people's lives. This course did not eliminate my frustrations. It intensified them. It forced me to look closely at things I may never be able to change. But in facing that, I was able to move past my frustration, to clarify my interests and abilities, and to imagine different ways of being and moving and speaking in this world." This student made a brave leap: she worked from the disorienting dilemma caused by entering and learning in a prison through her personal frustrations and on toward commitment. She did not necessarily resolve anything, yet she built a sense of working toward a goal. As Palmer notes, "Good education may leave students deeply dissatisfied, at least for a while. . . . [S]tudents who have been served by good teachers may walk away angry—angry that their prejudices have been challenged and their sense of self shaken. That sort of dissatisfaction may be a sign that real education has happened."[13]

Conclusion

The Inside-Out Prison Exchange Program strives not only to enable students from both sides of the wall to learn exciting new things about themselves, each other, and their society, but to prod them toward making a commitment to working for social change. As Freire has argued, liberatory pedagogy impels us "to create an education that enlarges and amplifies the horizon of critical understanding of the people, to create an education devoted to freedom." It is difficult to offer a blueprint for what that freedom might look like in the long run, but here is one student's description of its implications, based on our classroom experience:

> What a motley crew we made in that little program room at [the prison]. I often think about the incredible dynamic of our group and wonder what we must look like to the people outside that room. People of different colors, sexes, ages, education levels, social classes and opinions in a circle, laughing, talking, arguing and respecting each other for hours at a time. It has to make it difficult for anyone who watches to hold on to the status quo. The status quo says that doesn't happen. It says that people are different and that some things are never going to change. For two and a half hours every [week] this semester, we proved that untrue.

For college students who sometimes find themselves trapped inside the narrow expectations attached to ever-more-specialized career paths, the Inside-Out experience offers an opportunity to explore vistas that pull at the edges of what they already know, both about the subject at hand and about themselves. And in a world where individuals who are incarcerated wear wristbands with bar codes cataloguing their personal information, the experience of being treated as an equal can have a deeply liberating effect. And so both inside and outside students report that the Inside-Out program leaves them changed, motivated, eager to tackle the many problems of the prison-industrial complex.[14]

This approach to learning holds the promise of rehumanizing and reinvigorating the educational process, which in turn heralds new ways of relating to others and being in the world. In the words of a member of the Graterford Think Tank, "The Inside-Out experience . . . creates an alchemical transformation, fusing classroom learning with behind-the-bars reality, galvanizing students from both sides of the wall to look deeper into issues of criminal justice and deeper into themselves. The final product is a new educational alloy: students wanting to learn and eagerly seeking answers." These experiences feed our ultimate hope that growing numbers of Inside-Out students and alumni across the country will become emissaries of change and, in whatever situations they find themselves, begin to make the walls that we construct between us—so dramatically and tragically manifest in our prison walls—more and more permeable and, eventually, extinct.

Notes

1. In most cases, instructors teach their Inside-Out class as part of their usual course load, so there is no additional cost to the college or university. The issue of credit for inside students, however, presents both a challenge and an opportunity: Some educational institutions will fully or partially waive the fee for credits, while in other cases, the correctional institution may provide some limited financial assistance to the inside student. The key point is that instructors need to patch together whatever solutions are possible in their particular situations, including being creative about securing books and other materials for the inside students.

2. This passage, and all other quoted testimonies from Inside-Out participants, is used with permission of the author; for background on the pedagogical principles noted here, see Myles Horton and Paulo Freire, *We Make the Road by Walking: Conversations on Education and Social Change,* ed. Brenda Bell, John Gaventa, and John Peters (Philadelphia: Temple University Press, 1990).

3. A similar balancing act is discussed by Buzz Alexander in his essay in this volume (chapter 6); and see the dilemmas of boundaries in prison education and activism as discussed in Judith Tannenbaum, *Disguised as a Poem: My Years Teaching Poetry at San Quentin* (Boston: Northeastern University Press, 2000).

4. Paulo Freire, *Pedagogy of the Oppressed,* 30th anniv. ed., trans. Myra Bergman Ramos (New York: Continuum, 2000), 72; Alison Cook-Sather, *Education Is Transla-*

tion: A Metaphor for Change in Learning and Teaching (Philadelphia: University of Pennsylvania Press, 2006), 38.

5. bell hooks, *Teaching to Transgress: Education as the Practice of Freedom* (New York: Routledge, 1994), 39; and see Douglas L. Robertson, "Facilitating Transformative Learning: Attending to the Dynamics of the Educational Helping Relationship," *Adult Education Quarterly* 47, no. 1 (1996): 41–54; for the political implications of such work, see Henry A. Giroux, *Border Crossings: Cultural Workers and the Politics of Education* (New York: Routledge, 1992).

6. Parker J. Palmer, *The Courage to Teach: Exploring the Inner Landscape of a Teacher's Life* (San Francisco: Jossey-Bass, 1998), 33.

7. The claim that classrooms in prisons spur educational goals and creative pursuits throughout prisons as a whole is echoed in the essays herein by Buzz Alexander (chapter 6) and Robin Sohnen (chapter 7); for discussion of this outreach effect, see Stephen John Hartnett, "Lincoln and Douglas Engage the Abolitionist David Walker in Prison Debate: Empowering Education, Applied Communication, and Social Justice," *Journal of Applied Communication Research* 26, no. 2 (1998): 232–53.

8. Cook-Sather, *Education Is Translation*, 21; Palmer, *Courage to Teach*, 133. See the argument along these same lines in Freire, *Pedagogy of the Oppressed*, and hooks, *Teaching to Transgress*.

9. See Sidney Simon, *Values Clarification* (New York: Grand Central, 1995).

10. hooks, *Teaching to Transgress*, 150.

11. Hawkins quoted in Cook-Sather, *Education Is Translation*, 146.

12. On "disorienting dilemmas," see Jack Mezirow, "Transformation Theory of Adult Learning," in *In Defense of the Lifeworld: Critical Perspectives on Adult Learning*, ed. M. R. Welton (New York: SUNY Press, 1995), 39–70, quotation on 50; for more on the emotional work of entering and leaving prisons, see Tannenbaum, *Disguised as a Poem*, 11–14, and Stephen John Hartnett, *Incarceration Nation: Investigative Prison Poems of Hope and Terror* (Walnut Creek, CA: AltaMira, 2004), 33–41, 45–46, and 117–22.

13. Palmer, *Courage to Teach*, 94.

14. Paulo Freire, *Cultural Action for Freedom* (Cambridge, MA: Harvard Educational Review and Center for the Study of Development and Social Change, 1970), 219.

Appendix: Prisoner Art and the Work of Community Building

Janie Paul, PCAP Art Exhibition Curator

During the fifteen years of the Prison Creative Arts Project's Annual Exhibitions of Art by Michigan Prisoners, more than 1,500 men and women from nearly fifty Michigan prisons have exhibited their work at the University of Michigan. Some artists have exhibited many times, evolving and perfecting their work over the years, knowing that once a year they will be honored and appreciated. The exhibitions offer ways for incarcerated artists to grow as thinkers and creators; just as important, the exhibitions create spaces where imprisoned artists enter the world and help to break down the stereotypes that have come to dominate our national conversations about crime and punishment. If you could see the gallery space as it fills up with the family members of exhibiting artists, students and teachers, citizens of Ann Arbor and beyond (each year, between 3,700 and 4,100 people visit the gallery during a two-week period), then you would know how the exhibitions create community by redrawing the boundaries that normally separate those inside prisons and those who live "in the world."

When you walk into the gallery, you see people studying the biography books in which the artists have written statements about themselves and their work. You see a family looking for the art made by their son or brother or sister or mother; when they find the work, they might pose for a photograph in front of the piece, standing proud or amazed or grieving. You see a man quietly crying in front of a painting by his long-lost father. You see one of our staff or volunteers leading a tour for a group of developmentally disabled youth, a group of senior citizens, or youth from a drop-in center. Everywhere you look, you see groups of friends clustered in front of a piece of art, talking about it, debating its meanings, pulling other friends over to see what they have found. You see college students sitting before a work, taking notes for a letter that they will write to the artist. You see our community engaging in serious reflection about what the artists have put forth, about their own preconceptions and in some cases about the costs and consequences of how we respond to crime and violence. As the conversations roll on, they often turn to *what to do*, how to end the damage caused by our crisis of mass incarceration.

If you could see into the prison a few weeks later, you would see an incarcerated artist receiving her package in the mail, finding a quiet place to open it, and reading the comments in the guest book, perhaps one specifically written to her; she would then flip through the other materials sent to her, including local newspaper reviews, perhaps finding there an image of her work. You might see her go into her cell by herself to cry before tucking the package under her mattress or into her jacket. As the days pass, she will return to those materials again and again, both proud to have been seen as an artist and challenged to produce more work for next year's exhibition. Those of us who help organize these shows believe that they sustain these artists in their resistance to the hostile and dehumanizing world of prison, where almost everything works against their growth. We believe—and their art and words tell us—that each drawing and painting is a form of resistance against everyone who tells them they are nothing and that they are incapable of good. Working against such accusations, making art is a form of resistance to the barrenness, hostility, and meaninglessness of life in prison.

Each of the artists included in these pages has made a major contribution to the exhibitions. They have created beauty where there was none. They have created meaning where there was none. They have strived to perfect their craft through hours of labor. They have developed unique visual images for expressing what cannot be said in words. And so we honor their efforts and vision by including their work here. Readers who seek more information about the annual Prison Creative Arts Project's Exhibitions of Art by Michigan Prisoners may contact us at www.prisonarts.org.

Contributors

Buzz Alexander is the founder of the Prison Creative Arts Project and the Arthur A. Thurnau Professor of English at the University of Michigan. He is a member of the Sisters Within Theater Troupe at Huron Valley Correctional Facility and a cocurator of the Annual Exhibition of Art by Michigan Prisoners. He is the author of *William Dean Howells: The Realist as Humanist; Film on the Left: American Documentary Film from 1931 to 1942*; and numerous essays and poems. His *Is William Martinez Not Our Brother? Twenty Years of the Prison Creative Arts Project* will be published in 2010. In 2005 the Carnegie Foundation for the Advancement of Teaching and the Council for Advancement and Support of Education named him Professor of the Year. He can be contacted at the Department of English, 3187 Angell Hall, University of Michigan, Ann Arbor, MI 48109–1003; or at alexi@umich.edu; the website for PCAP is www.prisonarts.org.

Rose Braz was the campaign director for Critical Resistance, a national grassroots organization committed to abolishing the prison-industrial complex, for ten years. Prior to helping to found Critical Resistance, Braz graduated from the University of California at Berkeley School of Law and worked as a criminal defense attorney. She serves on the board of Justice Now and on the advisory board of the California Coalition for Women Prisoners, and she is climate campaign coordinator for the Center for Biological Diversity. She has published pieces in the *Los Angeles Times, San Francisco Chronicle, Radical History Review*, and *Women, Girls, and Criminal Justice*. Her work draws on personal experience supporting family members affected directly by the prison-industrial complex. She can be contacted at Critical Resistance, 1904 Franklin Street, Suite 504, Oakland, CA 94612; or at rose@criticalresistance.org; the Critical Resistance website is www.criticalresistance.org.

Travis L. Dixon is an associate professor in the Department of Communication at the University of Illinois–Urbana-Champaign. He studies the portrayal of people of color in the mass media and the effects of these images on audiences. His scholarly work has appeared in several journals in the field of communication, including the *Journal of Communication*, *Communication Research*, and *Communication Monographs*. He can be reached at tldixon@illinois.edu.

Garrett Albert Duncan is an associate professor of education in arts and sciences at Washington University in St. Louis, where he also holds appointments in African and African-American Studies, American Culture Studies, and Urban Studies. He is also the director of the Program in African and African-American Studies in Arts and Sciences. His work experiences include eight years teaching science in public secondary schools in Pomona, California; two years teaching ethics in St. Louis at the top-rated high school in Missouri; and a brief stint teaching GED courses to incarcerated male teenagers at the Fred C. Nelles School for Boys in Whittier, California. He has published in *Social Justice*, *Educational Theory*, *Journal of Negro Education*, *Anthropology and Education Quarterly*, and *Teachers College Record*, among other journals and edited and reference books. He can be contacted at gaduncan@wustl. edu, or at Washington University in St. Louis, One Brookings Drive, Campus Box 1183, St. Louis, MO 63130–4899.

Stephen John Hartnett is an associate professor and chair of the Department of Communication at the University of Colorado–Denver. He has spent the past twenty years teaching in, writing about, and protesting at America's prisons and is the editor of *Captured Words/Free Thoughts*, a biannual magazine produced by imprisoned writers and artists. His recent books include *Executing Democracy, volume 1: Capital Punishment and the Making of America* (2010), *Globalization and Empire* (2006), and *Incarceration Nation* (2004); his most recent articles about the prison-industrial complex have appeared in *Communication and Critical Cultural Studies*, *Rhetoric & Public Affairs*, and the *Common Review*. He may be reached at the Department of Communication, University of Colorado–Denver, 102-E Plaza Building, Denver, CO 80217; or at Stephen.hartnett@ucdenver.edu.

Julilly Kohler-Hausmann is a doctoral candidate in the history department at the University of Illinois–Urbana-Champaign. Focusing on the 1970s, she researches how and why punishment has become the dominant strategy in

American social and criminal policy. Her work has been published in the *Journal of Social History.* Prior to graduate school, Kohler-Hausmann spent six years organizing for labor, welfare, and antipoverty issues in Washington State. She can be contacted at kohlerha@illinois.edu.

Daniel Mark Larson is a doctoral candidate in the Department of Communication at the University of Illinois–Urbana-Champaign. His dissertation, "Twentieth Century Scarecrow: The Rhetorical Origins of the United States' War on Drugs," examines the 1950s to trace the arguments, meanings, and images that have collectively produced drug-war mythology. His work on the death penalty has appeared in *Communication and Critical Cultural Studies.* He may be contacted at dmlarson511@gmail.com.

Erica R. Meiners is a professor of education and Women's Studies at Northeastern Illinois University, where she works with a number of Chicago-based justice initiatives related to queer rights, educational justice, and resisting the prison-industrial complex. She works with a team of organizers and educators—Project 8—to support undocumented youth to gain access to higher education and resist criminalization, and with TAME (Teachers against Militarized Education, CivilianSchools@gmail.com), a group working against the militarization and privatization of public education in Chicago. Meiners is the author of *Right to Be Hostile: Schools, Prisons, and the Making of Public Enemies* (2007) and *Flaunt It! Queers Organizing for Public Education and Justice* (2009). She has published articles in, among others, *Rethinking Schools; Race, Ethnicity, and Education;* and *Meridians: Feminism, Race, Transnationalism.* She may be reached at the Department of Educational Foundations and Women's Studies, Northeastern Illinois University, 5500 North St. Louis Ave., Chicago, IL 60625; or at e-meiners@neiu.edu.

Janie Paul is a visual artist and an associate professor of the University of Michigan's School of Art and Design and its School of Social Work, where she teaches classes that send her students into prisons, juvenile centers, and Detroit elementary schools to facilitate art workshops. As a member of the Prison Creative Arts Project, she has facilitated art workshops at men's and women's facilities and is a cocurator of the Annual Exhibitions of Art by Michigan Prisoners. She exhibits her work at galleries in Michigan, New York, and New England and is represented by the River Gallery in Chelsea, Michigan. She can be contacted at the School of Art and Design, University of Michigan, 2000 Bonisteel Blvd, Ann Arbor, MI 48109; or at janiep@umich.edu. Her website is www.janiepaul.com.

Lori Pompa has been going in and out of prisons and jails since 1985. She is on the Criminal Justice faculty at Temple University and is founder and national director of The Inside-Out Prison Exchange Program, which, for the past fourteen years, has created opportunities for social change through dialogue between those inside and those outside our nation's correctional facilities. As a 2003 Soros Justice Senior Fellow, she collaborated with others on both sides of prison walls to develop the Inside-Out National Instructor Training Institute, which offers week-long, intensive training in this unique approach to teaching and learning. To date, more than 200 instructors from 120 colleges and universities in 35 states and abroad have taken part in the Inside-Out training, with scores of Inside-Out classes offered throughout the country each semester. The Inside-Out website is www.insideoutcenter.org; Pompa can be reached at lori.pompa@temple.edu.

Jonathan Shailor is the founder and lead facilitator of the Theater of Empowerment and the Shakespeare Prison Project (http://shakespeareprisonproject.blogspot.com/), two programs that provide opportunities for community groups to use performance and dialogue for personal and social development. Shailor is also the founder and director of the Certificate Program in Conflict Analysis and Resolution at the University of Wisconsin–Parkside, where he serves as an associate professor of communication. He is currently working on two books: the first is an expanded reflection on his prison teaching experiences; the second is an anthology on prison theater in the United States. His published work includes *Empowerment in Dispute Mediation* (1994) and essays in such venues as *PMLA* (the journal of the Modern Language Association). He may be contacted at the Department of Communication, University of Wisconsin–Parkside, 900 Wood Road, Kenosha, WI 53141–2000; or at jonathan.shailor@gmail.com.

Robin Sohnen is the founder and executive director of Each One Reach One. In addition to running EORO, she served for five years as the event producer for *The Waiting Room*, Richard Kamler's acclaimed political and artistic conversation about the death penalty, which toured nationally from 1998 to 2002. Sohnen is a member of the Skyline College Administration of Justice Advisory Committee and received the 1999 National Council on Crime and

Delinquency's *New American Community Award* for EORO's creative efforts to reduce crime. She served as a member of the Post-Adjudicated Youth Committee for San Francisco's Juvenile Detention Alternatives Initiative, which seeks alternatives to incarceration for the city's youth, and served on the Commission on the Status of Women of San Mateo County. She may be reached at Each One Reach One (www.eoro.org), 1486 Huntington Avenue #304, South San Francisco, CA 94080; or at info@eoro.org.

Myesha Williams graduated with a masters in social work from the University of Washington–Seattle. She has been working with Critical Resistance since May 2007; prior to that, she worked in Seattle with the Statewide Poverty Action Network advocating for and with low-income people in order to solve the root causes of poverty. She also works as a program associate for the Rose Foundation's New Voices are Rising program, working with youth to pursue environmental justice. She may be contacted at myeshawilliams@gmail.com.

Index

Mansker, Dennis, 41–42
Marcus Garvey School (Los Angeles), 222
marijuana, 77, 85, 87–88, 89–90
Marijuana Tax Act (1937), 73, 85, 87–88
Martinez, Dr., 62
Mason, Roseann, 231
Mastering Shakespeare (Kaiser), 244
Mauer, Marc, 28
Maxey Boys Training School, 156–58
May Day riot (Los Angeles, 2007), 2
Mays, Marvin, 72
McCarthy, Joe, 74
McCollum, Robert ("Chicago"), 201–2
McLaughlin, Joseph, 47–48
McLean, Andy, 241
Meiners, Erica, 4–6, 254
Mellon, Andrew, 73
*Mentally Ill Offenders in the Criminal Jus-
tice System* (Sentencing Project), 10n1
Mérida Initiative, 94–96
metal detectors, 136–37
methamphetamine, 77
Mexican drug war, 94–95
Mezirow, Jack, 268
"Miami Vice," 55
Michigan Battered Women, 172
Michigan Department of Corrections, 170,
178n13
Military Professional Resources, Inc.
(MPRI), 96
Miller, Katie, 169
Mills, Charles, 24
Milwaukee Journal-Sentinel, 241–42
Missouri Eastern Correctional Center,
239–40
Missouri Promise, 219–21
Monahan, Nicole, 228
Monday Shakespeare Club, 246
Monsanto, 96
Moore, Robert: *King, Warrior, Magician,
Lover*, 232–33
morphine, 85, 89–90
Morrell, David: *First Blood*, 56
Morris, Curtis, 209
Morris, Vivian Gunn, 209
Motorola, 49
Moy, Jin Fuey, 82
Muddy Flower Theatre Troupe (Racine

Correctional Institution), 229–30,
241
Mullin, Gene, 194–95
Mumford, F., 174
Muñoz, Manuel Jesus, 76
Murakawa, Naomi, 21, 23–24
Mural Arts Program (Philadelphia), 259
*The Murderers: The Shocking Story of the
Narcotic Gangs* (Anslinger), 88
Murphy Oil Promise, 221
Music Theatre Workshop, 246
Mwachofi, Ngure wa, 232

NAFTA (North American Free Trade Agree-
ment), 94–95
Narcotic Division (Prohibition Unit, Trea-
sury Department), 82
Narcotics Control Act (1956), 73, 88
Nast, Thomas, 38n17
National Association of State Budget Of-
ficers, 129–30
National Center for Schools and Communi-
ties (Fordham University), 133
National Council on Alcoholism and Drug
Dependence, 135
National Drug Control, 78
National Education Association, 135
National Endowment for the Humanities,
178n13
National Guard, 48
NCLB. *See* No Child Left Behind Act
Neal, Tracy, 157, 170
neoliberal economics. *See* economic infra-
structure
neoliberalism, 21–25, 32
New Deal, 21–22
Newsweek, 77
Newton, Huey, 52
New York City public schools, 136–37
New York Times, 90, 140
nihilism, 3–5
Nissen, Eugene, 150
Nixon, Jeremiah ("Jay"), 219–20
Nixon, Richard, 78, 88–91
No Child Left Behind Act (NCLB), 127–28,
138–40, 210–11
noose hangings, 132–33, 143n10
Noriega, Manuel, 92

sex offender registries, 31
Shailor, Christopher, 241
Shakespeare, William, 230
Shakespeare behind Bars (SBB), 241
Shakespeare Project, 242–46, 249–50
Shaver, George, 241
Shiebler, Bill, 128–29
The Show, 150
Silva, Eduardo Bonilla, 117
Simon, Sidney, 265
Sinclair, Upton: *The Jungle*, 47
Sisters within Theater Troupe, 150, 157,
    177n6
650-Lifer Law (Michigan, 1978), 90
Slave Codes, 70n32
slavery, 25, 38n.17, 203–10
"slippery banana" machine, 49
The Smartest Guys in the Room, 119
Smith, William T., 124–25
Sohnen, Robin, 254
Soler, Mark, 138
South Bronx Junior High School, 143n11
speed (drug), 77
SSAs (School Security Agents), 134,
    136–37
St. Leonard's Adult High School, 15–17,
    29, 34
Stallone, Sylvester, 56
Stanton, Elizabeth Cady, 80–81
State Correctional Institution (Graterford
    Prison; Pennsylvania), 258–60, 269
stereotypes, racial, 106–20; of the black
    criminal/social problem, on television
    news, 108–12, 114–18; and blue-collar
    vs. white-collar crime, 119; and crime
    news, 118–20; fair trials hindered by,
    110, 112; fear-based, 106–9, 118; the
    new racism, 117–18; news depictions as
    reinforcing, 113–18; in news program-
    ming, 108–12; overview of, 106–8; po-
    lice profiling, 106; and the profit motive
    of corporate media, 119–20; psychologi-
    cal appeal of, 113–14; reversing patterns
    of, 119–20; and scapegoating, 23–25;
    unconscious, 118
Street, Paul, 18, 20, 117, 192

Stroud, Alison, 169
supermax prisons, 17–18, 26, 34–35
Supreme Court, 51, 135
surveillance, fear-induced, 32–33
surveillance cameras, 136–37
systematic effects investigations, 113
Szasz, Thomas, 87

"Table of Voices" (Kamler), 171, 178n13
Tamms prison (Illinois), 17–18, 34–35
"Tarbaby" (V. Williams), 170
Taxi Driver, 55–56, 68n20
Taylor, Edmond, 171–72
television, 107, 108–12. *See also* stereo-
    types, racial
temperance movement, 80–81, 85
Temple University, 256, 258
terrorism, fear of, 32, 139
Theater of Empowerment, 231–39, 246
theater productions, 7, 229–50; King Lear
    Project, 240–42; overview of, 229–31;
    sanctuary, 246–47; Shakespeare Project,
    242–46, 249–50; social-capital building
    via the arts, 247–49; Theater of Empow-
    erment, 231–39, 246
Theatre Arts Department (UWP), 241
Thieme, Jean, 240
"Thinking of You," 187
Think Tank (State Correctional Institu-
    tion at Graterford Prison; Pennsylvania),
    258–60, 269
Thomson Correctional Center (Illinois), 27
Thousand Kites Project, 120
Tijuana/L.A. cocaine cartels, 2
Time, 53
Tofteland, Curt, 241
torture: at Abu Ghraib, 46; army field
    phone used for, 43–44, 46, 57–58, 60,
    69n23; burdens of testimony by, 61–62,
    70n32; and inner-city space as enemy
    territory, 45, 64, 65n4; as public, 44–45,
    58–59; racial elements of, 58–59; symp-
    toms of, 62
"tough on crime" stance, 19, 28, 121n6,
    129
Treasury Department, 82

Troy, Jacque, 241, 245–46
Tucker telephone. *See* army field phone used for torture
Turner, Herschell, 170–71

United Nations Education, Scientific, and Cultural Organization (UNESCO), 212
United Self-Defense Forces of Colombia (AUC), 93–94
Universal Declaration of Human Rights, 212
University of Chicago, 35n3
University of Illinois, 35n3
University of Illinois at Chicago (UIC), 15
University of Illinois at Urbana-Champaign (UIUC), 17–18
University of Michigan, 159, 178n13. *See also* PCAP
University of Missouri-Kansas City, 220
University of Wisconsin-Parkside (UWP), 231–32, 234–35, 248
urbanization, post-Reconstruction, 205–6
urban jungles, 44–45, 47–54, 64, 67n14
Urban League (Chicago), 54
urban-school achievement, 7, 203–23; academic achievement, fostering, 210–14; Hi-PASS school reform, 211; incarceration-to-college pipeline, 214–21; Kalamazoo Promise, 214–19, 222; Missouri Promise, 219–21; Murphy Oil Promise, 221; overview of, 203–4; race-making and legacies of slavery, 203–10; successes, 222–23
Uribe, Álvaro, 76
U.S. v. Doremus, 82
U.S. v. Jin Fuey Moy, 82

Vaca, Myrna, 157–58
Valentine, Danny, 173–74
Vargas, Martin, 170
Victoria's Secret, 26
Vietnam War: ambivalent legacy of, 56; police militarization influenced by, 43–44, 46–50, 52–60, 64; U.S. interrogation procedures in, 57–58; veterans of, 53–57, 59, 81

vigilantism: in popular culture, 44, 46, 54–57, 68nn20–22; right-wing support for, 51–52, 67n14
Violent Crime Control and Law Enforcement Act (1993), 254
voting rights of former inmates, 29–30

Wacquant, Loïc, 205–6
Walker, Vanessa Siddle, 209
Ward, Rick, 170
War on Drugs. *See* drug war
War on Poverty, 51
Washington Post, 90
Watts uprising (Los Angeles, 1965), 2, 48
Webb v. United States, 82
welfare state/programs, 21–24, 27–28, 63–64
West, Cornell, 3, 7, 183–84
West Englewood (Chicago), 29
Western Wayne Correctional Facility, 156–57, 162–63, 177n6
"When Can We Talk?" 149
"When I Was Young" (Ward), 170
Whiskey Act (1791), 82
Whiskey Rebellion, 82
white supremacy, 22–25
Wilcox, Agnes, 239–40
Williams, Myesha, 31, 254
Williams, Virgil, 170
Wilson, Andrew and Jackie, 43–44, 62
wiretapping, 49
Wisconsin Humanities Council (WHC), 231–32
Wolof, 205
Woodrow Wilson High School, 140
World War I, 83
Wright, Hamilton, 81

"Y2K and the Wicked Stepmother," 157
Young, Walter, 60
Youth Services Center (San Mateo, Calif.), 188, 192–93

zero-tolerance policies, 127–28, 130–34, 138
Zoot Suit riots (Los Angeles, 1943), 2

The University of Illinois Press
is a founding member of the
Association of American University Presses.
· ·

Composed in 9.5/13.5 Officina Serif Std Book
with Officina Serif Std display
by Celia Shapland
at the University of Illinois Press
Manufactured by Sheridan Books, Inc.

University of Illinois Press
1325 South Oak Street
Champaign, IL 61820-6903
www.press.uillinois.edu